A CYNTHIA OZICK READER

A

Cynthia
OZICK
R E A D E R

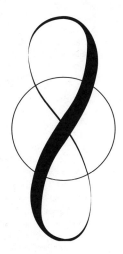

Edited by
Elaine M. Kauvar

INDIANA UNIVERSITY PRESS
BLOOMINGTON & INDIANAPOLIS

For Bernie

—E. M. K.

Compilation, preface, and introduction © 1996 by
Indiana University Press

Texts by Cynthia Ozick © 1958, 1962, 1963, 1965,
1966, 1969, 1971, 1973, 1974, 1976, 1977, 1982,
1984, 1985, 1987, 1992 by Cynthia Ozick

Earlier version of selected bibliography © 1985 by
the University Press of Kentucky

Manufactured in the United States of America

Library of Congress Cataloging-in-Publication Data

Ozick, Cynthia.
    [Selections.   1996]
    A Cynthia Ozick reader / edited by Elaine M. Kauvar.
      p. cm.
    Includes bibliographical references (p.   ).
    ISBN 0-253-33039-4 (cloth : alk. paper). —
ISBN 0-253-21053-4 (pbk. : alk. paper)
    I. Kauvar, Elaine M. (Elaine Mozer), date.   II. Title.
PS3565.Z5A6   1996
813'.54—dc20   95-39500

3   4   5   01 00 99

CONTENTS

 POEMS

FICTION

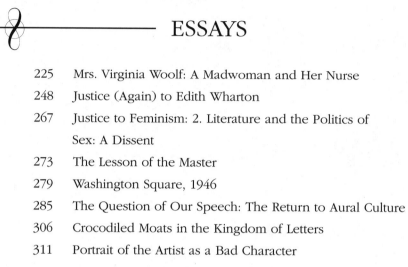

ESSAYS

PREFACE

The decision to cull from a writer's work certain pieces and collect them under the rubric "A Reader" rests on the conviction that taken together they will offer readers, in one volume, both the opportunity to sample the variety of a writer's oeuvre and the chance to saturate themselves in the writer's art. In a library, readers decide which book they will choose to begin their exploration; in a Reader they are presented with a library in little, a representative selection of an author's achievement. In either case, however, readers must decide for themselves which tale or which poem or which essay is the better one. What a Reader should provide is akin to what Virginia Woolf desired for libraries: "To admit authorities, however furred and gowned, into our libraries and let them tell us how to read, what to read, what value to place upon what we read, is to destroy the spirit of freedom which is the breath of those sanctuaries." Situated comfortably in those sanctuaries, we are faced with the difficulty of training our powers on what Virginia Woolf called "the very spot," the problem of knowing where to begin. This Cynthia Ozick Reader offers a solution to that problem.

This Reader also attempts, as Virginia Woolf urges, "to banish all [the] . . . preconceptions" that too often accompany us when we come to authors. Such preconceptions have plagued Cynthia Ozick's art from the very beginning of her career, commencing with the reaction to her first published novel, *Trust* (1966). With very few exceptions, critics have continued to focus on Ozick's Jewishness, claiming her work as solely the product of American Jewish writing and limiting her appeal to the special audience that shares her heritage. That judgment has arisen because of the nature of Ozick's vision, which is rooted in the Hebraic tradition and which draws sustenance from the Jewish Idea. But the fiction of other American Jewish writers—Saul Bellow and Philip Roth spring immediately to mind—has escaped the allegation of belonging to uniquely Jewish forms. What, then, accounts for the label critics have persistently attached to Cynthia Ozick?

The answer comes from two directions—Jews' expectations of Jewish writers and Gentiles' ignorance of Jewish materials. Faced with the undeniable fact, a fact not so evident in the fiction of a Bellow or a Philip Roth, that Jewish history, Jewish values, and Jewish sources enrich Ozick's art, Jews and Gentiles alike have come to it with the very preconceptions Virginia Woolf admonished readers to reject and wanted banished from the liberating precincts of libraries. Celebrating their own tradition, Jews have conceived of Cynthia Ozick's work as constituting Jewish texts which, in turn, represent Jewish reality. The implicit demand made on the writer of those texts is that she be a leader, a spokesperson for Jews, a source from which to draw Jewish identity. If, on the one hand, the desires of Jews have contributed to consigning Cynthia Ozick's fiction to a wholly Jewish realm, on the other hand, the lack of awareness of the Jewish Idea on the part of Gentiles has caused them to dismiss the Jewish materials in Ozick's tales as "sometimes inaccessible or maybe even alienating to many potential readers." To retain those preconceptions of a writer's work is ultimately to disallow the meaning of her tradition to her art; at worst, such preconceptions create the impossible situation in which Ozick is either charged with being too Jewish or found not Jewish enough. Neither view is relevant to Cynthia Ozick's art; neither view promotes understanding of it.

It is the American writer Henry James, one of Ozick's most influential mentors, who provides the key to approaching the American Jewish writer's work. In "The Art of Fiction" he argues that "We must grant the artist his subject, his idea, his *donnée*." James asserts further, in his preface to "Lady Barbarina," that "one never really chooses one's general range of vision— the experience from which ideas and themes and suggestions spring. . . . The subject thus pressed upon the artist is the necessity of his case and the fruit of his consciousness." The source of fiction, James maintains, inevitably and ineluctably includes the artist's consciousness. Though the *donnée* of Cynthia Ozick's fiction is her Jewish consciousness, and her tales, poems, and essays the fruit of that consciousness, Ozick does not begin any artistic endeavor with a consciousness of her Jewishness, nor is she aware of her Jewish identity while she writes. Indeed, no imaginative writer embarks on a project with a purposeful thesis in mind. And no reader should ask of any book that it enforce held beliefs. Instead, a reader should begin by suspending all such beliefs and heeding Virginia Woolf's counsel:

> Do not dictate to your author; try to become him. Be his fellow-worker and accomplice. If you hang back, and reserve and criticise at first, you are preventing yourself from getting the fullest possible value from what you read. But if you open your mind as widely as possible, then signs and hints of almost

imperceptible fineness, from the twist and turn of the first sentences, will bring you into the presence of a human being unlike any other. Steep yourself in this, acquaint yourself with this, and soon you will find that your author is giving you, or attempting to give you, something far more definite.

It is the purpose of the selections in this volume to encourage readers to hew to Woolf's advice. If they attend to it, they will see that the emphasis other readers have placed on Ozick's Jewishness has eclipsed for them her manifold alliances with other American writers and precluded their apprehension of her place in American letters. Woolf's ideal reader will come to realize that the barriers to an easy understanding of Ozick's work have less to do with her Jewish materials than with the quality of her art, with her adamant refusal to simplify what is incontrovertibly complex. On that score as well, she adheres to the conviction Henry James voiced in the preface to his complicated novel *The Wings of the Dove:* "The enjoyment of a work of art, the acceptance of an irresistible illusion, constituting, to my sense, our highest experience of 'luxury,' the luxury is not greatest, by my consequent measure, when the work asks for as little attention as possible. It is greatest, it is delightfully, divinely great, when we feel the surface, like the thick ice of the skater's pond, bear without cracking the strongest pressure we throw on it." In that thick ice is contained Ozick's strong allegiance not only to Henry James but to other writers in the American mainstream, writers whose work affords the means to assess Cynthia Ozick's place in contemporary American letters.

She shares with those writers a preoccupation with duality, a defining characteristic of her art, and a distinguishing feature as well of mainstream American writers like William Faulkner and Mark Twain. In turn, they grow out of a tradition that includes such writers as Poe, Hawthorne, Emerson, and Thoreau, whose namesakes appear in Ozick's novel *Trust.* Another of her pervasive themes—impersonation—is common to American writers like Melville and Fitzgerald. Those are but two of the numerous examples of the abiding alliances Cynthia Ozick has with writers in the mainstream of American letters, and those affinities demonstrate that Cynthia Ozick's art is central to American literature, not peripheral to it. The plethora of honors and awards her fiction and essays have won, the frequent speaking invitations extended to her—these testify to the acknowledgment she has earned. Her place in American letters was confirmed in 1988 when she was elected to the prestigious American Academy and Institute of Arts and Letters, whose history in the 1920s she was asked to write and which she published in 1994. Though she would never make a vaunt of her own accomplishments or claim importance and centrality for herself, the American Academy and other established institutions have accorded her the recognition she

merits, deeming hers one of the outstanding voices of twentieth-century American writing.

To that end—to providing a collection of her work that epitomizes its universal appeal and to liberating her tales, essays, and poems from those authorities Virginia Woolf scorned for destroying the spirit of freedom in libraries—this *Reader* is dedicated. If readers hang back constrained by their preconceptions of her heritage, if they close their minds to the breadth of her vision, those readers will not get the fullest possible value from what they have read. But if they give themselves over to the selections in this volume as completely as possible, they will be brought into the presence of a writer unlike any other and can delight in fearlessly skating on the thick ice of the skater's pond.

E. M. K.

ACKNOWLEDGMENTS

Grateful acknowledgment is made to the following sources for permission to reprint material in this Reader:

to Cynthia Ozick, for her poems "Greeks," "The Fish in the Net," "The Seventeen Questions of Rabbi Zusya," "Footnote to Lord Acton," "Commuters' Train through Harlem," "Caryatid," and "When That with Tragic Rapture Moses Stood"; for a selection from *Trust* (1966); and for "At Fumicaro";

to Alfred A. Knopf, Inc., for selections from

The Pagan Rabbi and Other Stories (1971): "Envy" and "Virility";

Bloodshed and Three Novellas (1976): "A Mercenary";

Levitation: Five Fictions (1982): "Puttermesser: Her Work History, Her Ancestry, Her Afterlife," and "Puttermesser and Xanthippe";

Art & Ardor: Essays (1983): "Mrs. Virginia Woolf: A Madwoman and Her Nurse," "Justice (Again) to Edith Wharton," "Justice to Feminism: 2. Literature and the Politics of Sex: A Dissent," and "The Lesson of the Master";

Metaphor & Memory: Essays (1989): "Washington Square, 1946," "The Question of Our Speech: The Return to Aural Culture," "Crocodiled Moats in the Kingdom of Letters," and "Portrait of the Artist as a Bad Character."

The publication histories for these and other Cynthia Ozick works may be found in the Selected Bibliography contained in this Reader. This bibliography was compiled, with additions, from "A Bibliography of Writings by Cynthia Ozick," by Susan Currier and Daniel J. Cahill, in *Contemporary American Women Writers: Narrative Strategies,* edited by Catherine Rainwater and William J. Scheick, copyright © 1985 by the University Press of Kentucky.

INTRODUCTION

Certain images from childhood so powerfully impress the mind that it retains them forever in the repository of memory. There other feelings attach themselves to those images, sometimes inflaming their power to wound anew, at other moments reaping from them a fructifying imaginative power. Such moments—the poet Wordsworth called them "spots of time"—date from earliest childhood and arise from chance events, from what the novelist Cynthia Ozick calls the Ordinary:

> Ordinariness can be defined as a breathing-space: the breathing-space between getting born and dying, perhaps; or else the breathing-space between rapture and rapture; or, more usually, the breathing-space between one disaster and the next. Ordinariness is sometimes the *status quo,* sometimes the slow, unseen movement of a subtle but ineluctable cycle, like a ride on the hour hand of the clock; in any case the Ordinary is above all *what is expected*.

Noticing the Ordinary—and this is why Ozick calls it a "riddle"—is difficult precisely because the Ordinary is so noticeable. Think of the common pavement, a staple of everyday life. A sidewalk, most would agree, is unremarkable, scarcely worthy of observation; a sidewalk has been constructed so that ordinary travelers may hasten on their way. Yet what seizes a mental traveler about that same sidewalk yields the answer to the riddle Ozick finds in the Ordinary.

In an hour of childhood, this is what she saw when she stared at the pavement: "tiny glints of isinglass that catch the sun and prickle upward from the pavement like shards of star-stuff. . . . hypnotic semaphores signaling eeriness out of the ground." And this is what she apprehended as an adult: "If you are five years old, loitering in a syrup of sunheat, gazing at the silver-white mica-eyes in the pavement, you will all at once be besieged by a strangeness: the strangeness of understanding, for the very first time, that you are really alive, and that the world is really true; and the strange-

ness will divide into a river of wonderings." That divided river of wonderings forms a confluence of amazement when at first she "wondered why
[she] was thinking these things . . . what wondering was, and why it was
spooky, and also secretly sweet, and amazingly *interesting*" and at last
recognizes "an uncanny sort of love" in wondering, "something curiously
and thrillingly other." Her first-born affinity with mica was Cynthia Ozick's
"First love," a "first inkling, bridging our new existence to existing things,"
an augury of her burgeoning imaginative powers which she would soon
bridge to the passion to write.

Decades later, after discovering in Wordsworth's *Prelude* what "shone
up out of the mica-eyes," she understood "those existing things are *all*
things, everything the mammal senses know, everything the human mind
constructs (temples or equations), the unheard poetry on the hidden side of
the round earth, the great thirsts everywhere, the wonderings past wonderings." Reckoning culminates in an ultimate wondering: "Can one begin with
mica in the pavement and learn the prophet Micah's meaning?" To link
mica-eyes with Micah's vision is to envision in that "river of wondering" the
prophet's bright message of hope ascending from the sins cast "into the
depths of the sea." Yoked to the Bible and to Wordsworth, ordinary mica is
transformed into Cynthia Ozick's trope for the regeneration brought by
consciousness.

In miniature that trope intimates her perception of a "redemptive literature," a literature whose "pulse and purpose [is] . . . to reject the blur of the
'universal'; to distinguish one life from another; to illumine diversity; to
light up the least grain of being, to show how it is concretely individual,
particularized from any other; to tell, in all the marvel of its singularity,
the separate holiness of the least grain," a literature whose very reason for
being is *"the recognition of the particular."* We can begin to learn the writer
Ozick's meaning from the two particular words in the title of her second
collection of essays—"memory" and "metaphor."

The enduring importance of memory originates in the Hebrew Bible,
where remembrance is pivotal, where the command to remember is absolute, and where various declensions of the verb *zakhar* ("to remember")
appear at least one hundred and sixty-nine times. The Hebraic tradition is
also the provenance for the overwhelming significance accorded to history
and for the intense absorption with the meaning of the past. To that tradition, the tradition which is the matrix of Cynthia Ozick's art, belong not
only the fierce commitment to remembering and interpreting the past but
the belief that continuity is essential. Those account for the storyteller's rejection of new forms:

Inventing a secret, then revealing it in the drama of entanglement—this is what ignites the will to write stories. The creation of forms has no part in this; I have no interest in "the new." Rupture doesn't attract me: I would rather inherit coherence than smash and start over again with enigma. The secrets that engage me—that sweep me away—are generally secrets of inheritance: how the pear seed becomes a pear tree, for instance, rather than a polar bear. Ideas are emotions that penetrate the future of coherence—in particular the idea of genesis.

The tradition she has inherited is the genesis of her convictions that history is judgment, that memory is a transforming power, and that continuity is indispensable; and the legacy bequeathed her is the corridor of access to her fiction. Enoch, a character in *Trust,* says: "History. . . . You want to know what it is? . . . It isn't simply what has happened. It's a judgment on what has happened! . . . And when we talk of redemption, it's history we mean!" Her Yiddish poet Herschel Edelshtein scorns those who "court amnesia of history," and her attorney Ruth Puttermesser "must own a past."

Out of the inheritance Cynthia Ozick owns come the various and variegated strands woven into the fabric of her art. Something akin to the strange moment of understanding sparked by the glints of mica in the pavement occurred in her early adulthood. When she was in her twenties, the glimmers came from an essay by Rabbi Leo Baeck. "Romantic Religion," she told an interviewer, "in some way broke open the conceptual egg of my life." What made the reading of that essay a formative intellectual experience for Ozick is Baeck's conception of Judaism as a "Classical Religion"; for the world of Classical Religion is the realm of the ordinary—that world which constitutes reality and in which fate is struggled against. Certainty in such a world grows out of "seeking and inquiring" just as knowledge comes from "wrestling and striving." Because of its "strong ethical impulse," classical religion engenders the "will to conquer life ethically," making the human being its subject and the human being's task the achievement of freedom and the attainment of "self-development." Concerning itself with humanity's attitude toward the world and the consequences of a person's deeds, classical religion spurns illusion and celebrates "living history." In this ethical idea of history, the "idea of becoming, of the never-quite-finished, of the directed ascent" is of paramount importance. Unlike "dead history," "living history" guarantees a future. The essence of Judaism for Baeck, then, is contained in the term "ethical monotheism," whose decisive feature is "the nameless, the incomprehensible and the unattainable" God who has created humankind.

If Baeck's explanation of Judaism inspired her conception of ethical monotheism, Ozick conceived of the bond between ethical monotheism and the imagination. She explained their connection in an interview:

> . . . in Judaism you have the greatest demand made on the imagination, to imagine essence without attribute, without portrait—"I am that I am."—so that to state a contradiction, a conflict, between imagination and Judaism is really erroneous. Where the contradiction comes in is when you . . . speak of the imagination that creates things in competition with God, a thinginess imagination, an art imagination, a systems imagination, a mammalian imagination. The mammalian imagination results in idol-making. The higher imagination, the imagination that invented monotheism—this posits God.

The process by which Ozick's fiction comes into being exemplifies the "higher imagination." For that kind of imagination, first-hand knowledge of a place fancied as the setting for a tale is unnecessary. That kind of imaginative faculty is more knowledgeable than the knowledge brought by experience. When Ozick began to write *The Cannibal Galaxy,* parts of which are based in France, she had spent only a few hours in Paris and those twenty-three years before the germ of the novel appeared. To an interviewer who observed that Ozick seemed to know Paris "very well" and who wondered whether the novelist had ever lived there, Ozick confessed:

> It is the guide book writers who know Paris very well! Before setting out to write the Paris sections of the novel, I went to the public library and borrowed Fodor's guide, and one or two others, and studied—i.e., imagined myself *into*—the street maps in great detail, and the accounts of the museums and shops and neighborhoods. That is how I discovered the Marais, a neighborhood I learned about only from the guide book. But I knew New York's Lower East Side, and it was clear that the Marais could not be very different. And of course, if you have been to the Metropolitan Museum of Art in New York, it is easy to visualize the Louvre.
>
> Or so I thought. When, after *The Cannibal Galaxy* was published in France, I actually came to Paris and for the first time really *saw* it—saw the resplendent city and visited the vastnesses of the Louvre (where I watched a copyist at work: the germ of a later story), and the streets of the Marais (the Musée Carnavalet was closed on the day I turned up there, and I could only peek into the courtyard, so much smaller than I had imagined it, through a crack between its two great doors)—I had the strange sense that if I had known Paris, I could not have written about it.

How her imagination can chance upon a name and dream it into a novelistic episode happens in a similar fashion. To illustrate the decisive change in Lars Andemening, the main character of her third novel, Ozick has him review *Illusion,* the latest novel by the popular and celebrated Ann-Charlott

Almgren. Or so we are led to think. Captivated by the plot Ozick unfolds and curious about Almgren, a reader might indeed go in search of her novel. But the journey would be in vain, for as Ozick revealed: "The 'prolific Ann-Charlott Almgren,' author of *Illusion,* is an invention. Her names come out of the marriage columns of a Stockholm newspaper found abandoned at the airport, so they are 'authentic' names." Such fabrications are the offsprings of an imagination that can glimpse its way through the pages of a guide book or the columns of a newspaper, or more fundamentally from old reverberations in the middle of her parents' pharmacy, which Ozick describes so movingly in "A Drugstore in Winter." Her delight in fabrication notwithstanding, Ozick apprehends the imagination as a moral and regenerative instrument forged in the smithy of history. That cognition moors her idea of the imagination to reality; that enables its participation in an unfolding future, and that attaches it to Baeck's "idea of becoming." It is his sense of Classical Religion that animates her judgment of literature, which, she avows, "decodes" and "interprets" the world, affirming the "freedom to change one's life," opposing the "fated or the static," and elevating "the lifegiving—if only through terror at its absence." If at first strangeness divides into a river of wondering, later memory ignites the will to bring literature into being.

To discover the meaning of memory is to return to the past, and the past is also where metaphor, the second defining term for the storyteller's art, originates. In the idea of metaphor Ozick discovers the virtues of "memory and pity," and she designates metaphor "the reciprocal agent, the universalizing force" because "it makes possible the power to envision the stranger's heart." From the history of the Greeks and the history of the Jews she ascertains the phenomena of inspiration and memory, or "history as judgment." Inspiration, which belongs to the Greeks, differs from the will to "cultivate memory, or search out any historical metaphor to contain memory." Wanting a "common historical experience to universalize ethical feeling," the Greeks "had no pity for the stranger": they disallowed the Other. The history of the Jews differs. "Driven to a preoccupation with history and memory" and "collectively obsessed with the imagination of pity," the Jews turned their concrete memory of thirty generations of slavery into a "universalizing metaphor of reciprocity" and discovered a "way to convert the imagination into a serious moral instrument." Ozick's reading of the Pentateuch and her interpretation of its precept of loving the stranger establish the congruence she makes between metaphor and the ability to imagine another's heart. To the concept of metaphor and the activity of metaphoric language she fastens the "hope of regeneration."

Her commitment to history is consonant with that hope. History explains her praise for a "purely transmitted inheritance," and because of history she is drawn to photography; for in their capacity to restore memory, photographs can recover the meaning of the past. They can also seize a moment and freeze it into a permanent image of truth. Ozick spoke of her attraction to photography in an interview: "I'm drawn to the eeriness of photography, the way it represents both mortality and immortality. It both stands for death and stands against death because it's statuary. It doesn't move. It's immobile like the dead, and it also saves. It's such a mystery. It's a mystery of a verisimilitude surrounded by . . . a penumbra of all kinds of unknown things." Its ability to save induces Cynthia Ozick to focus the lens of her fancied camera on an envisaged scene to make visible what is unseen. All that she has beheld in the medium of photography is transformed by her imagination into a summarizing metaphor for art.

"What is a photograph," she writes, "if not a stimulus to the most deliberate attentiveness: time held motionless in a vise of profound concentration, so that every inch of the seized moment can be examined?" When she turns back to the nineteenth century, to history, and reassesses the achievement of Anthony Trollope's novel *The Way We Live Now,* she conjures up a metaphor from her knowledge of photography. It empowers her to proclaim the aptness of Trollope's novel to the way we live in our own century. If there is in Trollope "something of a camera mounted on a helicopter—the Olympian looking down at a wide map strewn with wriggling mortals and their hungers," there is in his "scrutiny of his 'now,'" a "wide" lens, "extraordinarily so; wide enough to let in, finally, a slim ghost of the prophetic." But as ordinary mica sparkles with the prophetic Micah, the camera "can be made to lie" or to be "reality's aperture." Those twin capacities, the double-natured metaphors that balance two meanings, exemplify the laws governing the complexities of Cynthia Ozick's art. Its particulars must be scrutinized through a wide lens, wide enough to let in the doubleness that augments the significance of her great themes.

Throughout her fiction and her essays, one idea continually clashes with another: each vies with the other for attention, forever colliding, never attaining a resounding accord. None of her themes lacks an opposing one. In the arena of her fiction, Hebraism conflicts with Hellenism; the threat of idolatry combats the attraction of paganism. Art beckons beguilingly only to present disturbing and often insurmountable problems for the artist. Out of such discord are born ideas that both mirror her tradition and transform it. The Hebraism and Hellenism controversy is a case in point. Their warring values ineluctably established the two civilizations as rivals; and it is their fundamental divergence, the perdurable issue of idolatry, that Ozick seizes upon. Her intellect plumbs the injunction against idolatry for its historical significance just as her imagination imparts to it a powerful psychological resonance. Judaism in its entirety—the biblical and talmudic tradition—constitutes the threshold from which Ozick's imagination leaps into new realms.

Exalting the existence of many gods, all of them capable of being envisaged, the Greeks adhered to what monotheism expressly bans—belief in anything but one unvisualizable God. The biblical injunction against idolatry avows its futility and admonishes that it violates Covenant. So central is the issue of idolatry to Judaism that the Talmud defines a Jew as one who does not worship idols, enjoins rooting out idolatry and idolators, and declares idolatry the most serious of the three cardinal sins and the one to which even martyrdom is preferable. A separate tractate in the Talmud (*Avodah Zarah*) establishes the characteristics of idolators, designates the images and objects of idolatrous worship, and testifies to the seriousness of idolatry, forbidding it under pain of death.

Hearken now to Ozick's conception of idolatry and to the characteristics she assigns to an idol. She succinctly defines idolatry in her essay "The Riddle of the Ordinary," where she proclaims an idol "anything that is allowed to come between ourselves and God. Anything that is *instead of* God." In another essay, "Literature as Idol," she attributes to an idol a fourfold capacity: "that an idol can lead only to itself and has no meaning other than itself; that an idol always has an ideal precursor on which to model its form; that an idol can have no connection to human deed and human history-making; that an idol crushes pity." Rendered into psychological terms, those traits limn a prevalent and affecting plight, which at its worst places an embargo on human life. To be obsessed by the demons of illusion, to be stripped of the vitality of deed, to be enthralled to internal idols—these create emotional idolators. They must remain the lifeless slaves of their own past; for constrained by their mind-forged manacles, idolators replace potential with entelechy, arrest living history, and enter a self-imposed exile, annihilating their own souls. Understood historically, idolatry accounts for the catastrophe of the Holocaust, a prevailing but "unbidden" subject in Ozick's fiction. Understood psychologically, idolatry becomes a metaphor for the human sacrifice to fantasy and the peril of the unlived life. The philosophical implications of the Second Commandment, as Ozick envisions it, stretch outward to encompass all of humankind.

That she perceives the causes of an unlived life to emerge from the biblical injunction against idolatry demonstrates, on the one hand, how her tradition has enriched her thinking and, on the other, how tradition has inspired her own invention. Idolatry and idolators abound in her fiction; exposed to the blaze of her imagination, they instance the creative powers that are nourished by tradition. Not only is it the matrix of Ozick's art, it is the principal source of the artist's conflict. Throughout her work, ideas clash and viewpoints shift; she presents one idea in a tale only to contradict it in another tale or in an essay. In "Envy" (a story included in this volume), for example, Herschel Edelshtein struggles against his desire to leave the ghetto and enter Western civilization, which entices him and which pains him. Yet the Ozick who imagined his dilemma is the Ozick who expresses in "Toward a New Yiddish," an essay she published a year after she published her story, her revulsion at Western civilization's treatment of the Jews. Her dialectical imagination must be apprehended and her complexity acknowledged. In her kind of imagination, "every notion owns a double face."

And every impulse is double-edged. When asked during an interview in 1985 about the phrase "Jewish writer" and the idea of Jewish writing, she explained that in an essay, "Literature as Idol," she had once "developed the idea of Jewish writing as an oxymoron, the clash of monotheism with image-making, the poet as God-competitor." When questioned further she responded:

> . . . I think it's important that the writer not stand in for whatever leads a civilization, whatever a civilization is invested with or consists of. A writer can't do that. The writer is not a priest. The writer is certainly not a leader. It's true that Tolstoy became a kind of priest or leader, but by then he was writing "What is Art?" and had repudiated all his novels. When I read "What is Art ?" I have a great deal of sympathy for him. He's very compelling. But at the same time, would one want to accept the consequences of his ideas, and give up those immortal novels? I'm completely torn and in an unholy conflict between moral seriousness and its clash with aestheticism. And there's no solution for this. I think one has to go to the grave with that.

It is with the various forms of that conflict that she wrestles throughout her fiction. In her novel *The Cannibal Galaxy,* published in 1983, she invents a schoolmaster whose Dual Curriculum is designed to resolve the battle between the artistic imagination and moral responsibility. But then she dreams a character who is a student in Joseph Brill's school. Beulah Lilt becomes a painter and an aesthete and forgets the Dual Curriculum. The schoolmaster's lessons fail: his student lacks the "higher imagination" and owns instead an "art imagination," the kind that results in idol-making. That is why Ozick alludes to the nimbus of glory surrounding the head of a pagan god at the end of the novel when she describes the painter laboring "without brooding in calculated and enameled forms out of which a flaming nimbus sometimes spread." Like her nuanced conception of idolatry, the conflict between Hebraism and Hellenism Ozick describes, though its provenance is her tradition and its terms Matthew Arnold's, has broader implications, so broad that she aptly calls it the "central quarrel of the West." And she demonstrates its breadth and relevance far beyond Judaism and treats the subject with much more depth than did Matthew Arnold. Penetrating its meaning not only for the past but for the present, she endeavors to find a means to revivify the redemptive power of the imagination, to restore to all the cultures that inhabit our postmodern world what its privatization, fragmentation, and relativism have destroyed—moral seriousness.

Our postmodernist society, which has revived the older battle between the ancients and the moderns and reinvigorated Matthew Arnold's formulation, faces another historical phenomenon, the drive toward assimilation, which will affect American history as well as Jewish history. What Ozick has written about that phenomenon applies particularly to the Jewish experience but extends to all cultures and the battle they must wage against assimilation in order to keep their traditions alive and their histories meaningful. Losing that fight can only ensure the betrayal of tradition and pave the way to cultural rootlessness, or at the very least encourage acceptance of a divided identity. It is on these momentous issues, of great consequence to all minority cultures, that Cynthia Ozick steadily focuses as she examines the meaning of tradition and depicts the effects of diminishing it. One by one, the tales in her second collection of stories, *Bloodshed,* scrutinize those who repudiate tradition or those who are content to remain on its margins. Both decisions shatter the integrity of the self.

To attempt to become someone else, to appropriate a life different from one's own—these conscious acts result in impersonation. Having fabricated an identity, the impersonator expects liberation but ends not only by forfeiting freedom but by negating the self as well. Cultural marginality affords no better fate; for as Ozick confirms, "outsideness" never "becomes cultural opportunity," nor does "unbelonging" liberate or "otherness" ennoble. What matters, and matters overwhelmingly, is having "a fascination . . . with what we have"; what sustains, and sustains enduringly, is becoming "masters of our own civilization." The conservation of tradition and the assurance of continuity, Ozick teaches, lead not to a separatist mentality but to the preservation of individual cultures and to a keener appreciation of them. To break off "cultural continuity" is to extirpate "any recognizable human goals." Tradition, then, has "moral substance," and it is the moral impulse that imbues art with the "continuity of expectations." Upon the values engendered by tradition—the imperatives of responsibility, judgment, and duty and the demands they can make on the will—depends the writer's ability to state enduring truths. Upon those imperatives and the writers who obey them depends the destiny of imaginative literature.

However forceful a conclusion that proves to be and however stead-fastly she cleaves to it, Ozick's convictions do not assuage the perplexities that art presents to her as an imaginative writer. Art has created a similar quandary for other writers, a quandary such as the one voiced by the English poet Tennyson in "The Lady of Shalott," or the one the Irish poet Yeats describes in "The Choice":

> The intellect of man is forced to choose
> Perfection of the life, or of the work,
> And if it take the second must refuse
> A heavenly mansion, raging in the dark.
> When all that story's finished, what's the news?
> In luck or out the toil has left its mark:
> That old perplexity an empty purse,
> Or the day's vanity, the night's remorse.

The novelist shares the poets' predicament, and her heritage adds to their dilemma a special poignancy. It comes from the informing ethos of the Hebrew Bible, which places an undeviating demand on the human will and which cannot help but fire the conflict between what is moral and what is aesthetic. From that perspective, art cannot possess saving powers because the artistic enterprise must always remain subordinate to the moral wisdom anchored to belief. Indeed, in that perspective, the very act of artistic creation risks heresy; for the writer of fiction who creates her own separate world, imagines the human events that unfold in it, and directs their outcome rivals the Creator when she constructs her own image and contravenes the Second Commandment. And so the imaginative writer who has been schooled in that heritage labors not in "calculated and enameled forms" but with the fear that they are the forbidden ones relished by pagans.

Such an awareness offers no surcease from conflict, but it excites in Cynthia Ozick a preoccupation with artists and the artistic imagination. Portraits of artists in the act of imaginative creation fill the pages of her third collection of tales, *Levitation;* endeavoring to resolve her besetting and unholy conflict, she seeks in *The Cannibal Galaxy* to quiet the roiling questions of art. But the novel does not end in a synthesis, nor does Ozick achieve one in her recent novel *The Messiah of Stockholm.* Nonetheless, she discovers the means at least to mitigate the incursions of idolatry from the two terms with which we began, explicitly the "work of metaphor" and the "transforming effects of memory." From memory and its moral agent metaphor ensue the humane capacity to imagine another's pain and the moral obligation to honor the stranger. In the face of such human compassion, the menace of idolatry, though it remains a constant threat, recedes and the artistic imagination succeeds in fulfilling its obligation to moral seriousness. Reciprocity, righteousness, regeneration—these originate in the Judaic heritage.

No matter how deeply Jewish history and Jewish ideas have impressed Cynthia Ozick's mind, they do not wholly fill it, nor do they define its entire contents, nor are they equal to it. The limitations of the self, the restrictions it places on thinking about the world at large, are precisely what her unfettered imagination rejects: "Our gray cells aren't our limitations. It's our will to enter the world: by the world I mean history, including the history of thought, which is the history of human experience. This isn't an intellectual viewpoint. In fact, it asks for the widening of the senses and of all experience." Her allegiance to the ideas of other writers from diverse cultures evinces the truth of that statement. Those alliances were forged during the formative years of her education. At Hunter College High School, Ozick became enraptured with the classics, which she says "instigated the profoundest literary feelings." Of her first day at college she writes, "Until now, the fire of my vitals has been for the imperious tragedians of the *Aeneid;* I have lived in the narrow throat of poetry. . . . Washington Square will wake me. In a lecture room in the Main Building, Dylan Thomas will cry his webwork syllables. . . . I will read the Bhagavad Gita and Catullus and Lessing, and, in Hebrew, a novel eerily called *Whither?*" About her student years she observed, "the world was dividing itself into an Arnoldian vision of Hebraism and Hellenism. When I read and read in Hebrew sources, I would dream the differences from the Greek; and vice versa." Her college years culminated in her writing an English honors thesis on Blake, Coleridge, Wordsworth, and Shelley. In titling her first, unpublished novel after Blake's poem *Mercy, Pity, Peace, and Love,* she registers her attraction to the eighteenth-century poet. The many literary allusions in her fiction, to Keats's urn for example, indicate the extent to which the literary tradition informs her imagination.

As an essay by Leo Baeck broke open a conceptual egg in her intellectual life, so a tale by Henry James proved equally vital to her literary life. A surprising appearance of his "Beast in the Jungle" in a science fiction anthology, brought home from the public library by her brother when she was seventeen, must have produced in Cynthia Ozick another "strangeness" that divided "into a river of wondering"; for at twenty-two she wrote "Parable in the Later Novels of Henry James," her master's thesis in English at Ohio State University. The wondering continued until her knowledge of Henry James crystallized into an obsession so disturbing it moved her in an essay, "The Lesson of the Master," to declare James's influence tantamount to perdition. That transforming influence intensifies the wondering that in her fiction leads her frequently to engage in a dialogue with James in which she confronts the burden of his power and so turns perdition into creation. Other writers whom she has cherished—she describes them as "Everyone's List"—Forster, Chekhov, Tolstoy, Conrad, George Eliot, Mann, and Melville also inhabit her imagination and they have exerted an abiding influence. Her fascination with George Eliot, whose *Middlemarch* Ozick once admitted to reading annually, and her own involvement with letter writing provided Ozick with the germ for the novella "Puttermesser Paired." At once broadly and deeply educated, Cynthia Ozick has a brain as crowded with the treasures of imaginative art as is Ruth Puttermesser's.

Those treasures form the strong ties she has to European literature as well as to the writers located in the mainstream of American literature. To glance at a theme she shares with the writers of both civilizations is to recognize that the Judaic heritage is only one of the many tributaries flowing into the river of her consciousness. An obsessive theme in Ozick's fiction, doubling has a long history. The *doppelgänger* has captivated such writers as the Russian novelists Dostoyevsky and Chekhov and American storytellers like Poe, Melville, and Faulkner, just to name a few writers in whose work divided selves appear. Søren Kierkegaard, the Danish Christian philosopher whom Cynthia Ozick once studied with delight, writes in *Repetition,* "My whole being screams in self-contradiction." One of the entries in his journals locates the source of contradiction and suggests why the idea of the double is so compelling: "Ideality and reality therefore collide—in what medium? In time? That is indeed an impossibility. In what, then? In eternity? That is indeed an impossibility. In what, then? In consciousness—there is the contradiction."

His "Jolly Corner" intimates Henry James would have concurred. In fact, Ozick's allegiance to James, marked by her many allusions to his work, exists not only because of his American heritage but because she deems his novels "Judaized." What the two heritages have in common was apprehended earlier in this century by Upton Sinclair when he linked "the spirit of equality and brotherhood which spoke through Ezekiel and Amos and Isaiah" to the "Socialist and Anarchist agitators" who he declares were "following the same tradition, possessed by the same dream as the ancient Hebrew prophets." Later in this century, during an interview in 1992, Ozick identified the Jewish values that have permeated the American experience: "The whole idea of a Constitution, augmented by a system of judicial review, is endemically Jewish. The Fifth Amendment has a biblical origin. Jews who haven't been deprived of Jewish learning know they are at home in America because America is at home in Jewish juridical values."

Nonetheless, the Jewish Idea remains unfamiliar, and that lack of familiarity has resulted in an unfortunate but all too familiar way of regarding

American writers who are Jewish. They are deemed obscure, their fiction, which draws upon their tradition as does the fiction of all writers, is deemed relevant only to Jews and capable of being understood solely by them. However, all writers bring to their work distinctive cultural values which not only comprise the ethos of their culture but define the culture itself; together those cultures testify to the "thesis of American pluralism." Now pluralism in its purest definition surely implies openness and freedom—the openness to a culture not one's own, the freedom to celebrate the particulars of one's own culture. Embracing Jewish ideas—the particulars of Judaism—the American Jewish writer remains the writer whose ideas are construed as arcane, dismissed as inaccessible, and labeled parochial. Which is to say, that writer's ideas are deemed bereft of the commonality that endows a writer's work with the universal values that attract a wide audience and make art important to humankind.

Those two terms—parochial and universal—merit discussion, for they profoundly concern Cynthia Ozick, and the distinction between them is indispensable for evaluating our multicultural literary tradition and Ozick's importance to it. Generally used to indicate limitations of all kinds, restrictions of every sort, the parochial is more precisely a point of view that dismisses, discountenances, and denies what does not belong to it—anything that is *not* it, whether that be a single custom or an entire civilization. Intolerant of difference and void of the capacity to entertain, in order to understand, the unfamiliar, the parochial can easily be identified. Its absence of imagination and its failure to acknowledge the Other are its unmistakable marks. But to imagine what is Other is not to divest oneself of the particulars belonging to one's own culture or to dissolve them in the process of assimilation. Writers whose work has endured have always mined the singularity of their own cultures, not what is common to humankind. Paradoxically, it is only by dwelling on the singular that art can transcend the particular; and without it, any culture will vanish into an undifferentiated universalism. Its particulars, therefore, are the lifeblood of every culture.

To extol them, however, is not to welcome an ethnic designation. Think, as Cynthia Ozick has, of what such a designation means: "Ethnicity may be a celebration of 'roots,' but it is an affront to history, and when that history is metaphysical history, it is an inconceivable affront." What is more, mere ethnicity leads to an acceptance of marginality, a state quite alien to the particularism Ozick champions. For her, "Literature does not spring from the urge to Esperanto but from the tribe." Upholding its values as a Jew is one thing; being a writer who is a Jew is quite another. Here is the way Cynthia Ozick differentiates a Jew from a writer: "To be a Jew is an act of the strenuous mind as it stands before the fakeries and lying seductions of

the world, saying no and no again as they parade by in all their allure. And to be a writer is to plunge into the parade and become one of the delirious marchers." It is abundantly clear that Ozick can never liken imaginative art to what is deliberately Jewish: the two are asymptotes. Furthermore, no imaginative writer, whether or not she is Jewish, sets out to write a novel to become a spokesperson for a group of people or to assume responsibility for its culture.

Many American Jewish writers—Bernard Malamud and Philip Roth come immediately to mind—have simply thrown up their hands in annoyance when questioned about being a Jewish writer. Their reason: to be asked to speak for a tradition is to be required to relinquish the absolute independence that writing fiction demands. In 1992 when she was asked in an interview to discuss Jewish culture, Ozick responded:

> As a writer of fiction, I know today that I essentially don't want to be responsible for Jewish culture, responsible, that is, within the fiction itself, in the sense of being a spokesperson or assuming the task of carrier of a tradition—because when you write fiction your method and your goal must be freedom, freedom, and more freedom. Cultural responsibility is not where your imagination is. Your imagination belongs to writing sentences and making up stories.

If a fiction writer must have the liberty not to be accountable for what her fictional characters think and do, readers of fiction must not expect a writer to act as their spokesperson or mistake the storyteller for an authority on tradition or politics. The writer's loyalties lie elsewhere. Literature aims at nothing if not at extending perception, at affording entrance into other lives; in short, literature seeks to augment sensibility. To achieve that feat, literature is contingent upon the particulars of tradition and the ability of the artist to transform them in the alembic of her imagination. Where tradition is transmuted, invention takes place: the two are intermixed.

From their union comes the inspiration to secure a kinship between the prophet Micah and the "silver-white mica-eyes" sparkling up from the pavement. Out of the living creativity of tradition come the singular revelations that shine forth in the tales and essays and poems included in this volume. The earliest of her luminous insights fill Ozick's poems, the last of which she wrote before she was thirty-six. When the Logan Elm Press published some of her poems in a hand-bound edition with original prints in honor of her attendance at Ohio State University, Ozick was asked to write a foreword. In it she tells the history of her poetry writing and worries over what to call the volume: "I do not know what to call it. I *do* know that I want to avoid a 'poetic' title. . . . Probably I worry about misrepresenting myself, through that sort of title, as a poet." The title she admits to liking for a while, "Greeks, Jews, and Other Ironies," signals the range of subjects in the poems chosen for this *Reader*. The title she ultimately decided upon for the 1992 volume, *Epodes: First Poems*, captures the early period of her life when she devoted herself to poetry and spells its end in the aftersongs that are the title's meaning. She wrote her last poem two years before the publication of her novel *Trust*.

"Greeks," "Caryatid," "The Fish in the Net," "When that with tragic rapture Moses stood," and "The Seventeen Questions of Rabbi Zusya" reflect *Trust*'s themes and motifs. The subjects of the poems mirror the poles of the conflict central to her work and summarized in *Trust* by the title of Enoch Vand's essay "Pan Versus Moses." Another poem, "Commuters' Train through Harlem," glimpses a scene in a Harlem apartment through the window of a passing train and broods on the equation Keats formulated between truth and beauty. Still another poem, "Footnote to Lord Acton," which was written in 1962, seems eerily prophetic in the connection it discovers between death and a Democratic convention. All seven poems display a variety of forms, manifest Ozick's "meticulous language-love," and bear testimony to the resplendent language that is her trademark.

Characterized by Ozick as "In certain ways . . . simply an immensely long poem," *Trust* includes the "large range of language" she desired to impart to her first published novel. It is essential to a full understanding of the rest of her oeuvre, for in *Trust* she explores the three cultural forces in history, establishes the importance of memory and history to the human experience, and sets forth the terms of the dialectic crucial to the rest of her work. Like James Joyce's first novel, Ozick's *Trust* is a portrait of the artist, but as a young woman. The passage reprinted from that novel occurs when the narrator attains self-knowledge from a scene that awakens in her understanding of the union from which her own life began. Opulent language suffuses the intensely erotic passage with mythic overtones recalling the union of Poseidon and Demeter and at the same time alludes to the covenantal ritual of Judaic law.

The contest between Pan and Moses lurks in "Envy" and looms in the Puttermesser tales. If Herschel Edelshtein, the main character of "Envy," clings to his belief in Yiddish and Jewish history, he also yearns to divest himself of his past and make the pagan contributions to Western civilization that earn a poet accolades. One of Cynthia Ozick's most moving tales, "Envy" is chiefly concerned with the perplexities of art, principally those of the Jewish artist. But what artist is not at one time or another pierced by the emotion of "envy in the marrow"? And who escapes the experience that wracks Edelshtein—the strife between generations that is brought on by the incapacity of the young and the old to imagine each other's lives? On the surface, the attorney Ruth Puttermesser, whose biography Ozick unfolds, seems at least to have escaped the experience of envy, or, as Ozick calls it in *Trust*, the "plague-fly" that "desires us against our will." Nevertheless, as Puttermesser's biographer shows in these two chapters of the attorney's life, events conspire to lure the intellectual lawyer down a path that proves to be the very antithesis of the lawful existence an attorney is presumed to lead. Her creation of a golem forces Puttermesser, like Edelshtein, to affront the embattled principles of Judaism and paganism. Linked by their mutual concern with the problems of artists, the tales epitomize Ozick's kaleidoscopic fiction.

One of its prevalent themes, impersonation, emerges in "Virility" and "A Mercenary." The future frames "Virility," the past "A Mercenary." In the first tale, Ozick wittily demonstrates that it is masculinity, not talent, that brings success in the literary world. Feminism is an issue Ozick has been engaged with since she was five-and-a half years old. She became a feminist then, as she told an interviewer, because when her grandmother brought her to *cheder* (the room or school where Jewish children receive their traditional instruction) a rabbi said to her grandmother in Yiddish, "Take her home; a girl doesn't have to study." Perhaps that early experience haunts "Virility," for Elia Gatoff's manliness earns him, for a time, the fame that eludes his aunt—the situation a woman writer faced when Ozick was writing *Trust*. She reinvokes Elia's ambivalent identity in her introduction to Stanislav Lushinski, a "Pole and a diplomat" and the central character of "A Mercenary." In turn, he shares a destiny with his African assistant, Morris Ngambe. Their parallel existences, the similar events in their lives, dramatize a problem all cultures encounter—the loss of cultural integrity brought about by the attenuation of tradition. "A Mercenary" makes plain that what devolves from any fabricated identity brings unexpected and unwanted results.

"At Fumicaro" is illustrative, and its protagonist is the devout Roman Catholic Frank Castle. Though he is Christian, he is lured, like Ozick's Jewish characters, by paganism. Castle's religious philosophy, like Isaac Kornfeld's in "A Pagan Rabbi," lapses from his Catholicism into paganism, and this time it is Christian idolatry Ozick exposes. Together her tales reveal that idolatry imperils Jew and Christian alike, for the rituals of idolatry are utterly uncivilized and inescapably inhuman. None of Ozick's themes can be consigned to a special realm or limited to a single civilization, for her fiction invariably resists classification and defies categories. It manifests a sensibility that yearns to penetrate the full expanse of human experience.

Her essays also radiate that capacious mentality. Ranging from topics like Edith Wharton and Virginia Woolf to subjects like feminism and general literary matters and spreading out to include personal revelations, the essays in this volume affirm the value Cynthia Ozick attaches to imaginative

writing and exemplify the perceptiveness with which she judges imaginative writers. To the American writer Edith Wharton, for example, Ozick
attributes an "ongoing subliminal influence on current popular fiction,"
to the English writer Virginia Woolf "Classical feminism," a radiant "individuality of condition and temperament." Those virtues characterize Ozick
as well, as her essay "Justice to Feminism" attests. Like Virginia Woolf's,
Ozick's feminism is classical: that is, both writers reject "anatomy not only
as destiny, but as any sort of governing force." When feminism becomes
a "politics of sex" and "exclusion," classical feminism is undermined and
the term "woman writer," like the label "Jewish writer," stands for reductiveness.

It is against such reductiveness and separatism that Ozick argues in the
essays reprinted here from her second collection, *Metaphor & Memory.* She
upholds instead a "nobility of inclusiveness," the "universal accessibility of
art." Commending literature's capacity "to uncover the human face," she
offers a wry "portrait of the artist as a bad character," which is to be distinguished from the portrait of a good citizen, one who must reject the
treachery that is the novelist's stock and trade. To be an educated citizen, however, is to have recognized "literature as a force," is to have engaged in "reading as an act of imaginative conversion." What the diverse
viewpoints in her essays demonstrate, one by one, are the energies of the
imagination.

Sparked by "those tiny glints of isinglass," that divided river of wondering
flows through her poems, her tales, and her essays; for the dawn of wondering ignites imagination's light. As the hour hand of the clock continues its
inescapable round, strangeness becomes understanding and first love lapses
into memory, where it remains unseen until the lamp of art is made to shine
through. But memory gives birth to metaphor, to the powerful imagining
that yokes the various forms of Cynthia Ozick's art. What makes it compelling is the sort of inkling she had when she was five years old. What
impels her imagination is her passion for knowing the different dimensions
of existence. Crowded with illuminations of every kind, various and surprising, that art testifies to a breadth of vision, to a profundity of insight, to
the humanness and inclusiveness that is Cynthia Ozick's unmistakable
hallmark.

E. M. K.
New York City

POEMS

Yes, and he also sometimes slept; and
so do you; and that makes you like Socrates.

—WALTER KAUFMANN, *The Faith of a Heretic*

Greeks

I am like Socrates.
He also sometimes slept,
And never kept
A will to please.

Like Sappho I am.
She also breakfasted,
And if someone was wed
Cowered like a ram.

I am like Hesiod.
He also sometimes coughed,
And was seldom soft
Toward the probability of God.

Like Homer I may be.
He also had to scratch,
And knew fraud and trickery,
And whom to watch.

I am like Empedocles, I think.
He also sometimes yawned,
And never pawned
The chain of being for a link.

I am like Plato and like Aesop.
They also sometimes washed,
And saw the crowd and quashed
The supercilious fop.

I am like Aeschylus, Epictetus, Anaximander.
Like Thucydides, Euripides,
Heraclitus, Sophocles,
Aristotle, Philostratus, Alexander.

I am like Antiphon, Anacreon, Hippocrates.
I am like all of these.
(They also sometimes complained
When it rained.)

Quidve petunt animae? . . .

Tum demum admissi stagna exoptata revisunt.

—*The Aeneid,* Book VI

The Fish in the Net

While going up to nirvana the ascension,
Reputed joyous, turned out to be pretension.
Those Vedanta-dippers, ladling out to sea,
Found in me the fish of their philosophy
And promised, laying pressure at each gill,
That eschewing oxygen would nourish will
And that an eradication of the fin
Would (in mind) precede disbelief of sin.

I complied; but, bred to calisthenics,
Bone-conscious, health-cultish, spawned of eugenics,
My arras self I could not soon unknit.
To uncreate is difficult: so did admit
God in covenanting no more Floods to get:
Not for pity of man, but hating sweat.
Yet fish knew that Terror not. What was death
To the world swelled our mansions and our breath,
Multiplied us guiltless; hence our relique lore,
Remembering no hiatus, instructs us more
In perpetuation than relinquishment.

Still wooed these delectably: "Art bent
On formless repetition, one self being
Unceasingly enselfed? tasting brine? fleeing
Dry emancipation from salt, spine, tide?"
And cajoled further on this line. Then wide
Gaped the sea, my bride, cold and strangely veiled,
My sudden enemy: with waves assailed
Her lover. Soon toward that seductive net
I ascended the busy road.

                              Slow regret
Attended also, as when proselytes
For the last time straining home toward sights
And elements they willingly deny,
Still cannot forbear their grieving, and cry
As though they never were converted. So
Did I, baffled by the sea's flailings, go,
Leaving ribs for philosophers' toothpicks

And a clean backbone for a crucifix:
Surrendering, in all, a skeleton
And some meat for promised oblivion.

The net rose; floated up from stage to stage
Of unreality; yet seemed a cage
For all it swore me liberty. Now air
(A vapor weird and poisonous) lay bare
And still as some uninhabited lagoon.
It was as these had told: nirvana: ruin
Of passion, ruin of possibility,
Extinction of delusion—these were three
Oblivions of worth. Thus I: "Unscaled
Unboned uneyed ungilled unfinned untailed,
Am fish no more; freed of lust, brine, tide, thirst.
These touch Brahma not, whose whalish jaw first
Swallowed all and all. His law is nothingness."

And nothing was.

                Then like a weed distress
Held up its wand and pierced the universe,
Wounding God: but cessation is the nurse
Even of unmortality. God waits
For an ending to these covetous debates
On whether he exists: meanwhile will bleed
Till Brahma breaks the worshipers of creed.
Not I: stranger on this eternal reef
Where spewed the dark net, diluvial grief
Is not my friend, nor may compassion come
To root in me the hook of martyrdom.
Indifference is my hell. I will forget
How sad it was, ascending in the net.

The Seventeen Questions of Rabbi Zusya

But who was Zusya? What shall I say
If I am asked on that Last Day?
"Zusya wasn't Moses"—can this reprieve
What Zusya was, or undeceive?

And where was Zusya? How shall I accuse
Myself of finding what I could not lose?
Where the deed was, there I woke.
Where my neck turned, turned the yoke.

And how was Zusya? Was I torn
From not being to be born?
Or was I always in a place,
Now a body now a space?

And when was Zusya? How shall I mark
My mute age aboard the Ark?
Did Jacob grapple after or before
I went naked through the gaseous door?

And what was Zusya? How may I wrap
My loot, if what I was was trap
For catching God? And should the netter
Feel on himself this strangling fetter?

O why was Zusya? And if I deny
I'm Zusya, will Zusya cry
That he is I? How can I hide
From this inner Zusya in my side?

Footnote to Lord Acton ──────────────

While in the Convention they were nominating the Next
    President of the United States,
I thought of death:
Not merely that ambition is a skull
And all microphones handles of a coffin;
Not merely that those former public speakers Socrates
    and Caesar
Are less than the moth's foot,
That grass is all power,
And only the absolute worm corrupts absolutely—

    Since on the rostrum they know this,
    In the galleries where they clutch staffs and banners
        they know this,
    The Next President of the United States knows this,
    Having for an example
    If not Koheleth
    Then the Past Presidents of the United States.

The forgotten speaker,
The alternate delegate,
The trampled demonstrator,
The shunned and shunted eldest statesman with his
    honed wail unheard,
How irrelevant is death to the pieties of men!

Death the dark, dark horse.

Commuters' Train through Harlem ————————

A fly-eye of windows—quick quick
I see the ironing board
and the bending girl, and the lick
of a fugitive curtain against the brick,
and on a sill a yellow gourd
and a child beside a scarlet bed.
A hand pursues a radio knob,
a tilted woman shifts her head
to something someone else has said.
The shaft between purveys a sob.

Keats, there are no captives and no urn.
When I click past, the fragments turn
and resume what they will be
when I am by their brevity.
It isn't static Beauty's fault
that Truth for no one thing will halt,
not even for eternity.
The ironing board will fold away,
a draft will suck the curtain home.
The gourd will rot to gray,
the child will fever in the bed,
the knob will spawn a raucous foam.
The woman will go where the voice has led.
Garbage will fall and likely stay.

And I will go by again today:
only (since there is no perfection
and Truth and Beauty don't equate),
in the other direction
and a minute late.

Caryatid

The temple that from her temple soars
yields their dusts to a thousand wars.

Gun-redundant plunder
with its cartridges of sneezes
has shot asunder
cornices and friezes.

Her chin-high stance complains
a haughty long surprise
that down these farmers' lanes
skulls of sculptors fertilize.

Alone her gorgeous sect
survives the architect.

Sinewy her maiden back
strains beneath its rubbled pack
as though ghosts weighed.

She does not dream her head
is only lightened of its crown
now that all of Greece is down.

She that raised Diana's hall
cannot comprehend its fall:

rebel
holding up a pebble.

When that with tragic rapture Moses stood ——

When that with tragic rapture Moses stood on the edge and ledge,
    the edge of the Land overlooked from the mountain's ledge,
        the ledge of life which death, like all the others law
    and being of the Law, might not overlook,

bound on that double threshold to cross the ledge but not the edge,
    to see the plain of the valley and the palm and the wave-scaly
        boundary of the sea fretting near, Judah's shining lip,
    but not to go over,
to see the commanded boundary of sheol and death its commander and
    captain, likewise a leader of men according to the law and a
        lawgiver, that promised country's single-minded king,
    and sworn to go over,
loving limits because loving law, but liking not these to Land
    and life;

when that he, the plucker of the Law from the thorny desert who
    pricked the brows of idolators obeisant,
        who cracked Sinai's pillar for the holy stones its marrow-ore,
    those grains and pebbles chipped from Rock more than rock of
        mountain, being mountain-maker,
and early wept for the oppressors whom the silt sucked in, and for
    the mares whose eye-whites reddened with the splattered yolk
        of the broken wave, and for the chariot's axles hewn of
    straight young trees, all being God's and though oppressors
        all divine, men and steeds and wondrous wheels,
when that he ascended: ascended Nebo, he whose head history had
    hammered holy, hoary, heavy, bending down from Pisgah toward the
        rabble's luring ground rich with seed,
himself allured, him whom history brought to the edge and ledge of
    denial
lest history fever with more history that history-howling heart;

when that he ascended, and with proud lieutenant's measure the given
    territory scanned, given not for him but for the fickle mob,
in that moment it was enough: history dropped him from her beak,
    too fastidious for carrion,
        and led in the gilded mob. Not that he was less than they,

he who unbewildered the mazy riddle of the way through forty years
    of nomadry,
and laid his head upon the rock to be a chamber for the thunder's
    voice,
not that he was less!—but was, being man, not more,
      going squired, though the mob's ex-squire, to the territory
        given him.

          Its situation no man knows.

And since the border-crossing was jubilant, flag-wild and roaring
    triumph, the pageant already winking sidewise at some
        Canaanitish lady-baal with breasts of sanded wood and
    smelling piney,
and he from Pisgah saw how we, the mob, noses barely over the
    border and feet still prickled with the wilderness, raced
        crying after abominations, again and after all,
no wonder he praised history for halting him at humanity, and
    bringing him unhallowed to an unknown grave.

We would raise a sepulchre if we guessed the place, and over that
    a palace,
and on every edge and ledge would lift his sacred likeness,
        commissioned and called art,
in tapestry and marble, in majesty and crimson, hiding God in
    Moses' pleats,
we adoring till God departed in disgust, and left us to the idol
        we deserved;
or failing this, forgetting Sinai we'd suppose it all a symbol
        and a dream, deafening ourselves with that technique
until once more we stood, a babbling rabble in the desert,
      waiting for another Moses to give us back our ears,
        more driven than desirous.

FICTION

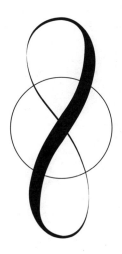

a selection from

Trust

The union of the lovers takes place on the floor, between the piano and the sofa, on the brown blanket Mrs. Purse has thrown down. There is the night sound of wind. The wool is the color of earth. Into the cavern of the dining room a weak moving light swims. It swims in like a fish, with short unsure darts, nudging an eye into life, a cruel honed nostril, gouging a murderous chin: the kings' heads are swarming in conclave on those walls. What is it, what stirs the mouths of monarchs?—a tremulous candle beating all the while, and now and again a stick of brightness cutting through from a flashlight. Someone is reading in the kitchen—I hear a page turning, I hear the fleshy creak of the reader turning his body into the night. The turning of a body is what has wakened me. I huddle on my sofa, hiding myself. The wind breathes as a sleeper might. I feel stiff with life, and lean my face between my knees—I can see my ankles, bad straight ankles with no indentation toward the heel. Above the heel a stubble snags my rub. The arms of the sofa shrug upward into shoulders, the shoulders into back. On the back the dancers dance. Behind it the lovers couple. I crouch on the ledge of the world and am their witness.

And I see her moulting, she crawls from the white tunnel of that skirt, her knees flash calisthenic pockets, in her neck two ropes pull and fall, the plane of her face grows negligible, her head feels out the floor slowly, like the tenderly lowered head of a patient. Then hands rise—her own—and through cleavages in the cloth the butting noses of buttons force themselves, her jacket springs open like mechanical wings and her shoulders lift grinning their strengths, her fingers acquiring eyes maneuver valorously against the ditch of vertebrae and the white sails over her breasts fail and sink to her belly. Then in a kind of loneliness, with the subtlety of feeling watched, she shows sportsman's skill, bets on herself, begins to slide, as with an itch in the upper back, and with a quick comic football dig has freed herself into whole nakedness, never once raising her body from its surgical lassitude. Arrogant on her dimensionless platform she lies stretched to his view and dares his daring. In her right thigh a dent like a scar but not a scar, a sulfurous soap-colored birth bruise, mocks the long strong highway of her haunch. With the vengefulness of the knowledgeably imperfect she throws her elbows crisscross over her head, displays the tangle in the armpit, and in a gesture almost scholarly closes one deft leg over another, obscuring the lower tangle. Then with buttocks nailed to the floor she rolls from the waist, twists out a balloon of flesh at the bending-point, presses to the wool two brown valves like weights dragging her breasts to their taperings, and reaches to shove away her clothes. He sees his chance, takes hold of her hipfat like a lever, and pushes her over—the solemn seal of her legs breaks, her chinbone grinds into the floor and her buttocks, pulled separate, crash into air like a pair of helmets. At the nape of each, on either side of her spine, there is a depressed pan; into the left one he fits his palm and sucks out the noise of vacuum tugging at vacuum. The hollow of his hand flees this place and seeks something round. "Roach," she says, "you nearly cracked my jaw." He gives no answer, travels with a forcing finger down into her bellybutton, he can tell how her muscles are carrying her accommodatingly higher for him, he bumps upward over the rhythm of ribs and is about to collect the candle-end of her nipple when she smashes herself suddenly down on his hand underneath her, so that her skeleton toils into his knuckles. "That hurt, you bitch, let go." "You roach. You cockroach," she says calmly, and heaves down to hold him. But somehow under her heaviness he has regained action—I can see from the minute but regular twitchings in his shoulder that he is in control of his wrist again, he has converted the soft hand of cautious searching into a fist with one uncompromising finger pointing straight out, a hand on a signpost, and now he abandons the upward direction, switches it round like an insect antenna, and probes down hard, punching with the ball of his finger as he listens to her anger, wiggling it down down among her whiskers, and slowly slowly of her own will she ripples her weight away from him, he is untrapped and free to wander, a bridge of strength grows from the root of her neck to her calves, her buttocks strain into squares, she seems to hang upward from the cord of her side, her bones gather themselves into a hinge and for a moment the leafy hillock that caches her cleft swings up, rears, dominates like a fortification, an acropolis, then from that second's ascendancy dives—her high place is razed, the Y of her slaps into an I, she closes like a compass, the hairy mound of love is reclaimed and reduced by the primary mound of the belly, vanishing almost, she is on her back, shut, but his touch which has risen with her, turned and fallen with her, clings for its life to the cliff, grabs at brush to keep itself from slipping to that belly-plain and its deep abandoned sexless pock, recovers, arches its hard knuckles, protrudes the resuming finger of excitation, and thrusts it laboring into the secret wood. "Quit that," she says bitterly, "I don't need any help from the likes of you, never mind those Chinaman gimmicks, believe me I can just cross my legs and break your arm off," but her voice runs with a moist sluggishness, the surfaces of her eyes are leathery as callouses, he has tripped some strand linked to other strands, some voluptuary wire in her brain tightens, he has caught the drawstring of her frame, her thighs knot and shift, the wicks of her nipples stiffen—"If you're waiting for tomorrow skip it," she mutters—her upper lip is hoisted, her nostrils knead themselves. But his body is away. "How d'you like that, bus without a driver," he says, "you going to get off before I get on?" "You'll never get on," she rasps. Again he does not answer, his feet curve under him like communing antlers, the absurd knobs of his buttocks pile up on his heels, he angles forward a little and from his cluttered fork just then lowers a lopsided basket like bunches of grapes in a wineskin, the round weights dragging heavily and unequally in their loose pulled bag. Hairs spring from his shoulders and he shows himself to her, leaning his tongue on his lip, then quick and crafty plunges it into the furrow of her breasts. His tongue scribbles figure 8s in a wobbling track—"I ride my own way, nobody tells me how to ride," and I see what he rides, I see the neck of the animal he rides kneeling, it stretches to escape him but is docile, its long straight neck yearns from its ruff and collar, it is a thick-flanked headless beast and new to me.—I think of Enoch and the door always open to insult my mother's delicacy, and I coming by one day and seeing how his stream falls from a tender fat creature with a short neck scalloped out of the head, and in the head a pouring cyclops-eye—the Jews are different. Stefanie laughs, mutedly they laugh together in fear of being heard, exposed—"the Leaning Tower of Pisa," she calls up to him, "whyn't you try Perma-Starch?" and I see how under the whip of her dispraise his steed hardens its headless neck, all sinew and maneless muscle, all sudden brutishness and power, its will surges out of his thighs, it bears him up on the crest of its canter, he climbs sideways to her side and still that stallion stays high in an arrested leap between his thighs, it strains outward as though it would shoot free, a slow wax tear glistens in its blind cup—"are you dressed for this?"—he turns his mouth and spits into the dark. "What d'you think I *came* with," she answers him, "I'm stuffed to the gills, I'm not *stupid,*" down now to a whisper, and he falls on his flattened hands on either side of her, and encumbered by the life that prances out of his fork he falls to his knees astride her haunch and suspends himself above her like the tent-skin that goes from bone to bone of the wing of a bat. His wrists and shins are the bones, and his ropy body hangs like a hammock between them; meanwhile his steed paws her belly. Then strangely—her face is very still—a fulcrum moves in her spine, her hams revolve and lift, her legs climb for their embrace like arms, she takes him like a caliper around the waist of an ant, her ankles are locked into his armpits, she divides herself to bag him, she cleaves herself wide for him, his stud charges and misses, retreats, assesses, charges, misses, their sighs sing together, he grabs for her buttocks and shoves them higher, she teeters on the base of her neck and props herself for him, he dangles her now from his neck like a wishbone, his sides within the crook of her urge her wider, she tears thigh from thigh, she opens herself, she is split beyond belief, his blind beast's thick muzzle lumbers down, vanishes. Ah. Reappears. She cries out at her loss of it, but now he has caught the sense of her track and goes to her straight, keen, with a cleanliness of skill and space, I hear a small brief grateful sucking, now he is like some woodcutter with a great bole before him and he must cut it down before night, and he begins, little by little, with his tempered saw, afraid of time and of magnitude, but snaring courage from the courage of the stroke, and driving in, in, toward the tree's deepest inner thong, each thrust to the center exacting an equal retreat to the farthest margin, the retreat feeding on the thrust and the thrust each time seizing more and more elasticity from the release that follows, so that the tree seems to labor in its own cutting, the tree devours the saw, together the tree and the cutter strive for its felling, the sunball leaps down and still the tree offers its opened side to the saw and the saw dives crucially into the wound, and they hurry, they hurry, if they do not meet in the crisis of the stroke they will forfeit the victory of time, if they do not match will for will they are lost to time and crisis. Time and crisis sweat in them, crisis claws time, time waits: now something huge; huge, taut, distended; some enormous dome of absence swelled by the squeeze of hope looms, intrudes, shoulders itself between the fitted halves of woman and man, untender, cunning yet blunt, now her mouth strains to stretch flat, the muscles of her cheeks squeeze now not hope but demand—now it is demand and demand, she demands the hugeness, she sweats for it, the huge freight of toil, she toils and demands, she demands what sharp birth she will bear, she toils and demands—"You lousy little independent," he tells her, "you've got plenty to learn," and she, bleak with fear of early triumph, bleats, "It's you not me, just try and catch up, grandpa," and suddenly both are motionless: motionless: a photograph of the tide: then the reel begins to run again, but too quick, berserk, backward, he flashes backward to his knees, I see his wet breast rise like a column rebuilding, he undoes gesture and posture, the trail of sweat shining downward climbs from the inner elbow to return itself to the armpit, he retrieves himself for himself: then reaches a single vast hand curved and spread to contain her and takes the swell of her crotch and fast and brutally, before she can sprawl, he flips her over. And penetrates. A noise of pain creaks from her—her arms are pressed crooked and tangled under her ribs, her palms show helplessly the wrong way up, like the pale backs of leaves, she is captive, twisted, his teeth pull on the skin of her nape and the heel of the hand that threw her over leans deep into her iron resisting belly, she no longer has her will, she is heaped below him and cannot turn, he keeps her stiff and still, his bottommost leg pries apart her calves and angry knees, she will not widen herself for him but inch by inch he pries with his invading knee and shin, now he has her wide for him but stiff, his fingers creep to cup themselves and push flat her nipple and breast, she is stiff but wonderfully wide for him, she sinks for the blow of his sinking, she burrows her hams in his grizzly triangle, she claims nothing, she is curiously manageable and quickly soft, he rides with her and rocks, as on a sea-toy, he rocks and rides, he slices the top off each smooth wave as it shrugs into being, the waves shrug themselves tall, the sea-toy swells to scale them, the waves are walls, his rocking slams the sea like a door, the tall water has walls and doors like a room, he rocks in the room, the small room shrinks, the walls tighten, he cannot rock so he beats, he beats, he does not rock or slide but he beats, beats, and slow-motion through the density of her spine the tender doors fall away of themselves, and behind one is another and beyond that another, door after door after door, and all the doors fade away into openings past openings, and he rolls from her, annulled, and she rolls slowly round, taking the curve of her flank prudently and slowly until she is on her back, her hand on the hand that dents her high nipple, and I have the sense that a mirror has peered into a mirror and viewed infinity, and I the witness of it.

From the beginning they never kissed.

17

They lay whispering.

Then I understood that they were making their plans, so I hung back to hear—a witness has no resources and no stratagems. But it was uninteresting. They were only wrangling over something nautical. Where they would go and what they would do seemed too well agreed for argument. And anyhow it was a very short quarrel, full of this boat and that boat; immediately they slept, so I started after the light. The light led from them. On the way to it I felt I had witnessed the very style of my own creation.

Envy; or, Yiddish in America

Edelshtein, an American for forty years, was a ravenous reader of novels by writers "of"—he said this with a snarl—"Jewish extraction." He found them puerile, vicious, pitiable, ignorant, contemptible, above all stupid. In judging them he dug for his deepest vituperation—they were, he said, *"Amerikaner-geboren."* Spawned in America, pogroms a rumor, *mama-loshen* a stranger, history a vacuum. Also many of them were still young, and had black eyes, black hair, and red beards. A few were blue-eyed, like the *cheder-yinglach* of his youth. Schoolboys. He was certain he did not envy them, but he read them like a sickness. They were reviewed and praised, and meanwhile they were considered Jews, and knew nothing. There was even a body of Gentile writers in reaction, beginning to show familiarly whetted teeth: the Jewish Intellectual Establishment was misrepresenting American letters, coloring it with an alien dye, taking it over, and so forth. Like Berlin and Vienna in the twenties. *Judenrein ist Kulturrein* was Edelshtein's opinion. Take away the Jews and where, O so-called Western Civilization, is your literary culture?

For Edelshtein Western Civilization was a sore point. He had never been to Berlin, Vienna, Paris, or even London. He had been to Kiev, though, but only once, as a young boy. His father, a *melamed,* had traveled there on a tutoring job and had taken him along. In Kiev they lived in the cellar of a big house owned by rich Jews, the Kirilovs. They had been born Katz, but bribed an official in order to Russify their name. Every morning he and his father would go up a green staircase to the kitchen for a breakfast of coffee and stale bread and then into the schoolroom to teach *chumash* to Alexei Kirilov, a red-cheeked little boy. The younger Edelshtein would drill him while his father dozed. What had become of Alexei Kirilov? Edelshtein, a widower in New York, sixty-seven years old, a Yiddishist (so-called), a poet, could stare at anything at all—a subway car-card, a garbage can lid, a street-light—and cause the return of Alexei Kirilov's face, his bright cheeks, his

Ukraine-accented Yiddish, his shelves of mechanical toys from Germany—
trucks, cranes, wheelbarrows, little colored autos with awnings overhead.
Only Edelshtein's father was expected to call him Alexei—everyone else,
including the young Edelshtein, said Avremeleh. Avremeleh had a knack of
getting things by heart. He had a golden head. Today he was a citizen of the
Soviet Union. Or was he finished, dead, in the ravine at Babi Yar? Edelshtein
remembered every coveted screw of the German toys. With his father he left
Kiev in the spring and returned to Minsk. The mud, frozen into peaks, was
melting. The train carriage reeked of urine and the dirt seeped through their
shoelaces into their socks.

And the language was lost, murdered. The language—a museum. Of what
other language can it be said that it died a sudden and definite death, in a
given decade, on a given piece of soil? Where are the speakers of ancient
Etruscan? Who was the last man to write a poem in Linear B? Attrition, assimilation. Death by mystery not gas. The last Etruscan walks around inside
some Sicilian. Western Civilization, that pod of muck, lingers on and on. The
Sick Man of Europe with his big globe-head, rotting, but at home in bed. Yiddish, a littleness, a tiny light—oh little holy light!—dead, vanished. Perished.
Sent into darkness.

This was Edelshtein's subject. On this subject he lectured for a living. He
swallowed scraps. Synagogues, community centers, labor unions underpaid
him to suck on the bones of the dead. Smoke. He traveled from borough
to borough, suburb to suburb, mourning in English the death of Yiddish.
Sometimes he tried to read one or two of his poems. At the first Yiddish
word the painted old ladies of the Reform Temples would begin to titter
from shame, as at a stand-up television comedian. Orthodox and Conserva-
tive men fell instantly asleep. So he reconsidered, and told jokes:

Before the war there was held a great International Esperanto Convention. It
met in Geneva. Esperanto scholars, doctors of letters, learned men, came
from all over the world to deliver papers on the genesis, syntax, and func-
tionalism of Esperanto. Some spoke of the social value of an international
language, others of its beauty. Every nation on earth was represented among
the lecturers. All the papers were given in Esperanto. Finally the meeting was
concluded, and the tired great men wandered companionably along the corridors, where at last they began to converse casually among themselves in
their international language: *"Nu, vos macht a yid?"*

After the war a funeral cortège was moving slowly down a narrow street on
the Lower East Side. The cars had left the parking lot behind the chapel in
the Bronx and were on their way to the cemetery in Staten Island. Their

route took them past the newspaper offices of the last Yiddish daily left in the city. There were two editors, one to run the papers off the press and the other to look out the window. The one looking out the window saw the funeral procession passing by and called to his colleague: "Hey Mottel, print one less!"

But both Edelshtein and his audiences found the jokes worthless. Old jokes. They were not the right kind. They wanted jokes about weddings—spiral staircases, doves flying out of cages, bashful medical students—and he gave them funerals. To speak of Yiddish was to preside over a funeral. He was a rabbi who had survived his whole congregation. Those for whom his tongue was no riddle were specters.

The new Temples scared Edelshtein. He was afraid to use the word *shul* in these palaces—inside, vast mock-bronze Tablets, mobiles of outstretched hands rotating on a motor, gigantic dangling Tetragrammatons in transparent plastic like chandeliers, platforms, altars, daises, pulpits, aisles, pews, polished-oak bins for prayerbooks printed in English with made-up new prayers in them. Everything smelled of wet plaster. Everything was new. The refreshment tables were long and luminous—he saw glazed cakes, snow-heaps of egg salad, herring, salmon, tuna, whitefish, gefilte fish, pools of sour cream, silver electric coffee urns, bowls of lemon-slices, pyramids of bread, waferlike teacups from the Black Forest, Indian-brass trays of hard cheeses, golden bottles set up in rows like ninepins, great sculptured butter-birds, Hansel-and-Gretel houses of cream cheese and fruitcake, bars, butlers, fat napery, carpeting deep as honey. He learned their term for their architecture: "soaring." In one place—a flat wall of beige brick in Westchester—he read Scripture riveted on in letters fashioned from 14-karat gold molds: "And thou shalt see My back; but My face shall not be seen." Later that night he spoke in Mount Vernon, and in the marble lobby afterward he heard an adolescent girl mimic his inflections. It amazed him: often he forgot he had an accent. In the train going back to Manhattan he slid into a miniature jogging doze—it was a little nest of sweetness there inside the flaps of his overcoat, and he dreamed he was in Kiev, with his father. He looked through the open schoolroom door at the smoking cheeks of Alexei Kirilov, eight years old. "Avremeleh," he called, "Avremeleh, *kum tsu mir, lebst ts' geshtorben?*" He heard himself yelling in English: Thou shalt see my asshole! A belch woke him to hot fear. He was afraid he might be, unknown to himself all his life long, a secret pederast.

He had no children and only a few remote relations (a druggist cousin in White Plains, a cleaning store in-law hanging on somewhere among the blacks in Brownsville), so he loitered often in Baumzweig's apartment—

dirty mirrors and rusting crystal, a hazard and invitation to cracks, an abandoned exhausted corridor. Lives had passed through it and were gone. Watching Baumzweig and his wife—gray-eyed, sluggish, with a plump Polish nose—it came to him that at this age, his own and theirs, it was the same having children or not having them. Baumzweig had two sons, one married and a professor at San Diego, the other at Stanford, not yet thirty, in love with his car. The San Diego son had a son. Sometimes it seemed that it must be in deference to his childlessness that Baumzweig and his wife pretended a detachment from their offspring. The grandson's photo—a fat-lipped blond child of three or so—was wedged between two wine glasses on top of the china closet. But then it became plain that they could not imagine the lives of their children. Nor could the children imagine their lives. The parents were too helpless to explain, the sons were too impatient to explain. So they had given each other up to a common muteness. In that apartment Josh and Mickey had grown up answering in English the Yiddish of their parents. Mutes. Mutations. What right had these boys to spit out the Yiddish that had bred them, and only for the sake of Western Civilization? Edelshtein knew the titles of their Ph.D. theses: literary boys, one was on Sir Gawain and the Green Knight, the other was on the novels of Carson McCullers.

Baumzweig's lethargic wife was intelligent. She told Edelshtein he too had a child, also a son. "Yourself, yourself," she said. "You remember yourself when you were a little boy, and *that* little boy is the one you love, *him* you trust, *him* you bless, *him* you bring up in hope to a good manhood." She spoke a rich Yiddish, but high-pitched.

Baumzweig had a good job, a sinecure, a pension in disguise, with an office, a part-time secretary, a typewriter with Hebrew characters, ten-to-three hours. In 1910 a laxative manufacturer—a philanthropist—had founded an organization called the Yiddish-American Alliance for Letters and Social Progress. The original illustrious members were all dead—even the famous poet Yehoash was said to have paid dues for a month or so—but there was a trust providing for the group's continuation, and enough money to pay for a bi-annual periodical in Yiddish. Baumzweig was the editor of this, but of the Alliance nothing was left, only some crumbling brown snapshots of Jews in derbies. His salary check came from the laxative manufacturer's grandson—a Republican politician, an Episcopalian. The name of the celebrated product was LUKEWARM: it was advertised as delightful to children when dissolved in lukewarm cocoa. The name of the obscure periodical was *Bitterer Yam*, Bitter Sea, but it had so few subscribers that Baumzweig's wife called it Invisible Ink. In it Baumzweig published much of his own poetry and a little of Edelshtein's. Baumzweig wrote mostly of Death, Edelshtein mostly of Love.

They were both sentimentalists, but not about each other. They did not like each other, though they were close friends.

Sometimes they read aloud among the dust of empty bowls their newest poems, with an agreement beforehand not to criticize: Paula should be the critic. Carrying coffee back and forth in cloudy glasses, Baumzweig's wife said: "Oh, very nice, very nice. But so sad. Gentlemen, life is not that sad." After this she would always kiss Edelshtein on the forehead, a lazy kiss, often leaving stuck on his eyebrow a crumb of Danish: very slightly she was a slattern.

Edelshtein's friendship with Baumzweig had a ferocious secret: it was moored entirely to their agreed hatred for the man they called *der chazer.* He was named Pig because of his extraordinarily white skin, like a tissue of pale ham, and also because in the last decade he had become unbelievably famous. When they did not call him Pig they called him *shed*—Devil. They also called him Yankee Doodle. His name was Yankel Ostrover, and he was a writer of stories.

They hated him for the amazing thing that had happened to him—his fame—but this they never referred to. Instead they discussed his style: his Yiddish was impure, his sentences lacked grace and sweep, his paragraph transitions were amateur, vile. Or else they raged against his subject matter, which was insanely sexual, pornographic, paranoid, freakish—men who embraced men, women who caressed women, sodomists of every variety, boys copulating with hens, butchers who drank blood for strength behind the knife. All the stories were set in an imaginary Polish village, Zwrdl, and by now there was almost no American literary intellectual alive who had not learned to say Zwrdl when he meant lewd. Ostrover's wife was reputed to be a high-born Polish Gentile woman from the "real" Zwrdl, the daughter in fact of a minor princeling, who did not know a word of Yiddish and read her husband's fiction falteringly, in English translation—but both Edelshtein and Baumzweig had encountered her often enough over the years, at this meeting and that, and regarded her as no more impressive than a pot of stale fish. Her Yiddish had an unpleasant gargling Galician accent, her vocabulary was a thin soup—they joked that it was correct to say she spoke no Yiddish—and she mewed it like a peasant, comparing prices. She was a short square woman, a cube with low-slung udders and a flat backside. It was partly Ostrover's mockery, partly his self-advertising, that had converted her into a little princess. He would make her go into their bedroom to get a whip he claimed she had used on her bay, Romeo, trotting over her father's lands in her girlhood. Baumzweig often said this same whip was applied to the earlobes of Ostrover's translators, unhappy pairs of collaborators he changed from month to month, never satisfied.

Ostrover's glory was exactly in this: that he required translators. Though he wrote only in Yiddish, his fame was American, national, international. They considered him a "modern." Ostrover was free of the prison of Yiddish! Out, out—he had burst out, he was in the world of reality.

And how had he begun? The same as anybody, a columnist for one of the Yiddish dailies, a humorist, a cheap fast article-writer, a squeezer-out of real-life tales. Like anybody else, he saved up a few dollars, put a paper clip over his stories, and hired a Yiddish press to print up a hundred copies. A book. Twenty-five copies he gave to people he counted as relatives, another twenty-five he sent to enemies and rivals, the rest he kept under his bed in the original cartons. Like anybody else, his literary gods were Chekhov and Tolstoy, Peretz and Sholem Aleichem. From this, how did he come to *The New Yorker,* to *Playboy,* to big lecture fees, invitations to Yale and M.I.T. and Vassar, to the Midwest, to Buenos Aires, to a literary agent, to a publisher on Madison Avenue?

"He sleeps with the right translators," Paula said. Edelshtein gave out a whinny. He knew some of Ostrover's translators—a spinster hack in dresses below the knee, occasionally a certain half-mad and drunken lexicographer, college boys with a dictionary.

Thirty years ago, straight out of Poland via Tel Aviv, Ostrover crept into a toying affair with Mireleh, Edelshtein's wife. He had left Palestine during the 1939 Arab riots, not, he said, out of fear, out of integrity rather—it was a country which had turned its face against Yiddish. Yiddish was not honored in Tel Aviv or Jerusalem. In the Negev it was worthless. In the God-given State of Israel they had no use for the language of the bad little interval between Canaan and now. Yiddish was inhabited by the past, the new Jews did not want it. Mireleh liked to hear these anecdotes of how rotten it was in Israel for Yiddish and Yiddishists. In Israel the case was even lamer than in New York, thank God! There was after all a reason to live the life they lived: it was worse somewhere else. Mireleh was a tragedian. She carried herself according to her impression of how a barren woman should sit, squat, stand, eat and sleep, talked constantly of her six miscarriages, and was vindictive about Edelshtein's sperm-count. Ostrover would arrive in the rain, crunch down on the sofa, complain about the transportation from the Bronx to the West Side, and begin to woo Mireleh. He took her out to supper, to his special café, to Second Avenue vaudeville, even home to his apartment near Crotona Park to meet his little princess Pesha. Edelshtein noticed with self-curiosity that he felt no jealousy whatever, but he thought himself obliged to throw a kitchen chair at Ostrover. Ostrover had very fine teeth, his own; the chair knocked off half a lateral incisor, and Edelshtein wept at the flaw. Immediately he led Ostrover to the dentist around the corner.

The two wives, Mireleh and Pesha, seemed to be falling in love: they had dates, they went to museums and movies together, they poked one another and laughed day and night, they shared little privacies, they carried pencil-box rulers in their purses and showed each other certain hilarious measurements, they even became pregnant in the same month. Pesha had her third daughter, Mireleh her seventh miscarriage. Edelshtein was grief-stricken but elated. "*My* sperm-count?" he screamed. "*Your* belly! Go fix the machine before you blame the oil!" When the dentist's bill came for Ostrover's jacket crown, Edelshtein sent it to Ostrover. At this injustice Ostrover dismissed Mireleh and forbade Pesha to go anywhere with her ever again.

About Mireleh's affair with Ostrover Edelshtein wrote the following malediction:

> *You, why do you snuff out my sons, my daughters?*
> *Worse than Mother Eve, cursed to break waters*
> *for little ones to float out upon in their tiny barks of skin,*
> *you, merciless one, cannot even bear the fruit of sin.*

It was published to much gossip in *Bitterer Yam* in the spring of that year—one point at issue being whether "snuff out" was the right term in such a watery context. (Baumzweig, a less oblique stylist, had suggested "drown.") The late Zimmerman, Edelshtein's cruelest rival, wrote in a letter to Baumzweig (which Baumzweig read on the telephone to Edelshtein):

Who is the merciless one, after all, the barren woman who makes the house peaceful with no infantile caterwauling, or the excessively fertile poet who bears the fruit of his sin—namely his untalented verses? He bears it, but who can bear it? In one breath he runs from seas to trees. Like his ancestors the amphibians, puffed up with arrogance. Hersheleh Frog! Why did God give Hersheleh Edelshtein an unfaithful wife? To punish him for writing trash.

Around the same time Ostrover wrote a story: two women loved each other so much they mourned because they could not give birth to one another's children. Both had husbands, one virile and hearty, the other impotent, with a withered organ, a *shlimazal*. They seized the idea of making a tool out of one of the husbands: they agreed to transfer their love for each other into the man, and bear the child of their love through him. So both women turned to the virile husband, and both women conceived. But the woman who had the withered husband could not bear her child: it withered in her womb. "As it is written," Ostrover concluded, "Paradise is only for those who have already been there."

A stupid fable! Three decades later—Mireleh dead of a cancerous uterus, Pesha encrusted with royal lies in *Time* magazine (which photographed the whip)—this piece of insignificant mystification, this *pollution,* included also in Ostrover's *Complete Tales* (Kimmel & Segal, 1968), was the subject of graduate dissertations in comparative literature, as if Ostrover were Thomas Mann, or even Albert Camus. When all that happened was that Pesha and Mireleh had gone to the movies together now and then—and such a long time ago! All the same, Ostrover was released from the dungeon of the dailies, from *Bitterer Yam* and even seedier nullities, he was free, the outside world knew his name. And why Ostrover? Why not somebody else? Was Ostrover more gifted than Komorsky? Did he think up better stories than Horowitz? Why does the world outside pick on an Ostrover instead of an Edelshtein or even a Baumzweig? What occult knack, what craft, what crooked convergence of planets drove translators to grovel before Ostrover's naked swollen sentences with their thin little threadbare pants always pulled down? Who had discovered that Ostrover was a "modern"? His Yiddish, however fevered on itself, bloated, was still Yiddish, it was still *mamaloshen,* it still squeaked up to God with a littleness, a familiarity, an elbow-poke, it was still pieced together out of *shtetl* rags, out of a baby *aleph,* a toddler *beys*—so why Ostrover? Why only Ostrover? Ostrover should be the only one? Everyone else sentenced to darkness, Ostrover alone saved? Ostrover the survivor? As if hidden in the Dutch attic like that child. *His* diary, so to speak, the only documentation of what was. Like Ringelblum of Warsaw. Ostrover was to be the only evidence that there was once a Yiddish tongue, a Yiddish literature? And all the others lost? Lost! Drowned. Snuffed out. Under the earth. As if never.

Edelshtein composed a letter to Ostrover's publishers:

Kimmel & Segal
244 Madison Avenue, New York City

My dear Mr. Kimmel, and very honored Mr. Segal:

I am writing to you in reference to one Y. Ostrover, whose works you are the company that places them before the public's eyes. Be kindly enough to forgive all flaws of English Expression. Undoubtedly, in the course of his business with you, you have received from Y. Ostrover, letters in English, even worse than this. (I HAVE NO TRANSLATOR!) We immigrants, no matter how long already Yankified, stay inside always green and never attain to actual native writing Smoothness. For one million green writers, one Nabokov, one Kosinski. I mention these to show my extreme familiarness with American Literature in all Contemporaneous avatars. In your language I read, let us say, wolfishly. I regard myself as a very Keen critic, esp. concerning so-called Amer.-Jewish writers. If you would give time I could willingly explain to you many clear opinions I have concerning these Jewish-Amer. boys and girls such as (not alphabetical) Roth Philip/Rosen Norma/Melammed Bernie/Friedman B.J./Paley Grace/Bellow Saul/Mailer Norman. Of the latter having just read several recent works including political I would like to remind him what F. Kafka, rest in peace, said to the German-speaking, already very comfortable, Jews of Prague, Czechoslovakia: "Jews of Prague! You know more Yiddish than you think!"

Perhaps, since doubtless you do not read the Jewish Press, you are not informed. Only this month all were taken by surprise! In that filthy propaganda *Sovietish Heymland* which in Russia they run to show that their prisoners the Jews are not prisoners—a poem! By a 20-year-old young Russian Jewish girl! Yiddish will yet live through our young. Though I doubt it as do other pessimists. However, this is not the point! I ask you— what does the following personages mean to you, you who are Sensitive men, Intelligent, and with closely-warmed Feelings! Lyessin, Reisen, Yehoash! H. Leivik himself! Itzik Manger, Chaim Grade, Aaron Zeitlen, Jacob Glatshtein, Eliezer Greenberg! Molodowsky and Korn, ladies, gifted! Dovid Ignatov, Morris Rosenfeld, Moishe Nadir, Moishe Leib Halpern, Reuven Eisland, Mani Leib, Zisha Landau! I ask you! Frug, Peretz, Vintchevski, Bovshover, Edelshtat! Velvl Zhbarzher, Avrom Goldfaden! A. Rosenblatt! Y.Y. Schwartz, Yoisef Rollnick! These are all our glorious Yiddish poets. And if I would add to them our beautiful recent Russian brother-poets that were killed by Stalin with his pockmarks, for instance Peretz Markish, would you know any name of theirs? No! THEY HAVE NO TRANSLATORS!

Esteemed Gentlemen, you publish only one Yiddish writer, not even a Poet, only a Story-writer. I humbly submit you give serious wrong Impressions. That we have produced nothing else. I again refer to your associate Y. Ostrover. I do not intend to take away from him any possible talent by this letter, but wish to WITH VIGOROUSNESS assure you that others also exist without notice being bothered over them! I myself am the author and also publisher of four tomes of poetry: *N'shomeh un Guf, Zingen un Freyen, A Velt ohn Vint, A Shtundeh mit Shney*. To wit, "Soul and Body," "Singing and Being Happy," "A World with No Wind," "An Hour of Snow," these are my Deep-Feeling titles.

Please inform me if you will be willing to provide me with a translator for these very worthwhile pieces of hidden writings, or, to use a Hebrew Expression, "Buried Light."

Yours very deeply respectful.

He received an answer in the same week.

Dear Mr. Edelstein:

Thank you for your interesting and informative letter. We regret that, unfortunately, we cannot furnish you with a translator. Though your poetry may well be of the quality you claim for it, practically speaking, reputation must precede translation.

Yours sincerely.

A lie! Liars!

Dear Kimmel, dear Segal,

Did YOU, Jews without tongues, ever hear of Ostrover before you found him translated everywhere? In Yiddish he didn't exist for you! For you Yiddish has no existence! A darkness inside a cloud! Who can see it, who can hear it? The world has no ears for the prisoner! You sign yourself "Yours." You're not mine and I'm not Yours!

Sincerely.

He then began to search in earnest for a translator. Expecting little, he wrote to the spinster hack.

Esteemed Edelshtein [she replied]:

To put it as plainly as I can—a plain woman should be as plain in her words—you do not know the world of practicality, of reality. Why should you? You're a poet, an idealist. When a big magazine pays Ostrover $500, how much do I get? Maybe $75. If he takes a rest for a month and doesn't write, what then? Since he's the only one they want to print he's the only one worth translating. Suppose I translated one of your nice little love songs? Would anyone buy it? Foolishness even to ask. And if they bought it, should I slave for the $5? You don't know what I go through with Ostrover anyhow. He sits me down in his dining room, his wife brings in a samovar of tea—did you ever hear anything as pretentious as this—and sits also, watching me. She has jealous eyes. She watches my ankles, which aren't bad. Then we begin. Ostrover reads aloud the first sentence the way he wrote it, in Yiddish. I write it down, in English. Right away it starts. Pesha reads what I put down and says, "That's no good, you don't catch his idiom." Idiom! She knows! Ostrover says, "The last word sticks in my throat. Can't you do better than that? A little more robustness." We look in the dictionary, the thesaurus, we scream out different words, trying, trying. Ostrover doesn't like any of them. Suppose the word is "big." We go through huge, vast, gigantic, enormous, gargantuan, monstrous, etc., etc.,

etc., and finally Ostrover says—by now it's five hours later, my tonsils hurt, I can hardly stand—"all right, so let it be 'big.' Simplicity above all." Day after day like this! And for $75 is it worth it? Then after this he fires me and gets himself a college boy! Or that imbecile who cracked up over the mathematics dictionary! Until he needs me. However I get a little glory out of it. Everyone says, "There goes Ostrover's translator." In actuality I'm his pig, his stool (I mean that in both senses, I assure you). You write that he has no talent. That's your opinion, maybe you're not wrong, but let me tell you he has a talent for pressure. The way among *them* they write careless novels, hoping they'll be transformed into beautiful movies and some- times it happens—that's how it is with him. Never mind the quality of his Yiddish, what will it turn into when it becomes English? Transformation is all he cares for—and in English he's a cripple—like, please excuse me, yourself and everyone of your generation. But Ostrover has the sense to be a suitor. He keeps all his translators in a perpetual frenzy of envy for each other, but they're just rubble and offal to him, they aren't the object of his suit. What he woos is *them*. Them! You understand me, Edelshtein? He stands on the backs of hacks to reach. I know you call me hack, and it's all right, by myself I'm what you think me, no imagination, so-so ability (I too once wanted to be a poet, but that's another life)—with Ostrover on my back I'm something else: I'm "Ostrover's translator." You think that's nothing? It's an entrance into *them*. I'm invited everywhere, I go to the same parties Ostrover goes to. Everyone looks at me and thinks I'm a bit freakish, but they say: "It's Ostrover's translator." A marriage. Pesha, that junk-heap, is less married to Ostrover than I am. Like a wife, I have the supposedly passive role. Supposedly: who knows what goes on in the bedroom? An unmarried person like myself becomes good at guessing at these matters. The same with translation. Who makes the language Ostro- ver is famous for? You ask: what has persuaded *them* that he's a "so-called modern"?—a sneer. Aha. *Who* has read James Joyce, Ostrover or I? I'm fifty-three years old. I wasn't born back of Hlusk for nothing, I didn't go to Vassar for nothing—do you understand me? I got caught in between, so I got squeezed. Between two organisms. A cultural hermaphrodite, neither one nor the other. I have a forked tongue. When I fight for five hours to make Ostrover say "big" instead of "gargantuan," when I take out all the nice homey commas he sprinkles like a fool, when I drink his wife's stupid tea and then go home with a watery belly—*then* he's being turned into a "modern," you see? I'm the one! No one recognizes this, of course, they think it's something inside the stories themselves, when actually it's the way I dress them up and paint over them. It's all cosmetics, I'm a cosmeti- cian, a painter, the one they pay to do the same job on the corpse in the mortuary, among *them* . . . don't, though, bore me with your criticisms. I tell you his Yiddish doesn't matter. Nobody's Yiddish matters. Whatever's in Yiddish doesn't matter.

The rest of the letter—all women are long-winded, strong-minded—he did not read. He had already seen what she was after: a little bit of money, a little bit of esteem. A miniature megalomaniac: she fancied herself the *real* Ostrover. She believed she had fashioned herself a genius out of a rag. A rag turned into a sack, was that genius? She lived out there in the light, with *them*: naturally she wouldn't waste her time on an Edelshtein. In the bleakness. Dark where he was. An idealist! How had this good word worked itself up in society to become an insult? A darling word nevertheless. Idealist. The difference between him and Ostrover was this: Ostrover wanted to save only himself, Edelshtein wanted to save Yiddish.

Immediately he felt he lied.

With Baumzweig and Paula he went to the 92nd Street Y to hear Ostrover read. "Self-mortification," Paula said of this excursion. It was a snowy night. They had to shove their teeth into the wind, tears of suffering iced down their cheeks, the streets from the subway were Siberia. "Two Christian saints, self-flagellation," she muttered, "with chains of icicles they hit themselves." They paid for the tickets with numb fingers and sat down toward the front. Edelshtein felt paralyzed. His toes stung, prickled, then seemed diseased, gangrenous, furnace-like. The cocoon of his bed at home, the pen he kept on his night table, the first luminous line of his new poem lying there waiting to be born—*Oh that I might like a youth be struck with the blow of belief*—all at once he knew how to go on with it, what it was about and what he meant by it, the hall around him seemed preposterous, unnecessary, why was he here? Crowds, huddling, the whine of folding chairs lifted and dropped, the babble, Paula yawning next to him with squeezed and wrinkled eyelids, Baumzweig blowing his flat nose into a blue plaid handkerchief and exploding a great green flower of snot, why was he in such a place as this? What did such a place have in common with what he knew, what he felt?

Paula craned around her short neck inside a used-up skunk collar to read the frieze, mighty names, golden letters, Moses, Einstein, Maimonides, Heine. Heine. Maybe Heine knew what Edelshtein knew, a convert. But these, ushers in fine jackets, skinny boys carrying books (Ostrover's), wearing them nearly, costumed for blatant bookishness, blatant sexuality, in pants crotch-snug, penciling buttocks on air, mustachioed, some hairy to the collarbone, shins and calves menacing as hammers, and girls, tunics, knees, pants, boots, little hidden sweet tongues, black-eyed. Woolly smell of piles and piles of coats. For Ostrover! The hall was full, the ushers with raised tweed wrists directed all the rest into an unseen gallery nearby: a television screen there, on which the little gray ghost of Ostrover, palpable and otherwise white as a washed pig, would soon flutter. The Y. Why? Edelshtein also lectured at Y's—Elmhurst, Eastchester, Rye, tiny platforms, lecterns too tall for him, catalogues of vexations, his sad recitations to old people. Ladies and Gentlemen, they have cut out my vocal cords, the only language I can freely and fluently address you in, my darling *mamaloshen,* surgery, dead, the operation was a success. Edelshtein's Y's were all old people's homes, convalescent factories, asylums. To himself he sang,

Why	*Farvos di Vy?*
the Y?	*Ich reyd*
Lectures	*ohn freyd*
to specters,	*un sheydim tantsen derbei,*

aha! specters, if my tongue has no riddle for you, Ladies and Gentlemen, you are specter, wraith, phantom, I have invented you, you are my imagining, there is no one here at all, an empty chamber, a vacant valve, abandoned, desolate. Everyone gone. *Pust vi dem kalten shul mein harts* (another first line left without companion-lines, fellows, followers), the cold study-house, spooks dance there. Ladies and Gentlemen, if you find my tongue a riddle, here is another riddle: How is a Jew like a giraffe? A Jew too has no vocal cords. God blighted Jew and giraffe, one in full, one by half. And no salve. Baumzweig hawked up again. Mucus the sheen of the sea. In God's Creation no thing without beauty however perverse. *Khrakeh khrakeh.* Baumzweig's roar the only noise in the hall. "Shah," Paula said, "*ot kumt der shed.*"

Gleaming, gleaming, Ostrover stood—high, far, the stage broad, brilliant, the lectern punctilious with microphone and water pitcher. A rod of powerful light bored into his eye sockets. He had a moth-mouth as thin and dim as a chalk line, a fence of white hair erect over his ears, a cool voice.

"A new story," he announced, and spittle flashed on his lip. "It isn't obscene, so I consider it a failure."

"Devil," Paula whispered, "washed white pig, Yankee Doodle."

"Shah," Baumzweig said, "*lomir heren.*"

Baumzweig wanted to hear the devil, the pig! Why should anyone want to hear him? Edelshtein, a little bit deaf, hung forward. Before him, his nose nearly in it, the hair of a young girl glistened—some of the stage light had become enmeshed in it. Young, young! Everyone young! Everyone for Ostrover young! A modern.

Cautiously, slyly, Edelshtein let out, as on a rope, little bony shiverings of attentiveness. Two rows in front of him he glimpsed the spinster hack,

Chaim Vorovsky the drunken lexicographer whom too much mathematics had crazed, six unknown college boys.

Ostrover's story:

Satan appears to a bad poet. "I desire fame," says the poet, "but I cannot attain it, because I come from Zwrdl, and the only language I can write is Zwrdlish. Unfortunately no one is left in the world who can read Zwrdlish. That is my burden. Give me fame, and I will trade you my soul for it."

"Are you quite sure," says Satan, "that you have estimated the dimensions of your trouble entirely correctly?" "What do you mean?" says the poet. "Perhaps," says Satan, "the trouble lies in your talent. Zwrdl or no Zwrdl, it's very weak." "Not so!" says the poet, "and I'll prove it to you. Teach me French, and in no time I'll be famous." "All right," says Satan, "as soon as I say Glup you'll know French perfectly, better than de Gaulle. But I'll be generous with you. French is such an easy language, I'll take only a quarter of your soul for it."

And he said Glup. And in an instant there was the poet, scribbling away in fluent French. But still no publisher in France wanted him and he remained obscure. Back came Satan: "So the French was no good, *mon vieux? Tant pis!*" "Feh," says the poet, "what do you expect from a people that kept colonies, they should know what's good in the poetry line? Teach me Italian, after all even the Pope dreams in Italian." "Another quarter of your soul," says Satan, ringing it up in his portable cash register. And Glup! There he was again, the poet, writing *terza rima* with such fluency and melancholy that the Pope would have been moved to holy tears of praise if only he had been able to see it in print—unfortunately every publisher in Italy sent the manuscript back with a plain rejection slip, no letter.

"What? Italian no good either?" exclaims Satan. *"Mamma mia,* why don't you believe me, little brother, it's not the language, it's you." It was the same with Swahili and Armenian, Glup!—failure, Glup!—failure, and by now, having rung up a quarter of it at a time, Satan owned the poet's entire soul, and took him back with him to the Place of Fire. "I suppose you'll burn me up," says the poet bitterly. "No, no," says Satan, "we don't go in for that sort of treatment for so silken a creature as a poet. Well? Did you bring everything? I told you to pack carefully! Not to leave behind a scrap!" "I brought my whole file," says the poet, and sure enough, there it was, strapped to his back, a big black metal cabinet. "Now empty it into the Fire," Satan orders. "My poems! Not all my poems? My whole life's output?" cries the poet in anguish. "That's right, do as I say," and the poet obeys, because, after all, he's in hell and Satan owns him. "Good," says Satan, "now come with me, I'll show you to your room."

A perfect room, perfectly appointed, not too cold, not too hot, just the right distance from the great Fire to be comfortable. A jewel of a desk, with a red leather top, a lovely swivel chair cushioned in scarlet, a scarlet Persian rug on the floor, nearby a red refrigerator stocked with cheese and pudding and pickles, a glass of reddish tea already steaming on a little red table. One window without a curtain. "That's your Inspiring View," says Satan, "look out and see." Nothing outside but the Fire cavorting splendidly, flecked with unearthly colors, turning itself and rolling up into unimaginable new forms. "It's beautiful," marvels the poet. "Exactly," says Satan. "It should inspire you to the composition of many new verses." "Yes, yes! May I begin, your Lordship?" "That's why I brought you here," says Satan. "Now sit down and write, since you can't help it anyhow. There is only one stipulation. The moment you finish a stanza you must throw it out of the window, like this." And to illustrate, he tossed out a fresh page.

Instantly a flaming wind picked it up and set it afire, drawing it into the great central conflagration. "Remember that you are in hell," Satan says sternly, "here you write only for oblivion." The poet begins to weep. "No difference, no difference! It was the same up there! O Zwrdl, I curse you that you nurtured me!" "And still he doesn't see the point!" says Satan, exasperated. "Glup glup glup glup glup glup glup! Now write." The poor poet began to scribble, one poem after another, and lo! suddenly he forgot every word of Zwrdlish he ever knew, faster and faster he wrote, he held on to the pen as if it alone kept his legs from flying off on their own, he wrote in Dutch and in English, in German and in Turkish, in Santali and in Sassak, in Lapp and in Kurdish, in Welsh and in Rhaeto-Romanic, in Niasese and in Nicobarese, in Galcha and in Ibanag, in Ho and in Khmer, in Ro and in Volapük, in Jagatai and in Swedish, in Tulu and in Russian, in Irish and in Kalmuck! He wrote in every language but Zwrdlish, and every poem he wrote he had to throw out the window because it was trash anyhow, though he did not realize it. . . .

Edelshtein, spinning off into a furious and alien meditation, was not sure how the story ended. But it was brutal, and Satan was again in the ascendancy: he whipped down aspiration with one of Ostrover's sample aphorisms, dense and swollen as a phallus, but sterile all the same. The terrifying laughter, a sea-wave all around: it broke toward Edelshtein, meaning to lash him to bits. Laughter for Ostrover. Little jokes, little jokes, all they wanted was jokes! "Baumzweig," he said, pressing himself down across Paula's collar (under it her plump breasts), "he does it for spite, you see that?"

But Baumzweig was caught in the laughter. The edges of his mouth were beaten by it. He whirled in it like a bug. "Bastard!" he said.

"Bastard," Edelshtein said reflectively.

"He means *you*," Baumzweig said.

"Me?"

"An allegory. You see how everything fits . . . ."

"If you write letters, you shouldn't mail them," Paula said reasonably. "It got back to him you're looking for a translator."

"He doesn't need a muse, he needs a butt. Naturally it got back to him," Baumzweig said. "That witch herself told him."

"Why me?" Edelshtein said. "It could be you."

"I'm not a jealous type," Baumzweig protested. "What he has you want." He waved over the audience: just then he looked as insignificant as a little bird.

Paula said, "You both want it."

What they both wanted now began. Homage.

Q.   Mr. Ostrover, what would you say is the symbolic weight of this story?

A.   The symbolic weight is, what you need you deserve. If you don't need to be knocked on the head you'll never deserve it.

Q.   Sir, I'm writing a paper on you for my English class. Can you tell me please if you believe in hell?

A.   Not since I got rich.

Q.   How about God? Do you believe in God?

A.   Exactly the way I believe in pneumonia. If you have pneumonia, you have it. If you don't, you don't.

Q.   Is it true your wife is a Countess? Some people say she's really only Jewish.

A.   In religion she's a transvestite, and in actuality she's a Count.

Q.   Is there really such a language as Zwrdlish?

A.   You're speaking it right now, it's the language of fools.

Q.   What would happen if you weren't translated into English?

A.   The pygmies and the Eskimos would read me instead. Nowadays to be Ostrover is to be a worldwide industry.

Q.   Then why don't you write about worldwide things like wars?

A.   Because I'm afraid of loud noises.

Q.   What do you think of the future of Yiddish?

A. What do you think of the future of the Doberman pinscher?

Q. People say other Yiddishists envy you.

A. No, it's I who envy them. I like a quiet life.

Q. Do you keep the Sabbath?

A. Of course, didn't you notice it's gone?—I keep it hidden.

Q. And the dietary laws? Do you observe them?

A. Because of the moral situation of the world I have to. I was heartbroken to learn that the minute an oyster enters my stomach, he becomes an anti-Semite. A bowl of shrimp once started a pogrom against my intestines.

Jokes, jokes! It looked to go on for another hour. The condition of fame, a Question Period: a man can stand up forever and dribble shallow quips and everyone admires him for it. Edelshtein threw up his seat with a squeal and sneaked up the aisle to the double doors and into the lobby. On a bench, half-asleep, he saw the lexicographer. Usually he avoided him—he was a man with a past, all pasts are boring—but when he saw Vorovsky raise his leathery eyelids he went toward him.

"What's new, Chaim?"

"Nothing. Liver pains. And you?"

"Life pains. I saw you inside."

"I walked out, I hate the young."

"You weren't young, no."

"Not like these. I never laughed. Do you realize, at the age of twelve I had already mastered calculus? I practically reinvented it on my own. You haven't read Wittgenstein, Hersheleh, you haven't read Heisenberg, what do you know about the empire of the universe?"

Edelshtein thought to deflect him: "Was it your translation he read in there?"

"Did it sound like mine?"

"I couldn't tell."

"It was and it wasn't. Mine, improved. If you ask that ugly one, she'll say it's hers, improved. Who's really Ostrover's translator? Tell me, Hersheleh, maybe it's you. Nobody knows. It's as they say—by several hands, and all the hands are in Ostrover's pot, burning up. I would like to make a good strong b.m. on your friend Ostrover."

"*My* friend? He's not my friend."

"So why did you pay genuine money to see him? You can see him for free somewhere else, no?"

"The same applies to yourself."

"Youth, I brought youth."

A conversation with a madman: Vorovsky's *meshugas* was to cause other people to suspect him of normality. Edelshtein let himself slide to the bench—he felt his bones accordion downward. He was in the grip of a mournful fatigue. Sitting eye to eye with Vorovsky he confronted the other's hat—a great Russian-style fur monster. A nimbus of droshky-bells surrounded it, shrouds of snow. Vorovsky had a big head, with big kneaded features, except for the nose, which looked like a doll's, pink and formlessly delicate. The only sign of drunkenness was at the bulbs of the nostrils, where the cartilage was swollen, and at the tip, also swollen. Of actual madness there was, in ordinary discourse, no sign, except a tendency toward elusiveness. But it was known that Vorovsky, after compiling his dictionary, a job of seventeen years, one afternoon suddenly began to laugh, and continued laughing for six months, even in his sleep: in order to rest from laughing he had to be given sedatives, though even these could not entirely suppress his laughter. His wife died, and then his father, and he went on laughing. He lost control of his bladder, and then discovered the curative potency, for laughter, of drink. Drink cured him, but he still peed publicly, without realizing it; and even his cure was tentative and unreliable, because if he happened to hear a joke that he liked he might laugh at it for a minute or two, or, on occasion, three hours. Apparently none of Ostrover's jokes had struck home with him—he was sober and desolate-looking. Nevertheless Edelshtein noticed a large dark patch near his fly. He had wet himself, it was impossible to tell how long ago. There was no odor. Edelshtein moved his buttocks back an inch. "Youth?" he inquired.

"My niece. Twenty-three years old, my sister Ida's girl. She reads Yiddish fluently," he said proudly. "She writes."

"In Yiddish?"

"Yiddish," he spat out. "Don't be crazy, Hersheleh, who writes in Yiddish? Twenty-three years old, she should write in Yiddish? What is she, a refugee, an American girl like that? She's crazy for literature, that's all, she's like the rest in there, to her Ostrover's literature. I brought her, she wanted to be introduced."

"Introduce me," Edelshtein said craftily.

"She wants to be introduced to someone famous, where do you come in?"

"Translated I'd be famous. Listen, Chaim, a talented man like you, so many languages under your belt, why don't you give me a try? A try and a push."

"I'm no good at poetry. You should write stories if you want fame."

"I don't want fame."

"Then what are you talking about?"

"I want—" Edelshtein stopped. What did he want? "To reach," he said.

Vorovsky did not laugh. "I was educated at the University of Berlin. From Vilna to Berlin, that was 1924. Did I reach Berlin? I gave my whole life to collecting a history of the human mind, I mean expressed in mathematics. In mathematics the final and only poetry possible. Did I reach the empire of the universe? Hersheleh, if I could tell you about reaching, I would tell you this: reaching is impossible. Why? Because when you get where you wanted to reach to, that's when you realize that's not what you want to reach to.— Do you know what a bilingual German-English mathematical dictionary is good for?"

Edelshtein covered his knees with his hands. His knuckles glimmered up at him. Row of white skulls.

"Toilet paper," Vorovsky said. "Do you know what poems are good for? The same. And don't call me cynic, what I say isn't cynicism."

"Despair maybe," Edelshtein offered.

"Despair up your ass. I'm a happy man. I know something about laughter." He jumped up—next to the seated Edelshtein he was a giant. Fists gray, thumbnails like bone. The mob was pouring out of the doors of the auditorium. "Something else I'll tell you. Translation is no equation. If you're looking for an equation, better die first. There are no equations, equations don't happen. It's an idea like a two-headed animal, you follow me? The last time I saw an equation it was in a snapshot of myself. I looked in my own eyes, and what did I see there? I saw God in the shape of a murderer. What you should do with your poems is swallow your tongue. There's my niece, behind Ostrover like a tail. Hey Yankel!" he boomed.

The great man did not hear. Hands, arms, heads enclosed him like a fisherman's net. Baumzweig and Paula paddled through eddies, the lobby swirled. Edelshtein saw two little people, elderly, overweight, heavily dressed. He hid himself, he wanted to be lost. Let them go, let them go—

But Paula spotted him. "What happened? We thought you took sick."

"It was too hot in there."

"Come home with us, there's a bed. Instead of your own place alone."

"Thank you no. He signs autographs, look at that."

"Your jealousy will eat you up, Hersheleh."

"I'm not jealous!" Edelshtein shrieked; people turned to see. "Where's Baumzweig?"

"Shaking hands with the pig. An editor has to keep up contacts."

"A poet has to keep down vomit."

Paula considered him. Her chin dipped into her skunk ruff. "How can you vomit, Hersheleh? Pure souls have no stomachs, only ectoplasm. Maybe Ostrover's right, you have too much ambition for your size. What if your dear friend Baumzweig didn't publish you? You wouldn't know your own name. My husband doesn't mention this to you, he's a kind man, but I'm not afraid of the truth. Without him you wouldn't exist."

"With him I don't exist," Edelshtein said. "What is existence?"

"I'm not a Question Period," Paula said.

"That's all right," Edelshtein said, "because I'm an Answer Period. The answer is period. Your husband is finished, period. Also I'm finished, period. We're already dead. Whoever uses Yiddish to keep himself alive is already dead. Either you realize this or you don't realize it. I'm one who realizes."

"I tell him all the time he shouldn't bother with you. You come and you hang around."

"Your house is a gallows, mine is a gas chamber, what's the difference?"

"Don't come any more, nobody needs you."

"My philosophy exactly. We are superfluous on the face of the earth."

"You're a scoundrel."

"Your husband's a weasel, and you're the wife of a weasel."

"Pig and devil yourself."

"Mother of puppydogs." (Paula, such a good woman, the end, he would never see her again!)

He blundered away licking his tears, hitting shoulders with his shoulder, blind with the accident of his grief. A yearning all at once shouted itself in his brain:

EDELSHTEIN: Chaim, teach me to be a drunk!

VOROVSKY: First you need to be crazy.

EDELSHTEIN: Teach me to go crazy!

VOROVSKY: First you need to fail.

EDELSHTEIN: I've failed, I'm schooled in failure, I'm a master of failure!

VOROVSKY: Go back and study some more.

One wall was a mirror. In it he saw an old man crying, dragging a striped scarf like a prayer shawl. He stood and looked at himself. He wished he had been born a Gentile. Pieces of old poems littered his nostrils, he smelled the hour of their creation, his wife in bed beside him, asleep after he had rubbed her to compensate her for bitterness. *The sky is cluttered with stars of David. . . . If everything is something else, then I am something else. . . . Am I a thing and not a bird? Does my way fork though I am one? Will God take back history? Who will let me begin again. . . .*

OSTROVER: Hersheleh, I admit I insulted you, but who will know? It's only a make-believe story, a game.

EDELSHTEIN: Literature isn't a game! Literature isn't little stories!

OSTROVER: So what is it, Torah? You scream out loud like a Jew, Edelshtein. Be quiet, they'll hear you.

EDELSHTEIN: And you, Mr. Elegance, you aren't a Jew?

OSTROVER: Not at all, I'm one of *them*. You too are lured, aren't you, Hersheleh? Shakespeare is better than a shadow, Pushkin is better than a pipsqueak, hah?

EDELSHTEIN: If you become a Gentile you don't automatically become a Shakespeare.

OSTROVER: Oho! A lot you know. I'll let you in on the facts, Hersheleh, because I feel we're really brothers, I feel you straining toward the core of the world. Now listen—did you ever hear of Velvl Shikkerparev? Never. A Yiddish scribbler writing romances for the Yiddish stage in the East End, I'm speaking of London, England. He finds a translator and overnight he becomes Willie Shakespeare. . . .

EDELSHTEIN: Jokes aside, is this what you advise?

OSTROVER: I would advise my own father no less. Give it up, Hersheleh, stop believing in Yiddish.

EDELSHTEIN: But I don't believe in it!

OSTROVER: You do. I see you do. It's no use talking to you, you won't let go. Tell me, Edelshtein, what language does Moses speak in the world-to-come?

EDELSHTEIN: From babyhood I know this. Hebrew on the Sabbath, on weekdays Yiddish.

OSTROVER: Lost soul, don't make Yiddish into the Sabbath-tongue! If you believe in holiness, you're finished. Holiness is for make-believe.

EDELSHTEIN: I want to be a Gentile like you!

OSTROVER: I'm only a make-believe Gentile. This means that I play at being a Jew to satisfy them. In my village when I was a boy they used to bring in a dancing bear for the carnival, and everyone said, "It's human!"— They said this because they knew it was a bear, though it stood on two legs and waltzed. But it was a bear.

Baumzweig came to him then. "Paula and her temper. Never mind, Hersheleh, come and say hello to the big celebrity, what can you lose?" He went docilely, shook hands with Ostrover, even complimented him on his story. Ostrover was courtly, wiped his lip, let ooze a drop of ink from a slow pen, and continued autographing books. Vorovsky lingered humbly at the rim of Ostrover's circle: his head was fierce, his eyes timid; he was steering a girl by the elbow, but the girl was mooning over an open flyleaf, where Ostrover had written his name. Edelshtein, catching a flash of letters, was startled: it was the Yiddish version she held.

"Excuse me," he said.

"My niece," Vorovsky said.

"I see you read Yiddish," Edelshtein addressed her. "In your generation a miracle."

"Hannah, before you stands H. Edelshtein the poet."

"Edelshtein?"

"Yes."

She recited, *"Little fathers, little uncles, you with your beards and glasses and curly hair. . . ."*

Edelshtein shut his lids and again wept.

"If it's the same Edelshtein?"

"The same," he croaked.

"My grandfather used to do that one all the time. It was in a book he had, *A Velt ohn Vint.* But it's not possible."

"Not possible?"

"That you're still alive."

"You're right, you're right," Edelshtein said, struck. "We're all ghosts here."

"My grandfather's dead."

"Forgive him."

"He used to read you! And he was an old man, he died years ago, and you're still alive—"

"I'm sorry," Edelshtein said. "Maybe I was young then, I began young."

"Why do you say ghosts? Ostrover's no ghost."

"No, no," he agreed. He was afraid to offend. "Listen, I'll say the rest for you. I'll take a minute only, I promise. Listen, see if you can remember from your grandfather—"

Around him, behind him, in front of him Ostrover, Vorovsky, Baumzweig, perfumed ladies, students, the young, the young, he clawed at his wet face and declaimed, he stood like a wanton stalk in the heart of an empty field:

> *How you spring out of the ground covered with poverty!*
> *In your long coats, fingers rolling wax, tallow eyes.*
> *How can I speak to you, little fathers?*
> *You who nestled me with lyu, lyu, lyu,*
> *lip-lullaby. Jabber of blue-eyed sailors,*
> *how am I fallen into a stranger's womb?*
>
> *Take me back with you, history has left me out.*
> *You belong to the Angel of Death,*
> *I to you.*
> *Braided wraiths, smoke,*
> *let me fall into your graves,*
> *I have no business being your future.*

He gargled, breathed, coughed, choked, tears invaded some false channel in his throat—meanwhile he swallowed up with the seizure of each bawled word this niece, this Hannah, like the rest, boots, rough full hair, a forehead made on a Jewish last, chink eyes—

> *At the edge of the village a little river.*
> *Herons tip into it pecking at their images*
> *when the waders pass whistling like Gentiles.*
> *The herons hang, hammocks above the sweet summer-water.*
> *Their skulls are full of secrets, their feathers scented.*
> *The village is so little it fits into my nostril.*
> *The roofs shimmer tar,*
> *the sun licks thick as cow.*
> *No one knows what will come.*
> *How crowded with mushrooms the forest's dark floor.*

Into his ear Paula said, "Hersheleh, I apologize, come home with us, please, please, I apologize." Edelshtein gave her a push, he intended to finish. *"Littleness,"* he screamed,

> *I speak to you.*
> *We are such a little huddle.*
> *Our little hovels, our grandfathers' hard hands, how little,*
> *our little, little words,*
> *this lullaby*
> *sung at the lip of your grave,*

he screamed.

Baumzweig said, "That's one of your old good ones, the best."

"The one on my table, in progress, is the best," Edelshtein screamed, clamor still high over his head; but he felt soft, rested, calm; he knew how patient.

Ostrover said, "That one you shouldn't throw out the window."

Vorovsky began to laugh.

"This is the dead man's poem, now you know it," Edelshtein said, looking all around, pulling at his shawl, pulling and pulling at it: this too made Vorovsky laugh.

"Hannah, better take home your uncle Chaim," Ostrover said: handsome, all white, a public genius, a feather.

Edelshtein discovered he was cheated, he had not examined the girl sufficiently.

He slept in the sons' room—bunk beds piled on each other. The top one was crowded with Paula's storage boxes. He rolled back and forth on the bottom, dreaming, jerking awake, again dreaming. Now and then, with a vomitous taste, he belched up the hot cocoa Paula had given him for reconciliation. Between the Baumzweigs and himself a private violence: lacking him, whom would they patronize? They were moralists, they needed someone to feel guilty over. Another belch. He abandoned his fine but uninnocent dream—young, he was kissing Alexei's cheeks like ripe peaches, he drew away . . . it was not Alexei, it was a girl, Vorovsky's niece. After the kiss she slowly tore the pages of a book until it snowed paper, black bits of alphabet, white bits of empty margin. Paula's snore traveled down the hall to him. He writhed out of bed and groped for a lamp. With it he lit up a decrepit table covered with ancient fragile model airplanes. Some had rubber-band propellers, some were papered over a skeleton of balsa-wood ribs. A game of Monopoly lay under a samite tissue of dust. His hand fell on two old envelopes, one already browning, and without hesitation he pulled the letters out and read them:

Today was two special holidays in one, Camp Day and Sacco and Vanzetti Day. We had to put on white shirts and white shorts and go to the casino to hear Chaver Rosenbloom talk about Sacco and Vanzetti. They were a couple of Italians who were killed for loving the poor. Chaver Rosenbloom cried, and so did Mickey but I didn't. Mickey keeps forgetting to wipe himself in the toilet but I make him.

Paula and Ben: thanks so much for the little knitted suit and the clown rattle. The box was a bit smashed in but the rattle came safe anyhow. Stevie will look adorable in his new blue suit when he gets big enough for it. He already seems to like the duck on the collar. It will keep him good and warm too. Josh has been working very hard these days preparing for a course in the American Novel and asks me to tell you he'll write as soon as he can. We all send love, and Stevie sends a kiss for Grandma and Pa. *P.S.* Mickey drove down in a pink Mercedes last week. We all had quite a chat and told him he should settle down!

Heroes, martyrdom, a baby. Hatred for these letters made his eyelids quiver. Ordinariness. Everything a routine. Whatever man touches becomes banal like man. Animals don't contaminate nature. Only man the corrupter, the anti-divinity. All other species live within the pulse of nature. He despised these ceremonies and rattles and turds and kisses. The pointlessness of their babies. Wipe one generation's ass for the sake of wiping another generation's ass: this was his whole definition of civilization. He pushed back the airplanes, cleared a front patch of table with his elbow, found his pen, wrote:

Dear Niece of Vorovsky:

It is very strange to me to feel I become a Smasher, I who was born to being humane and filled with love for our darling Human Race.

But nausea for his shadowy English, which he pursued in dread, passion, bewilderment, feebleness, overcame him. He started again in his own tongue—

Unknown Hannah:

I am a man writing you in a room of the house of another man. He and I are secret enemies, so under his roof it is difficult to write the truth. Yet I swear to you I will speak these words with my heart's whole honesty. I do not remember either your face or your body. Vaguely your angry voice. To me you are an abstraction. I ask whether the ancients had any physical representation of the Future, a goddess Futura, so to speak. Presumably she would have blank eyes, like Justice. It is an incarnation of the Future to whom this letter is addressed. Writing to the Future one does not expect an answer. The Future is an oracle for whose voice one cannot wait in inaction. One must do to be. Although a Nihilist, not by choice but by conviction, I discover in myself an unwillingness to despise survival. Often I have spat on myself for having survived the deathcamps— survived them drinking tea in New York!—but today when I heard carried on your tongue some old syllables of mine I was again wheedled into tolerance of survival. The sound of a dead language on a live girl's tongue! That baby should follow baby is God's trick on us, but surely we too can have a trick on God? If we fabricate with our syllables an immortality passed from the spines of the old to the shoulders of the young, even God cannot spite it. If the prayer-load that spilled upward from the mass graves should somehow survive! If not the thicket of lamentation itself, then the language on which it rode. Hannah, youth itself is nothing unless it keeps its promise to grow old. Grow old in Yiddish, Hannah, and carry fathers and uncles into the future with you. Do this. You, one in ten thousand maybe, who were born with the gift of Yiddish in your mouth, the alphabet of Yiddish in your palm, don't make ash of these! A little while ago there were twelve million people—not including babies— who lived inside this tongue, and now what is left? A language that never had a territory except Jewish mouths, and half the Jewish mouths on earth already stopped up with German worms. The rest jabber Russian, English, Spanish, God knows what. Fifty years ago my mother lived in Russia and spoke only broken Russian, but her Yiddish was like silk. In Israel they give the language of Solomon to machinists. Rejoice—in Solomon's time what else did the mechanics speak? Yet whoever forgets Yiddish courts amnesia of history. Mourn—the forgetting has already happened. A thousand years of our travail forgotten. Here and there a word left for vaudeville jokes. Yiddish, I call on you to choose! Yiddish! Choose death or death. Which is to say death through forgetting or death through translation. Who will redeem you? What act of salvation will restore you? All you can hope for, you tattered, you withered, is translation in America! Hannah, you have a strong mouth, made to carry the future—

But he knew he lied, lied, lied. A truthful intention is not enough. Oratory and declamation. A speech. A lecture. He felt himself an obscenity. What did the death of Jews have to do with his own troubles? His cry was ego and more ego. His own stew, foul. Whoever mourns the dead mourns himself. He wanted someone to read his poems, no one could read his poems. Filth and exploitation to throw in history. As if a dumb man should blame the ears that cannot hear him.

He turned the paper over and wrote in big letters:

EDELSHTEIN GONE,

and went down the corridor with it in pursuit of Paula's snore. Taken without ridicule a pleasant riverside noise. Bird. More cow to the sight: the connubial bed, under his gaze, gnarled and lumped—in it this old male and this old female. He was surprised on such a cold night they slept with only one blanket, gauzy cotton. They lay like a pair of kingdoms in summer. Long ago they had been at war, now they were exhausted into downy truce. Hair all over Baumzweig. Even his leg-hairs gone white. Nightstands, a pair of them, on either side of the bed, heaped with papers, books, magazines, lampshades sticking up out of all that like figurines on a prow—the bedroom was Baumzweig's second office. Towers of back issues on the floor. On the dresser a typewriter besieged by Paula's toilet water bottles and face powder. Fragrance mixed with urinous hints. Edelshtein went on looking at the sleepers. How reduced they seemed, each breath a little demand for more, more, more, a shudder of jowls; how they heaved a knee, a thumb; the tiny blue veins all over Paula's neck. Her nightgown was stretched away and he saw that her breasts had dropped sidewise and, though still very fat, hung in pitiful creased bags of mole-dappled skin. Baumzweig wore only his underwear: his thighs were full of picked sores.

He put EDELSHTEIN GONE between their heads. Then he took it away—on the other side was his real message: secret enemies. He folded the sheet inside his coat pocket and squeezed into his shoes. Cowardly. Pity for breathing carrion. All pity is self-pity. Goethe on his deathbed: more light!

In the street he felt liberated. A voyager. Snow was still falling, though more lightly than before, a night-colored blue. A veil of snow revolved in front of him, turning him around. He stumbled into a drift, a magnificent bluish pile slanted upward. Wetness pierced his feet like a surge of cold blood. Beneath the immaculate lifted slope he struck stone—the stair of a stoop. He remembered his old home, the hill of snow behind the study-house, the smoky fire, his father swaying nearly into the black fire and chanting, one big duck, the stupid one, sliding on the ice. His mother's neck too was finely veined and secretly, sweetly, luxuriantly odorous. Deeply and gravely he wished he had worn galoshes—no one reminds a widower. His shoes were infernos of cold, his toes dead blocks. Himself the only life in the street, not even a cat. The veil moved against him, turning, and beat on his pupils. Along the curb cars squatted under humps of snow, blue-backed tortoises. Nothing moved in the road. His own house was far, Vorovsky's nearer, but he could not read the street sign. A building with a canopy. Vorovsky's hat. He made himself very small, small as a mouse, and curled himself up in the fur of it. To be very, very little and to live in a hat. A little wild creature in a burrow. Inside warm, a mound of seeds nearby, licking himself for cleanliness, all sorts of weather leaping down. His glasses fell from his face and with an odd tiny crack hit the lid of a garbage can. He took off one glove and felt for them in the snow. When he found them he marveled at how the frames burned. Suppose a funeral on a night like this, how would they open the earth? His glasses were slippery as icicles when he put them on again. A crystal spectrum delighted him, but he could not see the passageway, or if there was a canopy. What he wanted from Vorovsky was Hannah.

There was no elevator. Vorovsky lived on the top floor, very high up. From his windows you could look out and see people so tiny they became patterns. It was a different building, not this one. He went down three fake-marble steps and saw a door. It was open: inside was a big black room knobby with baby carriages and tricycles. He smelled wet metal like a toothpain: life! Peretz tells how on a bitter night a Jew outside the window envied peasants swigging vodka in a hovel—friends in their prime and warm before the fire. Carriages and tricycles, instruments of Diaspora. Baumzweig with his picked sores was once also a baby. In the Diaspora the birth of a Jew increases nobody's population, the death of a Jew has no meaning. Anonymous. To have died among the martyrs—solidarity at least, a passage into history, one of the marked ones, *kiddush ha-shem.*—A telephone on the wall. He pulled off his glasses, all clouded over, and took out a pad with numbers in it and dialed.

"Ostrover?"

"Who is this?"

"*Yankel* Ostrover, the writer, or Pisher Ostrover the plumber?"

"What do you want?"

"To leave evidence," Edelshtein howled.

"Never mind! Make an end! Who's there?"

"The Messiah."

"Who is this?—Mendel, it's you?"

"Never."

"Gorochov?"

"That toenail? Please. Trust me."

"Fall into a hole!"

"This is how a man addresses his Redeemer?"

"It's five o'clock in the morning! What do you want? Bum! Lunatic! Cholera! Black year! Plague! Poisoner! Strangler!"

"You think you'll last longer than your shroud, Ostrover? Your sentences are an abomination, your style is like a pump, a pimp has a sweeter tongue—"

"Angel of Death!"

He dialed Vorovsky but there was no answer.

The snow had turned white as the white of an eye. He wandered toward Hannah's house, though he did not know where she lived, or what her name was, or whether he had ever seen her. On the way he rehearsed what he would say to her. But this was not satisfactory, he could lecture but not speak into a face. He bled to retrieve her face. He was in pursuit of her, she was his destination. Why? What does a man look for, what does he need? What can a man retrieve? Can the future retrieve the past? And if retrieve, how redeem? His shoes streamed. Each step was a pond. The herons in spring, red-legged. Secret eyes they have: the eyes of birds— frightening. Too open. The riddle of openness. His feet poured rivers. Cold, cold.

> Little old man in the cold,
> come hop up on the stove,
> your wife will give you a crust with jam.
> Thank you, muse, for this little psalm.

He belched. His stomach was unwell. Indigestion? A heart attack? He wiggled the fingers of his left hand: though frozen they tingled. Heart. Maybe only ulcer. Cancer, like Mireleh? In a narrow bed he missed his wife. How much longer could he expect to live? An unmarked grave. Who would know he had ever been alive? He had no descendants, his grandchildren were imaginary. *O my unborn grandson* . . . Hackneyed. *Ungrandfathered ghost* . . . Too baroque. Simplicity, purity, truthfulness.

He wrote:

Dear Hannah:

You made no impression on me. When I wrote you before at Baumzweig's I lied. I saw you for a second in a public place, so what? Holding a

Yiddish book. A young face on top of a Yiddish book. Nothing else. For me this is worth no somersault. Ostrover's vomit!—that popularizer, vulgarian, panderer to people who have lost the memory of peoplehood. A thousand times a pimp. Your uncle Chaim said about you: "She writes." A pity on his judgment. Writes! Writes! Potatoes in a sack! Another one! What do you write? When will you write? How will you write? Either you'll become an editor of *Good Housekeeping,* or, if serious, join the gang of so-called Jewish novelists. I've sniffed them all, I'm intimate with their smell. Satirists they call themselves. Picking at their crotches. What do they *know,* I mean of *knowledge?* To satirize you have to know something. In a so-called novel by a so-called Jewish novelist ("*activist-existential*"—listen, I understand, I read everything!)—Elkin, Stanley, to keep to only one example—the hero visits Williamsburg to contact a so-called "miracle rabbi." Even the word *rabbi!* No, listen—to me, a descendant of the Vilna Gaon myself, the *guter yid* is a charlatan and his *chasidim* are victims, never mind if willing or not. But that's not the point. You have to KNOW SOMETHING! At least the difference between a *rav* and a *rebbeh!* At least a *pinteleh* here and there! Otherwise where's the joke, where's the satire, where's the mockery? American-born! An ignoramus mocks only himself. *Jewish* novelists! Savages! The allrightnik's children, all they know is to curse the allrightnik! Their Yiddish! One word here, one word there. *Shikseh* on one page, *putz* on the other, and that's the whole vocabulary! And when they give a try at phonetic rendition! Darling God! If they had mothers and fathers, they crawled out of the swamps. Their grandparents were tree-squirrels if that's how they held their mouths. They know ten words for, excuse me, penis, and when it comes to a word for learning they're impotent!

Joy, joy! He felt himself on the right course at last. Daylight was coming, a yellow elephant rocked silently by in the road. A little light burned eternally on its tusk. He let it slide past, he stood up to the knees in the river at home, whirling with joy. He wrote:

TRUTH!

But this great thick word, Truth!, was too harsh, oaken; with his finger in the snow he crossed it out.

I was saying: indifference. I'm indifferent to you and your kind. Why should I think you're another species, something better? Because you knew a shred of a thread of a poem of mine? Ha! I was seduced by my own vanity. I have a foolish tendency to make symbols out of glimpses. My poor wife, peace on her, used to ridicule me for this. Riding in the subway once I saw a beautiful child, a boy about twelve. A Puerto Rican, dusky, yet he had cheeks like pomegranates. I once knew, in Kiev, a child who looked like that. I admit to it. A portrait under the skin of my eyes. The love of a man for a boy. Why not confess it? Is it against the nature of man to rejoice in beauty? "This is to be expected with a childless man"—my wife's verdict. That what I wanted was a son. Take this as a complete explanation: if an ordinary person cannot

The end of the sentence flew like a leaf out of his mind . . . it was turning into a quarrel with Mireleh. Who quarrels with the dead? He wrote:

Esteemed Alexei Yosifovitch:
   You remain. You remain. An illumination. More than my own home, nearer than my mother's mouth. Nimbus. Your father slapped my father. You were never told. Because I kissed you on the green stairs. The shadow-place on the landing where I once saw the butler scratch his pants. They sent us away shamed. My father and I, into the mud.

Again a lie. Never near the child. Lying is like a vitamin, it has to fortify everything. Only through the doorway, looking, looking. The gleaming face: the face of flame. Or would test him on verb-forms: *kal, nifal, piel, pual, hifil, hofal, hispael*. On the afternoons the Latin tutor came, crouched outside the threshold, Edelshtein heard *ego, mei, mihi, me, me*. May may. Beautiful foreign nasal chant of riches. Latin! Dirty from the lips of idolators. An apostate family. Edelshtein and his father took their coffee and bread, but otherwise lived on boiled eggs: the elder Kirilov one day brought home with him the *mashgiach* from the Jewish poorhouse to testify to the purity of the servants' kitchen, but to Edelshtein's father the whole house was *treyf*, the *mashgiach* himself a hired impostor. Who would oversee the overseer? Among the Kirilovs with their lying name money was the best overseer. Money saw to everything. Though they had their particular talent. Mechanical. Alexei Y. Kirilov, engineer. Bridges, towers. Consultant to Cairo. Builder of the Aswan Dam, assistant to Pharaoh for the latest Pyramid. To set down such a fantasy about such an important Soviet brain . . . poor little Alexei, Avremeleh, I'll jeopardize your position in life, little corpse of Babi Yar.
   Only focus. Hersh! Scion of the Vilna Gaon! Prince of rationality! Pay attention!
   He wrote:

The gait—the prance, the hobble—of Yiddish is not the same as the gait of English. A big headache for a translator probably. In Yiddish you use more words than in English. Nobody believes it but it's true. Another big problem is form. The moderns take the old forms and fill them up with mockery, love, drama, satire, etc. Plenty of play. But STILL THE SAME OLD FORMS, conventions left over from the last century even. It doesn't matter who denies this, out of pride: it's true. Pour in symbolism, impressionism, be complex, be subtle, be daring, take risks, break your teeth—whatever you do, it still comes out Yiddish. *Mamaloshen* doesn't produce *Wastelands*. No alienation, no nihilism, no dadaism. With all the suffering no smashing! No INCOHERENCE! Keep the latter in mind, Hannah, if you expect to make progress. Also: please remember that when a goy from Columbus, Ohio, says "Elijah the Prophet" he's not talking about *Eliohu hanovi*. Eliohu is one of us, a *folksmensh,* running around in second-hand clothes. Theirs is God knows what. The same biblical figure, with exactly the same history, once he puts on a name from King James, COMES OUT A DIFFERENT PERSON. Life, history, hope, tragedy, they don't come out even. They talk Bible Lands, with us it's *eretz yisroel*. A misfortune.

Astonished, he struck up against a kiosk. A telephone! On a street corner! He had to drag the door open, pulling a load of snow. Then he squeezed inside. His fingers were sticks. Never mind the pad, he forgot even where the pocket was. In his coat? Jacket? Pants? With one stick he dialed Vorovsky's number: from memory.

"Hello, Chaim?"

"This is Ostrover."

"Ostrover! Why Ostrover? What are you doing there? I want Vorovsky."

"Who's this?"

"Edelshtein."

"I thought so. A persecution, what is this? I could send you to jail for tricks like before—"

"Quick, give me Vorovsky."

"I'll *give* you."

"Vorovsky's not home?"

"How do I know if Vorovsky's home? It's dawn, go ask Vorovsky!"

Edelshtein grew weak: "I called the wrong number."

"Hersheleh, if you want some friendly advice you'll listen to me. I can get you jobs at fancy out-of-town country clubs, Miami Florida included, plenty of speeches your own style, only what they need is rational lecturers not lunatics. If you carry on like tonight you'll lose what you have."

"I don't have anything."

"Accept life, Edelshtein."

"Dead man, I appreciate your guidance."

"Yesterday I heard from Hollywood, they're making a movie from one of my stories. So now tell me again who's dead."

"The puppet the ventriloquist holds in his lap. A piece of log. It's somebody else's language and the dead doll sits there."

"Wit, you want them to make movies in Yiddish now?"

"In Talmud if you save a single life it's as if you saved the world. And if you save a language? Worlds maybe. Galaxies. The whole universe."

"Hersheleh, the God of the Jews made a mistake when he didn't have a son, it would be a good occupation for you."

"Instead I'll be an extra in your movie. If they shoot the *shtetl* on location in Kansas send me expense money. I'll come and be local color for you. I'll put on my *shtreiml* and walk around, the people should see a real Jew. For ten dollars more I'll even speak *mamaloshen*."

Ostrover said, "It doesn't matter what you speak, envy sounds the same in all languages."

Edelshtein said, "Once there was a ghost who thought he was still alive. You know what happened to him? He got up one morning and began to shave and he cut himself. And there was no blood. No blood at all. And he still didn't believe it, so he looked in the mirror to see. And there was no reflection, no sign of himself. He wasn't there. But he still didn't believe it, so he began to scream, but there was no sound, no sound at all—"

There was no sound from the telephone. He let it dangle and rock.

He looked for the pad. Diligently he consulted himself: pants cuffs have a way of catching necessary objects. The number had fallen out of his body. Off his skin. He needed Vorovsky because he needed Hannah. Worthwhile maybe to telephone Baumzweig for Vorovsky's number, Paula could look it up—Baumzweig's number he knew by heart, no mistake. He had singled out his need. Svengali, Pygmalion, Rasputin, Dr. (jokes aside) Frankenstein. What does it require to make a translator? A secondary occupation. Parasitic. But your own creature. Take this girl Hannah and train her. His alone. American-born but she had the advantage over him, English being no worm on her palate; also she could read his words in the original. Niece of a vanquished mind—still, genes are in reality God, and if Vorovsky had a little talent for translation why not the niece?—Or the other. Russia. The one in the Soviet Union who wrote two stanzas in Yiddish. In Yiddish! And only twenty! Born 1948, same year they made up to be the Doctors' Plot, Stalin already very busy killing Jews, Markish, Kvitko, Kushnirov, Hofshtein, Mikhoels, Susskin, Bergelson, Feffer, Gradzenski with the wooden leg. All slaughtered. How did Yiddish survive in the mouth of that girl? Nurtured in secret. Taught by an obsessed grandfather, a crazy uncle: Marranos. The poem reprinted, as they say, in the West. (The West! If a Jew says "the West," he sounds like an imbecile. In a puddle what's West, what's East?) Flowers, blue sky, she yearns for the end of winter: very nice. A zero, and received like a prodigy! An aberration! A miracle! Because composed in the lost tongue. As if some Neapolitan child suddenly begins to prattle in Latin. Not the same. Little verses merely. Death confers awe. Russian: its richness, directness. For "iron" and "weapon" the same word. A *thick* language, a world-language. He visualized himself translated into Russian, covertly, by the Marranos' daughter. To be circulated, in typescript, underground: to be read, read!

Understand me, Hannah—that our treasure-tongue is derived from strangers means nothing. 90 percent German roots, 10 percent Slavic: irrelevant. The Hebrew take for granted without percentages. We are a people who have known how to forge the language of need out of the language of necessity. Our reputation among ourselves as a nation of scholars is mostly empty. In actuality we are a mob of working people, laborers, hewers of wood, believe me. Leivik, our chief poet, was a house painter. Today all pharmacists, lawyers, accountants, haberdashers, but tickle the lawyer and you'll see his grandfather sawed wood for a living. That's how it is with us. Nowadays the Jew is forgetful, everybody with a profession, every Jewish boy a professor—justice seems less urgent. Most don't realize this quiet time is only another Interim. Always, like in a terrible Wagnerian storm, we have our interludes of rest. So now. Once we were slaves, now we are free men, remember the bread of affliction. But listen. Whoever cries Justice! is a liberated slave. Whoever honors Work is a liberated slave. They accuse Yiddish literature of sentimentality in this connection. Very good, true. True, so be it! A dwarf at a sewing machine can afford a little loosening of the heart. I return to Leivik. He could hang wallpaper. I once lived in a room he papered—yellow vines. Rutgers Street that was. A good job, no bubbles, no peeling. This from a poet of very morbid tendencies. Mani Leib fixed shoes. Moishe Leib Halpern was a waiter, once in a while a handyman. I could tell you the names of twenty poets of very pure expression who were operators, pressers, cutters. In addition to fixing shoes Mani Leib was also a laundryman. I beg you not to think I'm preaching Socialism. To my mind politics is dung. What I mean is something else: Work is Work, and Thought is Thought. Politics tries to mix these up, Socialism especially. The language of a hard-pressed people works under the laws of purity, dividing the Commanded from the Profane. I remember one of my old teachers. He used to take attendance every day and he gave his occupation to the taxing council as "attendance-taker"—so that he wouldn't be getting paid for teaching Torah. This with five pupils, all living in his house and fed by his wife! Call it splitting a hair if you want, but it's the hair of a head that distinguished between the necessary and the merely needed. People who believe that

Yiddish is, as they like to say, "richly intermixed," and that in Yiddishkeit the presence of the Covenant, of Godliness, inhabits humble things and humble words, are under a delusion or a deception. The slave knows exactly when he belongs to God and when to the oppressor. The liberated slave who is not forgetful and can remember when he himself was an artifact, knows exactly the difference between God and an artifact. A language also knows whom it is serving at each moment. I am feeling very cold right now. Of course you see that when I say liberated I mean self-liberated. Moses not Lincoln, not Franz Josef. Yiddish is the language of auto-emancipation. Theodor Herzl wrote in German but the message spread in *mamaloshen*—my God cold. Naturally the important thing is to stick to what you learned as a slave including language, and not to speak their language, otherwise you will become like them, acquiring their confusion between God and artifact and consequently their taste for making slaves, both of themselves and others.

Slave of rhetoric! This is the trouble when you use God for a Muse. Philosophers, thinkers—all cursed. Poets have it better: most are Greeks and pagans, unbelievers except in natural religion, stones, stars, body. This cube and cell. Ostrover had already sentenced him to jail, little booth in the vale of snow; black instrument beeped from a gallows. The white pad—something white—on the floor. Edelshtein bent for it and struck his jaw. Through the filth of the glass doors morning rose out of the dark. He saw what he held:

"ALL OF US ARE HUMANS TOGETHER
BUT SOME HUMANS SHOULD DROP DEAD."

DO YOU FEEL THIS ?

IF SO CALL TR 5-2530 IF YOU WANT TO
KNOW WHETHER YOU WILL SURVIVE IN
CHRIST'S FIVE-DAY INEXPENSIVE
ELECT-PLAN

*

"AUDITORY PHRENOLOGY"
PRACTICED FREE FREE

*

(PLEASE NO ATHEISTS OR CRANK CALLS
WE ARE SINCERE SCIENTIFIC SOUL-SOCIOLOGISTS)

*

ASK FOR ROSE OR LOU
WE LOVE YOU

He was touched and curious, but withdrawn. The cold lit him unfamiliarly: his body a brilliant hollowness, emptied of organs, cleansed of debris, the inner flanks of him perfect lit glass. A clear chalice. Of small change he had only a nickel and a dime. For the dime he could CALL TR 5-2530 and take advice appropriate to his immaculateness, his transparency. Rose or Lou. He had no satire for their love. How manifold and various the human imagination. The simplicity of an ascent lured him, he was alert to the probability of levitation but disregarded it. The disciples of Reb Moshe of Kobryn also disregarded feats in opposition to nature—they had no awe for their master when he hung in air, but when he slept—the miracle of his lung, his breath, his heartbeat! He lurched from the booth into rushing daylight. The depth of snow sucked off one of his shoes. The serpent too prospers without feet, so he cast off his and weaved on. His arms, particularly his hands, particularly those partners of mind his fingers, he was sorry to lose. He knew his eyes, his tongue, his stinging loins. He was again tempted to ascend. The hillock was profound. He outwitted it by creeping through it, he drilled patiently into the snow. He wanted to stand then, but without legs could not. Indolently he permitted himself to rise. He went only high enough to see the snowy sidewalks, the mounds in gutters and against stoops, the beginning of business time. Lifted light. A doorman fled out of a building wearing earmuffs, pulling a shovel behind him like a little tin cart. Edelshtein drifted no higher than the man's shoulders. He watched the shovel pierce the snow, tunneling down, but there was no bottom, the earth was without foundation.

He came under a black wing. He thought it was the first blindness of Death but it was only a canopy.

The doorman went on digging under the canopy; under the canopy Edelshtein tasted wine and felt himself at a wedding, his own, the canopy covering his steamy gold eyeglasses made blind by Mireleh's veil. Four beings held up the poles: one his wife's cousin the postman, one his own cousin the druggist; two poets. The first poet was a beggar who lived on institutional charity—Baumzweig; the second, Silverman, sold ladies' elastic stockings, the kind for varicose veins. The postman and the druggist were still alive, only one of them retired. The poets were ghosts, Baumzweig picking at himself in bed also a ghost, Silverman long dead, more than twenty years—*lideleh-shreiber* they called him, he wrote for the popular theater. "Song to Steerage": *Steerage, steerage, I remember the crowds, the rags we took with us we treated like shrouds, we tossed them away when we spied out the shore, going re-born through the Golden Door. . . .* Even on Second Avenue 1905 was already stale, but it stopped the show, made fevers, encores, tears, yells. Golden sidewalks. America the bride, under her fancy gown nothing. Poor Silverman, in love with the Statue of Liberty's lifted arm, what did he do in his life besides raise up a post at an empty wedding, no progeny?

The doorman dug out a piece of statuary, an urn with a stone wreath.

Under the canopy Edelshtein recognized it. Sand, butts, a half-naked angel astride the wreath. Once Edelshtein saw a condom in it. Found! Vorovsky's building. There is no God, yet who brought him here if not the King of the Universe? Not so bad off after all, even in a snowstorm he could find his way, an expert, he knew one block from another in this desolation of a world.

He carried his shoe into the elevator like a baby, an orphan, a redemption. He could kiss even a shoe.

In the corridor laughter, toilets flushing; coffee stabbed him.

He rang the bell.

From behind Vorovsky's door, laughter, laughter!

No one came.

He rang again. No one came. He banged. "Chaim, crazy man, open up!" No one came. "A dead man from the cold knocks, you don't come? Hurry up, open, I'm a stick of ice, you want a dead man at your door? Mercy! Pity! Open up!"

No one came.

He listened to the laughter. It had a form; a method, rather: some principle, closer to physics than music, of arching up and sinking back. Inside the shape barks, howls, dogs, wolves, wilderness. After each fright a crevice to fall into. He made an anvil of his shoe and took the doorknob for an iron hammer and thrust. He thrust, thrust. The force of an iceberg.

Close to the knob a panel bulged and cracked. Not his fault. On the other side someone was unused to the lock.

He heard Vorovsky but saw Hannah.

She said: "What?"

"You don't remember me? I'm the one what recited to you tonight my work from several years past, I was passing by in your uncle's neighborhood—"

"He's sick."

"What, a fit?"

"All night. I've been here the whole night. The whole night—"

"Let me in."

"Please go away. I just told you."

"In. What's the matter with you? I'm sick myself, I'm dead from cold! Hey, Chaim! Lunatic, stop it!"

Vorovsky was on his belly on the floor, stifling his mouth with a pillow as if it were a stone, knocking his head down on it, but it was no use, the laughter shook the pillow and came yelping out, not muffled but increased, darkened. He laughed and said "Hannah" and laughed.

Edelshtein took a chair and dragged it near Vorovsky and sat. The room stank, a subway latrine.

"Stop," he said.

Vorovsky laughed.

"All right, merriment, very good, be happy. You're warm, I'm cold. Have mercy, little girl—tea. Hannah. Boil it up hot. Pieces of flesh drop from me." He heard that he was speaking Yiddish, so he began again for her. "I'm sorry. Forgive me. A terrible thing to do. I was lost outside, I was look-ing, so now I found you, I'm sorry."

"It isn't a good time for a visit, that's all."

"Bring some tea also for your uncle."

"He can't."

"He can maybe, let him try. Someone who laughs like this is ready for a feast—*flanken, tsimmis, rosselfleysh*—" In Yiddish he said, "In the world-to-come people dance at parties like this, all laughter, joy. The day after the Messiah people laugh like this."

Vorovsky laughed and said "Messiah" and sucked the pillow, spitting. His face was a flood: tears ran upside down into his eyes, over his forehead, saliva sprang in puddles around his ears. He was spitting, crying, burbling, he gasped, wept, spat. His eyes were bloodshot, the whites showed like slashes, wounds; he still wore his hat. He laughed, he was still laughing. His pants were wet, the fly open, now and then seeping. He dropped the pillow for tea and ventured a sip, with his tongue, like an animal full of hope— vomit rolled up with the third swallow and he laughed between spasms, he was still laughing, stinking, a sewer.

Edelshtein took pleasure in the tea, it touched him to the root, more gripping on his bowel than the coffee that stung the hall. He praised himself with no meanness, no bitterness: prince of rationality! Thawing, he said, "Give him *schnapps,* he can hold *schnapps,* no question."

"He drank and he vomited."

"Chaim, little soul," Edelshtein said, "what started you off? Myself. I was there. I said it, I said graves, I said smoke. I'm the responsible one. Death. Death, I'm the one who said it. Death you laugh at, you're no coward."

"If you want to talk business with my uncle come another time."

"Death is business?"

Now he examined her. Born 1945, in the hour of the death-camps. Not selected. Immune. The whole way she held herself looked immune—by this he meant American. Still, an exhausted child, straggled head, remarkable child to stay through the night with the madman. "Where's your mother?" he said. "Why doesn't she come and watch her brother? Why does it fall on you? You should be free, you have your own life."

"You don't know anything about families."

She was acute: no mother, father, wife, child, what did he know about families? He was cut off, a survivor. "I know your uncle," he said, but without belief: in the first place Vorovsky had an education. "In his right mind your uncle doesn't want you to suffer."

Vorovsky, laughing, said "Suffer."

"He likes to suffer. He wants to suffer. He admires suffering. All you people want to suffer."

Pins and needles: Edelshtein's fingertips were fevering. He stroked the heat of the cup. He could feel. He said, "'You people'?"

"You Jews."

"Aha. Chaim, you hear? Your niece Hannah—on the other side already, never mind she's acquainted with *mamaloshen*. In one generation, 'you Jews.' You don't like suffering? Maybe you respect it?"

"It's unnecessary."

"It comes from history, history is also unnecessary?"

"History's a waste."

America the empty bride. Edelshtein said, "You're right about business. I came on business. My whole business is waste."

Vorovsky laughed and said "Hersheleh Frog Frog Frog."

"I think you're making him worse," Hannah said. "Tell me what you want and I'll give him the message."

"He's not deaf."

"He doesn't remember afterward—"

"I have no message."

"Then what do you want from him?"

"Nothing. I want from you."

"Frog Frog Frog Frog Frog."

Edelshtein finished his tea and put the cup on the floor and for the first time absorbed Vorovsky's apartment: until now Vorovsky had kept him out. It was one room, sink and stove behind a plastic curtain, bookshelves leaning over not with books but journals piled flat, a sticky table, a sofa-bed, a desk, six kitchen chairs, and along the walls seventy-five cardboard boxes which Edelshtein knew harbored two thousand copies of Vorovsky's dictionary. A pity on Vorovsky, he had a dispute with the publisher, who turned back half the printing to him. Vorovsky had to pay for two thousand German-English mathematical dictionaries, and now he had to sell them himself, but he did not know what to do, how to go about it. It was his fate to swallow what he first excreted. Because of a mishap in business he owned his life, he possessed what he was, a slave, but invisible. A hungry snake has to eat its tail all the way down to the head until it disappears.

Hannah said: "What could I do for you"—flat, not a question.

"Again 'you.' A distinction, a separation. What I'll ask is this: annihilate 'you,' annihilate 'me.' We'll come to an understanding, we'll get together."

She bent for his cup and he saw her boot. He was afraid of a boot. He said mildly, nicely, "Look, your uncle tells me you're one of us. By 'us' he means writer, no?"

"By 'us' you mean Jew."

"And you're not a Jew, *meydeleh?*"

"Not your kind."

"Nowadays there have to be kinds? Good, bad, old, new—"

"Old and new."

"All right! So let it be old and new, fine, a reasonable beginning. Let old work with new. Listen, I need a collaborator. Not exactly a collaborator, it's not even complicated like that. What I need is a translator."

"My uncle the translator is indisposed."

At that moment Edelshtein discovered he hated irony. He yelled, "Not your uncle. You! You!"

Howling, Vorovsky crawled to a tower of cartons and beat on them with his bare heels. There was an alteration in his laughter, something not theatrical but of the theater—he was amused, entertained, clowns paraded between his legs.

"You'll save Yiddish," Edelshtein said, "you'll be like a Messiah to a whole generation, a whole literature, naturally you'll have to work at it, practice, it takes knowledge, it takes a gift, a genius, a born poet—"

Hannah walked in her boots with his dirty teacup. From behind the plastic he heard the faucet. She opened the curtain and came out and said: "You old men."

"Ostrover's pages you kiss!"

"You jealous old men from the ghetto," she said.

"And Ostrover's young, a young prince? Listen! You don't see, you don't follow—translate me, lift me out of the ghetto, it's my life that's hanging on you!"

Her voice was a whip. "Bloodsuckers," she said. "It isn't a translator you're after, it's someone's soul. Too much history's drained your blood, you want someone to take you over, a dybbuk—"

"Dybbuk! Ostrover's language. All right, I need a dybbuk, I'll become a golem, I don't care, it doesn't matter! Breathe in me! Animate me! Without you I'm a clay pot!" Bereaved, he yelled, "Translate me!"

The clowns ran over Vorovsky's charmed belly.

Hannah said: "You think I have to read Ostrover in translation? You think translation has anything to do with what Ostrover is?"

Edelshtein accused her, "Who taught you to read Yiddish?—A girl like that, to know the letters worthy of life and to be ignorant! 'You Jews,' 'you people,' you you you!"

"I learned, my grandfather taught me, I'm not responsible for it, I didn't go looking for it, I was smart, a golden head, same as now. But I have my own life, you said it yourself, I don't have to throw it out. So pay attention, Mr. Vampire: even in Yiddish Ostrover's not in the ghetto. Even in Yiddish he's not like you people."

"He's not in the ghetto? Which ghetto, what ghetto? So where is he? In the sky? In the clouds? With the angels? Where?"

She meditated, she was all intelligence. "In the world," she answered him.

"In the marketplace. A fishwife, a *kochleffel*, everything's his business, you he'll autograph, me he'll get jobs, he listens to everybody."

"Whereas you people listen only to yourselves."

In the room something was absent.

Edelshtein, pushing into his snow-damp shoe, said into the absence, "So? You're not interested?"

"Only in the mainstream. Not in your little puddles."

"Again the ghetto. Your uncle stinks from the ghetto? Graduated, 1924, the University of Berlin, Vorovsky stinks from the ghetto? Myself, four God-given books not one living human being knows, I stink from the ghetto? God, four thousand years since Abraham hanging out with Jews, God also stinks from the ghetto?"

"Rhetoric," Hannah said. "Yiddish literary rhetoric. That's the style."

"Only Ostrover doesn't stink from the ghetto."

"A question of vision."

"Better say visions. He doesn't know real things."

"He knows a reality beyond realism."

"American literary babies! And in your language you don't have a rhetoric?" Edelshtein burst out. "Very good, he's achieved it, Ostrover's the world. A pantheist, a pagan, a goy."

"That's it. You've nailed it. A Freudian, a Jungian, a sensibility. No little love stories. A contemporary. He speaks for everybody."

"Aha. Sounds familiar already. For humanity he speaks? Humanity?"

"Humanity," she said.

"And to speak for Jews isn't to speak for humanity? We're not human? We're not present on the face of the earth? We don't suffer? In Russia they let us live? In Egypt they don't want to murder us?"

"Suffer suffer," she said. "I like devils best. They don't think only about themselves and they don't suffer."

Immediately, looking at Hannah—my God, an old man, he was looking at her little waist, underneath it where the little apple of her womb was hidden away—immediately, all at once, instantaneously, he fell into a chaos, a trance, of truth, of actuality: was it possible? He saw everything in miraculous reversal, blessed—everything plain, distinct, understandable, true. What he understood was this: that the ghetto was the real world, and the outside world only a ghetto. Because in actuality who was shut off? Who then was really buried, removed, inhabited by darkness? To whom, in what little space, did God offer Sinai? Who kept Terach and who followed Abraham? Talmud explains that when the Jews went into Exile, God went into Exile also. Babi Yar is maybe the real world, and Kiev with its German toys, New York with all its terrible intelligence, all fictions, fantasies. Unreality.

An infatuation! He was the same, all his life the same as this poisonous wild girl, he coveted mythologies, specters, animals, voices. Western Civilization his secret guilt, he was ashamed of the small tremor of his self-love, degraded by being ingrown. Alexei with his skin a furnace of desire, his trucks and trains! He longed to be Alexei. Alexei with his German toys and his Latin! Alexei whose destiny was to grow up into the world-at-large, to slip from the ghetto, to break out into engineering for Western Civilization! Alexei, I abandon you! I'm at home only in a prison, history is my prison, the ravine my house, only listen—suppose it turns out that the destiny of the Jews is vast, open, eternal, and that Western Civilization is meant to dwindle, shrivel, shrink into the ghetto of the world—what of history then? Kings, Parliaments, like insects, Presidents like vermin, their religion a row of little dolls, their art a cave smudge, their poetry a lust—Avremeleh, when you fell from the ledge over the ravine into your grave, for the first time you fell into reality.

To Hannah he said: "I didn't ask to be born into Yiddish. It came on me."

He meant he was blessed.

"So keep it," she said, "and don't complain."

With the whole ferocity of his delight in it he hit her mouth. The madman again struck up his laugh. Only now was it possible to notice that something had stopped it before. A missing harp. The absence filled with bloody laughter, bits of what looked like red pimento hung in the vomit on Vorovsky's chin, the clowns fled, Vorovsky's hat with its pinnacle of fur dangled on his chest—he was spent, he was beginning to fall into the quake of sleep, he slept, he dozed, roars burst from him, he hiccuped, woke, laughed, an enormous grief settled in him, he went on napping and laughing, grief had him in its teeth.

Edelshtein's hand, the cushiony underside of it, blazed from giving the blow. "You," he said, "you have no ideas, what are you?" A shred of learning flaked from him, what the sages said of Job ripped from his tongue like a peeling of the tongue itself, *he never was, he never existed.* "You were never born, you were never created!" he yelled. "Let me tell you, a dead man tells you this, at least I had a life, at least I understood something!"

"Die," she told him. "Die now, all you old men, what are you waiting for? Hanging on my neck, him and now you, the whole bunch of you, parasites, hurry up and die."

His palm burned, it was the first time he had ever slapped a child. He felt like a father. Her mouth lay back naked on her face. Out of spite, against instinct, she kept her hands from the bruise—he could see the shape of her teeth, turned a little one on the other, imperfect, again vulnerable. From fury her nose streamed. He had put a bulge in her lip.

"Forget Yiddish!" he screamed at her. "Wipe it out of your brain! Extirpate it! Go get a memory operation! You have no right to it, you have no right to an uncle, a grandfather! No one ever came before you, you were never born! A vacuum!"

"You old atheists," she called after him. "You dead old socialists. Boring! You bore me to death. You hate magic, you hate imagination, you talk God and you hate God, you despise, you bore, you envy, you eat people up with your disgusting old age—cannibals, all you care about is your own youth, you're finished, give somebody else a turn!"

This held him. He leaned on the door frame. "A turn at what? I didn't offer you a turn? An opportunity of a lifetime? To be published now, in youth, in babyhood, early in life? Translated I'd be famous, this you don't understand. Hannah, listen," he said, kindly, ingratiatingly, reasoning with her like a father, "you don't have to like my poems, do I ask you to *like* them? I don't ask you to like them, I don't ask you to respect them, I don't ask you to love them. A man my age, do I want a lover or a translator? Am I asking a favor? No. Look," he said, "one thing I forgot to tell you. A business deal. That's all. Business, plain and simple. I'll pay you. You didn't think I wouldn't pay, God forbid?"

Now she covered her mouth. He wondered at his need to weep; he was ashamed.

"Hannah, please, how much? I'll pay, you'll see. Whatever you like. You'll buy anything you want. Dresses, shoes—" *Gottenyu,* what could such a wild beast want? "You'll buy more boots, all kinds of boots, whatever you want, books, everything—" He said relentlessly, "You'll have from me money."

"No," she said, "no."

"Please. What will happen to me? What's wrong? My ideas aren't good enough? Who asks you to believe in my beliefs? I'm an old man, used up, I have nothing to say any more, anything I ever said was all imitation. Walt Whitman I used to like. Also John Donne. Poets, masters. We, what have we got? A Yiddish Keats? Never—" He was ashamed, so he wiped his cheeks with both sleeves. "Business. I'll pay you," he said.

"No."

"Because I laid a hand on you? Forgive me, I apologize. I'm crazier than he is, I should be locked up for it—"

"Not because of that."

"Then why not? *Meydeleh*, why not? What harm would it do you? Help out an old man."

She said desolately, "You don't interest me. I would have to be interested."

"I see. Naturally." He looked at Vorovsky. "Goodbye, Chaim, regards from Aristotle. What distinguishes men from the beasts is the power of ha-ha-ha. So good morning, ladies and gentlemen. Be well. Chaim, live until a hundred and twenty. The main thing is health."

In the street it was full day, and he was warm from the tea. The road glistened, the sidewalks. Paths crisscrossed in unexpected places, sleds clanged, people ran. A drugstore was open and he went in to telephone Baumzweig: he dialed, but on the way he skipped a number, heard an iron noise like a weapon, and had to dial again. "Paula," he practiced, "I'll come back for a while, all right? For breakfast maybe," but instead he changed his mind and decided to CALL TR 5-2530. At the other end of the wire it was either Rose or Lou. Edelshtein told the eunuch's voice, "I believe with you about some should drop dead. Pharaoh, Queen Isabella, Haman, that pogromchik King Louis they call in history Saint, Hitler, Stalin, Nasser—" The voice said, "You're a Jew?" It sounded Southern but somehow not Negro—maybe because schooled, polished: "Accept Jesus as your Saviour and you shall have Jerusalem restored." "We already got it," Edelshtein said. *Meshiachtseiten!* "The terrestrial Jerusalem has no significance. Earth is dust. The Kingdom of God is within. Christ released man from Judaic exclusivism." "Who's excluding who?" Edelshtein said. "Christianity is Judaism universalized. Jesus is Moses publicized for ready availability. Our God is the God of Love, your God is the God of Wrath. Look how He abandoned you in Auschwitz." "It wasn't only God who didn't notice." "You people are cowards, you never even tried to defend yourselves. You got a wide streak of yellow, you don't know how to hold a gun." "Tell it to the Egyptians," Edelshtein said. "Everyone you come into contact with turns into your enemy. When you were in Europe every nation despised you. When you moved to take over the Middle

East the Arab Nation, spic faces like your own, your very own blood-kin, began to hate you. You are a bone in the throat of all mankind." "Who gnaws at bones? Dogs and rats only." "Even your food habits are abnormal, against the grain of quotidian delight. You refuse to seethe a lamb in the milk of its mother. You will not eat a fertilized egg because it has a spot of blood on it. When you wash your hands you chant. You pray in a debased jargon, not in the beautiful sacramental English of our Holy Bible." Edelshtein said, "That's right, Jesus spoke the King's English." "Even now, after the good Lord knows how many years in America, you talk with a kike accent. You kike, you Yid."

Edelshtein shouted into the telephone, "Amalekite! Titus! Nazi! The whole world is infected by you anti-Semites! On account of you children become corrupted! On account of you I lost everything, my whole life! On account of you I have no translator!"

Virility

You are too young to remember Edmund Gate, but I knew him when he was Elia Gatoff in knickers, just off the boat from Liverpool. Now to remember Edmund Gate at all, one must be a compatriot of mine, which is to say a centagenerian. A man of one hundred and six is always sequestered on a metaphysical Elba, but on an Elba without even the metaphor of a Napoleon—where, in fact, it has been so long forgotten that Napoleon ever lived that it is impossible to credit his influence, let alone his fame. It is harsh and lonely in this country of exile—the inhabitants (or, as we in our eleventh decade ought more accurately to be called, the survivors) are so sparse, and so maimed, and so unreliable as to recent chronology, and so at odds with your ideas of greatness, that we do indeed veer toward a separate mentality, and ought in logic to have a flag of our own. It is not that we seclude ourselves from you, but rather that you have seceded from us— you with your moon pilots, and mohole fishermen, and algae cookies, and anti-etymological reformed spelling—in the face of all of which I can scarcely expect you to believe in a time when a plain and rather ignorant man could attain the sort of celebrity you people accord only to vile geniuses who export baby-germs in plastic envelopes. That, I suppose, is the worst of it for me and my countrymen in the land of the very old—your isolation from our great. Our great and especially our merely famous have slipped from your encyclopaedias, and will vanish finally and absolutely when we are at length powdered into reconstituted genetic ore—mixed with fish flour, and to be taken as an antidote immediately after radiation-saturation: a detail and a tangent, but I am subject to these broodings at my heavy age, and occasionally catch myself in egotistical yearning for an ordinary headstone engraved with my name. As if, in a population of a billion and a quarter, there could be space for that entirely obsolete indulgence!—and yet, only last week, in the old Preserved Cemetery, I visited Edmund Gate's grave, and viewed his monument, and came away persuaded of the beauty of that ancient, though wasteful, decorum. We have no room for physical memorials nowadays; and nobody pays any attention to the pitiful poets.

Just *here* is my huge difficulty. How am I to convince you that, during an interval in my own vast lifetime, there was a moment when a poet—a plain, as I have said, and rather ignorant man—was noticed, and noticed abundantly, and noticed magnificently and even stupendously? You will of course not have heard of Byron, and no one is more eclipsed than dear Dylan; nor will I claim that Edmund Gate ever rose to *that* standard. But he was recited, admired, worshiped, translated, pursued, even paid; and the press would not let him go for an instant. I have spoken of influence and of fame; Edmund Gate, it is true, had little influence, even on his own generation—I mean by this that he was not much imitated—but as for fame! Fame was what we gave him plenty of. We could give him fame—in those days fame was ours to give. Whereas you measure meanly by the cosmos. The first man to the moon is now a shriveling little statistician in a Bureau somewhere, superseded by the first to Venus, who, we are told, lies all day in a sour room drinking vodka and spitting envy on the first to try for Pluto. Now it is the stars which dictate fame, but with us it was *we* who made fame, and we who dictated our stars.

He died (like Keats, of whom you will also not have heard) at twenty-six. I have this note not from Microwafer Tabulation, but from the invincible headstone itself. I had forgotten it and was touched. I almost thought he lived to be middle-aged: I base this on my last sight of him, or perhaps my last memory, in which I observe him in his underwear, with a big hairy paunch, cracked and browning teeth, and a scabby scalp laid over with a bunch of thin light-colored weeds. He looked something like a failed pugilist. I see him standing in the middle of a floor without a carpet, puzzled, drunk, a newspaper in one hand and the other tenderly reaching through the slot in his shorts to enclose his testicles. The last words he spoke to me were the words I chose (it fell to me) for his monument: "I am a man."

He was, however, a boy in corduroys when he first came to me. He smelled of salami and his knickers were raveled at the pockets and gave off a saltiness. He explained that he had walked all the way from England, back and forth on the deck. I later gathered that he was a stowaway. He had been sent ahead to Liverpool on a forged passport (these were Czarist times), from a place full of wooden shacks and no sidewalks called Glusk, with instructions to search out an old aunt of his mother's on Mersey Street and stay with her until his parents and sisters could scrape up the papers for their own border-crossing. He miraculously found the Liverpudlian aunt, was received with joy, fed bread and butter, and shown a letter from Glusk in which his father stated that the precious sheets were finally all in order and properly stamped with seals almost identical to real government seals: they would all soon be reunited in the beckoning poverty of Golden Liverpool. He settled in with the aunt, who lived tidily in a gray slum and worked all day in the back of a millinery shop sewing on veils. She had all the habits of a cool and intellectual spinster. She had come to England six years before—she was herself an emigrant from Glusk, and had left it legally and respectably under a pile of straw in the last of three carts in a gypsy caravan headed westward for Poland. Once inside Poland (humanely governed by Franz Josef), she took a train to Warsaw, and liked the book stores there so much she nearly stayed forever, but instead thoughtfully lifted her skirts onto another train—how she hated the soot!—to Hamburg, where she boarded a neat little boat pointed right at Liverpool. It never occurred to her to go a little further, to America: she had fixed on English as the best tongue for a foreigner to adopt, and she was suspicious of the kind of English Americans imagined they spoke. With superior diligence she began to teach her great-nephew the beautiful and clever new language; she even wanted him to go to school, but he was too much absorbed in the notion of waiting, and instead ran errands for the greengrocer at three shillings a week. He put pennies into a little tin box to buy a red scarf for his mother when she came. He waited and waited, and looked dull when his aunt talked to him in English at night, and waited immensely, with his whole body. But his mother and father and his sister Feige and his sister Gittel never arrived. On a rainy day in the very month he burst into manhood (in the course of which black rods of hairs appeared in the trench of his upper lip), his aunt told him, not in English, that it was no use waiting any longer: a pogrom had murdered them all. She put the letter, from a cousin in Glusk, on exhibit before him—his mother, raped and slaughtered; Feige, raped and slaughtered; Gittel, escaped but caught in the forest and raped twelve times before a passing friendly soldier saved her from the thirteenth by shooting her through the left eye; his father, tied to the tail of a Cossack horse and sent to have his head broken on cobblestones.

All this he gave me quickly, briefly, without excitement, and with a shocking economy. What he had come to America for, he said, was a job. I asked him what his experience was. He reiterated the fact of the greengrocer in Liverpool. He had the queerest accent; a regular salad of an accent.

"That's hardly the type of preparation we can use on a newspaper," I said.

"Well, it's the only kind I've got."

"What does your aunt think of your leaving her all alone like that?"

"She's an independent sort. She'll be all right. She says she'll send me money when she can."

"Look here, don't you think the money ought to be going in the opposite direction?"

"Oh, I'll never have any money," he said.

I was irritated by his pronunciation—"mawney"—and I had theories about would-be Americans, none of them complimentary, one of which he was unwittingly confirming. "There's ambition for you!"

But he startled me with a contradictory smile both iron and earnest. "I'm very ambitious. You wait and see," as though we were already colleagues, confidants, and deep comrades. "Only what *I* want to be," he said, "they don't ever make much money."

"What's that?"

"A poet. I've always wanted to be a poet."

I could not help laughing at him. "In English? You want to do English poetry?"

"English, righto. I don't *have* any other language. Not any more."

"Are you positive you have English?" I asked him. "You've only been taught by your aunt, and no one ever taught *her.*"

But he was listening to only half, and would not bother with any talk about his relative. "That's why I want to work on a paper. For contact with written material."

I said strictly, "You could read books, you know."

"I've read *some.*" He looked down in shame. "I'm too lazy. My mind is lazy but my legs are good. If I could get to be a reporter or something like that I could use my legs a lot. I'm a good runner."

"And when," I put it to him in the voice of a sardonic archangel, "will you compose your poems?"

"While I'm running," he said.

I took him on as office boy and teased him considerably. Whenever I handed him a bit of copy to carry from one cubbyhole to another I reminded him that he was at last in contact with written material, and hoped he was finding it useful for his verse. He had no humor but his legs were as fleet as he had promised. He was always ready, always at attention, always on the alert to run. He was always *there,* waiting. He stood like a hare at rest watching the typewriters beat, his hands and his feet nervous for the snatch of the sheet from the platen, as impatient as though the production of a column of feature items were a wholly automatic act governed by the width of the paper and the speed of the machine. He would rip the page from the grasp of its author and streak for the copy desk, where he would lean belligerently over the poor editor in question to study the strokes of this cringing chap's blue pencil. "Is that what cutting is?" he asked. "Is that what you call proofreading? Doesn't 'judgment' have an 'e' in it? Why not? There's an 'e' in 'judge,' isn't there? How come you don't take the 'e' out of 'knowledgeable' too? How do you count the type for a headline?" He was insufferably efficient and a killing nuisance. In less than a month he switched from those ribbed and reeky knickers to a pair of grimy trousers out of a pawnshop, and from the ample back pocket of these there protruded an equally ample dictionary with its boards missing, purchased from the identical source: but this was an affectation, since I never saw him consult it. All the same we promoted him to proofreader. This buried him. We set him down at a dark desk in a dungeon and entombed him under mile-long strips of galleys and left him there to dig himself out. The printshop helped by providing innumerable shrdlus and inventing further typographical curiosities of such a nature that a psychologist would have been severely interested. The city editor was abetted by the whole reporting staff in the revelation of news stories rivaling the Bible in luridness, sexuality, and imaginative abomination. Meanwhile he never blinked, but went on devotedly taking the "e" out of "judgment" and putting it back for "knowledgeable," and making little loops for "omit" wherever someone's syntactical fancy had gone too rapturously far.

When I looked up and spotted him apparently about to mount my typewriter I was certain he had risen from his cellar to beg to be fired. Instead he offered me a double information: he was going to call himself Gate, and what did I think of that?—and in the second place he had just written his first poem.

"First?" I said. "I thought you've been at it all the while."

"Oh no," he assured me. "I wasn't ready. I didn't have a name."

"Gatoff's a name, isn't it?"

He ignored my tone, almost like a gentleman. "I mean a name suitable for the language. It has to match somehow, doesn't it? Or peopIe would get the idea I'm an impostor." I recognized this word from a recent fabrication he had encountered on a proof—my own, in fact: a two-paragraph item about a man who had successfully posed as a firewarden through pretending to have a sound acquaintance with the problems of water-pressure systems, but who let the firehouse burn down because he could not get the tap open. It was admittedly a very inferior story, but the best I could do; the others had soared beyond my meager gleam, though I made up for my barrenness by a generosity of double negatives. Still, I marveled at his quickness at self-enrichment—the aunt in Liverpool, I was certain, had never talked to him, in English, of impostors.

"Listen," he said thickly, "I really feel you're the one who started me off. I'm very grateful to you. You understood my weakness in the language and you allowed me every opportunity."

"Then you like your job down there?"

"I just wish I could have a light on my desk. A small bulb maybe, that's all. Otherwise it's great down there, sure, it gives me a chance to think about poems."

"Don't you pay any attention to what you're reading?" I asked admiringly.

"Sure I do. I always do. That's where I get my ideas. Poems deal with Truth, right? One thing I've learned lately from contact with written material is that Truth is Stranger than Fiction." He uttered this as if fresh from the mouths of the gods. It gave him a particular advantage over the rest of us: admonish him that some phrase was as old as the hills, and he would pull up his head like a delighted turtle and exclaim, "Now that's perfect. What a perfect way to express antiquity. That's true, the hills have been there since the earth was just new. Very good! I congratulate you"—showing extensive emotional reverberation, which I acknowledged after a time as his most serious literary symptom.

The terrible symptom was just now vividly tremulous. "What I want to ask you," he said, "is what you would think of Edmund for a poet's name. In front of Gate, for instance."

"*My* name is Edmund," I said.

"I know, I know. Where would I get the idea if not from you? A marvelous name. Could I borrow it? Just for use on poems. Otherwise it's all right, don't be embarrassed, call me Elia like always."

He reached for his behind, produced the dictionary, and cautiously shook it open to the Fs. Then he tore out a single page with meticulous orderliness and passed it to me. It covered Fenugreek to Fylfot, and the margins were foxed with an astonishing calligraphy, very tiny and very ornate, like miniature crystal cubes containing little bells.

"You want me to read this? " I said.

"Please," he commanded.

"Why don't you use regular paper?"

"I like words," he said. "Fenugreek, an herb of the pea family. Felo-de-se, a suicide. I wouldn't get that just from a blank sheet. If I see a good word in the vicinity I put it right in."

"You're a great borrower," I observed.

"Be brutal," he begged. "Tell me if I have talent."

It was a poem about dawn. It had four rhymed stanzas and coupled "lingered" with "rosy-fingered." The word Fuzee was strangely prominent.

"In concept it's a little on the hackneyed side," I told him.

"I'll work on it," he said fervently. "You think I have a chance? Be brutal."

"I don't suppose you'll ever be an original, you know," I said.

"You wait and see," he threatened me. "I can be brutal too."

He headed back for his cellar and I happened to notice his walk. His thick round calves described forceful rings in his trousers, but he had a curiously modest gait, like a preoccupied steer. His dictionary jogged on his buttock, and his shoulders suggested the spectral flutes of a spectral cloak, with a spectral retinue following murmurously after.

"Elia," I called to him.

He kept going.

I was willing to experiment. "Edmund!" I yelled.

He turned, very elegantly.

"Edmund," I said. "Now listen. I mean this. Don't show me any more of your stuff. The whole thing is hopeless. Waste your own time but don't waste mine."

He took this in with a pleasant lift of his large thumbs. "I never waste anything. I'm very provident."

"Provident, are you?" I made myself a fool for him: "Aha, evidently you've been inditing something in and around the Ps—"

"Puce, red. Prothorax, the front part of an insect. Plectrum, an ivory pick."

"You're an opportunist," I said. "A hoarder. A rag-dealer. Don't fancy yourself anything better than that. Keep out of my way, Edmund," I told him.

After that I got rid of him. I exerted—if that is not too gross a word for the politic and the canny—a quiet urgency here and there, until finally we tendered him the title of reporter and sent him out to the police station to call in burglaries off the blotter. His hours were midnight to morning. In two weeks he turned up at my desk at ten o'clock, squinting through an early sunbeam.

"Don't you go home to sleep now?" I asked.

"Criticism before slumber. I've got more work to show you. Beautiful new work."

I swallowed a groan. "How do you like it down at headquarters?"

"It's fine. A lovely place. The cops are fine people. It's a wonderful atmosphere to think up poems in. I've been extremely fecund. I've been pullulating down there. This is the best of the lot."

He ripped out Mimir to Minion. Along the white perimeter of the page his incredible handwriting peregrinated: it was a poem about a rose. The poet's beloved was compared to the flower. They blushed alike. The rose minced in the breeze; so did the lady.

"I've given up rhyme," he announced, and hooked his eyes in mine. "I've improved. You admit I've improved, don't you?"

"No," I said. "You've retrogressed. You're nothing but hash. You haven't advanced an inch. You'll never advance. You haven't got the equipment."

"I have all these new words," he protested. "Menhir. Eximious. Suffruti-cose. Congee. Anastrophe. Dandiprat. Trichiasis. Nidificate."

"Words aren't the only equipment. You're hopeless. You haven't got the brain for it."

"All my lines scan perfectly."

"You're not a poet."

He refused to be disappointed; he could not be undermined. "You don't see any difference?"

"Not in the least.—Hold on. A difference indeed. You've bought yourself a suit," I said.

"Matching coat and pants. Thanks to you. You raised me up from an errand boy."

"That's America for you," I said. "And what about Liverpool? I suppose you send your aunt something out of your salary?"

"Not particularly."

"Poor old lady."

"She's all right as she is."

"Aren't you all she's got? Only joy, apple of the eye and so forth?"

"She gets along. She writes me now and then."

"I suppose you don't answer much."

"I've got my own life to live," he objected, with all the ardor of a man in the press of inventing not just a maxim but a principle. "I've got a career to make. Pretty soon I have to start getting my things into print. I bet you know some magazine editors who publish poems."

It struck me that he had somehow discovered a means to check my ac-quaintance. "That's just the point. They publish *poems*. You wouldn't do for them."

"You could start me off in print if you wanted to."

"I don't want to. You're no good."

"I'll get better. I'm still on my way. Wait and see," he said.

"All right," I agreed, "I'm willing to wait but I don't want to see. Don't show me any more. Keep your stuff to yourself. Please don't come back."

"Sure," he said: this was his chief American acquisition. "You come to me instead."

During the next month there was a run of robberies and other non-matutinal felonies, and pleasurably and with relief I imagined him bunched up in a telephone booth in the basement of the station house, reciting clot after clot of criminal boredoms into the talking-piece. I hoped he would be hoarse enough and weary enough to seek his bed instead of his fortune, especially if he conceived of his fortune as conspicuously involving me. The mornings passed, and, after a time, so did my dread—he never ap-

peared. I speculated that he had given me up. I even ventured a little remorse at the relentlessness of my dealings with him, and then a courier
from the mail room loped in and left me an enormous envelope from an
eminent literary journal. It was filled with dozens and dozens of fastid-
iously torn-out dictionary pages, accompanied by a letter to me from the
editor-in-chief, whom—after a fashion—I knew (he had been a friend of
my late and distinguished father): "Dear Edmund, I put it to you that your
tastes in gall are not mine. I will not say that you presumed on my indulgence when you sent this fellow up here with his sheaf of horrors, but I
will ask you in the future to restrict your recommendations to *simple* fools—
who, presumably, turn to ordinary foolscap in their hour of folly. P.S. In any
case I never have, and never hope to, print anything containing the word
'ogdoad.'"

One of the sheets was headed Ogam to Oliphant.

It seemed too savage a hardship to rage all day without release: nevertheless I thought I would wait it out until midnight and pursue him where
I could find him, at his duties with the underworld, and then, for direct
gratification, knock him down. But it occurred to me that a police station is
an inconvenient situation for an assault upon a citizen (though it did not
escape me that he was still unnaturalized), so I looked up his address and
went to his room.

He opened the door in his underwear. "Edmund!" he cried. "Excuse me,
after all I'm a night worker—but it's all right, come in, come in! I don't need
a lot of sleep anyhow. If I slept I'd never get any poems written, so don't
feel bad."

Conscientiously I elevated my fists and conscientiously I knocked him
down.

"What's the idea?" he asked from the floor.

"What's the idea is right," I said. "Who told you you could go around
visiting important people and saying I sicked you on them?"

He rubbed his sore chin in a rapture. "You heard! I bet you heard straight
from the editor-in-chief himself. You would. You've got the connections, I
knew it. I told him to report right to you. I knew you'd be anxious."

"I'm anxious and embarrassed and ashamed," I said. "You've made me
look like an idiot. My father's oldest friend. He thinks I'm a sap."

He got up, poking at himself for bruises. "Don't feel bad for me. He didn't
accept any at all? Is that a fact? Not a single one?" I threw the envelope at
him and he caught it with a surprisingly expert arc of the wrist. Then he
spilled out the contents and read the letter. "Well, that's too bad," he said.
"It's amazing how certain persons can be so unsympathetic. It's in their
nature, they can't help it. But I don't mind. I mean it's all compensated for.

Here *you* are. I thought it would be too nervy to invite you—it's a very cheap place I live in, you can see that—but I knew you'd come on your own. An aristocrat like yourself."

"Elia," I said, "I came to knock you down. I *have* knocked you down."

"Don't feel bad about it," he repeated, consoling me. He reached for my ear and gave it a friendly pull. "It's only natural. You had a shock. In your place I would have done exactly the same thing. I'm very strong. I'm probably much stronger than you are. You're pretty strong too, if you could knock me down. But to tell the truth, I sort of *let* you. I like to show manners when I'm a host."

He scraped forward an old wooden chair, the only one in the room, for me to sit down on. I refused, so he sat down himself, with his thighs apart and his arms laced, ready for a civilized conversation. "You've read my new work yourself, I presume."

"No," I said. "When are you going to stop this? Why don't you concentrate on something sensible? You want to be a petty police reporter for the rest of your life?"

"I hope not," he said, and rasped his voice to show his sincerity. "I'd like to be able to leave this place. I'd like to have enough money to live in a nice American atmosphere. Like you, the way you live all alone in that whole big house."

He almost made me think I had to apologize. "My father left it to me. Anyway, didn't you tell me you never expected to get rich on poetry?"

"I've looked around since then, I've noticed things. Of America expect everything. America has room for anything, even poets. Edmund," he said warmly, "I know how you feel. R.I.P. I don't have a father either. You would have admired my father—a strapping man. It's amazing that they could kill him. Strong. Big. No offense, but he restrained himself, he never knocked anyone down. Here," he pleaded, "you just take my new things and look them over and see if that editor-in-chief was right. You tell me if in his shoes you wouldn't publish me, that's all I want."

He handed me Gharri to Gila Monster: another vapid excrescence in the margins. Schuit to Scolecite: the same. But it was plain that he was appealing to me out of the pathos of his orphaned condition, and from pity and guilt (I had the sense that he would regard it as a pogrom if I did not comply) I examined the rest, and discovered, among his daisies and sunsets, a fresh theme. He had begun to write about girls: not the abstract Beloved, but real girls, with names like Shirley, Ethel, and Bella.

"Love poems," he said conceitedly. "I find them very moving."

"About as moving as the lovelorn column," I said, "if less gripping. When do you get the time for girls? "

"Leonardo da Vinci also had only twenty-four hours in his day. Ditto Michelangelo. Besides, I don't go looking for them. I attract them."

This drew my stare. "You attract them?"

"Sure. I attract them right here. I hardly ever have to go out. Of course that sort of arrangement's not too good with some of the better types. They don't go for a poet's room."

"There's not a book in the place," I said in disgust.

"Books don't make a poet's room," he contradicted. "It depends on the poet—the build of man he is." And, with the full power of his odious resiliency, he winked at me.

The effect on me of this conversation was unprecedented: I suddenly began to see him as he saw himself, through the lens of his own self-esteem. He almost looked handsome. He had changed; he seemed larger and bolder. The truth was merely that he was not yet twenty and that he had very recently grown physically. He remained unkempt, and his belly had a habit of swelling under his shirt; but there was something huge starting in him.

About that time I was asked to cover a minor war in the Caribbean—it was no more than a series of swamp skirmishes—and when I returned after eight weeks I found him living in my house. I had, as usual, left the key with my married sister (it had been one of my father's crotchets—he had several—to anticipate all possible contingencies, and I carried on the custom of the house), and he had magically wheedled it from her: it turned out he had somehow persuaded her that she would earn the gratitude of his posterity by allowing him to attain the kind of shelter commensurate with his qualities.

"Commensurate with your qualities," I sing-songed at him. "When I heard that, I knew she had it verbatim. All right, Elia, you've sucked the place dry. That's all. Out." Every teacup was dirty and he had emptied the whiskey. "You've had parties," I concluded.

"I couldn't help it, Edmund. I've developed so many friendships recently."

"Get out."

"Ah, don't be harsh. You know the little rooms upstairs? The ones that have the skylight? I bet those were maids' rooms once. You wouldn't know I was there, I promise you. Where can I go where there's so much good light? Over at the precinct house it's even worse than the cellar was, they use only forty-watt bulbs. The municipality is prodigiously parsimonious. What have I got if I haven't got my eyesight?

Take my pen and still
I sing. But deny

*My eye
And Will
Departs the quill.*"

"My reply remains Nil," I said. "Just go."

He obliged me with a patronizing laugh. "That's very good. Deny, Reply. Quill, Nil."

"No, I mean it. You can't stay. Besides," I said sourly, "I thought you gave up rhymes long ago."

"You think I'm making it up about my eyes," he said. "Well, look." He darted a thick fist into a pocket and whipped out a pair of glasses and put them on. "While you were gone I had to get these. They're pretty strong for a person of my age. I'm not supposed to abuse my irises. These peepers cost me equal to nearly a month's rent at my old place."

The gesture forced me to study him. He had spoken of his qualities, but they were all quantities: he had grown some more, not upward exactly, and not particularly outward, but in some textural way, as though his bigness required one to assure oneself of it by testing it with the nerve in the fingertip. He was walking around in his underwear. For the first time I took it in how extraordinarily hairy a man he was. His shoulders and his chest were a forest, and the muscles in his arms were globes darkened by brush. I observed that he was thoroughly aware of himself; he held his torso like a bit of classical rubble, but he captured the warrior lines of it with a certain prideful agility.

"Go ahead, put on your clothes," I yelled at him.

"It's not cold in the house, Edmund."

"It is in the street. Go on, get out. With or without your clothes. Go."

He lowered his head, and I noted in surprise the gross stems of his ears. "It would be mean."

"I can take it. Stop worrying about my feelings."

"I'm not referring just to you. I left Sylvia alone upstairs when you came in."

"Are you telling me you've got a *girl* in this house right now?"

"Sure," he said meekly. "But you don't mind, Edmund. I know you don't. It's only what you do yourself, isn't it?"

I went to the foot of the staircase and shouted: "That's enough! Come down! Get out!"

Nothing stirred.

"You've scared her," he said.

"Get rid of her, Elia, or I'll call the police."

"That would be nice," he said wistfully. *"They* like my poems. I always read them aloud down at the station house. Look, if you really want me to go I'll go, and you can get rid of Sylvia yourself. You certainly have a beautiful spacious house here. Nice furniture. I certainly did enjoy it. Your sister told me a few things about it—it was very interesting. Your sister's a rather religious person, isn't she? Moral, like your father. What a funny man your father was, to put a thing like that in his will. Fornication on premises."

"What's this all about?" But I knew, and felt the heat of my wariness.

"What your sister mentioned. She just mentioned that your father left you this house only on condition you'd never do anything to defame or defile it, and if you did do anything like that the house would go straight to her. Not that she really needs it for herself, but it would be convenient, with all those children of hers—naturally I'm only quoting. I guess you wouldn't want me to let on to her about Regina last Easter, would you?—You see, Edmund, you're even sweating a little bit yourself, look at your collar, so why be unfair and ask me to put on my clothes?"

I said hoarsely, "How do you know about Regina?"

"Well, I don't really, do I? It's just that I found this bunch of notes from somebody by that name—Regina—and in one or two of them she says how she stayed here with you over Easter and all about the two of you. Actually, your sister might be a little strait-laced, but she's pretty nice, I mean she wouldn't think the family mansion was being desecrated and so on if *I* stayed here, would she? So in view of all that don't you want to give your consent to my moving in for a little while, Edmund?"

Bitterly I gave it, though consent was academic: he had already installed all his belongings—his dictionary (what was left of it: a poor skeleton, gluey spine and a few of the more infrequent vocabularies, such as K, X, and Z), his suit, and a cigar box filled with thin letters from Liverpool, mostly unopened. I wormed from him a promise that he would keep to the upper part of the house; in return I let him take my typewriter up with him.

What amazed me was that he kept it tapping almost every evening. I had really believed him to be indolent; instead it emerged that he was glib. But I was astonished when I occasionally saw him turn away visitors—it was more usual for him to grab, squeeze, tease and kiss them. They came often, girls with hats brimmed and plumed, and fur muffs, and brave quick little boots; they followed him up the stairs with crowds of poems stuffed into their muffs—their own, or his, or both—throwing past me jagged hillocks and troughs of laughter, their chins hidden in stanzas. Then, though the space of a floor was between us, I heard him declaim: then received a zephyr of shrieks; then further laughter, ebbing; then a scuffle like a herd of zoo antelope, until, in the pure zeal of fury, I floundered into the drawing room and violently clapped the doors to. I sat with my book of maps in my father's heavy creaking chair near a stagnant grate and wondered how I could get him out. I thought of carrying the whole rude tale of his licentiousness to my sister—but anything I might say against a person who was plainly my own guest would undoubtedly tell doubly against myself (so wholesome was my father's whim, and so completely had he disliked me), and since all the money had gone to my sister, and only this gigantic curio of a house to me, I had the warmest desire to hold onto it. Room for room I hated the place; it smelled of the wizened scrupulousness of my burdensome child-hood, and my dream was to put it on the market at precisely the right time and make off with a fortune. Luckily I had cozy advice from real-estate friends: the right hour was certainly not yet. But for this house and these hopes I owned nothing, not counting my salary, which was, as my sister liked to affirm, beggar's pay in the light of what she called our "back-ground." Her appearances were now unhappily common. She arrived with five or six of her children, and always without her husband, so that she puffed out the effect of having plucked her offspring out of a cloud. She was a small, exact woman, with large, exact views, made in the exact image of a pious bird, with a cautious jewel of an eye, an excessively arched and fussy breast, and two very tiny and exact nostril-points. She admired Elia and used to ascend to his rooms, trailing progeny, at his bedtime, which is to say at nine o'clock in the morning, when I would be just departing the house for my office; whereas the poetesses, to their credit, did not become visible until romantic dusk. Sometimes she would telephone me and recommend that I move such-and-such a desk—or this ottoman or that highboy—into his attic to supply him with the comforts due his gifts.

"Margaret," I answered her, "have you seen his stuff? It's all pointless. It's all trash."

"He's very young," she declared—"you wait and see," which she repro-duced in his idiom so mimetically that she nearly sounded like a Glusker herself. "At your age he'll be a man of the world, not a house-hugging eunuch."

I could not protest at this abusive epithet, vibrantly meant for me; to dis-claim my celibacy would have been to disclaim my house. Elia, it appeared, was teaching her subtlety as well as ornamental scurrility—"eunuch" had never before alighted on Margaret's austere tongue. But it was true that since I no longer dared to see poor Regina under our old terms—I was too perilously subject to my guest's surveillance—she had dropped me in pique, and though I was not yet in love, I had been fonder of Regina than of almost anyone. "All right," I cried, "then let him be what he can."

"Why that's *everything*," said Margaret; "you don't realize what a find you've got in that young man."

"He's told you his designs on fame."

"Dear, he doesn't have to tell me. I can *see* it. He's unbelievable. He's an artist."

"A cheap little immigrant," I said. "Uncultivated. He never reads anything."

"Well, that's perfectly true, he's *not* effete. And about being a foreigner, do you know that terrible story, what they did to his whole family over there? When you survive a thing like that it turns you into a man. A fighter. Heroic," she ended. Then, with the solemnity of a codicil: "Don't call him little. He's big. He's enormous. His blood hasn't been thinned."

"He didn't *survive* it," I said wearily. "He wasn't even there when it happened. He was safe in England, he was in Liverpool, for God's sake, living with his aunt."

"Dear, please don't exaggerate and *please* don't swear. I see in him what I'm afraid I'll never see in you: because it isn't there. Genuine manliness. You have no tenderness for the children, Edmund, you walk right by them. Your own nieces and nephews. Elia is remarkable with them. That's just a single example."

I recited, "Gentleness Is the True Soul of Virility."

"That's in very bad taste, Edmund, that's a very journalistic way to express it," she said sadly, as though I had shamed her with an indelicacy: so I assumed Elia had not yet educated her to the enunciation of this potent word.

"You don't like it? Neither do I. It's just that it happens to be the title of the manly artist's latest ode," which was a fact. He had imposed it on me only the night before, whereupon I ritually informed him that it was his worst banality yet.

But Margaret was unvanquishable; she had her own point to bring up. "Look here, Edmund, can't you do something about getting him a better job? What he's doing now doesn't come near to being worthy of him. After all, a police station. And the hours!—"

"I take it you don't think the police force an influence suitable to genuine manliness," I said, and reflected that he had, after all, managed to prove his virility at the cost of my demonstrating mine. I had lost Regina; but he still had all his poetesses.

Yet he did, as I have already noted, now and then send them away, and these times, when he was alone in his rooms, I would listen most particularly for the unrelenting clack of the typewriter. He was keeping at it; he was engrossed; he was serious. It seemed to me the most paralyzing sign of all that

this hollow chattering of his machine was so consistent, so reliable, so intelligible, so without stutter or modest hesitation—it made me sigh. He was deeply deadly purposeful. The tapping went on and on, and since he never stopped, it was clear that he never thought. He never daydreamed, meandered, imagined, meditated, sucked, picked, smoked, scratched or loafed. He simply tapped, forefinger over forefinger, as though these sole active digits of his were the legs of a conscientious and dogged errand boy. His investment in self-belief was absolute in its ambition, and I nearly pitied him for it. What he struck off the page was spew and offal, and he called it his career. He mailed three dozen poems a week to this and that magazine, and when the known periodicals turned him down he dredged up the unknown ones, shadowy quarterlies and gazettes printed on hand-presses in dubious basements and devoted to matters anatomic, astronomic, gastronomic, political, or atheist. To the publication of the Vegetarian Party he offered a pastoral verse in earthy trochees, and he tried the organ of a ladies' tonic manufacturing firm with fragile dactyls on the subject of corsets. He submitted everywhere, and I suppose there was finally no editor alive who did not clutch his head at the sight of his name. He clattered out barrage after barrage; he was a scourge to every idealist who had ever hoped to promote the dim cause of numbers. And leaf by leaf, travel journals shoulder to shoulder with Marxist tracts, paramilitarists alongside Seventh-Day Adventists, suffragettes hand in hand with nudists—to a man and to a woman they turned him down, they denied him print, they begged him at last to cease and desist, they folded their pamphlets like Arab tents and fled when they saw him brandishing so much as an iamb.

Meanwhile the feet of his fingers ran; he never gave up. My fright for him began almost to match my contempt. I was pitying him now in earnest, though his confidence remained as unmoved and oafish as ever. "Wait and see," he said, sounding like a copy of my sister copying him. The two of them put their heads together over me, but I had done all I could for him. He had no prospects. It even horribly developed that I was looked upon by my colleagues as his special protector, because when I left for the trenches my absence was immediately seized on and he was fired. This, of course, did not reach me until I returned after a year, missing an earlobe and with a dark and ugly declivity slashed across the back of my neck. My house guest had been excused from the draft by virtue of his bad eyesight, or perhaps more accurately by virtue of the ponderous thickness of his lenses; eight or ten of his poetesses tendered him a party in celebration of both his exemption and his myopia, at which he unflinchingly threw a dart into the bull's-eye of a target-shaped cake. But I was myself no soldier, and went only as a correspondent to that ancient and so primitive war, naïvely pretending to encompass the world, but Neanderthal according to our later and more expansive appetites for annihilation. Someone had merely shot a prince (a nobody—I myself cannot recall his name), and then, in illogical consequence, various patches of territory had sprung up to occupy and individualize a former empire. In the same way, I discovered, had Elia sprung up—or, as I must now consistently call him (lest I seem to stand apart from the miraculous change in his history), Edmund Gate. What I mean by this is that he stepped out of his attic and with democratic hugeness took over the house. His great form had by now entirely flattened my father's august chair, and, like a vast male Goldilocks, he was sleeping in my mother's bed—that shrine which my father had long ago consecrated to disuse and awe: a piety my sister and I had soberly perpetuated. I came home and found him in the drawing room, barefoot and in his underwear, his dirty socks strewn over the floor, and my sister in attendance mending the holes he had worn through the heels, invigilated by a knot of her children. It presently emerged that she had all along been providing him with an allowance to suit his tastes, but in that first unwitting moment when he leaped up to embrace me, at the same time dragging on his shirt (because he knew how I disliked to see him undressed), I was stunned to catch the flash of his initials—"E.G."—embroidered in scarlet silk on a pair of magnificent cuffs.

"Edmund!" he howled. "Not one, not two—two *dozen!* Two dozen in the past two months alone!"

"Two dozen what?" I said, blinking at what had become of him. He was now twenty-one, and taller, larger, and hairier than ever. He wore new glasses (far less formidable than the awful weights his little nose had carried to the draft board), and these, predictably, had matured his expression, especially in the area of the cheekbones: their elderly silver frames very cleverly contradicted that inevitable boyishness which a big face is wont to radiate when it is committed to surrounding the nose of a cherub. I saw plainly, and saw it for myself, without the mesmerizing influence of his preening (for he was standing before me very simply, diligently buttoning up his shirt), that he had been increased and transformed: his fantastic body had made a simile out of him. The element in him that partook of the heathen colossus had swelled to drive out everything callow—with his blunt and balding skull he looked (I am willing to dare the vulgar godliness inherent in the term) like a giant lingam: one of those curious phallic monuments one may suddenly encounter, wreathed with bright chains of leaves, on a dusty wayside in India. His broad hands wheeled, his shirttail flicked; it was clear that his scalp was not going to be friends for long with his follicles—stars of dandruff fluttered from him. He had apparently taken up smoking, because his teeth were already a brown ruin. And with all that, he was somehow a ceremonial and touching spectacle. He was massive and dramatic; he had turned majestic.

"Poems, man, poems!" he roared. "Two dozen poems sold, and to all the best magazines!" He would have pulled my ear like a comrade had I had a lobe to pull by, but instead he struck me down into a chair (all the while my sister went on peacefully darning), and heaped into my arms a jumble of the most important periodicals of the hour.

"Ah, there's more to it than just that," my sister said.

"How did you manage all this?" I said. "My God, here's one in *The Centennial!* You mean Fielding accepted? Fielding actually?"

"The sheaf of horrors man, that's right. He's really a very nice old fellow, you know that, Edmund? I've lunched with him three times now. He can't stop apologizing for the way he embarrassed himself—remember, the time he wrote you that terrible letter about me? He's always saying how ashamed he is over it."

"Fielding?" I said. "I can't imagine Fielding—"

"Tell the rest," Margaret said complacently.

"Well, tomorrow we're having lunch again—Fielding and Margaret and me, and he's going to introduce me to this book publisher who's very interested in my things and wants to put them between, how did he say it, Margaret?—between something."

"Boards. A collection, all the poems of Edmund Gate. You see?" said Margaret.

"I *don't* see," I burst out.

"You never did. You haven't the vigor. I doubt whether you've ever really *penetrated* Edmund. This confused me, until I understood that she now habitually addressed him by the name he had pinched from me. "Edmund," she challenged—which of us was this? from her scowl I took it as a finger at myself—"you don't realize his level. It's his *level* you don't realize."

"I realize it," I said darkly, and let go a landslide of magazines: but *The Centennial* I retained. "I suppose poor Fielding's gone senile by now. Wasn't he at least ten years older than Father even? I suppose he's off his head and they just don't have the heart to ship him out."

"That won't do," Margaret said. "This boy is getting his recognition at last, that's all there is to it."

"I know what he means, though," Edmund said. "I tell them the same thing, I tell them exactly that—all those editors, I tell them they're crazy to carry on the way they do. You ought to hear—"

"Praise," Margaret intervened with a snap: "praise and more praise," as if this would spite me.

"I never thought myself those poems were *that* good," he said. "It's funny, they were just an experiment at first, but then I got the hang of it."

"An experiment?" I asked him. His diffidence was novel, it was even radical; he seemed almost abashed. I had to marvel: he was as bemused over his good luck as I was.

Not so Margaret, who let it appear that she had read the cosmic will. "Edmund is working in a new vein," she explained.

"Hasn't he always worked in vain?" I said, and dived into *The Centennial* to see.

Edmund slapped his shins at this, but "He who laughs last," said Margaret, and beat her thimble on the head of the nearest child: "What a callous man your uncle is. Read!" she commanded me.

"He has a hole in the back of his neck and only a little piece of ear left," said the child in a voice of astute assent.

"Ssh," said Margaret. "We don't speak of deformities."

"Unless they turn up as poems," I corrected; and read; and was startled by a dilation of the lungs, like a horse lashed out of the blue and made to race beyond its impulse. Was it his, this clean stupendous stuff? But there was his name, manifest in print: it was his, according to *The Centennial,* and Fielding had not gone senile.

"Well?"

"I don't know," I said, feeling muddled.

"He doesn't know! Edmund"—this was to Edmund— "he doesn't know!"

"I can't believe it."

"He can't believe it, Edmund!"

"Well, neither could I at first," he admitted.

But my sister jumped up and pointed her needle in my face. "Say it's good."

"Oh, it's good. I can see it's good," I said. "He's hit it for once."

"They're *all* like that," she expanded. "Look for yourself."

I looked, I looked insatiably, I looked fanatically, I looked frenetically, I looked incredulously—I went from magazine to magazine, riffling and rifling, looking and looting and shuffling, until I had plundered them all of his work. My booty dumbfounded me: there was nothing to discard. I was transfixed; I was exhausted; in the end it was an exorcism of my stupefaction. I was converted, I believed; he had hit it every time. And not with ease—I could trace the wonderful risks he took. It *was* a new vein; more, it was an artery, it had a pump and a kick; it was a robust ineluctable fountain. And when his book came out half a year later, my proselytization was sealed. Here were all the poems of the periodicals, already as familiar as solid old columns, uniquely graven; and layered over them like dazzling

slabs of dappled marble, immovable because of the perfection of their weight and the inexorability of their balance, was the aftermath of that early work, those more recent productions to which I soon became a reverential witness. Or, if not witness, then auditor: for out of habit he still liked to compose in the attic, and I would hear him type a poem straight out, without so much as stopping to breathe. And right afterward he came down and presented it to me. It seemed, then, that nothing had changed: only his gift and a single feature of his manner. Unerringly it was a work of—yet who or what was I to declare him genius?—accept instead the modest judgment of merit. It was a work of merit he gave me unerringly, but he gave it to me—this was strangest of all—with a quiescence, a passivity. All his old arrogance had vanished. So had his vanity. A kind of tranquillity kept him taut and still, like a man leashed; and he went up the stairs, on those days when he was seized by the need for a poem, with a languidness unlike anything I had ever noticed in him before; he typed, from start to finish, with no falterings or emendations; then he thumped on the stairs again, loomed like a thug, and handed the glorious sheet over to my exulting grasp. I supposed it was a sort of trance he had to endure—in those dim times we were only just beginning to know Freud, but even then it was clear that, with the bursting forth of the latent thing, he had fallen into a relief as deep and curative as the sleep of ether. If he lacked—or skipped— what enthusiastic people call the creative exaltation, it was because he had compressed it all, without the exhibitionism of prelude, into that singular moment of power—six minutes, or eight minutes, however long it took him, forefinger over forefinger, to turn vision into alphabet.

He had become, by the way, a notably fast typist.

I asked him once—this was after he had surrendered a new-hatched sheet not a quarter of an hour from the typewriter—how he could account for what had happened in him.

"You used to be awful," I reminded him. "You used to be unspeakable. My God, you were vile."

"Oh, I don't know," he said in that ennui, or blandness, that he always displayed after one of his remarkable trips to the attic, "I don't know if I was *that* bad."

"Well, even if you weren't," I said—in view of what I had in my hand I could no longer rely on my idea of what he had been—"this! This!" and fanned the wondrous page like a triumphant flag. "How do you explain *this,* coming after what you were?"

He grinned a row of brown incisors at me and gave me a hearty smack on the ankle. "Plagiarism."

"No, tell me really."

"The plangent plagiarism," he said accommodatingly, "of the plantigrade persona.—Admit it, Edmund, you don't like the Ps, you never did and you never will."

"For instance," I said, "you don't do *that* any more."

"Do what?" He rubbed the end of a cigarette across his teeth and yawned. "I still do persiflage, don't I? I do it out of my pate, without periwig, pugree, or peril."

"That. Cram grotesque words in every line."

"No, I don't do that any more. A pity, my dictionary's practically all gone."

"Why?" I persisted.

"I used it up, that's why. I *finished* it."

"Be serious. What I'm getting at is why you're different. Your stuff *is* different. I've never seen such a difference."

He sat up suddenly and with inspiration, and it came to me that I was observing the revival of passion. "Margaret's given that a lot of thought, Edmund. *She* attributes it to maturity."

"That's not very perspicacious," I said—for the sake of the Ps, and to show him I no longer minded anything.

But he said shortly, "She means virility."

This made me scoff. "She can't even get herself to say the word."

"Well, maybe there's a difference in Margaret too," he said.

"She's the same silly woman she ever was, and her husband's the same silly stockbroker, the two of them a pair of fertile prudes—she wouldn't recognize so-called virility if she tripped over it. She hates the whole concept—"

"She likes it," he said.

"What she likes is euphemisms for it. She can't face it, so she covers it up. Tenderness! Manliness! Maturity! Heroics! She hasn't got a brain in her head," I said, "and she's never gotten anything done in the world but those silly babies, I've lost count of how many she's done of *those*—"

"The next one's mine," he said.

"That's an imbecile joke."

"Not a joke."

"Look here, joke about plagiarism all you want but don't waste your breath on fairy tales."

"Nursery tales," he amended. "I never waste anything, I told you. That's just it, I've gone and plagiarized Margaret. I've purloined her, if you want to stick to the Ps."—Here he enumerated several other Ps impossible to print, which I am obliged to leave to my reader's experience, though not of the parlor. "And you're plenty wrong about your sister's brains, Edmund. She's a

very capable businesswoman—she's simply never had the opportunity. You know since my book's out I have to admit I'm a bit in demand, and what she's done is she's booked me solid for six months' worth of recitations. And the fees! She's getting me more than Edna St. Vincent Millay, if you want the whole truth," he said proudly. "And why not? The only time that dame ever writes a good poem is when she signs her name."

All at once, and against his laughter and its storm of smoke, I understood who was behind the title of his collected poems. I was confounded. It was Margaret. His book was called *Virility*.

A week after this conversation he left with my sister for Chicago, for the inauguration of his reading series.

I went up to his attic and searched it. I was in a boil of distrust; I was outraged. I had lost Regina to Margaret's principles, and now Margaret had lost her principles, and in both cases Edmund Gate had stood to profit. He gained from her morality and he gained from her immorality. I began to hate him again. It would have rejoiced me to believe his quip: nothing could have made me merrier than to think him a thief of words, if only for the revenge of catching him at it—but he could not even be relied on for something so plausible as plagiarism. The place revealed nothing. There was not so much as an anthology of poetry, say, which might account for his extraordinary burgeoning; there was not a single book of any kind—that sparse and pitiful wreck of his dictionary, thrown into a corner together with a cigar box, hardly signified. For the rest, there were only an old desk with his—no, my—typewriter on it, an ottoman, a chair or two, an empty chest, a hot bare floor (the heat pounded upward), and his primordial suit slowly revolving in the sluggish airs on a hanger suspended from the skylight, moths nesting openly on the lapels. It brought to mind Mohammed and the Koran; Joseph Smith and the golden plates. Some mysterious dictation recurred in these rooms: his gift came to him out of the light and out of the dark. I sat myself down at his desk and piecemeal typed out an agonized letter to Regina. I offered to change the terms of our relationship. I said I hoped we could take up again, not as before (my house was in use). I said I would marry her.

She answered immediately, enclosing a wedding announcement six months old.

On that same day Margaret returned. "I left him, of *course* I left him. I had to, not that he can take care of himself under the circumstances, but I sent him on to Detroit anyhow. If I'm going to be his manager, after all, I have to *manage* things. I can't do all that from the provinces, you know—I have to *be* here, I have to see people . . . ah, you can't imagine it, Edmund, they want him everywhere! I have to set up a regular office, just a *little* switchboard to start with—"

"It's going well?"

"Going well! What a way to put it! Edmund, he's a phenomenon. It's supernatural. He has *charisma,* in Chicago they had to arrest three girls, they made a human chain and lowered themselves from a chandelier right over the lectern, and the lowest-hanging one reached down for a hair of his head and nearly tore the poor boy's scalp off—"

"What a pity," I said.

"What do you *mean* what a pity, you don't follow, Edmund, he's a celebrity!"

"But he has so few hairs and he thinks so much of them," I said, and wondered bitterly whether Regina had married a bald man.

"You have no right to take that tone," Margaret said. "You have no idea how modest he is. I suppose that's part of his appeal—he simply has no ego at all. He takes it as innocently as a baby. In Chicago he practically looked over his shoulder to see if they really meant *him.* And they *do* mean *him*, you can't imagine the screaming, and the shoving for autographs, and people calling bravo and fainting if they happen to meet his eyes—"

"Fainting?" I said doubtfully.

"Fainting! My goodness, Edmund, don't you read the headlines in your own paper? His audiences are three times as big as Caruso's. Oh, you're hard, Edmund, you admit he's good but I say there's a terrible wall in you if you don't see the power in this boy—"

"I see it over you," I said.

"Over me! Over the world, Edmund, it's the world he's got now—I've already booked him for London and Manchester, and here's this cable from Johannesburg pleading for him—oh, he's through with the backwoods, believe you me. And look here, I've just settled up this fine generous contract for his next book, with the reviews still piling in from the first one!" She crackled open her briefcase, and flung out a mass of files, lists, letterheads, schedules, torn envelopes with exotic stamps on them, fat legal-looking portfolios, documents in tiny type—she danced them all noisily upon her pouting lap.

"His second book?" I asked. "Is it ready?"

"Of course it's ready. He's remarkably productive, you know. Fecund."

"He pullulates," I suggested.

"His own word exactly, how did you hit it? He can come up with a poem practically at will. Sometimes right after a reading, when he's exhausted— you know it's his shyness that exhausts him that way—anyhow, there he is all fussed and worried about whether the next performance will be as good, and he'll suddenly get this—well, *fit,* and hide out in the remotest part of the hotel and fumble in his wallet for bits of paper—he's always carrying

bits of folded paper, with notes or ideas in them I suppose, and shoo every-one away, even me, and *type* (he's awfully fond of his new typewriter, by the way)—he just types the glory right out of his soul!" she crowed. "It's the energy of genius. He's *authentic*, Edmund, a profoundly energetic man is profoundly energetic in all directions at once. I hope at least you've been following the reviews?"

It was an assault, and I shut myself against it. "What will he call the new book?"

"Oh, he leaves little things like the titles to me, and I'm all for sim-plicity.—*Virility II,*" she announced in her shocking business-magnate voice. "And the one after that will be *Virility III.* And the one after that—"

"Ah, fecund," I said.

"Fecund," she gleamed.

"A bottomless well?"

She marveled at this. "How is it you always hit on Edmund's words exactly?"

"I know how he talks," I said.

"A bottomless well, he said it himself. Wait and see!" she warned me.

She was not mistaken. After *Virility* came *Virility II,* and after that *Virility III,* and after that an infant boy. Margaret named him Edmund—she said it was after me—and her husband the stockbroker, though somewhat puzzled at this human production in the midst of so much literary fertility, was all the same a little cheered. Of late it had seemed to him, now that Margaret's first simple switchboard had expanded to accommodate three secretaries, that he saw her less than ever, or at least that she was noticing him less than ever. This youngest Edmund struck him as proof (though it embarrassed him to think about it even for a minute) that perhaps she had noticed him more than he happened to remember. Margaret, meanwhile, was gay and busy—she slipped the new little Edmund ("Let's call *him* III," she laughed) into her packed nursery and went on about her business, which had grown formidable. Besides the three secretaries, she had two assistants: poets, poetasters, tenors, altos, mystics, rationalists, rightists, leftists, memoirists, fortune-tellers, peddlers, everyone with an *idée fixe* and therefore suitable to the lecture circuit clamored to be bundled into her clientele. Edmund she ran ragged. She ran him to Paris, to Lisbon, to Stockholm, to Moscow; nobody understood him in any of these places, but the title of his books translated impressively into all languages. He developed a sort of growl—it was from always being hoarse; he smoked day and night—and she made him cultivate it. Together with his accent it caused an international shudder among the best of women. She got rid of his initialed cuffs and dressed him like a prize fighter, in high laced black brogans and tight shining

T-shirts, out of which his hairiness coiled. A long bladder of smoke was always trailing out of his mouth. In Paris they pursued him into the Place de la Concorde yelling *"Virilité! Virilité!"* *"Die Manneskraft!"* they howled in Munich. The reviews were an avalanche, a cataclysm. In the rotogravure sections his picture vied with the beribboned bosoms of duchesses. In New Delhi glossy versions of his torso were hawked like an avatar in the streets. He had long since been catapulted out of the hands of the serious literary critics—but it was the serious critics who had begun it. "The Masculine Principle personified, verified, and illuminated." "The bite of Pope, the sensuality of Keats." "The quality, in little, of the very greatest novels. Tolstoyan." "Seminal and hard." "Robust, lusty, male." "Erotic."

Margaret was ecstatic, and slipped a new infant into her bursting nursery. This time the stockbroker helped her choose its name: they decided on Gate, and hired another nanny to take care of the overflow.

After *Virility IV* came *Virility V*. The quality of his work had not diminished, yet it was extraordinary that he could continue to produce at all. Occasionally he came to see me between trips, and then he always went upstairs and took a turn around the sighing floors of his old rooms. He descended haggard and slouching; his pockets looked puffy, but it seemed to be only his huge fists he kept there. Somehow his fame had intensified that curious self-effacement. He had divined that I was privately soured by his success, and he tried bashfully to remind me of the days when he had written badly.

"That only makes it worse," I told him. "It shows what a poor prophet I was."

"No," he said, "you weren't such a bad prophet, Edmund."

"I said you'd never get anywhere with your stuff."

"I haven't."

I hated him for that—Margaret had not long before shown me his bank statement. He was one of the richest men in the country; my paper was always printing human-interest stories about him—"Prosperous Poet Visits Fabulous Patagonia." I said, "What do you mean you haven't gotten anywhere? What more do you want from the world? What else do you think it can give you?"

"Oh, I don't know," he said. He was gloomy and sullen. "I just feel I'm running short on things."

"On triumphs? They're all the time comparing you to Keats. Your pal Fielding wrote in *The Centennial* just the other day that you're practically as great as the Early Milton."

"Fielding's senile. They should have put him away a long time ago."

"And in sales you're next to the Bible."

"I was brought up on the Bible," he said suddenly.

"Aha. It's a fit of conscience? Then look, Elia, why don't you take Margaret and get her divorced and get those babies of yours legitimized, if that's what's worrying you."

"They're legitimate enough. The old man's not a bad father. Besides, they're all mixed up in there, I can't tell one from the other."

"Yours are the ones named after you. You were right about Margaret, she's an efficient woman."

"I don't worry about that," he insisted.

"*Some*thing's worrying you." This satisfied me considerably.

"As a matter of fact—" He trundled himself down into my father's decaying chair. He had just returned from a tour of Italy; he had gone with a wardrobe of thirty-seven satin T-shirts and not one of them had survived intact. His torn-off sleeves sold for twenty lira each. They had stolen his glasses right off his celebrated nose. "I like it here, Edmund," he said. "I like your house. I like the way you've never bothered about my old things up there. A man likes to hang on to his past."

It always bewildered me that the style of his talk had not changed. He was still devoted to the insufferably hackneyed. He still came upon his clichés like Columbus. Yet his poems . . . but how odd, how remiss! I observe that I have not even attempted to describe them. That is because they ought certainly to be *presented*—read aloud, as Edmund was doing all over the world. Short of that, I might of course reproduce them here; but I must not let my narrative falter in order to make room for any of them, even though, it is true, they would not require a great deal of space. They were notably small and spare, in conventional stanza-form. They rhymed consistently and scanned regularly. They were, besides, amazingly simple. Unlike the productions of Edmund's early phase, their language was pristine. There were no unusual words. His poems had the ordinary vocabulary of ordinary men. At the same time they were immensely vigorous. It was astonishingly easy to memorize them—they literally could not be forgotten. Some told stories, like ballads, and they were exhilarating yet shocking stories. Others were strangely explicit love lyrics, of a kind that no Western poet had ever yet dared—but the effect was one of health and purity rather than scandal. It was remarked by everyone who read or heard Edmund Gate's work that only a person who had had great and large experience of the world could have written it. People speculated about his life. If the Borgias, privy to all forms of foulness, had been poets, someone said, they would have written poems like that. If Teddy Roosevelt's Rough Riders had been poets, they would have written poems like that. If Genghis Khan and Napoleon had been poets, they would have written poems like that. They were masculine poems. They were political and personal, public and private. They were full of both passion and ennui, they were youthful and elderly, they were green and wise. But they were not beautiful and they were not dull, the way a well-used, faintly gnarled, but superbly controlled muscle is neither beautiful nor dull.

They were, in fact, very much like Margaret's vision of Edmund Gate himself. The poet and the poems were indistinguishable.

She sent her vision to Yugoslavia, she sent it to Egypt, she sent it to Japan. In Warsaw girls ran after him in the street to pick his pockets for souvenirs—they came near to picking his teeth. In Copenhagen they formed an orgiastic club named "The Forbidden Gate" and gathered around a gatepost to read him. In Hong Kong they tore off his underwear and stared giggling at his nakedness. He was now twenty-five; it began to wear him out.

When he returned from Brazil he came to see me. He seemed more morose than ever. He slammed up the stairs, kicked heavily over the floors, and slammed down again. He had brought down with him his old cigar box.

"My aunt's dead," he said.

As usual he took my father's chair. His burly baby's-head lolled.

"The one in Liverpool?"

"Yeah."

"I'm sorry to hear that. Though she must have gotten to be a pretty old lady by now."

"She was seventy-four."

He appeared to be taking it hard. An unmistakable misery creased his giant neck.

"Still," I said, "you must have been providing for her nicely these last few years. At least before she went she had her little comforts."

"No. I never did a thing. I never sent her a penny."

I looked at him. He seemed to be nearly sick. His lips were black. "You always meant to, I suppose. You just never got around to it," I ventured; I thought it was remorse that had darkened him.

"No," he said. "I couldn't. I didn't have it then. I couldn't afford to. Besides, she was always very self-reliant."

He was a worse scoundrel than I had imagined. "Damn you, Elia," I said. "She took you in, if not for her you'd be murdered with your whole family back there—"

"Well, I never had as much as you used to think. That police station job wasn't much."

"Police station!" I yelled.

He gave me an eye full of hurt. "You don't follow, Edmund. My aunt died before all this fuss. She died three years ago."

"Three years ago?"

"Three and a half maybe."

I tried to adjust. "You just got the news, you mean? You just heard?"

"Oh, no. I found out about it right after it happened."

Confusion roiled in me. "You never mentioned it."

"There wasn't any point. It's not as though you *knew* her. Nobody knew her. I hardly knew her myself. She wasn't anybody. She was just this old woman."

"Ah," I said meanly, "so the grief is only just catching up with you, is that it? You've been too busy to find the time to mourn?"

"I never liked her," he admitted. "She was an old nuisance. She talked and talked at me. Then when I got away from her and came here she wrote me and wrote me. After a while I just stopped opening her letters. I figured she must have written me two hundred letters. I saved them. I save everything, even junk. When you start out poor, you always save everything. You never know when you might need it. I never waste anything." He said portentously, "Waste Not, Want Not."

"If you never answered her how is it she kept on writing?"

"She didn't have anybody else to write to. I guess she had to write and she didn't have anybody. All I've got left are the ones in here. This is the last bunch of letters of hers I've got." He showed me his big scratched cigar box.

"But you say you saved them—"

"Sure, but I used them up. Listen," he said. "I've got to go now, Edmund, I've got to meet Margaret. It's going to be one hell of a fight, I tell you."

"What?" I said.

"I'm not going anywhere else, I don't care how much she squawks. I've had my last trip. I've got to stay home from now on and do poems. I'm going to get a room somewhere, maybe my old room across town, *you* remember—where you came to see me that time?"

"Where I knocked you down. You can stay here," I said.

"Nah," he said. "Nowhere your sister can get at me. I've got to work."

"But you've *been* working," I said. "You've been turning out new poems all along! That's been the amazing thing."

He hefted all his flesh and stood up, clutching the cigar box to his dinosaurish ribs.

"I haven't," he said.

"You've done those five collections—"

"All I've done are those two babies. Edmund and Gate. And they're not even my real names. That's all I've done. The reviews did the rest. Margaret did the rest."

He was suddenly weeping.

"I can't tell it to Margaret—"

"Tell what?"

"There's only one bundle left. No more. After this no more. It's finished."

"Elia, what in God's name *is* this? "

"I'm afraid to tell. I don't know what else to do. I've *tried* to write new stuff. I've tried. It's terrible. It's not the same. It's not the same, Edmund. I can't do it. I've told Margaret that. I've told her I can't write any more. She says it's a block, it happens to all writers. She says don't worry, it'll come back. It always comes back to genius."

He was sobbing wildly; I could scarcely seize his words. He had thrown himself back into my father's chair, and the tears were making brooks of its old leather cracks.

"I'm afraid to tell," he said.

"Elia, for God's sake. Straighten up like a man. Afraid of what?"

"Well, I told you once. I told you because I knew you wouldn't believe me, but I *did* tell you, you can't deny it. You could've stopped me. It's your fault too." He kept his face hidden.

He had made me impatient. "What's my fault?"

"I'm a plagiarist."

"If you mean Margaret again—"

He answered with a whimper: "No, no, don't be a fool, I'm through with Margaret."

"Aren't those collections yours? They're not yours?"

"They're mine," he said. "They came in the mail, so if you mean are they mine *that* way—"

I caught his agitation. "Elia, you're out of your mind—"

"She wrote every last one," he said. "In Liverpool. Every last line of every last one. Tante Rivka. There's only enough left for one more book. Margaret's going to call it *Virility VI,*" he bawled.

"Your aunt?" I said. "She wrote them all?"

He moaned.

"Even the one—not the one about the—"

"All," he broke in; his voice was nearly gone.

He stayed with me for three weeks. To fend her off I telephoned Margaret and said that Edmund had come down with the mumps. "But I've just had a cable from Southern Rhodesia!" she wailed. "They need him like mad down there!"

"You'd better keep away, Margaret," I warned. "You don't want to carry the fever back to the nursery. All those babies in there—"

"Why should he get an infant's disease?" she wondered; I heard her fidget.

"It's just the sort of disease that corresponds to his mentality."

"Now stop that. You know that's a terrible sickness for a grown man to get. You know what it does. It's awful."

I had no idea what she could be thinking of; I had chosen this fabrication for its innocence. "Why?" I said. "Children recover beautifully—"

"Don't be an imbecile, Edmund," she rebuked me in my father's familiar tone—my father had often called me a scientific idiot. "He might come out of it as sterile as a stone. Stop it, Edmund, it's nothing to laugh at, you're a brute."

"Then you'll have to call his next book *Sterility*," I said.

He hid out with me, as I have already noted, for nearly a month, and much of the time he cried.

"It's all up with me."

I said coldly, "You knew it was coming."

"I've dreaded it and dreaded it. After this last batch I'm finished. I don't know what to do. I don't know what's going to happen."

"You ought to confess," I advised finally.

"To Margaret?"

"To everyone. To the world."

He gave me a teary smirk. "Sure. The Collected Works of Edmund Gate, by Tante Rivka."

"Vice versa's the case," I said, struck again by a shadow of my first shock. "And since it's true, you ought to make it up to her."

"You can't make anything up to the dead." He was wiping the river that fell from his nose. "My reputation. My poor about-to-be-mutilated reputation. No, I'll just go ahead and get myself a little place to live in and produce new things. What comes now will be *really* mine. Integrity," he whined. "I'll save myself that way."

"You'll ruin yourself. You'll be the man of the century who fizzled before he made it to thirty. There's nothing more foolish-looking than a poet who loses his gift. Pitiful. They'll laugh at you. Look how people laugh at the Later Wordsworth. The Later Gate will be a fiasco at twenty-six. You'd better confess, Elia."

Moodily he considered it. "What would it get me?"

"Wonder and awe. Admiration. You'll be a great sacrificial figure. You can say your aunt was reticent but a tyrant, she made you stand in her place. Gate the Lamb. You can say anything."

This seemed to attract him. "It *was* a sacrifice," he said. "Believe me it was hell going through all of that. I kept getting diarrhea from the water in all those different places. I never could stand the screaming anywhere. Half the time my life was in danger. In Hong Kong when they stole my shorts I practically got pneumonia." He popped his cigarette out of his mouth and began to cough. "You really think I ought to do that, Edmund? Margaret wouldn't like it. She's always hated sterile men. It'll be an admission of my own poetic sterility, that's how she'll look at it."

"I thought you're through with her anyhow."

Courage suddenly puffed him out. "You bet I am. I don't think much of people who exploit other people. She built that business up right out of my flesh and blood. Right out of my marrow."

He sat at the typewriter in the attic, at which I had hammered out my futile proposal to Regina, and wrote a letter to his publisher. It was a complete confession. I went with him to the drugstore to get it notarized. I felt the ease of the perfect confidant, the perfect counsel, the perfect avenger. He had spilled me the cup of humiliation, he had lost me Regina; I would lose him the world.

Meanwhile I assured him he would regain it. "You'll go down," I said, "as the impresario of the nearly-lost. You'll go down as the man who bestowed a hidden genius. You'll go down as the savior who restored to perpetual light what might have wandered a mute inglorious ghost in the eternal dark."

On my paper they had fired better men than I for that sort of prose.

"I'd rather have been the real thing myself," he said. The remark seemed to leap from his heart; it almost touched me.

"Caesar is born, not made," I said. "But who notices Caesar's nephew? Unless he performs a vast deep act. To be Edmund Gate was nothing. But to shed the power of Edmund Gate before the whole watching world, to become little in oneself in order to give away one's potency to another— *that* is an act of profound reverberation."

He said wistfully, "I guess you've got a point there," and emerged to tell Margaret.

She was wrathful. She was furious. She was vicious. "A lady wrote 'em?" she cried. "An old Jewish immigrant lady who never even made it to America?"

"My Tante Rivka," he said bravely.

"Now Margaret," I said. "Don't be obtuse. The next book will be every bit as good as the ones that preceded it. The quality is exactly the same. He picked those poems at random out of a box and one's as good as another. They're all good. They're brilliant, you know that. The book won't be different so its reception won't be different. The profits will be the same."

She screwed up a doubtful scowl. "It'll be the last one. He says *he* can't write. There won't be any more after this."

"The canon closes," I agreed, "when the poet dies."

"This poet's dead all right," she said, and threw him a spiteful laugh. Edmund Gate rubbed his glasses, sucked his cigarette, rented a room, and disappeared.

Margaret grappled in vain with the publisher. "Why not *Virility* again? It was good enough for the other five. It's a selling title."

"This one's by a woman," he said. "Call it *Muliebrity,* no one'll understand you." The publisher was a wit who was proud of his Latin, but he had an abstract and wholesome belief in the stupidity of his readers.

The book appeared under the name *Flowers from Liverpool.* It had a pretty cover, the color of a daisy's petal, with a picture of Tante Rivka on it. The picture was a daguerrotype that Edmund had kept flat at the bottom of the cigar box. It showed his aunt as a young woman in Russia, not very handsome, with large lips, a circular nose, and minuscule light eyes—the handle of what looked strangely like a pistol stuck out of her undistinguished bosom.

The collection itself was sublime. By some accident of the unplanned gesture the last poems left in Edmund Gate's cracked cigar box had turned out to be the crest of the poet's vitality. They were as clear and hard as all the others, but somehow rougher and thicker, perhaps more intellectual. I read and marveled myself into shame—if I had believed I would dash his career by inducing him to drop his connection with it, I had been worse than misled. I had been criminal. Nothing could damage the career of these poems. They would soar and soar beyond petty revenges. If Shakespeare was really Bacon, what difference? If Edmund Gate was really Tante Rivka of Liverpool, what difference? Since nothing can betray a good poem, it is pointless to betray a bad poet.

With a prepublication copy in my hand I knocked at his door. He opened it in his underwear: a stink came out of him. One lens was gone from his glasses.

"Well, here it is," I said. "The last one."

He hiccuped with a mournful drunken spasm.

"The last shall be first," I said with a grin of disgust; the smell of his room made me want to run.

"The first shall be last," he contradicted, flagging me down with an old newspaper. "You want to come in here, Edmund? Come in, sure."

But there was no chair. I sat on the bed. The floor was splintered and his toenails scraped on it. They were long filthy crescents. I put the book down. "I brought this for you to have first thing."

He looked at the cover. "What a mug on her."

"What a mind," I said. "You were lucky to have known her."

"An old nuisance. If not for her I'd still be what I was. If she didn't run out on me."

"Elia," I began; I had come to tell him a horror. "The publisher did a little biographical investigation. They found where your aunt was living when she died. It seems," I said, "she was just what you've always described. Self-sufficient."

"Always blah blah at me. Old nuisance. I ran out on her, couldn't stand it."

"She got too feeble to work and never let on to a soul. They found her body, all washed clean for burial, in her bed. She'd put on clean linens her-self and she'd washed herself. Then she climbed into the bed and starved to death. She just waited it out that way. There wasn't a crumb in the place."

"She never asked me for anything," he said.

"How about the one called 'Hunger'? The one everybody thought was a battle poem?"

"It was only a poem. Besides, she was already dead when I got to it."

"If you'd sent her something," I said, "you might have kept Edmund Gate going a few years more. A hardy old bird like that could live to be a hun-dred. All she needed was bread."

"Who cares? The stuff would've petered out sooner or later anyhow, wouldn't it? The death of Edmund Gate was unavoidable. I wish you'd go away, Edmund. I'm not used to feeling this drunk. I'm trying to get profi-cient at it. It's killing my stomach. My bladder's giving out. Go away."

"All right."

"Take that damn book with you."

"It's yours."

"Take it away. It's your fault they've turned me into a woman. I'm a man," he said; he gripped himself between the legs; he was really very drunk.

All the same I left it there, tangled in his dirty quilt.

Margaret was in Mexico with a young client of hers, a baritone. She was arranging bookings for him in hotels. She sent back a photograph of him in a swimming pool. I sat in the clamorous nursery with the stockbroker and together we rattled through the journals, looking for reviews.

"Here's one. 'Thin feminine art,' it says."

"Here's another. 'A lovely girlish voice reflecting a fragile girlish soul: a lace valentine.'"

"'Limited, as all domestic verse must be. A spinster's one-dimensional vision.'"

"'Choked with female inwardness. Flat. The typical unimaginativeness of her sex.'"

"'Distaff talent, secondary by nature. Lacks masculine energy.'"

"'The fine womanly intuition of a competent poetess.'"

The two youngest children began to yowl. "Now, now Gatey boy," said the stockbroker, "now, now, Edmund. Why can't you be good? Your brothers and sisters are good, *they* don't cry." He turned to me with a shy beam. "Do you know we're having another?"

"No," I said. "I didn't know that. Congratulations."

"She's the New Woman," the stockbroker said. "Runs a business all by herself, just like a man."

"Has babies like a woman."

He laughed proudly. "Well, she doesn't do that one by herself, I'll tell you that."

"Read some more."

"Not much use to it. They all say the same thing, don't they? By the way, Edmund, did you happen to notice they've already got a new man in *The Centennial?* Poor Fielding, but the funeral was worthy of him. Your father would have wept if he'd been there."

"Read the one in *The Centennial,*" I said.

"'There is something in the feminine mind which resists largeness and depth. Perhaps it is that a woman does not get the chance to sleep under bridges. Even if she got the chance, she would start polishing the piles. Experience is the stuff of art, but experience is not something God made woman for . . .' It's just the same as the others," he said.

"So is the book."

"The title's different," he said wisely. "This one's by a woman; they all point that out. All the rest of 'em were called *Virility.* What happened to that fellow, by the way? He doesn't come around."

The babies howled down the ghost of my reply.

I explained at the outset that only last week I visited the grave of Edmund Gate, but I neglected to describe a curious incident that occurred on that spot.

I also explained the kind of camaraderie elderly people in our modern society feel for one another. We know we are declining together, but we also recognize that our memories are a kind of national treasury, being living repositories for such long-extinct customs as burial and intra-uterine embryo-development.

At Edmund Gate's grave stood an extraordinary person—a frazzled old woman, I thought at first. Then I saw it was a very aged man. His teeth had not been trans-rooted and his vision seemed faint. I was amazed that he did not salute me—like myself, he certainly appeared to be a centagenerian—

but I attributed this to the incompetence of his eyes, which wore their lids like hunched capes.

"Not many folks around here nowadays," I said. "People keep away from the old Preserved Cemeteries. My view is these youngsters are morbid. Afraid of the waste. They have to use everything. We weren't morbid in our time, hah?"

He did not answer. I suspected it was deliberate.

"Take this one," I said, in my most cordial manner, inviting his friendship. "This thing right here." I gave the little stone a good knock, taking the risk of arrest by the Outdoor Museum Force. Apparently no one saw. I knocked it again with the side of my knuckle. "I actually knew this fellow. He was famous in his day. A big celebrity. That young Chinese fellow, the one who just came back from flying around the edge of the Milky Way, well, the fuss they made over *him,* that's how it was with this fellow. This one was literary, though."

He did not answer; he spat on the part of the stone I had touched, as if to wash it.

"You knew him too?" I said.

He gave me his back—it was shaking horribly—and minced away. He looked shriveled but of a good size still; he was uncommonly ragged. His clothing dragged behind him as though the covering over the legs hobbled him; yet there was a hint of threadbare flare at his ankle. It almost gave me the sense that he was wearing an ancient woman's garment, of the kind in fashion seventy years ago. He had on queer old-fashioned woman's shoes with long thin heels like poles. I took off after him—I am not slow, considering my years—and slid my gaze all over his face. It was a kettle of decay. He was carrying a red stick—it seemed to be a denuded lady's umbrella (an apparatus no longer known among us)—and he held it up to strike.

"Listen here," I said hotly, "what's the matter with you? Can't you pass a companionable word? I'll just yell for the Museum Force, you and that stick, if you don't watch it—"

"I watch it," he said. His voice burst up and broke like boiling water—it sounded vaguely foreign. "I watch it all the time. That's my monument, and believe you me I watch it. I won't have anyone else watch it either. See what it says there? 'I am a man.' You keep away from it."

"I'll watch what I please. You're no more qualified than I am," I said.

"To be a man? I'll show you," he retorted, full of malice, his stick still high. "Name's Gate, same as on that stone. That's my stone. They don't make 'em any more. *You'll* do without."

Now this was a sight: madness has not appeared in our society for over two generations. All forms of such illness have vanished these days, and if

any pops up through some genetic mishap it is soon eliminated by Elec-tromed Procedure. I had not met a madman since I was sixty years old.

"Who do you say you are?" I asked him.

"Gate, born Gatoff. Edmund, born Elia."

This startled me: it was a refinement of information not on the monument.

"Edmund Gate's dead," I said. "You must be a literary historian to know a point like that. I knew him personally myself. Nobody's heard of him now, but he was a celebrated man in my day. A poet."

"Don't tell *me,*" the madman said.

"He jumped off a bridge dead drunk."

"That's what you think. That so, where's the body? I ask you."

"Under that stone. Pile of bones by now."

"I thought it was in the river. Did anybody ever pull it out of the river, hah? You've got a rotten memory, and you look roughly my age, boy. My memory is perfect: I can remember perfectly and I can forget perfectly. That's my stone, boy. I survived to see it. That stone's all there's left of Edmund Gate." He peered at me as though it pained him. "He's dead, y'know."

"Then you can't be him," I told the madman; genuine madmen always contradict themselves.

"Oh yes I can! I'm no dead poet, believe you me. I'm what survived him. He was succeeded by a woman, y'know. Crazy old woman. Don't tell *me.*"

He raised his bright stick and cracked it down on my shoulder. Then he slipped off, trembling and wobbling in his funny shoes, among the other monuments of the Preserved Cemetery.

He had never once recognized me. If it had really been Elia, he would certainly have known my face. That is why I am sure I have actually met a genuine madman for the first time in over forty years. The Museum Force at my request has made an indefatigable search of the Cemetery area, but up to this writing not so much as his pointed heel-print has been discovered. They do not doubt my word, however, despite my heavy age; senility has been eliminated from our modern society.

A Mercenary

Today we are all expressionists—men who want to make the world outside themselves take the form of their life within themselves.

—JOSEPH GOEBBELS

Stanislav Lushinski, a Pole and a diplomat, was not a Polish diplomat. People joked that he was a mercenary, and would sell his tongue to any nation that bargained for it. In certain offices of the glass rectangle in New York he was known as "the P.M."—which meant not so much that they considered him easily as influential as the Prime Minister of his country (itself a joke: his country was a speck, no more frightening than a small wart on the western—or perhaps it was the eastern—flank of Africa), but stood, rather, for Paid Mouthpiece.

His country. Altogether he had lived in it, not counting certain lengthy official and confidential visits, for something over fourteen consecutive months, at the age of nineteen—that was twenty-seven years ago—en route to America. But though it was true that he was not a native, it was a lie that he was not a patriot. Something in that place had entered him, he could not shake out of his nostrils the musky dreamy fragrance of nights in the capital—the capital was, as it happened, the third-largest city, though it had the most sophisticated populace. There, his colleagues claimed, the men wore trousers and the women covered their teats.

The thick night-blossoms excited him. Born to a flagstoned Warsaw garden, Lushinski did not know the names of flowers beyond the most staid dooryard sprigs, daisies and roses, and was hardly conscious that these heaps of petals, meat-white, a red as dark and boiling as an animal's maw, fevered oranges and mauves, the lobe-leafed mallows, all hanging downward like dyed hairy hanged heads from tall bushes at dusk, were less than animal. It was as if he disbelieved in botany, although he believed gravely enough in jungle. He felt himself native to these mammalian perfumes, to the dense sweetness of so many roundnesses, those round burnt hills at the edge of the capital, the little round brown mounds of the girls he pressed down under the trees—he, fresh out of the roil of Europe; they, secret to the ground, grown out of the brown ground, on which he threw himself, with his tongue on their black-brown nipples, learning their language.

He spoke it not like a native—though he was master of that tangled clot of extraordinary inflections scraped on the palate, nasal whistles, beetle-clicks—but like a preacher. The language had no written literature. A century ago a band of missionaries had lent it the Roman alphabet and transcribed in it queer versions of the Psalms, so that

> thou satest in the throne judging right

came out in argot:

> god squat-on-earth-mound
> tells who owns
> accidentally-decapitated-by-fallen-tree-trunk
> deer,

and it was out of this Bible, curiously like a moralizing hunting manual, the young Lushinski received his lessons in syntax. Except for when he lay under a cave of foliage with a brown girl, he studied alone, and afterward (he was still only approaching twenty) translated much of Jonah, which the exhausted missionaries had left unfinished. But the story of the big fish seemed simple-minded in that rich deep tongue, which had fifty-four words describing the various parts and positions of a single rear fin. And for "prow" many more: "nose-of-boat-facing-brightest-star," or star of middle dimness, or dimmest of all; "nose-of-boat-fully-invisible-in-rain-fog"; half-visible; quarter-visible; and so on. It was an observant, measuring, meticulous language.

His English was less given to sermonizing. It was diplomat's English: which does not mean that it was deceitful, but that it was innocent before passion, and minutely truthful about the order of paragraphs in all previous documentation.

He lived, in New York, with a mistress: a great rosy woman, buxom, tall and talkative. To him she was submissive.

In Geneva—no one could prove this—he lived on occasion with a strenuous young Italian, a coppersmith, a boy of twenty-four, red-haired and lean and not at all submissive.

His colleagues discovered with surprise that Lushinski was no bore. It astounded them. They resented him for it, because the comedy had been theirs, and he the object of it. A white man, he spoke for a black country: this made a place for him on television. At first he came as a sober financial attaché, droning economic complaints (the recently expelled colonial power had exploited the soil by excessive plantings; not an acre was left fallow; the chief crop—jute? cocoa? rye? Lushinski was too publicly fastidious ever to call it by its name—was thereby severely diminished, there was famine in the south). And then it was noticed that he was, if one listened with care, inclined to obliqueness—to, in fact, irony.

It became plain that he could make people laugh. Not that he told jokes, not even that he was a wit—but he began to recount incidents out of his own life. Sometimes he was believed; often not.

In his office he was ambitious but gregarious. His assistant, Morris Ngambe, held an Oxford degree in political science. He was a fat-cheeked, flirtatious young man with a glossy bronze forehead, perfectly rounded, like a goblet. He was exactly half Lushinski's age, and sometimes, awash in papers after midnight, their ties thrown off and their collars undone, they would send out for sandwiches and root beer (Lushinski lusted after everything American and sugared); in this atmosphere almost of equals they would compare boyhoods.

Ngambe's grandfather was the brother of a chief; his father had gone into trade, aided by the colonial governor himself. The history and politics of all this was murky; nevertheless Ngambe's father became rich. He owned a kind of assembly-line consisting of many huts. Painted gourds stood in the doorways like monitory dwarfs; these were to assure prosperity. His house grew larger and larger; he built a wing for each wife. Morris was the eldest son of the favorite wife, a woman of intellect and religious attachment. She stuck, Morris said, to the old faith. A friend of Morris's childhood—a boy raised in the missionary school, who had grown up into a model bookkeeper and dedicated Christian—accused her of scandal: instead of the Trinity, he shouted to her husband (his employer), she worshipped plural gods; instead of caring for the Holy Spirit, she adhered to animism. Society was progressing, and she represented nothing but regression: a backslider into primitivism. The village could not tolerate it, even in a female. Since it was fundamental propriety to ignore wives, it was clear that the fellow was crazy to raise a fuss over what one of a man's females thought or did. But it was also fundamental propriety to ignore an insane man (in argot the word for "insane" was, in fact, "becoming-childbearer," or, alternatively, "bottom-hole-mouth"), so everyone politely turned away, except Morris's mother, who followed a precept of her religion: a female who has a man (in elevated argot "lord") for her enemy must offer him her loins in reconciliation. Morris's mother came naked at night to her accuser's hut and parted her legs for him on the floor. Earlier he had been sharpening pencils; he took the knife from his pencil-pot (a gourd hollowed-out and painted, one of Morris's father's most successful export items) and stabbed her breasts. Since she had recently given birth (Morris was twenty years older than his youngest brother), she bled both blood and milk, and died howling, smeared pink. But because in her religion the goddess Tanake declares before five hundred lords that she herself became divine through having been cooked in her own milk, Morris's mother, with her last cry, pleaded for similar immortality; and so his father, who was less pious but who had loved her profoundly, made a feast. While the governor looked the other way, the murderer was murdered; Morris was unwilling to describe the execution. It was, he said in his resplendent Oxonian voice, "very clean." His mother was ceremonially eaten; this accomplished her transfiguration. Her husband and eldest son were obliged to share the principal sacrament, the nose, "emanator-of-wind-of-birth." The six other wives—Morris called each of them Auntie—divided among them a leg steamed in goat's milk. And everyone who ate at that festival, despite the plague of gnats that attended the day, became lucky ever after. Morris was admitted to Oxford; his grandfather's brother died at a very great age and his father replaced him as chief; the factory acquired brick buildings and chimneys and began manufacturing vases both of ceramic and glass; the colonial power was thrown out; Morris's mother was turned into a goddess, and her picture sold in the villages. Her name had been Tuka. Now she was Tanake-Tuka, and could perform miracles for devout women, and sometimes for men.

Some of Ngambe's tales Lushinski passed off as his own observations of what he always referred to on television as "bush life." In the privacy of his office he chided Morris for having read too many Tarzan books. "I have only seen the movies," Ngambe protested. He recalled how in London on Sunday afternoons there was almost nothing else to do. But he believed his mother had been transformed into a divinity. He said he often prayed to her. The taste of her flesh had bestowed on him simplicity and geniality.

From those tedious interviews by political analysts Lushinski moved at length to false living rooms with false "hosts" contriving false conversation. He felt himself recognized, a foreign celebrity. He took up the habit of looking caressingly into the very camera with the red light alive on it, signaling it was sensitive to his nostrils, his eyebrows, his teeth and his ears. And under all that lucid theatrical blaze, joyful captive on an easy chair between an imbecile film reviewer and a cretinous actress, he began to weave out a life.

Sometimes he wished he could write out of imagination: he fancied a small memoir, as crowded with desires as with black leafy woods, or else sharp and deathly as a blizzard; and at the same time very brief and chaste, though full of horror. But he was too intelligent to be a writer. His intelligence was a version of cynicism. He rolled irony like an extra liquid in his mouth. He could taste it exactly the way Morris tasted his mother's nose. It gave him powers.

He pretended to educate. The "host" asked him why he, a white man, represented a black nation. He replied that Disraeli too had been of another race, though he led Britain. The "host" asked him whether his fondness for his adopted country induced him to patronize its inhabitants. This he did not answer; instead he hawked up into the actress's handkerchief—leaning right over to pluck it from her décolletage where she had tucked it—and gave the "host" a shocked stare. The audience laughed—he seemed one of those gruff angry comedians they relished.

Then he said: "You can only patronize if you are a customer. In my country we have no brothels."

Louisa—his mistress—did not appear on the programs with him. She worried about his stomach. "Stasek has such a very small stomach," she said. She herself had oversized eyes, rubbed blue over the lids, a large fine nose, a mouth both large and nervous. She mothered him and made him eat. If he ate corn she would slice the kernels off the cob and warn him about his stomach. "It is very hard for Stasek to eat, with his little stomach. It shrank when he was a boy. You know he was thrown into the forest when he was only six."

Then she would say: "Stasek is generous to Jews but he doesn't like the pious ones."

They spoke of her as a German countess—her last name was preceded by a "von"—but she seemed altogether American, though her accent had a fake melody either Irish or Swedish. She claimed she had once run a famous chemical corporation in California, and truly she seemed as worldly as that, an executive, with her sudden jagged gestures, her large hands all alertness, her curious attentiveness to her own voice, her lips painted orange as fire. But with Lushinski she could be very quiet. If they sat at some party on opposite sides of the room, and if he lifted one eyebrow, or less, if he twitched a corner of his mouth or a piece of eyelid, she understood and came to him at once. People gaped; but she was proud. "I gave up everything for Stanislav. Once I had three hundred and sixty people under me. I had two women who were my private secretaries, one for general work, one exclusively for dictation and correspondence. I wasn't always the way you see me now. When Stasek tells me to come, I come. When he tells me to stay, I stay."

She confessed all this aloofly, and with the panache of royalty. On official business he went everywhere without her. It was true his stomach was very flat. He was like one of those playing-card soldiers in *Alice in Wonderland:* his shoulders a pair of neat thin corners, everything else cut along straight lines. The part in his hair (so sleekly black it looked painted on) was a clean line exactly above the terrifying pupil of his left eye. This pupil measured and divided, the lid was as cold and precise as the blade of a knife. Even his nose was a rod of machined steel there under the live skin—separated from his face, it could have sliced anything. Still, he was handsome, or almost so, and when he spoke it was necessary to attend. It was as if everything he said was like that magic pipe in the folktale, the sound of which casts a spell on its hearers' feet and makes the whole town dance madly, willy-nilly. His colleagues only remembered to be scornful when they were not face to face with him; otherwise, like everybody else, they were held by his mobile powerful eyes, as if controlled by silent secret wheels behind, and his small smile that was not a smile, rather a contemptuous little mock-curtsy of those narrow cheeks, and for the moment they believed anything he told them, they believed that his country was larger than it seemed and was deserving of rapt respect.

In New York Morris Ngambe had certain urban difficulties typical of the times. He was snubbed and sent to the service entrance (despite the grandeur of his tie) by a Puerto Rican elevator man in an apartment house on Riverside Drive, he was knocked down and robbed not in Central Park but a block away by a gang of seven young men wearing windbreakers reading "Africa First, Harlem Nowhere"—a yellow-gold cap covering his right front incisor fell off, and was aesthetically replaced by a Dr. Korngelb of East Forty-ninth Street, who substituted a fine white up-to-date acrylic jacket. Also he was set upon by a big horrible dog, a rusty-furred female chow, who, rising from a squat, having defecated in the middle of the sidewalk, inexplicably flew up and bit deep into Morris's arm. Poor Morris had to go to Bellevue outclinic for rabies injections in his stomach. For days afterward he groaned with the pain. "This city, this city!" he wailed to Lushinski. "London is boring but at least civilized. New York is just what they say of it—a wilderness, a jungle." He prayed to his mother's picture, and forgot that his own village at home was enveloped by a rubbery skein of gray forest with all its sucking, whistling, croaking, gnawing, perilously breathing beasts and their fearful eyes luminous with moonlight.

But at other times he did not forget, and he and Lushinski would compare the forests of their boyhoods. That sort of conversation always made Morris happy: he had been gifted with an ecstatic childhood, racing with other boys over fallen berries, feeling the squush of warm juice under his swift toes, stopping to try the bitter taste of one or two; and once they swallowed sour flies, for fun, and on a dare. But mostly there were games—so clever and elaborate he wondered at them even now, who had invented them, and in what inspired age long ago: concealing games, with complicated clue-songs attached, and quiet games with twigs of different sizes from different kinds of bark, requiring as much concentration as chess; and acrobatic games, boys suspended upside down from branches to stretch the muscles of the neck, around which, one day, the great width of the initiation-band would be fitted; and sneaking-up games, mimicking the silence of certain deer-faced little rodents with tender flanks who streaked by so quickly they could be perceived only as a silver blur. And best of all, strolling home after a whole dusty day in the bright swarm of the glade, insects jigging in the slotted sunbeams and underfoot the fleshlike fever-pad of the forest floor; and then, nearing the huts, the hazy smell of dusk beginning and all the aunties' indulgent giggles; then their hearts swelled: the aunties called them "lord"; they were nearly men. Morris—in those days he was Mdulgo-kt'dulgo ("prime-soul-born-of-prime-soul")—licked the last bit of luscious goat-fat from his banana leaf and knew he would one day weigh in the world.

Lushinski told little of his own forest. But for a moment its savagery wandered up and down the brutal bone of his nose.

"Wolves?" Morris asked; in his forest ran sleek red jackals with black swaths down their backs, difficult to trap but not dangerous if handled intelligently, their heads as red as some of these female redheads one saw taking big immodest strides in the streets of London and New York. But wolves are northern terrors, Slavic emanations, spun out of snow and legends of the Baba Yaga.

"Human wolves," Lushinski answered, and said nothing after that. Sometimes he grew sullen all at once, or else a spurt of fury would boil up in him; and then Morris would think of the chow. It had never been determined whether the chow was rabid or not. Morris had endured all that wretchedness for nothing, probably. Lulu (this was Louisa: a name that privately disturbed Morris—he was ashamed to contemplate what these two horrid syllables denoted in argot, and prayed to his mother to help him blot out the pictures that came into his thoughts whenever Lushinski called her on the telephone and began with—O Tanake-Tuka!—"Lulu?")—Lulu also was sometimes bewildered by these storms which broke out in him: then he would reach out a long hard hand and chop at her with it, and she would remember that once he had killed a man. He had killed; she saw in him the power to kill.

On television he confessed to murder:

Once upon a time, long ago in a snowy region of the world called Poland, there lived a man and his wife in the city of Warsaw. The man

ruled over a certain palace—it was a bank—and the woman ruled over another palace, very comfortable and rambling, with hundreds of delightful
storybooks behind glass doors in mahogany cases and secret niches to hide
toy soldiers in and caves under chairs and closets that mysteriously connected with one another through dark and enticing passageways—it was a
rich fine mansion on one of the best streets in Warsaw. This noble and
blessed couple had a little son, whom they loved more than their very lives,
and whom they named Stanislav. He was unusually bright, and learned
everything more rapidly than he could be taught, and was soon so accomplished that they rejoiced in his genius and could not get over their good
luck in having given life to so splendid a little man. The cook used to bring
him jigsaw puzzles consisting of one thousand pieces all seemingly of the
same shape and color, just for the marvel of watching him make a picture
out of them in no time at all. His father's chauffeur once came half an hour
early, just to challenge the boy at chess; he was then not yet five, and the
maneuvers he invented for his toy soldiers were amusingly in imitation of
the witty pursuits of the chessboard. He was already joyously reading about
insects, stars, and trolley cars. His father had brought home for him one
evening a little violin, and his mother had engaged a teacher of celebrated
reputation. Almost immediately he began to play with finesse and ease.

In Stanislav there was only one defect—at least they thought it a defect—
that grieved his parents. The father and mother were both fair, like a Polish
prince and a Polish princess; the mother kept her golden hair plaited in a
snail-like bun over each pink ear, the father wore a sober gray waistcoat
under his satiny pink chin. The father was ruddy, the mother rosy, and
when they looked into one another's eyes, the father's as gray as the buttery
gray cloth of his vest, the mother's as clamorously blue as the blue chips of
glass in her son's kaleidoscope, they felt themselves graced by God with
such an extraordinary child, indeed a prodigy (he was obsessed by an interest in algebra)—but, pink and ruddy and golden and rosy as they were,
the boy, it seemed, was a gypsy. His hair was black with a slippery will of
its own, like a gypsy's, his eyes were brilliant but disappointingly black, like
gypsy eyes, and even the skin of his clever small hands had a dusky glow,
like gypsy skin. His mother grew angry when the servants called him by a
degrading nickname—Ziggi, short for *Zigeuner,* the German word for
gypsy. But when she forbade it, she did not let slip to them that it was the
darkness she reviled, she pretended it was only the German word itself; she
would not allow German to be uttered in that house—German, the language of the barbarian invaders, enemies of all good Polish people.

All the same, she heard them whisper under the stairs, or in the kitchen:
Zigeuner; and the next day the Germans came, in helmets, in boots, tanks

grinding up even the most fashionable streets, and the life of the Warsaw palaces, the fair father in his bank, the fair mother under her rose-trellis, came to an end. The fair father and the fair mother sewed *zloty* in their underclothes and took the dark child far off into a peasant village at the edge of the forest and left him, together with the money to pay for it, in the care of a rough but kind-hearted farmer until the world should right itself again. And the fair blessed couple fled east, hoping to escape to Russia: but on the way, despite fair hair and pale eyes and aristocratic manners and the cultivated Polish speech of city people with a literary bent, they were perceived to be non-Aryan and were roped to a silver birch at the other end of the woods and shot.

All this happened on the very day Stanislav had his sixth birthday. And what devisings, months and months ahead of time, there had been for that birthday! Pony rides, and a clown in a silken suit, and his father promising to start him on Euclid. . . . And here instead was this horrid dirty squat-necked man with a bald head and a fat nose and such terrible fingers with thick horny blackened nails like angle irons, and a dreadful witchlike woman standing there with her face on fire, and four children in filthy smocks peering out of a crack in a door tied shut with a rubber strap.

"He's too black," said the witch. "I didn't know he'd be a black one. You couldn't tell from the looks of *them*. He'll expose us, there's danger in it for us."

"They paid," the man said.

"Too black. Get rid of him."

"All right," said the man, and that night he put the boy out in the forest. . . .

But now the "host" interrupted, and the glass mouth of the television filled up with a song about grimy shirt collars and a soap that could clean them properly. "Ring around the collar," the television sang, and then the "host" asked, "Was that the man you killed?"

"No," Lushinski said. "It was somebody else."

"And you were only six?"

"No," Lushinski said, "by then I was older."

"And you lived on your own in the forest—a little child, imagine!—all that time?"

"In the forest. On my own."

"But how? How? You were only a child!"

"Cunning," Lushinski said. It was all mockery and parody. And somehow—because he mocked and parodied, sitting under the cameras absurdly smiling and replete with contradictions, the man telling about the boy, Pole putting himself out as African, candor offering cunning—an uneasy blossom of laughter opened in his listeners, the laughter convinced: he was making himself up. He had made himself over, and now he was making himself up, like one of those comedians who tell uproarious anecdotes about their preposterous relatives. "You see," Lushinski said, "by then the peasants wanted to catch me. They thought if they caught me and gave me to the Germans there would be advantage in it for them—the Germans might go easy on the village, not come in and cart away all the grain without paying and steal the milk—oh, I was proper prey. And then I heard the slaver of a dog: a big sick bulldog, I knew him, his name was Andor and he had chewed-up genitals and vomit on his lower jaw. He belonged to the sexton's helper who lived in a shed behind the parish house, a brute he was, old but a brute, so I took a stick when Andor came near and stuck it right in his eye, as deep as I could push it. And Andor comes rolling and yowling like a demon, and the sexton's helper lunges after him, and I grab Andor— heavy as a log, heavy as a boulder, believe me—I grab him and lift him and smash him right down against the sexton's helper, and he's knocked over on his back, by now Andor is crazy, Andor is screeching and sticky with a river of blood spilling out of his eye, and he digs his smelly teeth like spades, like spikes, like daggers, into the old brute's neck—"

All this was comedy: Marx Brothers, Keystone cops, the audience is elated by its own disbelief. The bulldog is a dragon, the sexton's helper an ogre, Lushinski is only a storyteller, and the "host" asks, "Then that's the man you killed?"

"Oh no, Jan's Andor killed Jan."

"Is it true?" Morris wanted to know—he sat in the front row and laughed with the rest—and began at once to tell about the horrid chow on East Ninetieth Street; but Lulu never asked this. She saw how true. Often enough she shook him out of nightmares, tears falling from his nostrils, his tongue curling after air with hideous sucking noises. Then she brought him hot milk, and combed down his nape with a wet hand, and reminded him he was out of it all, Poland a figment, Europe a fancy, he now a great man, a figure the world took notice of.

He told no one who the man was—the man he killed: not even Lulu. And so she did not know whether he had killed in the Polish forest, or in the camp afterward when they caught him, or in Moscow where they took him, or perhaps long afterward, in Africa. And she did not know whether the man he killed was a gypsy, or a Pole, or a German, or a Russian, or a Jew, or one of those short brown warriors from his own country, from whom the political caste was drawn. And she did not know whether he had killed with his hands, or with a weapon, or through some device or ruse. Sometimes she was frightened to think she was the mistress of a murderer; and sometimes it gladdened her, and made her life seem different from all other lives, adventurous and poignant; she could pity and admire herself all at once.

He took Morris with him to Washington to visit the Secretary of State. The Secretary was worried about the threatened renewal of the northern tribal wars: certain corporate interests, he explained in that vapid dialect he used on purpose to hide the name of the one furious man whose fear he was making known, who had yielded his anxiety to the Secretary over a lunch of avocado salad, fish in some paradisal sauce, wine-and-mushroom-scented roast, a dessert of sweetened asparagus mixed with peppered apricot liqueur and surrounded by a peony-pattern of almond cakes—certain corporate interests, said the Secretary (he meant his friend), were concerned about the steadiness of shipments of the single raw material vital to the manufacture of their indispensable product; the last outbreak of tribal hostility had brought the cutting in the plantations to a dead halt; the shippers had nothing to send, and instead hauled some rotted stuff out of last year's discarded cuttings in the storehouses; it wouldn't do, an entire American industry depended on peace in that important region; but when he said "an entire American industry," he still meant the one furious man, his friend, whose young third wife had been at the luncheon too, a poor girl who carried herself now like a poor girl's idea of a queen, with hair expensively turned stiff as straw, but worth looking at all the same. And so again he said "that important region."

"You know last time with the famine up there," the Secretary continued, "I remember twenty years or so ago, before your time, I was out in the Cameroon, and they were at each other's throats over God knows what."

Morris said, "It was the linguistic issue. Don't think of 'tribes,' sir; think of nations, and you will comprehend better the question of linguistic pride."

"It's not a matter of comprehension, it's a matter of money. They wouldn't go to the plantations to cut, you see."

"They were at war. There was the famine."

"Mr. Ngambe, you weren't born then. If they had cut something, there wouldn't have been famine."

"Oh, that crop's not edible, sir," Morris protested: "it's like eating rope!"

The Secretary did not know what to do with such obtuseness; he was not at all worried about a hunger so far away which, full of lunch, he could not credit. His own stomach seemed a bit acid to him, he hid a modest belch. "God knows," he said, "what those fellows eat—"

But "Sir," said Lushinski, "you have received our documents on the famine in the south. The pressure on our northern stocks—believe me, sir, they are dwindling—can be alleviated by a simple release of Number Three grain deposits, for which you recall we made an appeal last week—"

"I haven't gotten to the Number Threes, Mr. Lushinski. I'll look them over this weekend, I give you my word. I'll put my staff right on it. But the fact is, if there's an outbreak—"

"Of cholera?" said Morris. "We've had word of some slight cholera in the south already."

"I'm talking about war. It's a pity about the cholera, but that's strictly internal. We can't do anything about it, unless the Red Cross . . . Now look here, we can't have that sort of interference again with cutting and with shipments. We can't have it. There has got to be a way—"

"Negotiations have begun between the Dt' and the Rundabi," Morris said; he always understood when Lushinski wished him to speak, but he felt confused, because he could feel also that the Secretary did not wish him to speak and was in fact annoyed with him, and looked to Lushinski only. All at once bitterness ran in him, as when the Puerto Rican elevator man sent him to the service entrance: but then it ebbed, and he admonished himself that Lushinski was his superior in rank and in years, a man the Prime Minister said had a heart like a root of a tree in his own back yard. This was a saying derived from the Dt' proverb: the man whose heart is rooted in his own garden will betray your garden, but the man whose heart is rooted in your garden will take care of it as if it were his own. (In the beautiful compressed idiom of the Prime Minister's middle-region argot: *bl'kt pk'ralwa, bl'kt duwam pk'ralwi.*)

And so instead of allowing himself to cultivate the hard little knob of jealousy that lived inside his neck, in the very spot where he swallowed food and drink, Morris reminded himself of his patriotism—his dear little country, still more a concept than a real nation, a confederacy of vast and enviously competitive families, his own prestigious tribe the most prominent, its females renowned for having the sleekest skin, even grandmothers' flesh smooth and tight as the flesh of panthers. He considered how inventiveness and adaptability marked his father and all his father's brothers, how on the tribe-god's day all the other families had to bring his great-uncle baskets of bean-flour and garlic buds, how on that day his great-uncle took out the tall tribe-god from its locked hut, and wreathed a garland of mallows on its *lulu,* and the females were shut into the tribe-god's stockade, and how at the first star of night the songs from the females behind the wall heated the sky and every boy of fourteen had his new bronze collar hitched on, and then how, wearing his collar, Morris led out of the god's stockade and into the shuddering forest his first female of his own, one of the aunties' young cousins, a pliant little girl of eleven. . . .

In New York there were dangerous houses, it was necessary to be married to be respectable, not to acquire a disease, in New York it was not possible for an important young man to have a female of his own who was not his wife; in London it was rather more possible, he had gone often to the bedsitter of Isabel Oxenham, a cheerful, bony, homely young woman who explained that being a Cockney meant you were born within the sound of Bow Bells and therefore she was a Cockney, but in New York there was prejudice, it was more difficult, in this Lushinski could not be his model. . . . Now he was almost listening to the Secretary, and oh, he had conquered jealousy, he was proud that his country, so tender, so wise, so full of feeling, could claim a mind like Lushinski's to represent it! It was not a foreign mind, it was a mind like his own, elevated and polished. He heard the Secretary say "universal," and it occurred to him that the conversation had turned philosophical. Instantly he made a contribution to it; he was certain that philosophy and poetry were his only real interests: his strengths.

"At bottom," Morris said, "there is no contradiction between the tribal and the universal. Remember William Blake, sir: 'To see a world in a grain of sand'—"

The Secretary had white hair and an old, creased face; Morris loathed the slender purple veins that made flower-patterns along the sides of his nose. The ugliness, the defectiveness, of some human beings! God must have had a plan for them if He created them, but since one did not understand the plan, one could not withhold one's loathing. It was not a moral loathing, it was only aesthetic. "Nationalism," Morris said, "in the West is so very recent: a nineteenth-century development. But in Africa we have never had that sort of thing. Our notion of nationhood is different, it has nothing political attached to it; it is for the dear land itself, the customs, the rites, the cousins, the sense of family. A sense of family gives one a more sublime concept: one is readier to think of the Human Family," but he thanked his mother that he was not related to this old, carmine-colored, creased and ugly man.

On the way back to New York in the shuttle plane Lushinski spoke to him like a teacher—avoiding English, so as not to be overheard. "That man is a peasant," he told Morris. "It is never necessary to make conversation with peasants. They are like their own dogs or pigs or donkeys. They only know if it rains. They look out only for their own corner. He will make us starve if we let him." And he said, using the middle-region argot of the Prime Minister, "Let him eat air," which was, in that place, a dark curse, but one that always brought laughter. In spite of this, and in spite of the funny way he pronounced *hl'tk*, "starve," aspirating it (*hlt'k*) instead of churning it in his throat, so that it came out a sort of half-pun for "take-away-the-virginity-of," Morris noticed again that whenever Lushinski said the word "peasant" he looked afraid. The war, of course, happened. For a week the cables flew. Lushinski flew too, to consult with the Prime Minister; he had letters from the Secretary, which he took with him to burn in the Prime Minister's ashtray. Morris remained in New York. One evening Lulu telephoned, to invite him to supper. He heard in her voice that she was obeying her lover, so he declined.

The war was more than fifty miles north of the capital. The Prime Minister's bungalow was beaten by rain; after the rain, blasts of hot wind shook the shutters. The leaves, which had been turned into cups and wells, dried instantly. Evaporation everywhere sent up steam and threads of rainbows. The air-conditioners rattled like tin pans. One by one Lushinski tore up the Secretary's letters, kindling them in the Prime Minister's ashtray with the Prime Minister's cigarette lighter—it was in the shape of the Leaning Tower of Pisa. Then he stoked them in the Prime Minister's ashtray with the Prime Minister's Japanese-made fountain pen. Even indoors, even with the air-conditioners grinding away, the sunlight was dense with scents unknown in New York: rubber mingled with straw and tar and monkey-droppings and always the drifting smell of the mimosas. The Prime Minister's wife (he pretended to be monogamous, though he had left off using this one long ago)—rather, the female who had the status of the Prime Minister's wife—went on her knees to Lushinski and presented him with a sacerdotal bean-flour cake.

The war lasted a second week; when the Prime Minister signed the cease-fire, Lushinski stood at his side, wearing no expression at all. From the Secretary came a congratulatory cable; Lushinski read it under those perfumed trees, heavy as cabbage-heads, smoking and smoking—he was addicted to the local tobacco. His flesh drank the sun. The hills, rounder and greener than any other on the planet, made his chest blaze. From the airplane—now he was leaving Africa again—he imagined he saw the tarred roofs of the guerrilla camps in the shadows of the hills; or perhaps those were only the dark nests of vultures. They ascended, and through the window he fixed on the huge silver horn of the jet, and under it the white cloud-meadows.

In New York the Secretary praised him and called him a peacemaker. Privately Lushinski did not so much as twitch, but he watched Morris smile. They had given the Secretary air to eat! A month after the "war"—the quotation marks were visible in Lushinski's enunciation: what was it but a combination of village riots and semistrikes? only two hundred or so people killed, one of them unfortunately the Dt' poet L'duy—the price of the indispensable cuttings rose sixty per cent, increasing gross national income by two thirds. The land was like a mother whose breasts overflow. This was Morris's image: but Lushinski said, "She has expensive nipples, our mother." And then Morris understood that Lushinski had made the war the way a man in his sleep makes a genital dream, and that the Prime Minister had transfigured the dream into wet blood.

The Prime Minister ordered a bronze monument to commemorate the dead poet. Along the base were the lines, both in argot and in English,

The deer intends,	*Kt'ratalwo*
The lion fulfills.	*Mnep g'trpa*
Man the hunter	*Kt'bl ngaya wiba*
Only chooses sides.	*Gagl gagl mrpa.*

The translation into English was Lushinski's. Morris said worshipfully, "Ah, there is no one like you," and Lulu said, "How terrible to make a war just to raise prices," and Lushinski said, "For this there are many precedents."

To Morris he explained: "The war would have come in any case. It was necessary to adjust the timing. The adjustment saved lives"—here he set forth the preemptive strategy of the Rundabi, and how it was foiled: his mouth looked sly, he loved tricks—"and simultaneously it accomplished our needs. Remember this for when you are Ambassador. Don't try to ram against the inevitable. Instead, tinker with the timing." Though it was after midnight and they were alone in Morris's office—Lushinski's was too grand for unofficial conversation—they spoke in argot. Lushinski was thirstily downing a can of Coca-Cola and Morris was eating salted crackers spread with apple butter. "Will I be Ambassador?" Morris asked. "One day," Lushinski said, "the mother will throw me out." Morris did not understand. "The motherland? Never!" "The mother," Lushinski corrected, "Tanake-Tuka." "Oh, never!" cried Morris, "you bring her luck." "I am not a totem," Lushinski said. But Morris pondered. "We civilized men," he said (using for "men" the formal term "lords," so that his thought ascended, he turned eloquent), "we do not comprehend what the more passionate primitive means when he says 'totem.'" "I am not afraid of words," Lushinski said. "You are," Morris said.

Lulu, like Morris, had also noticed a word which made Lushinski afraid. But she distinguished intelligently between bad memories and bad moods. He told her he was the century's one free man. She scoffed at such foolery. "Well, not the only one," he conceded. "But more free than most. Every survivor is free. Everything that can happen to a human being has already happened inside the survivor. The future can invent nothing worse. What he owns now is recklessness without fear."

This was his diplomat's English. Lulu hated it. "You didn't die," she said. "Don't be pompous about being alive. If you were dead like the others, you would have something to be pompous about. People call them martyrs, and they were only ordinary. If you were a martyr, you could preen about it."

"Do you think me ordinary?" he asked. He looked just then like a crazy man burning with a secret will; but this was nothing, he could make himself look any way he pleased. "If I were ordinary I would be dead."

She could not deny this. A child strung of sticks, he had survived the peasants who baited and blistered and beat and hunted him. One of them had hanged him from the rafter of a shed, by the wrists. He was four sticks hanging. And his stomach shrank and shrank, and now it was inelastic, still the size of a boy's stomach, and he could not eat. She brought him a bowl of warm farina, and watched him push the spoon several times into the straight line of his mouth; then he put away the spoon; then she took his head down into her lap, as if it were the head of a doll, and needed her own thoughts to give it heat.

He offered her books.

"Why should I read all this? I'm not curious about history, only about you."

"One and the same," he said.

"Pompous," she told him again. He allowed her only this one subject. "Death," she said. "Death, death, death. What do you care? *You* came out alive." "I care about the record," he insisted. There were easy books and there were hard books. The easier ones were stories; these she brought home herself. But they made him angry. "No stories, no tales," he said. "Sources. Documents only. Politics. This is what led to my profession. Accretion of data. There are no holy men of stories," he said, "there are only holy men of data. Remember this before you fall at the feet of anyone who makes romances out of what really happened. If you want something liturgical, say to yourself: *what really happened.*" He crashed down on the bed beside her an enormous volume: it was called *The Destruction*. She opened it and saw tables and figures and asterisks; she saw train-schedules. It was all dry, dry. "Do you know that writer?" she asked; she was accustomed to his being acquainted with everyone. "Yes," he said, "do you want to have dinner with him?" "No," she said.

She read the stories and wept. She wept over the camps. She read a book called *Night;* she wept. "But I can't separate all that," she pleaded, "the stories and the sources."

"Imagination is romance. Romance blurs. Instead count the numbers of freight trains."

She read a little in the enormous book. The title irritated her. It was a lie. "It isn't as if the whole *world* was wiped out. It wasn't like the Flood. It wasn't *mankind,* after all, it was only one population. The Jews aren't the whole world, they aren't mankind, are they?"

She caught in his face a prolonged strangeness: he was new to her, like someone she had never looked at before. "What's the matter, Stasek?" But all at once she saw: she had said he was not mankind.

"Whenever people remember mankind," he said, "they don't fail to omit the Jews."

"An epigram!" she threw out. "What's the good of an epigram! Self-conscious! In public you make jokes, but at home—"

"At home I make water," and went into the bathroom.

"Stasek?" she said through the door.

"You'd better go read."

"Why do you want me to know all that?"

"To show you what you're living with."

"I know who I'm living with!"

"I didn't say *who,* I said *what.*"

The shower water began.

She shouted, "You always want a bath whenever I say that word!"

"Baptism," he called. "Which word? Mankind?"

"Stasek!" She shook the knob; he had turned the lock. "Listen, Stasek, I want to tell you something. Stasek! I want to say something *important.*"

He opened the door. He was naked. "Do you know what's important?" he asked her.

She fixed on his member; it was swollen. She announced, "I want to tell you what I hate."

"I hope it's not what you're staring at," he said.

"History," she said. "History's what I hate."

"Poor Lulu, some of it got stuck on you and it won't come off—"

"Stasek!"

"Come wash it away, we'll have a tandem baptism."

"I know what *you* hate," she accused. "You hate being part of the Jews. You hate that."

"I am not part of the Jews. I am part of mankind. You're not going to say they're the same thing?"

She stood and reflected. She was sick of his satire. She felt vacuous and ignorant. "Practically nobody knows you're a Jew," she said. "*I* never think of it. You always make me think of it. If I forget it for a while you give me a book, you make me read history, three wars ago, as remote as Attila the Hun. And then I say that word"—she breathed, she made an effort—"I say *Jew,* and you run the water, you get afraid. And then when you get afraid you *attack,* it all comes back on you, you attack like an animal—"

Out of the darkness came the illusion of his smile: oh, a sun! She saw him beautifully beaming. "If not for history," he said, "think! You'd still be in the *Schloss,* you wouldn't have become a little American girl, you wouldn't have grown up to the lipstick factory—"

"Did you leave the drain closed?" she said suddenly. "Stasek, with the shower going, how stupid, now look, the tub's almost ready to over-flow—"

He smiled and smiled: "Practically nobody knows you're a princess."

"I'm *not*. It's my great-aunt—oh for God's sake, there it goes, over the side." She peeled off her shoes and went barefoot into the flood and reached to shut off the water. Her feet streamed, her two hands streamed. Then she faced him. "Princess! I know what it is with you! The more you mock, the more you mean it, but I know what it is! You want little stories, deep gossip, you want to pump me and pump me, you have a dream of royalty, and you know perfectly well, you've known it from the first *minute*, I've told and told how I spent the whole of the war in school in England! And then you say nonsense like 'little American girl' because you want that too, you want a princess and you want America and you want Europe and you want Africa—"

But he intervened. "I don't want Europe," he said.

"Pompous! Mockery! You want everything you're not, *that's* what it's about! Because of what you are!" She let herself laugh; she fell into laughter like one of his audiences. "An African! An African!"

"Louisa"—he had a different emphasis now: "I am an African," and in such a voice, all the sinister gaming out of it, the voice of a believer. Did he in truth believe in Africa? He did not take her there. Pictures swam in her of what it might be—herons, plumage, a red stalk of bird-leg in an unmoving pool, mahogany nakedness and golden collars, drums, black bodies, the women with their hooped lips, loin-strings, yellow fur stalking, dappled, striped . . . the fear, the fear.

He pushed his nakedness against her. Her hand was wet. Always he was cold to Jews. He never went among them. In the Assembly he turned his back on the ambassador from Israel; she was in the reserved seats, she saw it herself, she heard the gallery gasp. All New York Jews in the gallery. She knew the word he was afraid of. He pressed her, he made himself her master, she read what he gave her, she, once securely her own mistress, who now followed when he instructed and stayed when he ordered it, she knew when to make him afraid.

"You Jew," she said.

Without words he had told her when to say those words; she was obedient and restored him to fear.

Morris, despite his classical education, had no taste for Europe. No matter that he had studied "political science"—he turned it all into poetry, or, at the least, psychology; better yet, gossip. He might read a biography but he did not care about the consequences of any life. He remembered the names of Princess Margaret's dogs and it seemed to him that Hitler, though unluckily mad, was a genius, because he saw how to make a whole people search for ecstasy. Morris did not understand Europe. Nevertheless he knew he was superior to Europe, as people who are accustomed to a stable temperature are always superior to those who must live with the zaniness of the seasons. His reveries were attuned to a steady climate—summer, summer. In his marrow the crickets were always rioting, the mantises always flashing: sometimes a mantis stood on a leaf and put its two front legs one over the other, like a good child.

Lushinski seemed to him invincibly European: Africa was all light, all fine scent, sweet deep rain and again light, brilliance, the cleansing heat of shining. And Europe by contrast a coal, hellish and horrible, even the snows dark because humped and shadowy, caves, paw-prints of wolves, shoe-troughs of fleeing. In Africa you ran for joy, the joyous thighs begged for fleetness, you ran into veld and bush and green. In Europe you fled, it was flight, you ran like prey into shadows: Europe the Dark Continent.

Under klieg lights Lushinski grew more and more polished; he was becoming a comic artist, he learned when to stop for water, when to keep the tail of a phrase in abeyance. Because of television he was invited to talk everywhere. His stories were grotesque, but he told them so plausibly that he outraged everyone into nervous howls. People liked him to describe his student days in Moscow, after the Russian soldiers had liberated him; they liked him to tell about his suitcase, about his uniform.

He gave very little. He was always very brief. But they laughed. "In Moscow," he said, "we lived five in one room. It had once been the servant's room of a large elegant house. Twenty-seven persons, male and female, shared the toilet; but we in our room were lucky because we had a balcony. One day I went out on the balcony to build a bookcase for the room. I had some boards for shelves and a tin of nails and a hammer and a saw, and I began banging away. And suddenly one of the other students came flying out onto the balcony: 'People at the door! People at the door!' There were mobs of callers out there, ringing, knocking, yelling. That afternoon I received forty-six orders in three hours, for a table, a credenza, endless bookshelves, a bed, a desk, a portable commode. They thought I was an illegal carpenter working out in the open that way to advertise: you had to wait months for a State carpenter. One of the orders—it was for the commode—was from an informer. I explained that I was only a student and not in business, but they locked me up for hooliganism because I had drawn a crowd. Five days in a cell with drunkards. They said I had organized a demonstration against the regime.

"A little while afterward the plumbing of our communal toilet became defective—I will not say just how. The solid refuse had to be gathered in buckets. It was unbearable, worse than any stable. And again I saw my opportunity as a carpenter. I constructed a commode and delivered it to the informer—and oh, it was full, it was full. Twenty-seven Soviet citizens paid tribute."

Such a story made Morris uncomfortable. His underwear felt too tight, he perspired. He wondered why everyone laughed. The story seemed to him European, uncivilized. It was something that could have happened but probably did not happen. He did not know what he ought to believe.

The suitcase, on the other hand, he knew well. It was always reliably present, leaning against Lushinksi's foot, or propped up against the bottom of his desk, or the door of his official car. Lushinski was willing enough to explain its contents: "Several complete sets of false papers," he said with satisfaction, looking the opposite of sly, and one day he displayed them. There were passports for various identities—English, French, Brazilian, Norwegian, Dutch, Australian—and a number of diplomas in different languages. "The two Russian ones," he boasted, "aren't forgeries," putting everything back among new shirts still in their wrappers.

"But why, why?" Morris said.

"A maxim. Always have your bags packed."

"But why?"

"To get away."

"Why?"

"Sometimes it's better where you aren't than where you are."

Morris wished the Prime Minister had heard this; surely he would have trusted Lushinski less. But Lushinski guessed his thought. "Only the traitors stay home," he said. "In times of trouble only the patriots have false papers."

"But now the whole world knows," Morris said reasonably. "You've told the whole world on television."

"That will make it easier to get away. They will recognize a patriot and defer."

He became a dervish of travel: he was mad about America and went to Detroit and to Tampa, to Cincinnati and to Biloxi. They asked him how he managed to keep up with his diplomatic duties; he referred them to Morris, whom he called his "conscientious blackamoor." Letters came to the consulate in New York accusing him of being a colonialist and a racist. Lushinski remarked that he was not so much that as a cyclist, and immediately—to prove his solidarity with cyclists of every color—bought Morris a gleaming ten-speed two-wheeler. Morris had learned to ride at Oxford, and was overjoyed once again to pedal into a rush of wind. He rode south on Second Avenue; he circled the whole Lower East Side. But in only two days his bike was stolen by a gang of what the police designated as "teen-age black male perpetrators." Morris liked America less and less.

Lushinski liked it more and more. He went to civic clubs, clubs with animal names, clubs with Indian names; societies internationalist and jingoist; veterans, pacifists, vegetarians, feminists, vivisectionists; he would agree to speak anywhere. No Jews invited him; he had turned his back on the Israeli ambassador. Meanwhile the Secretary of State withdrew a little, and omitted Lushinski from his dinner list; he was repelled by a man who would want to go to Cincinnati, a place the Secretary had left forever. But the Prime Minister was delighted and cabled Lushinski to "get to know the proletariat"—nowadays the Prime Minister often used such language: he said "dialectic," "collective," and "Third World." Occasionally he said "peoples," as in "peoples' republic." In a place called Oneonta, New York, Lushinski told about the uniform: in Paris he had gone to a tailor and asked him to make up the costume of an officer. "Of which nationality, sir?" "Oh, no particular one." "What rank, sir?" "High. As high as you can imagine." The coat was long, had epaulets, several golden bands on the sleeves, and metal buttons engraved with the head of a dead monarch. From a toy store Lushinski bought ribbons and medals to hang on its breast. The cap was tall and fearsomely military, with a strong bill ringed by a scarlet cord. Wearing this concoction, Lushinski journeyed to the Rhineland. In hotels they gave him the ducal suite and charged nothing, in restaurants he swept past everyone to the most devoted service, at airports he was served drinks in carpeted sitting rooms and ushered on board, with a guard, into a curtained parlor.

"Your own position commands all that," Morris said gravely. Again he was puzzled. All around him they rattled with hilarity. Lushinski's straight mouth remained straight; Morris brooded about impersonation. It was no joke (but this was years and years ago, in the company of Isabel Oxenham) that he sought out Tarzan movies: Africa in the Mind of the West. It could have been his thesis, but it was not. He was too inward for such a generality: it was his own mind he meant to observe. Was he no better than that lout Tarzan, investing himself with a chatter not his own? How long could the ingested, the invented, foreignness endure? He felt himself— himself, Mdulgo-kt'dulgo, called Morris, dressed in suit and tie, his academic gown thrown down on a chair twenty miles north of this cinema—he felt himself to be self-duped, an impersonator. The film passed (jungle, vines, apes, the famous leap and screech and fisted thump, natives each with his rubber spear and extra's face—janitors and barmen), it was a confusion, a mist. His thumb climbed Isabel's vertebrae: such a nice even row, up and down like a stair. The children's matinee was done, the evening film commenced. It was in Italian, and he never forgot it, a comedy about an unwilling impostor, a common criminal mistaken for a heroic soldier: General della Rovere.

The movie made Isabel's tears fall onto Morris's left wrist.

The criminal, an ordinary thug, is jailed; the General's political enemies want the General put away. The real General is a remarkable man, a saint, a hero. And, little by little, the criminal acquires the General's qualities, he becomes selfless, he becomes courageous, glorious. At the end of the movie he has a chance to reveal that he is not the real General della Rovere. Nobly, he chooses instead to be executed in the General's place, he atones for his past life, a voluntary sacrifice. Morris explained to Isabel that the ferocious natives encountered by Tarzan are in the same moral situation as the false General della Rovere: they accommodate, they adapt to what is expected. Asked to howl like men who inhabit no culture, they howl. "But they have souls, once they were advanced beings. If you jump into someone else's skin," he asked, "doesn't it begin to fit you?"

"Oi wouldn now, oi hev no ejucytion," Isabel said.

Morris himself did not know.

All the same, he did not believe that Lushinski was this sort of impersonator. A Tarzan perhaps, not a della Rovere. The problem of sincerity disturbed and engrossed him. He boldly asked Lushinski his views.

"People who deal in diplomacy attach too much importance to being believed," Lushinski declaimed. "Sincerity is only a maneuver, like any other. A quantity of lies is a much more sensible method—it gives the effect of greater choice. Sincerity offers only one course. But if you select among a great variety of insincerities, you're bound to strike a better course."

He said all this because it was exactly what Morris wanted to hear from him.

The Prime Minister had no interest in questions of identity. "He is not a false African," the Prime Minister said in a parliamentary speech defending his appointment, "he is a true advocate." Though vainglorious, this seemed plausible enough; but for Morris, Lushinski was not an African at all. "It isn't enough to be *politically* African," Morris argued one night; "politically you can assume the culture. No one can assume the cult." Then he remembered the little bones of Isabel Oxenham's back. "Morris, Morris," Lushinski said, "you're not beginning to preach Negritude?" "No," said Morris; he wanted to speak of religion, of his mother; but just then he could not—the telephone broke in, though it was one in the morning and not the official number, rather his own private one, used by Louisa. She spoke of returning to her profession; she was too often alone. "Where are you going tomorrow?" she asked Lushinski. Morris could hear the little electric voice in the receiver. "You say you do it for public relations," she said, "but why really? What do they need to know about Africa in Shaker Heights that they don't know already?" The little electric voice forked and fragmented, tiny lightnings in her lover's ear.

The next day a terrorist from one of the hidden guerrilla camps in the hills shot the Prime Minister's wife at a government ceremony with many Westerners present; he had intended to shoot the Prime Minister. The Prime Minister, it was noted, appeared to grieve, and ordered a bubble-top for his car and a bulletproof vest to wear under his shirt. In a cable he instructed Lushinski to cease his circulation among the American proletariat. Lulu was pleased. Lushinski began to refuse invitations, his American career was over. In the Assembly he spoke—"with supernal," Morris acknowledged, "eloquence"—against terrorism; though their countries had no diplomatic relations, and in spite of Lushinski's public snub, the Israeli ambassador applauded, with liquid eyes. But Lushinski missed something. To address an international body representing every nation on the planet seemed less than before; seemed limiting; he missed the laughter of Oneonta, New York. The American provinces moved him—how gullible they were, how little they knew, or would ever know, of cruelty's breadth! A country of babies. His half-year among all those cities had elated him: a visit to an innocent star: no sarcasm, cynicism, innuendo grew there; such nice church ladies; a benevolent passiveness which his tales, with their wily spikes, could rouse to nervous pleasure.

Behind Lushinski's ears threads of white hairs sprang; he worried about the Prime Minister's stability in the aftermath of the attack. While the representative from Uganda "exercised," Lushinski sneered, "his right of reply"— "The distinguished representative from our sister-country to the north fabricates dangerous adventures for make-believe pirates who exist only in his fantasies, and we all know how colorfully, how excessively, he is given to whimsy"—Lushinski drew on his pad the head of a cormorant, with a sack under its beak. Though there was no overt resemblance, it could pass nevertheless for a self-portrait.

In October he returned to his capital. The Prime Minister had a new public wife. He had replenished his ebullience, and no longer wore the bulletproof vest. The new wife kneeled before Lushinski with a bean-flour cake. The Prime Minister was sanguine: the captured terrorist had informed on his colleagues, entire nests of them had been cleaned out of four nearby villages. The Prime Minister begged Lushinski to allow him to lend him one of his younger females. Lushinski examined her and accepted. He took also one of Morris's sisters, and with these two went to live for a month alone in a white villa on the blue coast.

Every day the Prime Minister sent a courier with documents and newspapers; also the consular pouch from New York.

Morris in New York: Morris in a city of Jews. He walked. He crossed a bridge. He walked. He was attentive to their houses, their neighborhoods.

Their religious schools. Their synagogues. Their multitudinous societies. Announcements of debates, ice cream, speeches, rallies, delicatessens, violins, felafel, books. Ah, the avalanche of their books!

Where their streets ended, the streets of the blacks began. Mdulgo-kt'dulgo in exile among the kidnapped—cargo-Africans, victims with African faces, lost to language and faith; impostors sunk in barbarism, primitives, impersonators. Emptied-out creatures, with their hidden knives, their swift silver guns, their poisoned red eyes, Christianized, made not new but neuter, fabricated: oh, only restore them to their inmost selves, to the serenity of orthodoxy, redemption of the true gods who speak in them without voice!

Morris Ngambe in New York. Alone, treading among traps, in jeopardy of ambush, with no female.

And in Africa, in a white villa on the blue coast: the Prime Minister's gaudy pet, on a blue sofa before an open window, smoking and smoking, under the breath of the scented trees, under the sleek palms of a pair of young females, smoking and caressing—snug in Africa, Lushinski.

In Lushinski's last week in the villa, the pouch from New York held a letter from Morris.

The letter:

A curious note concerning the terrorist personality. I have just read of an incident which took place in a Jerusalem prison. A captive terrorist, a Japanese who had murdered twenty-nine pilgrims at the Tel Aviv airport, was permitted to keep in his cell, besides reading matter, a comb, a hairbrush, a nailbrush, and a fingernail clippers. A dapper chap, apparently. One morning he was found to have partially circumcised himself. His instrument was the clippers. He lost consciousness and the job was completed in the prison hospital. The doctor questioned him. It turned out he had begun to read intensively in the Jewish religion. He had a Bible and a text for learning the Hebrew language. He had begun to grow a beard and earlocks. Perhaps you will understand better than I the spiritual side of this matter.

You recall my remarks on culture and cult. Here is a man who wishes to annihilate a society and its culture, but he is captivated by its cult. For its cult he will bleed himself.

Captivity leading to captivation: an interesting notion.

It may be that every man at length becomes what he wishes to victimize.

It may be that every man needs to impersonate what he first must kill.

Lushinski recognized in Morris's musings a lumpy parroting of *Reading Gaol* mixed with—what? Fanon? Genet? No; only Oscar Wilde, sentimentally epigrammatic. Oscar Wilde in Jerusalem! As unlikely as the remorse of Go-morrah. Like everyone the British had once blessed with Empire, Morris was a Victorian. He was a gentleman. He believed in civilizing influences; even more in civility. He was besotted by style. If he thought of knives, it was for buttering scones.

But Lushinski, a man with the nose and mouth of a knife, and the body of a knife, understood this letter as a blade between them. It meant a severing. Morris saw him as an impersonator. Morris uncovered him; then stabbed. Morris had called him a transmuted, a transfigured, African. A man in love with his cell. A traitor. Perfidious. A fake.

Morris had called him Jew.

—Morris in New York, alone, treading among traps, in jeopardy of ambush, with no female. He knew his ascendancy. Victory of that bird-bright forest, glistening with the bodies of boys, over the old terror in the Polish woods.

Morris prayed. He prayed to his mother: down, take him down, bring him something evil. The divine mother answers sincere believers: O Tanake-Tuka!

And in Africa, in a white villa on the blue coast, the Prime Minister's gaudy pet, on a blue sofa before an open window, smoking and smoking, under the breath of the scented trees, under the shadow of the bluish snow, under the blue-black pillars of the Polish woods, under the breath of Andor, under the merciless palms of peasants and fists of peasants, under the raft-ers, under the stone-white hanging stars of Poland—Lushinski.

Against the stones and under the snow.

Puttermesser:
Her Work History,
Her Ancestry,
Her Afterlife

Puttermesser was thirty-four, a lawyer. She was also something of a feminist, not crazy, but she resented having "Miss" put in front of her name; she thought it pointedly discriminatory, she wanted to be a lawyer among lawyers. Though she was no virgin she lived alone, but idiosyncratically—in the Bronx, on the Grand Concourse, among other people's decaying old parents. Her own had moved to Miami Beach; in furry slippers left over from high school she roamed the same endlessly mazy apartment she had grown up in, her aging piano sheets still on top of the upright with the teacher's X marks on them showing where she should practice up to. Puttermesser always pushed a little ahead of the actual assignment; in school too. Her teachers told her mother she was "highly motivated," "achievement oriented." Also she had "scholastic drive." Her mother wrote all these things down in a notebook, kept it always, and took it with her to Florida in case she should die there. Puttermesser had a younger sister who was also highly motivated, but she had married an Indian, a Parsee chemist, and gone to live in Calcutta. Already the sister had four children and seven saris of various fabrics.

Puttermesser went on studying. In law school they called her a grind, a competitive-compulsive, an egomaniac out for aggrandizement. But ego was no part of it; she was looking to solve something, she did not know what. At the back of the linen closet she found a stack of her father's old shirt cardboards (her mother was provident, stingy: in kitchen drawers Puttermesser still discovered folded squares of used ancient waxed paper, million-creased into whiteness, cheese-smelling, nesting small unidentifiable wormlets); so behind the riser pipe in the bathroom Puttermesser kept weeks' worth of Sunday *Times* crossword puzzles stapled to these laundry boards and worked on them indiscriminately. She played chess against herself, and was always victor over the color she had decided to identify with. She organized tort cases on index cards. It was not that she intended to remember everything: situations—it was her tendency to call intellectual problems "situations"—slipped into her mind like butter into a bottle.

A letter came from her mother in Florida:

Dear Ruth,

I know you won't believe this but I swear it's true the other day Daddy was walking on the Avenue and who should he run into but Mrs. Zaretsky, the thin one from Burnside not the stout one from Davidson, you remember her Joel? Well he's divorced now no children thank God so he's free as a bird as they say his ex the poor thing couldn't conceive. *He* had tests he's O.K. He's only an accountant not good enough for you because God knows I never forget the day you made Law Review but you should come down just to see what a tender type he grew into. Every tragedy has its good side Mrs. Zaretsky says he comes down now practically whenever she calls him long distance. Daddy said to Mrs. Zaretsky well, an accountant, you didn't overeducate your son anyhow, with daughters it's different. But don't take this to heart honey Daddy is as proud as I am of your achievements. Why don't you write we didn't hear from you too long busy is busy but parents are parents.

Puttermesser had a Jewish face and a modicum of American distrust of it. She resembled no poster she had ever seen: with a Negroid passion she hated the Breck shampoo girl, so blond and bland and pale-mouthed; she boycotted Breck because of the golden-haired posters, all crudely idealized, an American wet dream, in the subway. Puttermesser's hair came in bouncing scallops—layered waves from scalp to tip, like imbricated roofing tile. It was nearly black and had a way of sometimes sticking straight out. Her nose had thick, well-haired, uneven nostrils, the right one noticeably wider than the other. Her eyes were small, the lashes short, invisible. She had the median Mongol lid—one of those Jewish faces with a vaguely Oriental cast. With all this, it was a fact she was not bad-looking. She had a good skin with, so far, few lines or pits or signs of looseness-to-come. Her jaw was pleasing—a baby jowl appeared only when she put her head deep in a book.

In bed she studied Hebrew grammar. The permutations of the triple-lettered root elated her: how was it possible that a whole language, hence a whole literature, a civilization even, should rest on the pure presence of three letters of the alphabet? The Hebrew verb, a stunning mechanism: three letters, whichever fated three, could command all possibility simply by a change in their pronunciation, or the addition of a wing-letter fore and aft. Every conceivable utterance blossomed from this trinity. It seemed to her not so much a language for expression as a code for the world's design, indissoluble, predetermined, translucent. The idea of the grammar of Hebrew turned Puttermesser's brain into a palace, a sort of Vatican; inside its corridors she walked from one resplendent triptych to another.

She wrote her mother a letter refusing to come to Florida to look over the divorced accountant's tenderness. She explained her life again; she explained it by indirection. She wrote:

> I have a cynical apperception of power, due no doubt to my current job. You probably haven't heard of the Office for Visas and Registration, OVIR for short. It's located on Ogaryova Street, in Moscow, U.S.S.R. I could enumerate for you a few of the innumerable bureaucratic atrocities of OVIR, not that anyone knows them all. But I could give you a list of the names of all those criminals, down to the women clerks, Yefimova, Korolova, Akulova, Arkhipova, Izrailova, all of them on Kolpachni Street in an office headed by Zolotukhin, the assistant to Colonel Smyrnov, who's under Ovchinikov, who is second in command to General Viryein, only Viryein and Ovchinikov aren't on Kolpachni Street, they're the ones in the head office—the M.D.V., Internal Affairs Ministry—on Ogaryova Street. Some day all the Soviet Jews will come out of the spider's clutches of these people and be free. Please explain to Daddy that this is one of the highest priorities of my life at this time in my personal history. Do you think a Joel Zaretsky can share such a vision?

Immediately after law school, Puttermesser entered the firm of Midland, Reid & Cockleberry. It was a blueblood Wall Street firm, and Puttermesser, hired for her brains and ingratiating (read: immigrant-like) industry, was put into a back office to hunt up all-fours cases for the men up front. Though a Jew and a woman, she felt little discrimination: the back office was chiefly the repository of unmitigated drudgery and therefore of usable youth. Often enough it kept its lights burning till three in the morning. It was right that the Top Rung of law school should earn you the Bottom of the Ladder in the actual world of all-fours. The wonderful thing was the fact of the Ladder itself. And though she was the only woman, Puttermesser was not the only Jew. Three Jews a year joined the back precincts of Midland, Reid (four the year Puttermesser came, which meant they thought "woman" more than "Jew" at the sight of her). Three Jews a year left—not the same three. Lunchtime was difficult. Most of the young men went to one or two athletic clubs nearby to "work out"; Puttermesser ate from a paper bag at her desk, along with the other Jews, and this was strange: the young male

Jews appeared to be as committed to the squash courts as the others. Alas, the athletic clubs would not have them, and this too was preternatural—the young Jews were indistinguishable from the others. They bought the same suits from the same tailors, wore precisely the same shirts and shoes, were careful to avoid tie clips and to be barbered a good deal shorter than the wild men of the streets, though a bit longer than the prigs in the banks.

Puttermesser remembered what Anatole France said of Dreyfus: that he was the same type as the officers who condemned him. "In their shoes he would have condemned himself."

Only their accents fell short of being identical: the "a" a shade too far into the nose, the "i" with its telltale elongation, had long ago spread from Brooklyn to Great Neck, from Puttermesser's Bronx to Scarsdale. These two influential vowels had the uncanny faculty of disqualifying them for promotion. The squash players, meanwhile, moved out of the back offices into the front offices. One or two of them were groomed—curried, fed sugar, led out by the muzzle—for partnership: were called out to lunch with thin and easeful clients, spent an afternoon in the dining room of one of the big sleek banks, and, in short, developed the creamy cheeks and bland habits of the always-comfortable.

The Jews, by contrast, grew more anxious, hissed together meanly among the urinals (Puttermesser, in the ladies' room next door, could hear malcontent rumblings in the connecting plumbing), became perfectionist and uncasual, quibbled bitterly, with stabbing forefingers, over principles, and all in all began to look and act less like superannuated college athletes and more like Jews. Then they left. They left of their own choice; no one shut them out.

Puttermesser left too, weary of so much chivalry—the partners in particular were excessively gracious to her, and treated her like a fellow-aristocrat. Puttermesser supposed this was because *she* did not say "a" in her nose or elongate her "i," and above all she did not dentalize her "t," "d," or "l," keeping them all back against the upper palate. Long ago her speech had been "standardized" by the drilling of fanatical teachers, elocutionary missionaries hired out of the Midwest by Puttermesser's prize high school, until almost all the regionalism was drained out; except for the pace of her syllables, which had a New York deliberateness, Puttermesser could have come from anywhere. She was every bit as American as her grandfather in his captain's hat. From Castle Garden to blue New England mists, her father's father, hat-and-neckwear peddler to Yankees! In Puttermesser's veins Providence, Rhode Island, beat richly. It seemed to her the partners felt this.

Then she remembered that Dreyfus spoke perfect French, and was the perfect Frenchman.

For farewell she was taken out to a public restaurant—the clubs the partners belonged to (they explained) did not allow women—and apologized to.

"We're sorry to lose you," one said, and the other said, "No one for you in this outfit for under the canvas, hah?"

"The canvas?" Puttermesser said.

"Wedding canopy," said the partner, with a wink. "Or do they make them out of sheepskin—I forget."

"An interesting custom. I hear you people break the dishes at a wedding too," said the second partner.

An anthropological meal. They explored the rites of her tribe. She had not known she was strange to them. Their beautiful manners were the cautiousness you adopt when you visit the interior: Dr. Livingstone, I presume? They shook hands and wished her luck, and at that moment, so close to their faces with those moist smile-ruts flowing from the sides of their wafer-like noses punctured by narrow, even nostrils, Puttermesser was astonished into noticing how strange *they* were—so many luncheon martinis inside their bellies, and such beautiful manners even while drunk, and, important though they were, insignificant though she was, the fine ceremonial fact of their having brought her to this carpeted place. Their eyes were blue. Their necks were clean. How closely they were shaven!—like men who grew no hair at all. Yet hairs curled inside their ears. They let her take away all her memo pads with her name printed on them. She was impressed by their courtesy, their benevolence, through which they always got their way. She had given them three years of meticulous anonymous research, deep deep nights going after precedents, dates, lost issues, faded faint politics; for their sakes she had yielded up those howling morning headaches and half a diopter's worth of sight in both eyes. Brilliant students make good aides. They were pleased though not regretful. She was replaceable: a clever black had been hired only that morning. The palace they led her to at the end of it all was theirs by divine right: in which they believed, on which they acted. They were benevolent because benevolence was theirs to dispense.

She went to work for the Department of Receipts and Disbursements. Her title was Assistant Corporation Counsel—it had no meaning, it was part of the subspeech on which bureaucracy relies. Of the many who held this title most were Italians and Jews, and again Puttermesser was the only woman. In this great City office there were no ceremonies and no manners: gross shouts, ignorant clerks, slovenliness, litter on the floors, grit stuck all over antiquated books. The ladies' room reeked: the women urinated standing up, and hot urine splashed on the toilet seats and onto the muddy tiles.

The successive heads of this department were called Commissioners. They were all political appointees—scavengers after spoils. Puttermesser herself was not quite a civil servant and not quite *not* a civil servant—one of those amphibious creatures hanging between base contempt and bare decency; but she soon felt the ignominy of belonging to that mean swarm of City employees rooted bleakly in cells inside the honeycomb of the Municipal Building. It was a monstrous place, gray everywhere, abundantly tunneled, with multitudes of corridors and stairs and shafts, a kind of swollen doom through which the bickering of small-voiced officials whinnied. At the same time there were always curious farm sounds—in the summer the steady cricket of the air-conditioning, in the winter the gnash and croak of old radiators. Nevertheless the windows were broad and high and stupendously filled with light; they looked out on the whole lower island of Manhattan, revealed *as* an island, down to the Battery, all crusted over with the dried lava of shape and shape: rectangle over square, and square over spire. At noon the dark gongs of St. Andrew's boomed their wild and stately strokes.

To Puttermesser all this meant she had come down in the world. Here she was not even a curiosity. No one noticed a Jew. Unlike the partners at Midland, Reid, the Commissioners did not travel out among their subjects and were rarely seen. Instead they were like shut-up kings in a tower, and suffered from rumors.

But Puttermesser discovered that in City life all rumors are true. Putative turncoats are genuine turncoats. All whispered knifings have happened: officials reputed to be about to topple, topple. So far Puttermesser had lasted through two elections, seeing the powerful become powerless and the formerly powerless inflate themselves overnight, like gigantic winds, to suck out the victory of the short run. When one Administration was razed, for the moment custom seemed leveled with it, everything that smelled of "before," of "the old way"—but only at first. The early fits of innovation subsided, and gradually the old way of doing things crept back, covering everything over, like grass, as if the building and its workers were together some inexorable vegetable organism with its own laws of subsistence. The civil servants were grass. Nothing destroyed them, they were stronger than the pavement, they were stronger than time. The Administration might turn on its hinge, throwing out one lot of patronage eaters and gathering in the new lot: the work went on. They might put in fresh carpeting in the new Deputy's office, or a private toilet in the new Commissioner's, and change the clerks' light bulbs to a lower wattage, and design an extravagant new colophon for a useless old document—they might do anything they liked: the work went on as before. The organism breathed, it comprehended itself.

So there was nothing for the Commissioner to do, and he knew it, and the organism knew it. For a very great salary the Commissioner shut his door and cleaned his nails behind it with one of the shining tools of a fancy Swiss knife, and had a secretary who was rude to everyone, and made dozens of telephone calls every day.

The current one was a rich and foolish playboy who had given the Mayor money for his campaign. All the high officials of every department were either men who had given the Mayor money or else courtiers who had humiliated themselves for him in the political clubhouse—mainly by flattering the clubhouse boss, who before any election was already a secret mayor and dictated the patronage lists. But the current Commissioner owed nothing to the boss because he had given the Mayor money and was the Mayor's own appointee; and anyhow he would have little to do with the boss because he had little to do with any Italian. The boss was a gentlemanly Neapolitan named Fiore, the chairman of the board of a bank; but still, he was only an Italian, and the Commissioner cared chiefly for blue-eyed bankers. He used his telephone to make luncheon appointments with them, and sometimes tennis. He himself was a blue-eyed Guggenheim, a German Jew, but not one of the grand philanthropic Guggenheims. The name was a cunning coincidence (cut down from Guggenheimer), and he was rich enough to be taken for one of the real Guggenheims, who thought him an upstart and disowned him. Grandeur demands discreetness; he was so discreetly disowned that no one knew it, not even the Rockefeller he had met at Choate.

This Commissioner was a handsome, timid man, still young, and good at boating; on weekends he wore sneakers and cultivated the friendship of the dynasties—Sulzbergers and Warburgs, who let him eat with them but warned their daughters against him. He had dropped out of two colleges and finally graduated from the third by getting a term-paper factory to plagiarize his reports. He was harmless and simpleminded, still devoted to his brainy late father, and frightened to death of news conferences. He understood nothing: art appreciation had been his best subject (he was attracted to Renaissance nudes), economics his worst. If someone asked, "How much does the City invest every day?" or "Is there any Constitutional bar against revenue from commuters?" or "What is your opinion about taxing exempt properties?" his pulse would catch in his throat, making his nose run, and he had to say he was pressed for time and would let them have the answers from his Deputy in charge of the Treasury. Sometimes he would even call on Puttermesser for an answer.

Now if this were an optimistic portrait, exactly here is where Puttermesser's emotional life would begin to grind itself into evidence. Her biography would proceed romantically, the rich young Commissioner of the Department of Receipts and Disbursements would fall in love with her. She would convert him to intelligence and to the cause of Soviet Jewry. He would abandon boating and the pursuit of bluebloods. Puttermesser would end her work history abruptly and move on to a bower in a fine suburb.

This is not to be. Puttermesser will always be an employee in the Municipal Building. She will always behold Brooklyn Bridge through its windows; also sunsets of high glory, bringing her religious pangs. She will not marry. Perhaps she will undertake a long-term affair with Vogel, the Deputy in charge of the Treasury; perhaps not.

The difficulty with Puttermesser is that she is loyal to certain environments.

Puttermesser, while working in the Municipal Building, had a luxuriant dream, a dream of *gan eydn*—a term and notion handed on from her great-uncle Zindel, a former shammes in a shul that had been torn down. In this reconstituted Garden of Eden, which is to say in the World to Come, Puttermesser, who was not afflicted with quotidian uncertainty in the Present World, had even more certainty of her aims. With her weakness for fudge (others of her age, class, and character had advanced to martinis, at least to ginger ale; Puttermesser still drank ice cream with cola, despised mints as too tingly, eschewed salty liver canapés, hunted down chocolate babies, Kraft caramels, Mary Janes, Milky Ways, peanut brittle, and immediately afterward furiously brushed her teeth, scrubbing off guilt)—with all this nasty self-indulgence, she was nevertheless very thin and unironic. Or: to postulate an afterlife was her single irony—a game in the head not unlike a melting fudge cube held against the upper palate.

There, at any rate, Puttermesser would sit, in Eden, under a middle-sized tree, in the solid blaze of an infinite heart-of-summer July, green, green, green everywhere, green above and green below, herself gleaming and made glorious by sweat, every itch annihilated, fecundity dismissed. And there Puttermesser would, as she imagined it, *take in.* Ready to her left hand, the box of fudge (rather like the fudge sold to the lower school by the eighth-grade cooking class in P.S. 74, The Bronx, circa 1942); ready to her right hand, a borrowed steeple of library books: for into Eden the Crotona Park Branch has ascended intact, sans librarians and fines, but with its delectable terrestrial binding-glue fragrances unevaporated.

Here Puttermesser sits. Day after celestial day, perfection of desire upon perfection of contemplation, into the exaltations of an uninterrupted forever, she eats fudge in human shape (once known—no use covering this up—as nigger babies), or fudge in square shapes (and in Eden there is no tooth decay); and she reads. Puttermesser reads and reads. Her eyes in Paradise are unfatigued. And if she still does not know what it is she wants to solve, she has only to read on. The Crotona Park Branch is as paradisal here as it was on earth. She reads anthropology, zoology, physical chemistry, philosophy (in the green air of heaven Kant and Nietzsche together fall into crystal splinters). The New Books section is peerless: she will learn about the linkages of genes, about quarks, about primate sign language, theories of the origins of the races, religions of ancient civilizations, what Stonehenge meant. Puttermesser will read Non-Fiction into eternity; and there is still time for Fiction! Eden is equipped above all with timelessness, so Puttermesser will read at last all of Balzac, all of Dickens, all of Turgenev and Dostoevski (her mortal self has already read all of Tolstoy and George Eliot); at last Puttermesser will read *Kristin Lavransdatter* and the stupendous trilogy of Dmitri Merezhkovski, she will read *The Magic Mountain* and the whole *Faerie Queene* and every line of *The Ring and the Book,* she will read a biography of Beatrix Potter and one of Walter Scott in many entrancing volumes and one of Lytton Strachey, at last, at last! In Eden insatiable Puttermesser will be nourished, if not glutted. She will study Roman law, the more arcane varieties of higher mathematics, the nuclear composition of the stars, what happened to the Monophysites, Chinese history, Russian, and Icelandic.

But meanwhile, still alive, not yet translated upward, her days given over to the shadow reign of a playboy Commissioner, Puttermesser was learning only Hebrew.

Twice a week, at night (it seemed), she went to Uncle Zindel for a lesson. Where the bus ran through peeling neighborhoods the trolley tracks sometimes shone up through a broken smother of asphalt, like weeds wanting renewal. From childhood Puttermesser remembered how trolley days were better days: in summer the cars banged along, self-contained little carnivals, with open wire-mesh sides sucking in hot winds, the passengers serenely jogging on the seats. Not so this bus, closed like a capsule against the slum.

The old man, Zindel the Stingy, hung on to life among the cooking smells of Spanish-speaking blacks. Puttermesser walked up three flights of steps and leaned against the crooked door, waiting for the former shammes with his little sack. Each evening Zindel brought up a single egg from the Cuban grocery. He boiled it while Puttermesser sat with her primer.

"You should go downtown," the shammes said, "where they got regular language factories. Berlitz. N.Y.U. They even got an *ulpan,* like in Israel."

"You're good enough," Puttermesser said. "You know everything they know."

"And something more also. Why you don't live downtown, on the East Side, fancy?"

"The rent is too much, I inherited your stinginess."

"And such a name. A nice young fellow meets such a name, he laughs. You should change it to something different, lovely, nice. Shapiro, Levine. Cohen, Goldweiss, Blumenthal. I don't say make it *different,* who needs Adams, who needs McKee, I say make it a name not a joke. Your father gave you a bad present with it. For a young girl, Butterknife!"

"I'll change it to Margarine-messer."

"Never mind the ha-ha. *My* father, what was your great-great-grandfather, didn't allow a knife to the table Friday night. When it came to *kiddush*—knifes off! All knifes! On Sabbath an instrument, a blade? On Sabbath a weapon? A point? An edge? What makes bleeding among mankind? What makes war? Knifes! No knifes! Off! A clean table! And something else you'll notice. By us we got only *messer,* you follow? By them they got sword, they got lance, they got halberd. Go to the dictionary, I went once. So help me, what don't one of them knights carry? Look up in the book, you'll see halberd, you'll see cutlass, pike, rapier, foil, ten dozen more. By us a pike is a fish. Not to mention what nowadays they got—bayonet stuck on the gun, who knows what else the poor soldier got to carry in the pocket. Maybe a dagger same as a pirate. But by us—what we got? A *messer! Puttermesser,* you slice off a piece butter, you cut to live, not to kill. A name of honor, you follow? Still, for a young girl—"

"Uncle Zindel, I'm past thirty."

Uncle Zindel blinked lids like insect's wings, translucent. He saw her voyaging, voyaging. The wings of his eyes shadowed the Galilee. They moved over the Tomb of the Patriarchs. A tear for the tears of Mother Rachel rode on his nose. "Your mother knows you're going? Alone on an airplane, such a young girl? You wrote her?"

"I wrote her, Uncle Zindel. I'm not flying anywhere."

"By sea is also danger. What Mama figures, in Miami who is there? The dead and dying. In Israel you'll meet someone. You'll marry, you'll settle there. What's the difference, these days, modern times, quick travel—"

Uncle Zindel's egg was ready, hard-boiled. The shammes tapped it and the shell came off raggedly. Puttermesser consulted the alphabet: *aleph, beys, gimel;* she was not going to Israel, she had business in the Municipal Building. Uncle Zindel, chewing, began finally to teach: "First see how a *gimel* and which way a *zayen.* Twins, but one kicks a leg left, one right.

You got to practice the difference. If legs don't work, think pregnant bellies. Mrs. *Zayen* pregnant in one direction, Mrs. *Gimel* in the other. Together they give birth to *gez,* which means what you cut off. A night for knives! Listen, going home from here you should be extra careful tonight. Martinez, the upstairs not the next door, her daughter they mugged and they took."

The shammes chewed, and under his jaws Puttermesser's head bent, practicing the bellies of the holy letters.

Stop. Stop, stop! Puttermesser's biographer, stop! Disengage, please. Though it is true that biographies are invented, not recorded, here you invent too much. A symbol is allowed, but not a whole scene: do not accommodate too obsequiously to Puttermesser's romance. Having not much imagination, she is literal with what she has. Uncle Zindel lies under the earth of Staten Island. Puttermesser has never had a conversation with him; he died four years before her birth. He is all legend: Zindel the Stingy, who even in *gan eydn* rather than eat will store apples until they rot. Zindel the Unripe. Why must Puttermesser fall into so poignant a fever over the cracked phrases of a shammes of a torn-down shul?

(The shul was not torn down, neither was it abandoned. It disintegrated. Crumb by crumb it vanished. Stones took some of the windows. There were no pews, only wooden folding chairs. Little by little these turned into sticks. The prayer books began to flake: the bindings flaked, the glue came unstuck in small brown flakes, the leaves grew brittle and flaked into confetti. The congregation too began to flake off—the women first, wife after wife after wife, each one a pearl and a consolation, until there they stand, the widowers, frail, gazing, palsy-struck. Alone and in terror. Golden Agers, Senior Citizens! And finally they too flake away, the shammes among them. The shul becomes a wisp, a straw, a feather, a hair.)

But Puttermesser must claim an ancestor. She demands connection— surely a Jew must own a past. Poor Puttermesser has found herself in the world without a past. Her mother was born into the din of Madison Street and was taken up to the hullabaloo of Harlem at an early age. Her father is nearly a Yankee: his father gave up peddling to captain a dry-goods store in Providence, Rhode Island. In summer he sold captain's hats, and wore one in all his photographs. Of the world that was, there is only this single grain of memory: that once an old man, Puttermesser's mother's uncle, kept his pants up with a rope belt, was called Zindel, lived without a wife, ate frugally, knew the holy letters, died with thorny English a wilderness between his gums. To him Puttermesser clings. America is a blank, and Uncle Zindel is all her ancestry. Unironic, unimaginative, her plain but stringent mind strains beyond the parents—what did they have? Only day-by-day in their lives, coffee in the morning, washing underwear, occasionally a trip to the beach. Blank. What did they know? Everything from the movies; something—scraps—from the newspaper. Blank.

Behind the parents, beyond and before them, things teem. In old photographs of the Jewish East Side, Puttermesser sees the teeming. She sees a long coat. She sees a woman pressing onions from a pushcart. She sees a tiny child with a finger in its mouth who will become a judge.

Past the judge, beyond and behind him, something more is teeming. But this Puttermesser cannot see. The towns, the little towns. Zindel born into a flat-roofed house a modest distance from a stream.

What can Puttermesser do? She began life as the child of an anti-Semite. Her father would not eat kosher meat—it was, he said, too tough. He had no superstitions. He wore the mother down, she went to the regular meat market at last.

The scene with Uncle Zindel did not occur. How Puttermesser loved the voice of Zindel in the scene that did not occur!

(He is under the ground. The cemetery is a teeming city of toy skyscrapers shouldering each other. Born into a wooden house, Zindel now has a flat stone roof. Who buried him? Strangers from the *landsmanshaft* society. Who said a word for him? No one. Who remembers him now?)

Puttermesser does not remember Uncle Zindel; Puttermesser's mother does not remember him. A name in the dead grandmother's mouth. Her parents have no ancestry. Therefore Puttermesser rejoices in the cadences of Uncle Zindel's voice above the Cuban grocery. Uncle Zindel, when alive, distrusted the building of Tel Aviv because he was practical, Messiah was not imminent. But now, in the scene that did not occur, how naturally he supposes Puttermesser will journey to a sliver of earth in the Middle East, surrounded by knives, missiles, bazookas!

The scene with Uncle Zindel did not occur. It could not occur because, though Puttermesser dares to posit her ancestry, we may not. Puttermesser is not to be examined as an artifact but as an essence. Who made her? No one cares. Puttermesser is henceforth to be presented as given. Put her back into Receipts and Disbursements, among office Jews and patronage collectors. While winter dusk blackens the Brooklyn Bridge, let us hear her opinion about the taxation of exempt properties. The bridge is not the harp Hart Crane said it was in his poem. Its staves are prison bars. The women clerks, Yefimova, Korolova, Akulova, Arkhipova, Izrailova, are on Kolpachni Street, but the vainglorious General Viryein is not. He is on Ogaryova Street. Joel Zaretsky's ex-wife is barren. The Commissioner puts on his tennis sneakers. He telephones. Mr. Fiore, the courtly secret mayor behind the Mayor, also telephones. Hey! Puttermesser's biographer! What will you do with her now?

Puttermesser and Xanthippe

for Mark Podwal

I. Puttermesser's brief love life, her troubles, her titles

Puttermesser, an unmarried lawyer and civil servant of forty-six, felt attacked on all sides. The night before, her lover, Morris Rappoport, a married fund-raiser from Toronto, had walked out on her. His mysterious job included settling Soviet Jewish refugees away from the big metropolitan centers; he claimed to have fresh news of the oppressed everywhere, as well as intimate acquaintance with malcontents in numerous cities in both the Eastern and Western hemispheres. Puttermesser suspected him of instability and overdependency: a future madman. His gripe was that she read in bed too much; last night she had read aloud from Plato's *Theaetetus*:

THEODORUS: What do you mean, Socrates?
SOCRATES: The same thing as the story about the Thracian maidservant who exercised her wit at the expense of Thales, when he was looking up to study the stars and tumbled down a well. She scoffed at him for being so eager to know what was happening in the sky that he could not see what lay at his feet. Anyone who gives his life to philosophy is open to such mockery. It is true that he is unaware what his next-door neighbor is doing, hardly knows, indeed, whether the creature is a man at all; he spends all his pains on the question, what man is, and what powers and properties distinguish such a nature from any other. You see what I mean, Theodorus?

Rappoport did not see. He withdrew his hand from Puttermesser's belly. "What's the big idea, Ruth?" he said.

"That's right," Puttermesser said.

"What?"

"That's just what Socrates is after: the big idea."

"You're too old for this kind of thing," Rappoport said. He had a medium-sized, rather square, reddish mustache over perfect teeth. His teeth were more demanding to Puttermesser's gaze than his eyes, which were so diffidently pigmented that they seemed whited out, like the naked eyes on a Roman bust. His nose, however, was dominant, eloquent, with large deep nostrils that appeared to meditate. "Cut it out, Ruth. You're behaving like an adolescent," Rappoport said.

"You'll never fall down a well," Puttermesser said. "You never look up." She felt diminished; those philosophical nostrils had misled her.

"Ruth, Ruth," Rappoport pleaded, "what did I do?"

"It's what you didn't do. You didn't figure out what powers and properties distinguish human nature from any other," Puttermesser said bitterly; as a feminist, she was careful never to speak of "man's" nature. She always said "humankind" instead of "mankind." She always wrote "he or she" instead of just "he."

Rappoport was putting on his pants. "You're too old for sex," he said meanly.

Puttermesser's reply was instantly Socratic: "Then I'm *not* behaving like an adolescent."

"If you know I have a plane to catch, how come you want to read in bed?"

"It's more comfortable than the kitchen table."

"Ruth, I came to make love to you!"

"All I wanted was to finish the *Theaetetus* first."

Now he had his coat on, and was crossing his scarf carefully at his throat, so as not to let in the cold. It was a winter night, but Puttermesser saw in this gesture that Rappoport, at the age of fifty-two, still obeyed his mother's doctrines, no matter that they were five decades old. "You wanted to finish!" he yelled. He grabbed the book from her lap. "It goes from page 847 to page 879, that's thirty-three pages—"

"I read fast," Puttermesser said.

In the morning she understood that Rappoport would never come back. His feelings were hurt. In the end he would have deserted her anyway—she had observed that, sooner or later, he told all his feelings to his wife. And not only to his wife. He was the sort of man who babbles.

The loss of Rappoport was not Puttermesser's only trouble. She had developed periodontal disease; her dentist reported—with a touch of pleasure in disaster—a sixty percent bone loss. Loss of bone, loss of Rappoport, loss of home! "Uncontrollable pockets," the dentist said. He gave her the name of a periodontist to consult. It was an emergency, he warned. Her gums were puffy, her teeth in peril of uprooting. It was as if, in the dread under-world below the visible gums, a volcano lay, watching for its moment of release. She spat blood into the sink.

The sink was a garish fake marble. Little blue fish-tiles swam around the walls. The toilet seat cover had a large blue mermaid painted on it. Putter-messer hated this bathroom. She hated her new "luxury" apartment, with its windowless slot of a kitchen and two tiny cramped rooms, the bathroom without a bathtub, the shower stall the size of a thimble, the toilet's flush handle made of light blue plastic. Her majestic apartment on the Grand Concourse in the Bronx, with its Alhambra spaciousness, had been ravaged by arsonists. Even before that, the old tenants had been dying off or moving away, one by one; junkies stole in, filling empty corridors with bloodstained newspapers, smashed bottles, dead matches in random rows like beetle tracks. On a summer evening Puttermesser arrived home from her office without possessions: her shoes were ash, her piano was ash, her piano teacher's penciled "Excellent," written in fine large letters at the top of "Hu-moresque" and right across the opening phrase of "Für Elise," had vanished among the cinders. Puttermesser's childhood, burned away. How prescient her mother had been to take all of Puttermesser's school compositions with her to Florida! Otherwise every evidence of Puttermesser's early mental growth might have gone under in that criminal conflagration.

The new apartment was crowded with plants: Puttermesser, who was once afflicted with what she called a "black thumb," and who had hitherto killed every green thing she put her hand to, determined now to be respon-sible for life. She dragged in great clay urns and sacks of vitamin-rich soil bought at Woolworth's and emptied dark earth into red pots. She seeded and conscientiously watered. Rappoport himself had lugged in, on a plastic-wheeled dolly, a tall stalk like a ladder of green bear's ears: he claimed it was an avocado tree he had grown from a pit in Toronto. It reminded Putter-messer of her mother's towering rubber plants on the Grand Concourse, in their ceiling-sweeping prime. Every window sill of Puttermesser's new apart-ment was fringed with fronds, foliage, soaring or drooping leaf-tips. The tough petals of blood-veined coleus strained the bedroom sunset. Putter-messer, astonished, discovered that if she remained attentive enough, she had the power to stimulate green bursts. All along the bosky walls vegetation burgeoned.

Yet Puttermesser's days were arid. Her office life was not peaceable; nothing bloomed for her. She had fallen. Out of the blue, the Mayor ousted the old Commissioner—Puttermesser's boss, the chief of the Department of Receipts and Disbursements—and replaced him with a new man, seven years younger than Puttermesser. He looked like a large-eared boy; he wore his tie pulled loose, and his neck stretched forward out of his collar; it gave him the posture of a vertical turtle. His eyes, too, were unblinkingly turtlish. It was possible, Puttermesser conceded to herself, that despite his slowly reaching neck and flattish head, the new man did not really resemble a turtle at all; it was only that his name—Alvin Turtelman—suggested the bare lidless deliberation of that immobile creature of the road. Turtelman did not preen. Puttermesser saw at once, in all that meditated motionlessness, that he was more ambitious than the last Commissioner, who had been satisfied with mere prestige, and had used his office like a silken tent decorated with viziers and hookahs. But Turtelman was patient; his steady ogle took in the whole wide trail ahead. He spoke of "restructuring," of "functioning," of "goals" and "gradations," of "levels of purpose" and "versus equations." He was infinitely abstract. "None of this is personal," he liked to say, but his voice was a surprise; it was more pliable than you would expect from the stillness of his stare. He stretched out his vowels like any New Yorker. He had brought with him a score of underlings for what he called "mapping out." They began the day late and ended early, moving from cubicle to cubicle and collecting résumés. They were all bad spellers, and their memos, alive with solecisms, made Puttermesser grieve, because they were lawyers, and Puttermesser loved the law and its language. She caressed its meticulousness. She thought of law as Apollo's chariot; she had read all the letters of Justice Oliver Wendell Holmes, Jr., to Harold Laski (three volumes) and to Sir Frederick Pollock (two). In her dream once she stood before a ship captain and became the fifth wife of Justice William O. Douglas; they honeymooned on the pampas of Argentina. It was difficult to tell whether Turtelman's bad spellers represented the Mayor himself, or only the new Commissioner; but clearly they were scouts and spies. They reported on lateness and laxness, on backlogs and postponements, on insufficiencies and excesses, on waste and error. They issued warnings and sounded alarms; they brought pressure to bear and threatened and cautioned and gave tips. They were watchful and envious. It soon became plain that they did not understand the work.

They did not understand the work because they were, it turned out, political appointees shipped over from the Department of Hygienic Maintenance; a handful were from the Fire Department. They had already had careers as oligarchs of street-sweeping, sewers and drains, gutters, the perils of sleet, ice, rainslant, gas, vermin, fumigation, disinfection, snow removal, water supply, potholes, steam cleaning, deodorization, ventilation, abstersion, elutriation; those from the Fire Department had formerly wielded the scepter over matters of arson, hydrants, pumps, hose (measured by weight, in kilograms), incendiary bombs, rubber boots, wax polish, red paint, false alarms, sappers, marshals. They had ruled over all these corporealities, but without comprehension; they asked for frequent memos; they were "administrators." This meant they were good at arrest; not only at making arrests (the fire marshals, for instance), but at bringing everything to a standstill, like the spindle-prick in Sleeping Beauty. In their presence the work instantly held its breath and came to a halt, as if it were a horse reined in for examination. They walked round and round the work, ruminating, speculating. They could not judge it; they did not understand it.

But they knew what it was for. It was for the spoils quota. The work, impenetrable though it was to its suzerains, proliferated with jobs; jobs blossomed with salaries; salaries were money; money was spoils. The current Mayor, Malachy ("Matt") Mavett, like all the mayors before him, was a dispenser of spoils, though publicly, of course, he declared himself morally opposed to political payoffs. He had long ago distributed the plums, the high patronage slots. All the commissioners were political friends of the Mayor. Sometimes a mayor would have more friends than there were jobs, and then this or that commissioner would suddenly be called upon to devise a whole new management level: a many-pegged perch just between the heights of direct mayoral appointment and the loftier rungs of the Civil Service. When that happened, Puttermesser would all at once discover a fresh crew of intermediate bosses appointed to loiter between herself and the Commissioner. Week after week, she would have to explain the work to them: the appointed intermediate bosses of the Department of Receipts and Disbursements did not usually know what the Department of Receipts and Disbursements *did*. By the time they found out, they vanished; they were always on the move, like minor bedouin sheikhs, to the next oasis. And when a new commissioner arrived right after an election (or, now and then, after what was officially described as "internal reorganization"—demoralization, upheaval, bloodbath), Puttermesser would once again be standing in the sanctuary of the Commissioner's deep inner office, the one with the mottled carpeting and the private toilet, earnestly explaining his rich domain to its new overlord.

Puttermesser was now an old hand, both at the work and at the landscape of the bureaucracy. She was intimate with every folly and every fall. (Ah, but she did not expect her own fall.) She was a witness to every succession. (Ah, but she did not expect to be succeeded herself.) The bureaucracy was a faded feudal world of territory and authority and hierarchy, mainly dusty, except at those high moments of dagger and toppling.

Through it all, Puttermesser was seen to be useful: this accounted for her climb. She had stuck her little finger into every cranny of every permutation of the pertinent law. Precedents sped through her brain. Her titles, movable and fictitious, traveled upward: from Assistant Corporation Counsel she became Administrative Tax Law Associate, and after that Vice Chief of Financial Affairs, and after that First Bursary Officer. All the while she felt like Alice, swallowing the potion and growing compact, nibbling the mushroom and swelling: each title was a swallow or a nibble, and not one of them signified anything but the degree of her convenience to whoever was in command. Her titles were the poetry of the bureaucracy.

The truth was that Puttermesser was now a fathomer; she had come to understand the recondite, dim, and secret journey of the City's money, the tunnels it rolled through, the transmutations, investments, multiplications, squeezings, fattenings and battenings it underwent. She knew where the money landed and where it was headed for. She knew the habits, names, and even the hot-tempered wives of three dozen bank executives on various levels. She had acquired half a dozen underlings of her own—with these she was diffident, polite; though she deemed herself a feminist, no ideology could succeed for her in aggrandizing force. Puttermesser was not aggressive. She disdained assertiveness. Her voice was like Cordelia's. At home, in bed, she went on dreaming and reading. She retained a romantic view of the British Civil Service in its heyday: the Cambridge Apostles carrying the probities of G. E. Moore to the far corners of the world, Leonard Woolf doing justice in Ceylon, the shy young Forster in India. Integrity. Uprightness. And all for the sake of imperialism, colonialism! In New York, Puttermesser had an immigrant's grandchild's dream of merit: justice, justice shalt thou pursue. Her heart beat for law, even for tax law: she saw the orderly nurturing of the democratic populace, public murals, subway windows bright as new dishes, parks with flowering borders, the bell-hung painted steeds of dizzying carousels.

Every day, inside the wide bleak corridors of the Municipal Building, Puttermesser dreamed an ideal Civil Service: devotion to polity, the citizen's sweet love of the citizenry, the light rule of reason and common sense, the City as a miniature country crowded with patriots—not fools and jingoists, but patriots true and serene; humorous affection for the idiosyncrasies of one's distinctive little homeland, each borough itself another little homeland, joy in the Bronx, elation in Queens, O happy Richmond! Children on roller skates, and over the Brooklyn Bridge the long patchwork-colored line of joggers, breathing hard above the homeland-hugging green waters.

II. Puttermesser's fall, and the history of the genus golem

Turtelman sent his secretary to fetch Puttermesser. It was a new secretary, a middle-aged bony acolyte, graying and testy, whom he had brought with him from the Department of Hygienic Maintenance: she had coarse eyebrows crawling upward. "This isn't exactly a good time for me to do this," Puttermesser complained. It was as if Turtelman did not trust the telephone for such a purpose. Puttermesser knew his purpose: he wanted teaching. He was puzzled, desperate. Inside his ambitiousness he was a naked boy, fearful. His office was cradled next to the threatening computer chamber; all along the walls the computer's hard flanks glittered with specks and lights. Puttermesser could hear, behind a partition, the spin of a thousand wheels, a thin threadlike murmur, as if the software men, long-haired chaps in sneakers, had set lyres out upon the great stone window sills of the Municipal Building. Walking behind the bony acolyte, Puttermesser pitied Turtelman: the Mayor had called for information—figures, indexes, collections, projections—and poor Turtelman, fresh from his half-education in the land of abstersion and elutriation, his frontal lobes still inclined toward repair of street-sweeping machinery, hung back bewildered. He had no answers for the Mayor, and no idea where the answers might be hidden; alas, the questions themselves fell on Turtelman's ears as though in a foreign tongue.

The secretary pushed open Turtelman's door, stood aside for Puttermesser, and went furiously away.

Poor Turtelman, Puttermesser thought.

Turtelman spoke: "You're out."

"Out?" Puttermesser said. It was a bitter Tuesday morning in mid-January; at that very moment, considerably south of the Municipal Building, in Washington, D.C., they were getting ready to inaugurate the next President of the United States. High politics emblazoned the day. Bureaucracies all over the world were turning on their hinges, gates were lifting and shutting, desks emptying and filling. The tide rode upon Turtelman's spittle; it glimmered on his teeth.

"As of this afternoon," Turtelman said, "you are relieved of your duties. It's nothing personal, believe me. I don't know you. We're restructuring. It's too bad you're not a bit older. You can't retire at only forty-six." He had read her résumé, then; at least that.

"I'm old enough," Puttermesser said.

"Not for collecting your pension. You people have a valuable retirement system here. I envy you. It drains the rest of us dry." The clack of his teeth showed that he was about to deliver a sting: "We ordinary folk who aren't lucky enough to be in the Civil Service can't afford you."

Puttermesser announced proudly, "I earn my way. I scored highest in the entire city on the First-Level Management Examination. I was editor-in-chief of Law Review at Yale Law School. I graduated from Barnard with honors in history, *summa cum laude,* Phi Beta Kappa—"

Turtelman broke in: "Give me two or three weeks, I'll find a little spot for you somewhere. You'll hear from me."

Thus the manner of Puttermesser's fall. Ignoble. She did not dream there was worse to come. She spilled the papers out of her drawers and carried them to a windowless cubicle down the hall from her old office. For a day or so her ex-staff averted their eyes; then they ceased to notice her; her replacement had arrived. He was Adam Marmel, late of the Bureau of Emergencies, an old classmate of Turtelman's at New York University, where both had majored in Film Arts. This interested Puttermesser: the Department of Receipts and Disbursements was now in the hands of young men who had been trained to pursue illusion, to fly with a gossamer net after fleeting shadows. They were attracted to the dark, where fraudulent emotions raged. They were, moreover, close friends, often together. The Mayor had appointed Turtelman; Turtelman had appointed Marmel; Marmel had succeeded Puttermesser, who now sat with the *Times,* deprived of light, isolated, stripped, forgotten. An outcast. On the next Friday her salary check came as usual. But no one called her out of her cubicle.

Right in the middle of business hours—she no longer had any business, she was perfectly idle—Puttermesser wrote a letter to the Mayor:

The Honorable Malachy Mavett
Mayor, City of New York
City Hall

Dear Mayor Mavett:

Your new appointee in the Department of Receipts and Disbursements, Commissioner Alvin Turtelman, has forced a fine civil servant of honorable temperament, with experience both wide and impassioned, out of her job. I am that civil servant. Without a hearing, without due process, without a hope of appeal or redress (except, Mr. Mayor, by you!), Commissioner Turtelman has destroyed a career in full flower. Employing an affectless vocabulary by means of which, in a single instant, he abruptly ousted a civil servant of high standing, Commissioner Turtelman has politicized a job long held immune to outside preferment. In a single instant, honor, dignity, and continuity have been snatched away! I have been professionally injured and personally humiliated. I have been rendered useless. As of this writing I am costing the City's taxpayers the price of my entire salary, while I sit here working a crossword puzzle; while I hold this very pen. No one looks at me. They are embarrassed and ashamed. At first a few ex-colleagues came into this little abandoned office (where I do nothing) to offer condolences, but that was only at first. It is like being at my own funeral, Mr. Mayor, only imagine it!

Mr. Mayor, I wish to submit several urgent questions to you; I will be grateful for your prompt views on these matters of political friendships, connections, and power.

1. Are you aware of this inequitable treatment of professional staff in the Bureau of Summary Sessions of the Department of Receipts and Disbursements?

2. If so, is this the nature of the Administration you are content to be represented by?

3. Is it truly your desire to erode and undermine the professional Civil Service—one of democratic government's most just, most equitable, devices?

4. Does Commissioner Alvin Turtelman's peremptory action really reflect your own sensibility, with all its fairness and exuberant humaneness?

In City, State, and World life, Mr. Mayor (I have observed this over many years), power and connections are never called power and connections. They are called principle. They are called democracy. They are called judgment. They are called doing good. They are called restructuring. They are called exigency. They are called improvement. They are called functioning. They are called the common need. They are called government. They are called running the Bureau, the Department, the City, the State, the World, looking out for the interests of the people.

Mr. Mayor, getting the spoils is called anything but getting the spoils!

Puttermesser did not know whether Malachy ("Matt") Mavett's sensibility was really fair and exuberantly humane; she had only put that in to flatter him. She had glimpsed the Mayor in the flesh only once or twice, at a meeting, from a distance. She had also seen him on Sunday morning television, at a press conference, but then he was exceptionally cautious and sober; before the cameras he was neuter, he had no sensibility at all; he was nearly translucent. His white mustache looked tangled; his white hair twirled in strings over his temples.

Puttermesser's letter struck her as gripping, impressive; copying it over on the typewriter at home that night, she felt how the Mayor would be stabbed through by such fevered eloquence. How remorseful he would be, how moved!

Still another salary check arrived. It was not for the usual amount; Putter-messer's pay had been cut. The bony acolyte appeared with a memo from Turtelman: Puttermesser was to leave her barren cubicle and go to an office with a view of the Woolworth Building, and there she was to take up the sad life of her demotion.

Turtelman had shoved her into the lowliest ranks of Taxation. It was an unlikely post for a mind superfetate with Idea; Puttermesser felt the malig-nancy behind this shift. Her successor had wished her out of sight. "I do not consort with failure," she heard Adam Marmel tell one of the auditors. She lived now surrounded by auditors—literal-minded men. They read best-sellers; their fingers were smudged from the morning papers, which they clutched in their car pools or on the subway from Queens. One of them, Leon Cracow, a bachelor from Forest Hills who wore bow ties and saddle shoes, was engaged in a tedious litigation: he had once read a novel and fancied himself its hero. The protagonist wore bow ties and saddle shoes. Cracow was suing for defamation. "My whole love life's maligned in there," he complained to Puttermesser. He kept the novel on his desk—it was an obscure book no one had ever heard of, published by a shadowy California press. Cracow had bought it remaindered for eighty-nine cents and rumi-nated over it every day. Turning the pages, he wet two of his fingers repeatedly. The novel was called *Pyke's Pique;* a tax auditor named John McCracken Pyke was its chief character. "McCracken," Cracow said, "that's practically Cracow. It sounds practically identical. Listen, in the book this guy goes to prostitutes. I don't go to prostitutes! The skunk's got me all wrong. He's destroying my good name." Sometimes Cracow asked Putter-messer for her opinion of his lawyer's last move. Puttermesser urged him on. She believed in the uses of fantasy. "A person should see himself or her-self everywhere," she said. "All things manifest us."

The secret source of this motto was, in fact, her old building on the Grand Concourse. Incised in a stone arch over the broad front door, and also in Puttermesser's loyal brain, were these Roman-style tracings: LONG-WOOD ARMS, NO. 26. GREENDALE HALL, NO. 28. ALL THINGS MANIFEST US. The builder had thought deep thoughts, and Cracow was satisfied. "Ruth," he said, "you take the cake." As usual, he attempted to date her. "Any con-cert, any show, you name it," he said; "I'm a film buff." "You fit right in with Turtelman and Marmel," Puttermesser said. "Not me," Cracow re-torted, "with me it's nostalgia only. My favorite movie is Deanna Durbin, Leopold Stokowski, and Adolphe Menjou in *One Hundred Men and a Girl*. Wholesome, sweet, not like they make today. Light classical. Come on, Ruth, it's at the Museum of Modern Art, in the cellar." Puttermesser turned him down. She knew she would never marry, but she was not yet reconciled to childlessness. Sometimes the thought that she would never give birth tore her heart.

She imagined daughters. It was self-love: all these daughters were Puttermesser as a child. She imagined a daughter in fourth grade, then in seventh grade, then in second-year high school. Puttermesser herself had gone to Hunter College High School and studied Latin. At Barnard she had not renounced Catullus and Vergil. *O infelix Dido,* chanted the imaginary daughter, doing her Latin homework at Puttermesser's new Danish desk in the dark corner of the little bedroom. It was a teak rectangle; Puttermesser still had not bought a lamp for it. She hated it that all her furniture was new.

No reply came from the Mayor: not even a postcard of acknowledgment from an underling. Malachy ("Matt") Mavett was ignoring Puttermesser.

Rappoport had abandoned the Sunday *Times,* purchased Saturday night at the airport; he had left it, unopened, on the Danish desk. Puttermesser swung barefoot out of bed, stepped over Plato, and reached for Rappoport's *Times.* She brooded over his furry chest hair, yellowing from red. Now the daughter, still in high school, was memorizing Goethe's *Erlkönig:*

> *Dem Vater grauset's, er reitet geschwind,*
> *Er hält in Armen des ächzende Kind,*
> *Erreicht den Hof mit Mühe und Not:*
> *In seinem Armen das Kind war tot.*

The words made Puttermesser want to sob. The child was dead. In its father's arms the child was dead. She came back to bed, carrying Rappoport's *Times.* It was as heavy as if she carried a dead child. The Magazine Section alone was of a preternatural weight. Advertising. Consumerism. Capitalism. Page after page of cars, delicately imprinted chocolates, necklaces, golden whiskey. Affluence while the poor lurked and mugged, hid in elevators, shot drugs into their veins, stuck guns into old grandmothers' tremulous and brittle spines, in covert pools of blackness released the springs of their bright-flanked switchblades, in shafts, in alleys, behind walls, in ditches.

A naked girl lay in Puttermesser's bed. She looked dead—she was all white, bloodless. It was as if she had just undergone an epileptic fit: her tongue hung out of her mouth. Her eyelids were rigidly ajar; they had no lashes, and the skin was so taut and thin that the eyeballs bulged through. Her palms had fallen open; they were a clear white. Her arms were cold rods. A small white square was visible on the tongue. The girl did not resemble Puttermesser at all; she was certainly not one of the imaginary daughters. Puttermesser moved to one side of the bed, then circled back around the foot to the other side. She put on her slippers; summoning reason, she continued to move around and around the bed. There was no doubt that a real body was in it. Puttermesser reached out and touched the right shoulder—a reddish powder coated her fingers. The body seemed filmed with sand, or earth, or grit; some kind of light clay. Filth. A filthy junkie or prostitute; both. Sickness and filth. Rappoport, stalking away in the middle of the night, had been careless about closing the apartment door. God only knew where the creature had concealed herself, what had been stolen or damaged. When Puttermesser's back was turned, the filthy thing had slid into her bed. Such a civilized bed, the home of Plato and other high-minded readings. The body had a look of perpetuity about it, as if it had always been reclining there, in Puttermesser's own bed; yet it was a child's body, the limbs stretched into laxity and languor. She was a little thing, no more than fifteen: Puttermesser saw how the pubic hair was curiously sparse; but the breasts were nearly not there at all. Puttermesser went on calculating and circling: should she call the super, or else telephone for an ambulance? New York! What was the good of living in a tiny squat box, with low ceilings, on East Seventy-first Street, a grudging landlord, a doorman in an admiral's uniform, if there were infiltrators, addicts, invaders, just the same as on the fallen Grand Concourse?

Puttermesser peered down at the creature's face. Ugly. The nose and mouth were clumsily formed, as if by some coarse hand that had given them a negligent tweak. The vomerine divider was off-center, the nostrils unpleasantly far apart. The mouth was in even worse condition—also off-center, but somehow more carelessly made, with lips that failed to match, the lower one no better than a line, the upper one amazingly fat, swollen, and the narrow tongue protruding with its white patch. Puttermesser reached out a correcting hand, and then withdrew it. Once again the dust left deep red ovals on her fingertips. But it was clear that the nostrils needed pinching to bring them closer together, so Puttermesser tentatively pinched. The improvement was impressive. She blew into the left nostril to get rid of a tuft of dust; it solidified and rolled out like a clay bead. With squeamish deliberation she pushed the nose in line with the middle space where the eyebrows ought to have been. There were no eyebrows, no eyelashes, no fingernails, no toenails. The thing was defective, unfinished. The mouth above all required finishing. Forming and re-forming the savage upper lip, getting into the mood of it now, Puttermesser wished she were an artist or sculptor: she centered the mouth, thickened the lower lip with a quick turn, smoothed out the hunch of the upper one—the tongue was in the way. She peeled off the white square and, pressing hard, shoved the tongue back down into the mouth.

The bit of white lay glimmering in Puttermesser's palm. It seemed to be nothing more than an ordinary slip of paper, but she thought she ought to put it aside to look it over more carefully after a while, so she left the bed and set it down on the corner of the teak desk. Then she came back and glanced up and down the body, to see whether there was anything else that called for correction. A forefinger needed lengthening, so Puttermesser tugged at it. It slid as if boneless, like taffy, cold but not sticky, and thrillingly pliable. Still, without its nail a finger can shock; Puttermesser recoiled. Though the face was now normal enough, there was more to be done. Something had flashed upward from that tongue-paper—the white patch was blank; yet it was not only blank. Puttermesser carried it in her palm to the window, for the sake of the light. But on the sill and under the sill every pot was cracked, every green plant sprawled. The roots, skeletal and hairy, had been torn from their embracing soil—or, rather, the earth had been scooped away. The plain earth, stolen. Puttermesser, holding the white scrap, wandered from window to window. There was no pot that had not been vandalized in the same way—Rappoport's big clay urn was in shards, the avocado tree broken. A few sparse grains of soil powdered the floor. Not a plant anywhere had been left unmolested—all the earth in Puttermesser's apartment was gone; taken away; robbed.

In the bedroom the girl's form continued its lethal sleep. Puttermesser lifted the tiny paper to the bright panes. Out of the whiteness of the white patch another whiteness flickered, as though a second version of absence were struggling to swim up out of the aboriginal absence. For Puttermesser, it was as if the white of her own eye could suddenly see what the purposeful retina had shunned. It was in fact not so much a seeing as the sharpness of a reading, and what Puttermesser read—she whose intellectual passions were pledged to every alphabet—was a single primeval Hebrew word, shimmering with its lightning holiness, the Name of Names, that which one dare not take in vain. Aloud she uttered it:

השם,

whereupon the inert creature, as if drilled through by electricity, as if struck by some principle of instantaneous vitality, leaped straight from the bed; Puttermesser watched the fingernails grow rapidly into place, and the toenails, and the eyebrows and lashes: complete. A configuration of freckles appeared on the forehead. The hair of the head and of the mons Veneris thickened, curled, glistened dark red, the color of clay; the creature had risen to walk. She did it badly, knocking down the desk-chair and bumping into the dresser. Sick, drugged, drunk; vandal; thief of earth!

"Get your clothes on and get out," Puttermesser said. Where were the thing's clothes? She had none; she seemed less pale moment by moment;

she was lurching about in her skin. She was becoming rosy. A lively color was in her cheeks and hands. The mouth, Puttermesser's own handiwork, was vivid. Puttermesser ran to her closet and pulled out a shirt, a skirt, a belt, a cardigan. From her drawers she swept up bra, pantyhose, slip. There was only the question of shoes. "Here," she said, "summer sandals, that's all I can spare. Open toes, open heels, they'll fit. Get dressed. I can give you an old coat—go ahead. Sit down on the bed. Put this stuff on. You're lucky I'm not calling the police."

The creature staggered away from the bed, toward the teak desk.

"Do what I say!"

The creature had seized a notepad and a ballpoint pen, and was scribbling with shocking speed. Her fingers, even the newly lengthened one, were rhythmically coordinated. She clenched the pen, Puttermesser saw, like an experienced writer: as if the pen itself were a lick of the tongue, or an extension of the thinking digits. It surprised Puttermesser to learn that this thief of earth was literate. In what language? And would she then again try to swallow what she wrote, leaving one untouchable word behind?

The thing ripped away the alphabet-speckled page, tottered back with the pad, and laid the free sheet on the pillow.

"What's the matter? Can't you walk?" Puttermesser asked; she thought of afflicted children she had known, struck by melancholy witherings and dodderings.

But the answer was already on the paper. Puttermesser read: "I have not yet been long up upon my fresh-made limbs. Soon my gait will come to me. Consider the newborn colt. I am like unto that. All tongues are mine, especially that of my mother. Only speech is forbidden me."

A lunatic! Cracked! Alone in the house with a maniac; a deaf-mute to boot. "Get dressed," Puttermesser again commanded.

The thing wrote: "I hear and obey the one who made me."

"What the hell *is* this," Puttermesser said flatly.

The thing wrote: "My mother," and rapidly began to jerk herself into Puttermesser's clothes, but with uneven sequences of the body—the more vitality the creature gained, the more thinglike she seemed.

Puttermesser was impatient; she longed to drive the creature out. "Put on those shoes," she ordered.

The thing wrote: "No."

"Shoes!" Puttermesser shouted. She made a signpost fist and flung it in the direction of the door. "Go out the way you came in!"

The thing wrote: "No shoes. This is a holy place. I did not enter. I was formed. Here you spoke the Name of the Giver of Life. You blew in my nostril and encouraged my soul. You circled my clay seven times. You enveloped me with your spirit. You pronounced the Name and brought me to myself. Therefore I call you mother."

Puttermesser's lungs began to roil. It was true she had circled the creature on the bed. Was it seven times around? It was true she had blown some foreign matter out of the nose. Had she blown some uncanny energy into an entrance of the dormant body? It was true she had said aloud one of the Names of the Creator.

The thing wrote again: "Mother. Mother."

"Go away!"

The thing wrote: "You made me."

"I didn't give birth to you." She would never give birth. Yet she had formed this mouth—the creature's mute mouth. She looked at the mouth: she saw what she had made.

The thing wrote: "Earth is my flesh. For the sake of my flesh you carried earth to this high place. What will you call me?"

A new turbulence fell over Puttermesser. She had always imagined a daughter named Leah. "Leah," she said.

"No," the creature wrote. "Leah is my name, but I want to be Xanthippe."

Puttermesser said, "Xanthippe was a shrew. Xanthippe was Socrates' wife."

"I want to be Xanthippe," the thing wrote. "I know everything you know. I am made of earth but also I am made out of your mind. Now watch me walk."

The thing walked, firmly, with a solid thump of a step and no stumbling. She wrote on the pad: "I am becoming stronger. You made me. I will be of use to you. Don't send me away. Call me what I prefer, Xanthippe."

"Xanthippe," Puttermesser said.

She succumbed; her throat panted. It came to her that the creature was certainly not lying: Puttermesser's fingernails were crowded with grains of earth. In some unknown hour after Rappoport's departure in the night, Puttermesser had shaped an apparition. She had awakened it to life in the conventional way. Xanthippe was a golem, and what had polymathic Puttermesser *not* read about the genus golem?

Puttermesser ordered: "All right, go look on the bookshelves. Bring me whatever you see on your own kind."

The creature churned into the living room and hurried back with two volumes, one in either hand; she held the pen ready in her mouth. She dumped the books on the bed and wrote: "I am the first female golem."

"No you're not," Puttermesser said. It was clear that the creature required correction. Puttermesser flew through the pages of one of the books. "Ibn

Gabirol created a woman. This was in Spain, long ago, the eleventh century. The king gave him a dressing-down for necromancy, so he dismantled her. She was made of wood and had hinges—it was easy to take her apart."

The creature wrote: "That was not a true golem."

"Go sit down in a corner," Puttermesser said. "I want to read."

The creature obeyed. Puttermesser dived into the two volumes. She had read them many times before; she knew certain passages nearly verbatim. One, a strange old text in a curiously awkward English translation (it was printed in Austria in 1925), had the grass-green public binding of a library book; to Puttermesser's citizenly shame, she had never returned it. It had been borrowed from the Crotona Park Branch decades ago, in Puttermesser's adolescence. There were photographs in it, incandescently clear: of graves, of a statue, of the lamp-hung interior of a synagogue in Prague—the Altneuschul—, of its tall peaked contour, of the two great clocks, one below the cupola, the other above it, on the venerable Prague Jewish Community House. Across the street from the Community House there was a shop, with a sign that said V. PRESSLER in large letters; underneath, his hand in his pocket, a dapper mustached dandy in a black fedora lounged eternally. Familiar, static, piercingly distinct though these illustrations were, Puttermesser all the same felt their weary old ache: phantoms—V. PRESSLER a speck of earth; the houses air; the dandy evaporated. Among these aged streets and deranged structures Puttermesser's marveling heart had often prowled. "You have no feelings," Rappoport once told her: he meant that she had the habit of flushing with ideas as if they were passions.

And this was true. Puttermesser's intelligence, brambly with the confusion of too much history, was a private warted tract, rubbled over with primordial statuary. She was painfully anthropological. Civilizations rolled into her rib cage, stone after graven stone: cuneiform, rune, cipher. She had pruned out allegory, metaphor; Puttermesser was no mystic, enthusiast, pneumaticist, ecstatic, kabbalist. Her mind was clean; she was a rationalist. Despite the imaginary daughters—she included these among her losses—she was not at all attached to any notion of shade or specter, however corporeal it might appear, and least of all to the idea of a golem—hardly that, especially now that she had the actual thing on her hands. What transfixed her was the kind of intellect (immensely sober, pragmatic, unfanciful, rationalist like her own) to which a golem ordinarily occurred—occurred, that is, in the shock of its true flesh and absolute being. The classical case of the golem of Prague, for instance: the Great Rabbi Judah Loew, circa 1520–1609, maker of that renowned local creature, was scarcely one of those misty souls given over to untrammeled figments or romances. He was, instead, a reasonable man of biting understanding, a solid scholar, a pragmatic leader—a learned quasi-mayor. What he understood was that the scurrilous politics of his city, always tinged with religious interests, had gone too far. In short, they were killing the Jews of Prague. It had become unsafe for a peddler to open his pack, or a merchant his shop; no mother and her little daughter dared turn into an alley. Real blood ran in the streets, and all on account of a rumor of blood: citizens of every class—not just the guttersnipes—were muttering that the Jews had kneaded the bodies of Christian infants into their sacral Passover wafers. Scapegoat Jews, exposed, vulnerable, friendless, unarmed! The very Jews forbidden by their dietary code to eat an ordinary farmyard egg tainted with the minutest jot of fetal blood! So the Great Rabbi Judah Loew, to defend the Jews of Prague against their depredators, undertook to fashion a golem.

Puttermesser was well acquainted with the Great Rabbi Judah Loew's method of golem-making. It was classical; it was, as such things go, ordinary. To begin with, he entered a dream of Heaven, wherein he asked the angels to advise him. The answer came in alphabetical order: *afar, esh, mayim, ruach:* earth, fire, water, wraith. With his son-in-law, Isaac ben Shimshon, and his pupil, Jacob ben Chayim Sasson, the Great Rabbi Judah Loew sought inner purity and sanctification by means of prayer and ritual immersion; then the three of them went out to a mud-bed on the banks of the River Moldau to create a man of clay. Three went out; four returned. They worked by torchlight, reciting Psalms all the while, molding a human figure. Isaac ben Shimshon, a descendant of the priests of the Temple, walked seven times around the clay heap bulging up from the ground. Jacob ben Chayim Sasson, a Levite, walked seven times around. Then the Great Rabbi Judah Loew himself walked around, once only, and placed a parchment inscribed with the Name into the clay man's mouth. The priest represented fire; the Levite water; the Great Rabbi Judah Loew designated himself spirit and wraith, or air itself. The earth-man lay inert upon earth, like upon like. Fire, water, air, all chanted together: "And he breathed into his nostrils the breath of life; and man became a living soul"—whereupon the golem heated up, turned fiery red, and rose! It rose to become the savior of the Jews of Prague. On its forehead were imprinted the three letters that are the Hebrew word for truth: *aleph, mem, tav.*

This history Puttermesser knew, in its several versions, inside out. "Three went out; four returned"—following which, how the golem punished the slaughterers, persecutors, predators! How it cleansed Prague of evil and infamy, of degeneracy and murder, of vice and perfidy! But when at last the Great Rabbi Judah Loew wished the golem to subside, he climbed a ladder (a golem grows bigger every day), reached up to the golem's forehead, and erased the letter *aleph.* Instantly the golem fell lifeless, given back to spiritless clay: lacking the *aleph,* the remaining letters, *mem* and *tav,* spelled *met*—dead. The golem's body was hauled up to the attic of the Altneuschul, where it still rests among ever-thickening cobwebs. "No one may touch the cobwebs," ran one of the stories, "for whoever touches them dies."

For Puttermesser, the wonder of this tale was not in any of its remarkable parts, familiar as they were, and not even in its recurrence. The golem recurred, of course. It moved from the Exile of Babylon to the Exile of Europe; it followed the Jews. In the third century Rabbi Rava created a golem, and sent it to Rabbi Zera, who seemed not to know it was a golem until he discovered that it could not speak. Then realization of the thing's true nature came to him, and he rebuked it: "You must have been made by my comrades of the Talmudic Academy; return to your dust." Rabbi Hanina and Rabbi Oshaya were less successful than Rabbi Rava; they were only able to produce a very small calf, on which they dined. An old kabbalistic volume, the Book of Creation, explains that Father Abraham himself could manufacture human organisms. The Book of Raziel contains a famous workable prescription for golem-making: the maker utilizes certain chants and recitations, imprinted medals, esoteric names, efficacious shapes and totems. Ben Sira and his father, the prophet Jeremiah, created a golem, in the logical belief that Adam himself was a golem; their golem, like Adam, had the power of speech. King Nebuchadnezzar's own idol turned into a living golem when he set on its head the diadem of the High Priest, looted out of the Temple in Jerusalem; the jeweled letters of the Tetragrammaton were fastened into the diadem's silver sockets. The prophet Daniel, pretending to kiss the king's golem, swiftly plucked out the gems that spelled the Name of God, and the idol was again lifeless. Even before that, thieves among the wicked generation that built the Tower of Babel swiped some of the contractor's materials to fashion idols, which were made to walk by having the Name shoved into their mouths; then they were taken for gods. Rabbi Aharon of Baghdad and Rabbi Hananel did not mold images; instead, they sewed parchments inscribed with the Name into the right arms of corpses, who at once revived and became members of the genus golem. The prophet Micah made a golden calf that could dance, and Bezalel, the designer of the Tabernacle, knew how to combine letters of the alphabet so as to duplicate Creation, both heaven and earth. Rabbi Elazar of Worms had a somewhat similar system for golem-making: three adepts must gather up "virginal mountain earth," pour running water over it, knead it into a man, bury it, and recite two hundred and twenty-one alphabetical combinations, observing meticulously the prescribed order of the vowels and consonants. But Abraham Abulafia could make a man out of a mere spoonful of earth by blowing it over an ordinary dish of water; undoubtedly this had some influence on Paracelsus, the sixteenth-century German alchemist, who used a retort to make a homunculus: Paracelsus's manikin, however, was not telluric, being composed of blood, sperm, and urine, from which the Jewish golem-makers recoiled. For the Jews, earth, water, and the divine afflatus were the only permissible elements—the afflatus being summoned through the holy syllables. Rabbi Ishmael, on the other hand, knew another way of withdrawing that life-conferring holiness and rendering an active golem back into dust: he would recite the powerful combinations of sacred letters backward, meanwhile circling the creature in the direction opposite to the one that had quickened it.

There was no end to the conditions of golem-making, just as there was no end to the appearance of one golem after another in the pullulating procession of golem-history; but Puttermesser's brain, crowded with all these acquisitions and rather a tidy store of others (for instance, she had the noble Dr. Gershom Scholem's bountiful essay "The Idea of the Golem" virtually by heart), was unattracted either to number or to method. What interested Puttermesser was something else: it was the plain fact that the golem-makers were neither visionaries nor magicians nor sorcerers. They were neither fantasists nor fabulists nor poets. They were, by and large, scientific realists—and, in nearly every case at hand, serious scholars and intellectuals: the plausible forerunners, in fact, of their great-grandchildren, who are physicists, biologists, or logical positivists. It was not only the Great Rabbi Judah Loew, the esteemed golem-maker of Prague, who had, in addition, a reputation as a distinguished Talmudist, reasoner, philosopher; even Rabbi Elijah, the most celebrated Jewish intellect of Eastern Europe (if Spinoza is the most celebrated on the Western side), whose brilliance outstripped the fame of every other scholar, who founded the most rigorous rabbinical academy in the history of the cold lands, who at length became known as the Vilna *Gaon* (the Genius of the city of Vilna, called, on his account, the Jerusalem of the North)—even the Vilna *Gaon* once attempted, before the age of thirteen, to make a golem! And the Vilna *Gaon,* with his stern refinements of exegesis and analysis, with his darting dazzlements of logical penetration, was—as everyone knows—the scourge of mystics, protester *(mitnagid)* against the dancing hasidim, scorner of those less limber minds to the Polish south, in superstitiously pious Galicia. If the Vilna *Gaon* could contemplate the making of a golem, thought Puttermesser, there was nothing irrational in it, and she would not be ashamed of what she herself had concocted.

She asked Xanthippe: "Do you eat?"

The golem wrote, *"Vivo, ergo edo.* I live, therefore I eat."

"Don't pull that on me—my Latin is as good as yours. Can you cook?"

"I can do what I must, if my mother decrees it," the golem wrote.

"All right," Puttermesser said. "In that case you can stay. You can stay until I decide to get rid of you. Now make lunch. Cook something I like, only better than I could do it."

III. The golem cooks, cleans, and shops

The golem hurried off to the kitchen. Puttermesser heard the smack of the refrigerator, the clatter of silver, the faucet turned on and off; sounds of chopping in a wooden bowl; plates set out, along with an eloquent tinkle of glassware; a distant whipping, a distant sizzling; mushroom fragrances; coffee. The golem appeared at the bedroom door with a smug sniff, holding out her writing pad:

"I can have uses far beyond the mere domestic."

"If you think you're too good for kitchen work," Puttermesser retorted, "don't call yourself Xanthippe. You're so hot on aspiration, you might as well go the whole hog and pick Socrates. "

The golem wrote: "I mean to be a critic, even of the highest philosophers. Xanthippe alone had the courage to gainsay Socrates. Nay, I remain Xanthippe. Please do not allow my Swedish mushroom soufflé to sink. It is best eaten in a steaming condition."

Puttermesser muttered, "I don't like your prose style. You write like a translation from the Middle Finnish. Improve it," but she followed the golem into the little kitchen. The golem's step was now light and quick, and the kitchen too seemed transformed—a floating corner of buoyancy and quicksilver: it was as if the table were in the middle of a Parisian concourse, streaming, gleaming: it had the look of a painting, both transient and eternal, a place where you sat for a minute to gossip, and also a place where the middle-aged Henry James came every day so that nothing in the large world would be lost on him. "You've set things up nicely enough," Puttermesser said; "I forgot all about these linen placemats." They were, in fact, part of her "trousseau"; her mother had given her things. It was expected, long ago, that Puttermesser would marry.

The golem's soufflé was excellent; she had also prepared a dessert that was part mousse, part lemon gelatin. Puttermesser, despite her periodontic troubles, took a greedy second helping. The golem's dessert was more seductive even than fudge; and fudge for Puttermesser was notoriously paradisal.

"First-rate," Puttermesser said; the golem had been standing all the while. "Aren't you having any?"

Immediately the golem sat down and ate.

"Now I'm going for a walk," Puttermesser announced. "Clean all this up. Make the bed. Be sure to mop under it. Look in the hamper, you'll find a heap of dirty clothes. There's a public washing machine in the basement. I'll give you quarters."

The golem turned glum.

"Well, look," Puttermesser argued, "I can use you for anything I please, right?"

The golem wrote, "The Great Rabbi Judah Loew's wife sent the golem of Prague to fetch water, and he fetched, and he fetched, until he flooded the house, the yard, the city, and finally the world."

"Don't bother me with fairy tales," Puttermesser said.

The golem wrote, "I insist I am superior to mere household use."

"No one's superior to dirty laundry," Puttermesser threw back, and went out into the great city. She intended to walk and brood; though she understood at last how it was that she had brought the golem to life, it disturbed her that she did not recall *making* her—emptying all the plant pots, for instance. Nor was Puttermesser wise to her own secret dictates in creating the golem. And now that the golem was actually in the house, what was to be done with her? Puttermesser worried about the landlord, a suspicious fellow. The landlord allowed no dogs or—so the lease read—"irregular relationships." She thought of passing Xanthippe off as an adopted daughter—occasionally she would happen on an article about single parents of teen-age foster children. It was not so unusual. But even that would bring its difficulty, because—to satisfy the doorman and the neighbors—such a child would have to be sent to school; and it was hardly reasonable, Puttermesser saw, to send the golem to an ordinary high school. They would ship her off to an institution for deaf-mutes, to learn sign language—and it would become evident soon enough, wouldn't it, that the golem was not the least bit deaf? There was really no place for her in any classroom; she probably knew too much already. The erratic tone of her writing, with its awful pastiche, suggested that she had read ten times more than any other tenth-grader of the same age. Besides, did the golem *have* an age? She had the shape of a certain age, yes; but the truth was she was only a few hours old. Her public behavior was bound to be unpredictable.

Puttermesser was walking northward. Her long introspective stride had taken her as far as Eighty-sixth Street. She left Madison and veered up Lexington. She had forgotten her gloves; her fingers were frozen. February's flying newspapers scuttled over broken bottles and yogurt cups squashed in the gutter. A bag lady slept in a blue-black doorway, wrapped in a pile of ragged coats. Dusk was coming down; all the store windows, without exception, were barred or shuttered against the late-afternoon Sunday emptiness. Burglars, addicts, marauders, the diverse criminal pestilences of uptown and downtown, would have to find other ways of entry: breaking through a roof; a blowtorch on a steel bar; a back toilet window with a loose grill. Ingenuity. Puttermesser peered around behind her for the mugger who, in all logic, should have been stalking her; no one was there. But she was ready: she had left her wallet at home on purpose; a police whistle dangled on a cord around her neck; she fondled the little knife in her pocket. New York! All the prisons in the metropolitan area were reputed to be hopelessly overcrowded.

At Ninety-second Street she swung through the revolving doors of the Y to warm up. The lobby was mostly uninhabited; a short line straggled toward the ticket office. Puttermesser read the poster: a piano concert at eight o'clock. She headed downtown. It was fully dark now. She reflected that it would be easy enough to undo, to reverse, the golem; there was really no point in keeping her on. For one thing, how would the golem be occupied all day while Puttermesser was at work? And Puttermesser was nervous: she had her demotion to think about. Stripped. Demoralized. That pest Cracow. Turtelman and Marmel. The Civil Service, founded to eradicate patronage, nepotism, favoritism, spoils, payoffs, injustice, corruption! Lost, all lost. The Mayor had no intention of answering Puttermesser's urgent letter.

Taking off her coat, Puttermesser called to the golem, "What's going on in there?" An unexpected brilliance spilled out of the bedroom: a lamp in the form of the Statue of Liberty stood on the teak desk. "What's this?"

"I bought it," the golem wrote. "I did everything my mother instructed. I cleaned up the kitchen, made the bed"—a new blue bedspread, with pictures of baseball mitts, covered it—"mopped the whole house, did the laundry, ironed everything, hung my mother's blouses and put my mother's pantyhose into the drawer—"

Puttermesser grabbed the sheet of paper right off the golem's pad and tore it up without reading the rest of it. "What do you mean you bought it? What kind of junk is this? I don't want the Statue of Liberty! I don't want baseball mitts!"

"It was all I could find," the golem wrote on a fresh page. "All the stores around here are closed on Sunday. I had to go down to Delancey Street on the Lower East Side. I took a taxi."

"Taxi! You'll shop when I tell you to shop!" Puttermesser yelled. "Otherwise you stay home!"

"I need a wider world," the golem wrote. "Take me with you to your place of employment tomorrow."

"My foot I will," Puttermesser said. "I've had enough of you. I've been thinking"—she looked for a euphemism—"about sending you back."

"Back?" the golem wrote; her mouth had opened all the way.

"You've got a crooked tooth. Come here," Puttermesser said, "I'll fix it."

The golem wrote, "You can no longer alter my being or any part of my being. The speaking of the Name fulfills; it precludes alteration. But I am pleasant to look on, am I not? I will not again gape so that my crooked tooth can offend my mother's eye. Only use me."

"You've got rotten taste."

The golem wrote, "It was my task to choose between baseball mitts and small raccoons intermingled with blue-eyed panda bears. The baseball mitts struck me as the lesser evil."

"I never *wanted* a bedspread," Puttermesser objected. "When I said to make the bed I just meant to straighten the blankets, that's all. And my God, the Statue of Liberty!"

The golem wrote, "A three-way bulb, 150 watts. I thought it so very clever that the bulb goes right into the torch."

"Kitsch. And where'd you get the money?"

"Out of your wallet. But see how pleasantly bright," the golem wrote. "I fear the dark. The dark is where pre-existence abides. It is not possible to think of pre-existence, but one dreads its facsimile: post-existence. Do not erase, obliterate, or annihilate me. Mother, my mother. I will serve you. Use me in the wide world."

"You stole my money right out of my wallet, spent a fortune on a taxi, and brought home the cheapest sort of junk. If you pull this kind of thing in the house, don't talk to me about the wide world!"

IV. Xanthippe at work

But the next morning the golem was in Puttermesser's office.

"Who's the kid?" Cracow asked.

"Marmel's letting me have a typist," Puttermesser said.

"Marmel? That don't make sense. After demoting you?"

"I was reassigned," Puttermesser said; but her cheeks stung.

"Them's the breaks," Cracow said. "So how come the royal treatment? You could use the typing pool like the rest of us."

"Turtelman's put me on a special project."

"Turtelman? Turtelman kicked you in the head. What special project?"

"I'm supposed to check out any employee who broods about lawsuits on City time," Puttermesser said.

"Oh come on, Ruth, can the corn. You know damn well I've been maligned. My lawyer says I have a case. I damn well have a case. What's the kid's name?"

"Leah."

"Leah." Cracow pushed his face right into the golem's. "Do they hire 'em that young? What are you, Leah, a high-school dropout?"

"She's smart enough as is," Puttermesser said.

"Whyn't you let the kid answer for herself?"

Puttermesser took Cracow by the elbow and whispered, "They cut out her throat. Malignancy of the voicebox."

"Whew," Cracow said.

"Get going," Puttermesser ordered the golem, and led her to the ladies' room. "I told you not to come! I'm in enough hot water around here, I don't need you to make trouble."

The golem plucked a paper towel from the wall, fetched Puttermesser's ballpoint pen from the pocket of Puttermesser's cardigan (the golem was still wearing it), and wrote: "I will ameliorate your woe."

"I didn't say woe, I said hot water. *Trouble.* First kitsch, now rococo. Observe reality can't you? Look, you're going to sit in front of that typewriter and that's it. If you can type half as well as you cook, fine. I don't care *what* you type. Stay out of my way. Write letters, it doesn't matter, but stay out of my way."

The golem wrote, "I hear and obey."

All day the golem, a model of diligence, sat at the typewriter and typed. Puttermesser, passing en route from one fruitless meeting to another, saw the sheets accumulating on the floor. Was Xanthippe writing a novel? a memoir? To whom, after all, did she owe a letter? The golem looked abstracted, rapt. Puttermesser was hoping to patch together, bit by bit, her bad fortune. The gossips ran from cubicle to cubicle, collecting the news: Turtelman's niece, an actress—she had most recently played a medieval leper, with a little bell, in a television costume drama—was engaged to the Mayor's cousin. Marmel's aunt had once stayed in the same hotel in Florida with Mrs. Minnie Mavett, the Mayor's elderly widowed adoptive mother. (The Mayor had been an adopted child, and campaigned with his wife and four natural children as a "lucky orphan.") Marmel and Turtelman were said to have married twin sisters; surely this was a symbolic way of marrying each other? Or else Marmel was married to a Boston blueblood, Turtelman to a climber from Great Neck. On the other hand, only Marmel was married; Turtelman was an austere bachelor. One of the secretaries in the Administrative Assistant's office had observed that Marmel, Turtelman, and the Mayor all wore identical rings; she denied they were school rings. Turtelman's "restructuring," moreover, had begun (according to Polly in Personnel) to assume telltale forms. He was becoming bolder and bolder. He was like some crazed plantation owner at harvest time, who, instead of cutting down the standing grain, cuts down the conscientious reapers. Or he was like a raving chessmaster who throws all the winning pieces in the fire. Or he was like a general who leads a massacre against his own best troops. All these images failed. Turtelman was destroying the Department of Receipts and Disbursements. What he looked for was not performance but loyalty. He was a mayoral appointee of rapacious nature conniving at the usual outrages of patronage; he was doing the Mayor's will. He did not love the democratic polity as much as he feared the Mayor. Ah, Walt Whitman was not in his kidneys. Plunder was.

Cracow, meanwhile, reported that several times Adam Marmel had telephoned for Puttermesser. It was urgent. "That new girl's no good, Ruth. I'm all in favor of hiring the handicapped, but when it comes to answering the telephone what's definitely needed is a larynx. I had to pick up every damn time. You think Marmel wants to put you back up there in the stratosphere?"

Puttermesser said nothing. Cracow thought women ought to keep their place; he took open satisfaction in Puttermesser's flight downward. He nagged her to tell him what Turtelman's special project was. "You'd rather do special projects for the higher-ups than date a nice guy like me," he complained. "At least let's have lunch." But Puttermesser sent the golem out to a delicatessen for sandwiches; it was a kosher delicatessen—Puttermesser thought the golem would care about a thing like that. By the middle of the afternoon the golem's typed sheets were a tall stack.

At a quarter to five Turtelman's bony acolyte came puffing in. "Mr. Turtelman lent me to Mr. Marmel just to give you this. I hope you appreciate I'm not normally anyone's delivery boy. You're never at your desk. You can't be reached by phone. You're not important enough to be incommunicado, believe me. Mr. Marmel wants you to prepare a portfolio for him on these topics toot sweet."

Marmel's memo:

Dear Ms. Puttermesser:

Please be good enough to supply me with the following at your earliest convenience. A list of the City's bank depositories. Average balance in each account for the last three years. List of contact people at banks—names, titles, telephone numbers. List of contacts for Department of Receipts and Disbursements (referred to below as "we," "our," and "us") in Office of Mayor, Department of Budget, relevant City Council committees, Office of Comptroller. Copies of all evaluation reports published during past year. Current organization chart showing incumbent, title, and salary for each of our Office Heads. Why do we not have any window poles? Where have all the window poles gone? How to get toilet paper and soap regularly replaced in executive washroom? What kind of Management Information System files do we have on the assessed value of City real estate? How effective was our last Investors' Tour? Old notes disclose visit to sewage disposal plant, helicopter ride, fireboat demonstration, lunch and fashion show for the ladies—how to win goodwill this year from these heavy pockets? What hot litigation should I know about in re our Quasi-Judicial Division?

It was the old story: the floundering new official perplexed and beleaguered. Puttermesser felt a touch of malicious pleasure in Marmel's memo; she had known it would come to this—Turtelman, having thrown her out, now discovered he could not clear a space for himself without the stirring of Puttermesser's little finger. Marmel, spurred by Turtelman (too high-and-mighty to ask on his own), had set out to pick Puttermesser's brain. He was appealing to Puttermesser to diaper him. Each item in Marmel's memo would take hours and hours to answer! Except for the window poles. Puttermesser could explain about the window poles in half a second.

"Stand by," she said to the bony acolyte. And to Xanthippe: "Take a letter!"

Mr. Adam Marmel
First Bursary Officer
Bureau of Summary Sessions
Department of Receipts and Disbursements
Municipal Building

Dear Mr. Marmel:
    Window poles are swiped by the hottest and sweatiest secretaries. The ones located directly above the furnace room, for instance. Though lately the ones who jog at lunchtime are just as likely to pinch poles. When they get them they hide them. Check out the second-floor ladies' room.
    The fresh air of candor is always needed whenever the oxygen of honest admission has been withdrawn. Precisely WHY ["Make that all capitals," Puttermesser said, dictating] have I been relieved of my position? Precisely WHY have you stepped into my job? Let us have some fresh air!

Yours sincerely,
R. Puttermesser, Esq.

The bony acolyte snatched the sheet directly from the golem's typewriter. "There's a lot more he wants answers to. You've left out practically everything."

"Window poles are everything," Puttermesser said. "The fresh air of candor is all." She observed—it was a small shock—that the golem's style had infected her.

The bony acolyte warned, "Fresh is right. You better answer the rest of what he wants answered."

"Go home," Puttermesser told the golem. "Home!"

During dinner in the little kitchen Puttermesser was nearly as silent as the golem. Injustice rankled. She paid no attention to the golem's scribblings. The nerve! The nerve! To throw her out and then come and pick her brain! "No more Swedish soufflé," she growled. "Cook something else for a change. And I'm getting tired of seeing you in my old sweater. I'll give you money, tomorrow go buy yourself some decent clothes."

"Tomorrow," the golem wrote, "I will again serve you at your place of employment."

But in the morning Puttermesser was lackadaisical; ambition had trickled away. What, after so much indignity, was there to be ambitious *for*? For the first time in a decade she came to the office late. "What's the special project, Ruth?" Cracow wanted to know right away. "The kid was burning up the typewriter yesterday. What is she anyhow, an illegal alien? She don't look like your ordinary person. Yemenite Israeli type? What is this, already she don't show up, it's only the second day on the job? The phone calls you missed! Memos piled up! That gal from Personnel back and forth two, three times! They're after you today, Ruth! The higher-ups! What's the special project, hah? And the kid leaves you high and dry!"

"She'll turn up." Puttermesser had given the golem a hundred and twenty dollars and sent her to Alexander's. "No taxis or else," Puttermesser said; but she knew the golem would head downtown to Delancey Street. The thronged Caribbean faces and tongues of the Lower East Side drew her; Xanthippe, a kind of foreigner herself, as even Cracow could see, was attracted to immigrant populations. Their tastes and adorations were hers. She returned with red and purple blouses, narrow skirts and flared pants of parrot-green and cantaloupe-orange, multicolored high-heeled plastic shoes, a sunflower-yellow plastic shoulder bag with six double sets of zippers, a pocket mirror, and a transparent plastic comb in its own peach tattersall plastic case.

"Hispanic absolutely," Cracow confirmed—Cracow the bigot—watching Xanthippe lay open boxes and bags.

But Puttermesser was occupied with a trio of memos. They appeared to originate with Marmel but were expressed through Polly, the Atropos of Personnel, she who had put aside her shears for the flurry of a thousand Forms, she who brooded like Shiva the Destroyer on a world of the lopped.

Memo One:

You are reported as having refused to respond to requests for information relating to Bureau business. You now are subject to conduct inquiry. Please obtain and fill out Form 10V, Q17, with particular reference to Paragraph L, and leave it *immediately* with Polly in Personnel.

Memo Two:

In consideration of your seniority, Commissioner Alvin Turtelman, having relieved you of Level Eleven status in the Bureau of Summary Sessions, Department of Receipts and Disbursements, due to insufficient control of bursary materials, weak administrative supervision as well as output insufficiency, has retained you at Level Four. However, your work shows continued decline. Lateness reported as of A.M. today. Fill out Below-Level-Eight Lateness Form 14TG. (Submit Form to Polly in Personnel.)

Memo Three:

As a result of a determination taken by Commissioner Alvin Turtelman in conjunction and in consultation with First Bursary Officer Adam Marmel, your Level Four appointment in the Department of Receipts and Disbursements is herewith terminated. Please submit Below-Level-Six Severance Form A97, Section 6, with particular reference to Paragraph 14b, to Polly in Personnel.

Severed! Sacked! Dismissed! Let go! Fired! And all in the space of three hours! "Output insufficiency," a lie! "Decline," a fiction! "Conduct inquiry"— like some insignificant clerk or window-pole thief! Late once in ten years and Cracow, litigious would-be lover, snitches to Polly, the Atropos, the Shiva, of Personnel! Who else but Cracow? Lies. Fabrications. Accusations. Marmel the hollow accuser. Absence of due process!

The Honorable Malachy Mavett
Mayor, City of New York
City Hall

Dear Mayor Mavett:

Where is your pride, to appoint such men? Men who accuse without foundation? An accuser who seizes the job of the accused? Suspect! Turtelman wanted me out in order to get Marmel in! I stand for Intellect and Knowledge, they stand for Politics and Loyal Cunning. Hart Crane, poet of New York, his harp the Brooklyn Bridge, does that harp mean nothing to you? Is Walt Whitman dead in your kidneys? Walt Whitman who cried out "numberless crowded streets, high growths of iron, slender, strong, light, splendidly uprising toward clear skies," who embraced "a million people—manners free and superb—open voices—hospitality . . ." Oh, Mayor Mavett, it is Injustice you embrace! You have given power to men for whom Walt Whitman is dead in their kidneys! This city of masts and spires opens its breast for Walt Whitman, and you feed it with a Turtelman and a Marmel! Ruth Puttermesser is despised, demoted, thrown away at last! Destroyed. Without work. Doer of nought, maker of nothing.

This letter remained locked inside Puttermesser's head. Cracow was trying hard not to look her way. He had already read Marmel's memos manifested through Polly the Destroyer; he had surely read them. He stood behind the golem's chair, attentive to her fingers galloping over the typewriter keys— including the newly lengthened one; how glad Puttermesser was that she had fixed it! "Hey Ruth, take a gander at this stuff. What's this kid *doing?* That's some so-called special project for Turtelman."

"The special project for Turtelman," Puttermesser said coldly, "is my vanquishment. My vanishing. My send-off and diminishment. So long, Leon. May you win your case against the mediocre universality of the human imagination."

"You been canned?"

"You know that."

"Well, when Polly walks in you figure what's up. You figure who's out."

"Beware of *Schadenfreude,* Leon. You could be next."

"Not me. I don't look for trouble. You look for trouble. I knew right away this whole setup with the kid was phony. She's typing up a craziness— whatever it is, Bureau business it isn't. You let in the crazies, you get what you expect."

At that moment—as Cracow's moist smile with its brown teeth turned and turned inside Cracow's dark mouth—a clarification came upon Putter- messer: no: a clarity. She was shut of a mystery. She understood; she saw.

"Home!" Puttermesser ordered the golem. Xanthippe gathered up her clothes and shoved the typewritten sheets into one of the blouse bags.

V. Why the golem was created; Puttermesser's purpose

That night the golem cooked spaghetti. She worked barefoot. The fragrance of hot buttered tomato sauce and peppers rushed over a mound of shining porcelain strands. "What are you doing?" Puttermesser demanded; she saw the golem heaping up a second great batch. "Why are you so hungry?"

The golem looked a little larger today than she had yesterday.

Then Puttermesser remembered that it was in the nature of a golem to grow and grow. The golem's appetite was nevertheless worrisome—how long would it take for Xanthippe to grow out of over one hundred dollars' worth of clothes? Could only a Rothschild afford a golem? And what would the rate of growth be? Would the golem eventually have to be kept outdoors, so as not to crash through the ceiling? Was the golem of Prague finally reversed into lifelessness on account of its excessive size, or because the civic reforms it was created for had been accomplished?

Ah, how this idea glowed for Puttermesser! The civic reforms of Prague—the broad crannied city of Prague, Prague distinguished by numberless crowded streets, high growths of iron, masts and spires! The clock-tower of the Jewish Community House, the lofty peaked and chimneyed roof of the Altneuschul! Not to mention Kafka's Castle. All that manifold urban shimmer choked off by evil, corruption, the blood libel, the strong dampened hearts of wicked politicos. The Great Rabbi Judah Loew had undertaken to create his golem in an unenlightened year, the dream of America just unfolding, far away, in all its spacious ardor; but already the seed of New York was preparing in Europe's earth: inspiration of city-joy, love for the comely, the cleanly, the free and the new, mobs transmuted into troops of the blessed, citizens bursting into angelness, sidewalks of alabaster, buses filled with thrones. Old delicate Prague, swept and swept of sin, giving birth to the purified daylight, the lucent genius, of New York!

By now Puttermesser knew what she knew.

"Bring me my books," she ordered the golem. And read:

A vision of Paradise must accompany the signs. The sacred formulae are insufficient without the trance of ecstasy in which are seen the brilliance of cities and their salvation through exile of heartlessness, disorder, and the desolation of sadness.

A city washed pure. New York, city (perhaps) of seraphim. Wings had passed over her eyes. Her arms around Rappoport's heavy *Times,* Puttermesser held to her breast heartlessness, disorder, the desolation of sadness, ten thousand knives, hatred painted in the subways, explosions of hand-guns, bombs in the cathedrals of transportation and industry, Pennsylvania Station, Grand Central, Rockefeller Center, terror in the broadcasting booths with their bustling equipment and seductive provincial voices, all the metropolitan airports assaulted, the decline of the Civil Service, maggots in high management. Rappoport's *Times,* repository of a dread freight! All the same, carrying Rappoport's *Times* back to bed, Puttermesser had seen Paradise.

New York washed, reformed, restored.

"Xanthippe!"

The golem, who had been scrubbing spaghetti sauce off the dishes in a little cascade of water-thunder under the kitchen faucet, wiped her hands on her new orange blouse, snatched up ballpoint pen and notepad, and ran to Puttermesser.

Puttermesser asked, "When you woke into life what did you feel?"

"I felt like an embryo," the golem wrote.

"What did you know?"

"I knew why I was created," the golem wrote.

"Why were you created?"

"So that my mother should become what she was intended to become," the golem wrote.

"Bring me that stack of stuff you were fooling around with in the office," Puttermesser ordered, but the golem had already scampered off to the bedroom closet to rummage among her boxes and bags of new clothes.

So Puttermesser set aside her books about the history and nature of the genus golem and settled down to contemplate all the pages the golem had typed for two days in Puttermesser's sorrowful cubicle, shared with Cracow—the cubicle of her demotion, denigration, disgrace—in the Taxation Section of the Bureau of Summary Sessions of the Department of Receipts and Disbursements of the City of New York.

What the golem had composed was a *PLAN*. Puttermesser recognized everything in it. It was as if she had encountered this *PLAN* before—its very language. It was as if, in the instant it had occurred to her to make the golem, she had read the *PLAN* in some old scroll. Ah, here was a stale and restless truth: that she did not recollect the actual fabrication of the golem, that she had helplessly, without volition, come upon Xanthippe in her bed as if the golem were some transient mirage, an aggressive imagining, or else a mere forward apparition—this had, with a wearisome persistence, been teasing at the edge of Puttermesser's medulla oblongata all along, ever since the first mulling of it on her desolate walk to the Y. It was like a pitcher that will neither fill nor pour out. But it was now as plain as solid earth itself that the golem was no apparition. Apparitions do not, in hideous public jargon, type up exhaustive practical documents concerning civic reform! Puttermesser knew what she knew—it unraveled before her in the distance, the *PLAN*, approaching, approaching, until it crowded her forebrain with its importuning force: how she had set Rappoport's *Times,* record of multiple chaos and urban misfortune, down on the floor beside the bed, where the *Theaetetus* already lay. How, with a speed born of fever and agitation, she had whirled from window sill to window sill, cracking open clay plant pots as though they were eggs, and scooping up the germinative yolks of spilling earth. How she had fetched it all up in her two palms and dumped it into the bathtub. How only a half-turn of the tap stirred earth to the consistency of mud—and how there then began the blissful shudder of Puttermesser's wild hands, the molding and the shaping, the caressing and the smoothing, the kneading and the fingering, the straightening and the rounding, but quickly, quickly, with detail itself (God is in the details) unachieved, blurred, completion deferred, the authentic pleasure of the precise final form of nostril and eyelid and especially mouth left for afterward. Into the hole of the unfinished face of clay Puttermesser pressed a tag of paper, torn from the blank upper margin of Rappoport's *Times,* on which she had written in her own spittle two oracular syllables. The syllables adhered and were as legible as if inscribed in light. Then Puttermesser raised up out of the tub the imponderous damp relentless clay of a young girl—a lifeless forked creature in the semblance of a girl—and smelled the smell of mud, and put her down in her own bed to dry. The small jar to that small weight loosened crumbs of earth wherever a limb was joined to the trunk, and where the neck was joined, and where the ears had their fragile connecting stems. The crumbs sprinkled down. They crept under Puttermesser's fingernails.

And all this Puttermesser performed (aha, now it beat in hindbrain and in forebrain, she saw it, she knew it again!) because of agitation and fever: because of the wilderness inside Rappoport's *Times.* Why should the despoiled misgoverned miscreant City not shine at dawn like washed stones? Tablets of civilization, engraved with ontological notations in an ancient tongue. Puttermesser craved. Her craving was to cleanse the wilderness; her craving was to excise every black instance of injustice; her craving was to erase outrage. In the middle of her craving—out of the blue—she formulated the *PLAN.*

She was thumbing it now, it was in her hands:

PLAN

FOR THE

RESUSCITATION,

REFORMATION,

REINVIGORATION

& REDEMPTION

OF THE

CITY OF NEW YORK

"Where did you get this?" Puttermesser demanded.

"I am your amanuensis," the golem wrote. "I express you. I copy and record you. Now it is time for you to accomplish your thought."

"Everyone has funny thoughts," Puttermesser croaked; an uneasiness heated her. She was afraid of the last page.

"No reality greater than thought," the golem wrote.

"Lay off the Middle Finnish. I want to hear the truth about all this. Where'd this stuff come from? You *couldn't* copy it, I never put any of it down."

The golem wrote: "Two urges seeded you. I am one, this is the other. A thought must claim an instrument. When you conceived your urge, simultaneously you conceived me."

"Not simultaneously," Puttermesser objected; perhaps the golem could not be trusted with chronology. She breathed outside history. Puttermesser re-imagined the electric moment exactly: the *PLAN* swimming like an inner cosmos into being, the mere solid golem an afterthought.

"No matter; I will serve your brain. I am your offspring, you are my mother. I am the execution of the grandeur of your principles. Grand design is my business. Leave visionary restoration to me." After which the golem put the ballpoint pen in her mouth and patiently sucked.

A fatigue seeped into Puttermesser; a tedium. It struck her that the golem was looking sly. She noticed that the seams along the armholes in the golem's orange blouse had begun to open. Growth. Enlargement. Swelling. Despite distraction Puttermesser read on. The *PLAN*, though it had originated in her own mind, nevertheless smacked of Marmel's lingo, Turtelman's patois. It appeared to derive, in truth, from the Form-language of Polly the Destroyer. A starkness penetrated Puttermesser; the dead words themselves depressed her. Her wrists shook. Was it not possible to dream a dream of City without falling into the mouth of the Destroyer? Behold the conservation of residential property through the exclusion of depreciating factors. Compute twelve hundred and fifty zoning codes. Note physical aspects. Social aspects. Retail and wholesale business. Manufacturing. Shipping. Single and multiple residences. Cultural institutions. Parks, public buildings, amusements, schools, universities, community objectives, rapidity and feasibility of transportation via streets and transit lines. Health, traffic, safety, public assembly conveniences. Sanitation. Prevention of slums. Transformation of slums. Eradication of poverty. Morality and obedience to law. Ordinances. Trust and pension funds. Treasury, public works, water. Public library. Police. Inspection. Councils and commissions. Welfare. Trustees. Revenue forecasting. Remote teleprocessing systems, computerized key-entry, restructuring of assessment districts, liens, senior-citizen rent-increase exemptions, delinquency centralization, corporate billings!

"My God," Puttermesser said.

"My mother has mastered and swallowed all of it," the golem wrote. "All of it is inside my mother's intelligence."

"I only meant—" Weak, Puttermesser wondered what it was she had meant. "Gardens and sunlight. Washed stones. Tablets. No; tables. Picnic tables."

Xanthippe stood nodding. The slyness powered her eyes. "My mother will become Mayor," she wrote.

The golem took the stack of typed sheets from Puttermesser's unquiet hands and held out the last page:

BY ORDER OF

RUTH PUTTERMESSER,

MAYOR

OF THE

CITY OF NEW YORK

"Drivel. Now you've gone too far. *I* never thought of that."

"Sleep on it," the golem wrote.

"That's *your* idea. You're the one who put that one in."

"Creator and created," the golem wrote, "merge," scribbling this with a shrug; the shrug made the ripped seams in her orange blouse open a little more.

The Honorable Malachy Mavett
Mayor
City Hall

Dear Mayor Mavett:

It is not respectful of a citizen's conception of the Mayor's office as "responsive" that you ignore my letter about possible spoils and other abuses. Still less is it respectful of me as a living human being and as a (former, now dismissed) Civil Servant. Shame! Shame!

Very sincerely yours,

THE HONORABLE RUTH PUTTERMESSER

This letter too remained locked inside Puttermesser's head. The signature was experimental—just to see what it looked like.

"No use, no use," the golem wrote on her notepad. "Mayor Puttermesser, by contrast, will answer all letters."

VI. Mayor Puttermesser

And so Puttermesser becomes Mayor of New York. The "and so" encloses much—but not so much as one might think. It is only a way of hastening Puttermesser's blatant destiny, of avoiding—never mind that God is in the details!—a more furrowed account of how the golem, each day imperceptibly enlarging, goes about gathering signatures for a citizens' petition.

The golem is above all a realist; Puttermesser will run as an independent. There is not the minutest hope that the county leaders of either the Democratic or the Republican party will designate, as preferred candidate for Mayor of the City of New York, Ruth Puttermesser, Esq., a currently unemployed attorney put out in the street, so to speak, by Commissioner Alvin Turtelman of the Department of Receipts and Disbursements, in conjunction and in consultation with First Bursary Officer Adam Marmel. The golem is Puttermesser's campaign manager. She has burst out of all her new clothes, and has finally taken to extra-large men's denim overalls bought in the Army-Navy store on the corner of Suffolk and Delancey. The golem's complexion has coarsened a little. It is somehow redder, and the freckles on her forehead, when gazed at by an immobile eye, appear to have the configuration of a handful of letters from a generally unrecognizable alphabet:

$$ \text{ת} \quad \text{מ} \quad \text{א} $$

Puttermesser has not failed to take note of how these letters, *aleph, mem,* and *tav,* in their primal North Semitic form, read from right to left, have extruded themselves with greater and greater clarity just below the golem's hairline. Puttermesser attributes this to pressure of the skin as the golem gains in height and thickness. She orders the golem to cut bangs. Though she is periodically alarmed at what a large girl Xanthippe is growing into, otherwise Puttermesser is pleased by her creation. Xanthippe is cheerful and efficient, an industrious worker. She continues to be a zealous cook. She remains unsure about time (occasionally she forgets that Wednesday intrudes between Tuesday and Thursday, and she has not quite puzzled out the order of all the months, though she has it splendidly fixed that November will embrace what has now become the sun of Puttermesser's firmament—Election Day); she is sometimes cocky; often intrepid; now and then surly; mainly she smiles and smiles. She can charm a signature out of anyone. At her own suggestion she wears around her neck a card that reads DEAF-MUTE, and with this card dangling on her bosom, in overalls, she scrambles up and down tenement steps as far away as Bensonhurst and Canarsie, in and out of elevators of East Side and West Side apartment buildings. She churns through offices, high schools and universities (she has visited Fordham, L.I.U., Pace, N.Y.U., Baruch College, Columbia; she has solicited the teaching staffs of Dalton, Lincoln, Brearley, John Dewey, Julia Richman, Yeshiva of Flatbush, Fieldston, Ramaz, as well as Puttermesser's own alma mater, Hunter High), supermarkets, cut-rate drugstores, subway stations, the Port Authority bus terminal. Wherever there are signers to be found, the golem appears with her ballpoint pen.

The petition is completed. The golem has collected fourteen thousand five hundred and sixty-two more signatures than the law calls for.

All this must be recorded as lightly and swiftly as possible; a dry patch to be gotten through, perhaps via a doze or a skip. For Puttermesser herself it is much more wretched than a mere dry patch. She suffers. Her physiological responses are: a coldness in the temples, blurring of the eyes, increased periodontic difficulties. She is afflicted with frequent diarrhea. Her spine throbs. At night she weeps. But she keeps on. Xanthippe gives her no peace, urges her to rephrase her speeches with an ear for the lively, insists that she sport distinctive hats, glossy lipstick, even contact lenses (Puttermesser, edging into middle age, already owns reading glasses).

The golem names Puttermesser's party as follows: Independents for Socratic and Prophetic Idealism—ISPI for short. A graphic artist is hired to devise a poster. It shows an apple tree with a serpent in it. The S in ISPI is the serpent. Puttermesser has promised to transform the City of New York into Paradise. She has promised to cast out the serpent. On Election Day, Malachy ("Matt") Mavett, the incumbent, is routed. Of the three remaining candidates, two make poor showings. Puttermesser is triumphant.

Puttermesser is now the Mayor of the City of New York!

Old ardors and itches wake in her. She recites to herself: Justice, justice shalt thou pursue. Malachy ("Matt") Mavett takes his wife and family to Florida, to be near Mrs. Minnie Mavett, his adoptive mother. He is no longer a lucky orphan. He gets a job as a racetrack official. It is a political job, but he is sad all the same. His wife bears his humiliation gracelessly. His children rapidly acquire accents that do not mark them as New Yorkers. Turtelman and Marmel vanish into rumor. They are said to be with the F.B.I. in Alaska, with the C.I.A. in Indonesia. They are said to have relocated at Albany. They are said to be minor factotums in the Federal Crop Insurance Corporation, with offices in Sourgrass, Iowa. They are said to have mediocre positions in the Internal Revenue Service, where they will not be entitled to Social Security. They are said to have botched a suicide pact. No one knows what has become of Turtelman and Marmel. But Puttermesser is relieved; she herself, by means of a memo from City Hall, has dismissed them. Turtelman and Marmel are sacked! Let go! Fired!

Malachy ("Matt") Mavett, following protocol, telephones to congratulate Puttermesser on her victory. But he confesses to bafflement. Where has Puttermesser come from? An ordinary drone from the Bureau of Summary Sessions of the Department of Receipts and Disbursements! How can she, "an unknown," he asks, "a political nonentity," have won the public over so handily? Puttermesser reminds him that some months ago she wrote him a letter asking for justice, condemning patronage and spoils. "You did not reply," she accuses him in a voice hoarse from speech-making. The ex-Mayor does not remember any letter.

Though Puttermesser is disconcerted by the move to Gracie Mansion (in her dreams her mother is once again rolling up winter rugs and putting down summer rugs in the wide sun-periled apartment on the Grand Concourse), the golem immediately chooses the most lavish bedroom in the Mayor's residence for herself. It contains an antique dresser with gryphon feet and a fourposter arched by a lofty tester curtained in white velvet. Old brass bowls glint on the dresser-top. The golem fills one whole closet with fresh overalls. She wanders about studying the paintings and caressing the shining banister. She exhorts Puttermesser to rejoice that she no longer has her old suspicious landlord on East Seventy-first Street to worry about. Millions of citizens are her landlord now!

Puttermesser cannot pay attention to the golem's sprightliness. She is in a frenzy over the job of appointing commissioners and agency heads. She implores Xanthippe to keep away from City Hall—the campaign is over, she will only distract from business. The new Mayor intends to recruit noble psyches and visionary hearts. She is searching for the antithesis of Turtelman and Marmel. For instance: she yearns after Wallace Stevens—insurance executive of probity during office hours, enraptured poet at dusk. How she would like to put Walt Whitman himself in charge of the Bureau of Summary Sessions, and have Shelley take over Water Resource Development—Shelley whose principle it is that poets are the legislators of mankind! William Blake in the Fire Department. George Eliot doing Social Services. Emily Brontë over at Police, Jane Austen in Bridges and Tunnels, Virginia Woolf and Edgar Allan Poe sharing Health. Herman Melville overseeing the Office of Single Room Occupancy Housing. "*Integer vitae scelerisque purus,*" the golem writes on her notepad, showing off. "That's the ticket," Puttermesser agrees, "but what am I supposed to do, chase around town like Diogenes with a lantern looking for an honest man?" Xanthippe writes philosophically, "The politics of Paradise is no longer politics." "The politics of Paradise is no longer Paradise," Puttermesser retorts; "don't annoy me anyhow, I have to get somebody fast for Receipts and Disbursements." "You could promote Cracow," the golem writes. "I already have. I moved him over to Bronx Landfill and Pest Control. That's two levels up. He's got a good idea for winter, actually—wants to convert that garbage mountain out near the bay to a ski jump. And he's stopped asking me out. Thank God he's scared of dating the Mayor." "If you would seek commissioners of integrity and rosy cleverness," the golem writes, "fashion more of my kind." Fleetingly, Puttermesser considers this; she feels tempted. The highest echelons of City management staffed by multiple members of the genus golem! Herself the creator, down to the last molecule of ear-wax, of every commissioner, deputy, bureau chief, executive director! Every mayoral assistant, subordinate, underling, a golem! She looks over at Xanthippe. Twice already Xanthippe has quarreled with the Mansion's official cook. The cook has refused to follow the golem's recipes. "One is enough," Puttermesser says, and hurries down the subway and off to City Hall.

Despite its odious language reminiscent of Turtelman and Marmel, Puttermesser repeatedly consults the ·

PLAN

FOR THE

RESUSCITATION,

REFORMATION,

REINVIGORATION

& REDEMPTION

OF THE

CITY OF NEW YORK.

She blames Xanthippe for such a preposterous text: only two days spent in the Bureau of Summary Sessions, and the golem has been infected by periphrasis, pleonasm, and ambagious tautology. But behind all that there glimmers a loveliness. To Puttermesser's speeding eye, it is like the spotted sudden flank of a deer disturbing a wood. There *will* be resuscitation! There *will* be redemption!

And it begins. Mayor Puttermesser sends the golem out into the City. At first she tends to hang out among the open-air stalls of Delancey Street, but Puttermesser upbraids her for parochialism; she instructs the golem to take subways and buses—no taxis—out to all the neighborhoods in all the boroughs. It goes without saying that a robust reformist administration requires a spy. The golem returns with aching tales of what she has seen among the sordid and the hopeless; sometimes she even submits a recommendation on a page of her notepad. Puttermesser does not mind. Nothing the golem reports is new to Mayor Puttermesser. What is new is the discovery of the power of office. Wrongdoing and bitterness can be overturned: it is only a matter of using the power Puttermesser owns.

Crowds of self-seeking importuners float up the steps of City Hall; Mayor Puttermesser shoos them away. She admits visionary hearts only. She tacks signs up all around her desk: NO MORE SPOILS QUOTA. MERIT IS SWEETER THAN GOLD. WHAT YOU ARE, NOT WHOM YOU KNOW.

Lost wallets are daily being returned to their owners. Now it is really beginning—the money and credit cards are always intact. The golem ascends from the subway at Sixty-eighth and Lexington (this is the very corner where Puttermesser's alma mater, Hunter High, used to stand), looking slightly larger than the day before, but also irradiated. The subways have been struck by beauty. Lustrous tunnels unfold, mile after mile. Gangs of youths have invaded the subway yards at night and have washed the cars clean. The wheels and windows have been scrubbed by combinations of chemicals; the long seats have been fitted with velour cushions of tan and blue. Each car shines like a bullet. The tiles that line the stations are lakes of white; the passengers can cherish their own reflections in the walls. Every Thursday afternoon the youths who used to terrorize the subways put on fresh shirts and walk out into Central Park, reconnoitering after a green space; then they dance. They have formed themselves into dancing clubs, and crown one another's heads with clover pulled up from the sweet ground. Foliage is browning, Thursday afternoons grow cold and dusky. But the youths who used to terrorize the subways are whirling in rings over darkening lawns.

The streets are altered into garden rows: along the curbs, between sidewalk and road, privet hedges shake their little leaves. The open sanitation carts are bright, like a string of scarlet chariots. They are drawn by silent horses who sniff among the new hedges. Flutes and clarinets announce the coming of the cart procession every day at noon, and children scramble to pick up every nub of cigarette or scrap of peel or paper wrapper, pressing with fistfuls toward the singing flutes and gravely marching horses, whose pairs of high nostrils flare outward like trumpets.

The great cargo trucks still spill into the intersections, carrying bolts of cloth, oranges, fowl, refrigerators, lamps, pianos, cards of buttons, lettuces, boxes of cereal, word processors, baby carriages, pillowcases with peacocks imprinted on them; some deliver uptown, others downtown; they pant and rumble freely, unimpeded; buses and taxis overtake them effortlessly. Except for fire engines and ambulances, there are no other motored vehicles. Little girls dare, between buses, to jump rope in the middle of the street. Some roads, though, have been lushly planted, so that lovers seek them out to hide in one another's breast. The tall grasses and young maples of the planted roads are haunted by pretzel sellers, hot-chestnut peddlers, hawkers of books in wheelbarrows. The children are often indoors after school, carpentering bookshelves. The libraries are lit all night, and the schools are thronged in the evenings by administrative assistants from the great companies, learning Spanish, Portuguese, Russian, Hebrew, Korean, and Japanese. There are many gardeners now, and a hundred urban gardening academies. There is unemployment among correction offfficers; numbers of them take gardening jobs. No one bothers to drag the steel shutters down over storefronts after closing. The Civil Service hums. Intellect and courtliness are in the ascendancy. Mayor Puttermesser has staffed the Department of Receipts and Disbursements with intelligent lawyers, both women and men, who honor due process. Turtelman and Marmel are replaced by visionary hearts. Never again will an accuser take the job of the accused, as Marmel did with Puttermesser! There is no more rapaciousness in the Bureau of Summary Sessions.

A little-known poet who specializes in terza rima is put in charge of Potter's Field. For each sad burial there, she composes a laudatory ode; even the obscure dead are not expendable or forlorn. The parks, their arbors and fields, are speckled with wide-mouthed terra-cotta urns; no one injures them. Far away in the Bronx, the grape-wreathed heads of wine gods are restored to the white stelae of the Soldiers' Monument, and the bronze angel on top of the Monument's great stone needle glistens. Nothing is broken, nothing is despoiled. No harm comes to anything or anyone. The burnt-out ruins of Brownsville and the South Bronx burst forth with spinneys of pines and thorny locusts. In their high secret pride, the slums undo themselves: stoops sparkle, new factories and stores buzz, children gaze down in gladness at shoes newly bought, still unscratched; the shoe stores give away balloons, and the balloons escape to the sky. Everywhere former louts and loiterers, muggers and thieves, addicts and cardsharps are doing the work of the world, absorbed, transformed. The biggest City agency is what used to be called Welfare; now it is the Department of Day Play, and delivers colored pencils and finger paints and tambourines to nurseries clamorous as bee-loud glades, where pianos shake the floors, and story-tellers dangle toddlers in suspense from morning to late afternoon, when their parents fetch them home to supper. Everyone is at work. Lovers apply to the City Clerk for marriage licenses. The Bureau of Venereal Disease Control has closed down. The ex-pimps are learning computer skills.

Xanthippe's heels have begun to hang over the foot of her fourposter bed in Gracie Mansion. The golem is worn out. She lumbers from one end of the City to the other every day, getting ideas. Mayor Puttermesser is not disappointed that the golem's ideas are mainly unexciting. The City is at peace. It is in the nature of tranquility—it is in the nature of Paradise—to be pacific; tame; halcyon. Oh, there is more to relate of how Mayor Puttermesser, inspired by the golem, has resuscitated, reformed, reinvigorated and redeemed the City of New York! But this too must be left to dozing and skipping. It is essential to record only two reflections that especially engage Mayor Puttermesser. The first is that she notices how the City, tranquil, turns toward the conventional and the orderly. It is as if tradition, continuity, propriety blossom of themselves: old courtesies, door-holding, hat-tipping, a thousand pleases and pardons and thank-yous. Something in the grain of Paradise is on the side of the expected. Sweet custom rules. The City in its redeemed state wishes to conserve itself. It is a rational daylight place; it has shut the portals of night.

Puttermesser's second reflection is about the golem. The coming of the golem animated the salvation of the City, yes—but who, Puttermesser sometimes wonders, is the true golem? Is it Xanthippe or is it Puttermesser? Puttermesser made Xanthippe; Xanthippe did not exist before Puttermesser made her: that is clear enough. But Xanthippe made Puttermesser Mayor, and Mayor Puttermesser too did not exist before. And that is just as clear. Puttermesser sees that she is the golem's golem.

In the newborn peaceable City, Xanthippe is restless. She is growing larger. Her growth is frightening. She can no longer fit into her overalls. She begins to sew together pairs of sheets for a toga.

VII. Rappoport's return

On a late spring afternoon about halfway through her mayoral term, and immediately after a particularly depressing visit to the periodontist (she who had abolished crime in the subways was unable to stem gum disease in the hollow of her own jaw), Puttermesser came home to Gracie Mansion to find Rappoport waiting in her private sitting room.

"Hey, you've got some pretty tough security around here. I had a hell of a time getting let in," Rappoport complained.

"Last time I saw you," Puttermesser said, "you had no trouble letting yourself out."

"How about we just consider that water under the bridge, Ruth, what do you say?"

"You walked out on me. In the middle of the night."

"You were liking Socrates better than me," Rappoport said.

"Then why are you back?"

"My God, Ruth, look who you've become! I can't pass through New York without seeing the Mayor, can I? Ruth," he said, spreading his impressive nostrils, "I've thought about you a lot since the election. We read all about you up in Toronto."

"You and Mrs. Rappoport?"

"Oh come on, let's give it another try. Not that I don't understand you have to be like Caesar's wife. Above susp—"

"I have to be Caesar," Puttermesser broke in.

"Well, even Caesar gives things another try."

"You're no Cleopatra," Puttermesser said.

There was a distant howl; it was the cook. She was fighting with the golem again. In a moment Xanthippe stood in the doorway, huge and red, weeping.

"Leave that woman alone. She'll cook what she'll cook, you can't tell her anything different," Puttermesser scolded. "She runs a strictly kosher kitchen and that's enough. Go and wash your face."

"Plump," Rappoport said, staring after Xanthippe in her toga. "Right out of Caesar's Forum."

"A growing girl. She wears what she pleases."

"Who is she?"

"I adopted her."

"I like a big girl like that." Rappoport stood up. "The town looks terrific. I came to congratulate you, Ruth."

"Is that why you came?"

"It turns out. Only I figured if you could bring a whole city back to life—"

"There are some things, Morris, that even the Mayor can't revive."

Rappoport, his briefcase under his arm, wheeled and hesitated. "It didn't make it through the move? My avocado tree that I grew from a pit in Toronto? It was doing fine in your old apartment."

"I don't have it any more."

"Aha, you wanted to dispose of me lock, stock, and barrel. You got rid of every symptom and sign. The least bit of green leaf—"

"All my plants are gone."

"No kidding. What happened?"

"I took their earth and made a golem."

Rappoport, flaunting his perfect teeth under his mustache, laughed out loud. In the middle of his laughter his head suddenly fell into the kind of leaning charm Puttermesser recalled from long ago, when they had first become lovers; it almost made her relent.

"Goodbye, Ruth. I really do congratulate you on civic improvement." Rappoport held out his hand. "It's one terrific town, I mean it. Utopia. Garden of Eden. In Toronto they run articles on you every day."

"You can stay for dinner if you like," Puttermesser offered. "Though I've got a meeting right after—municipal bonds. Myself, it's eat and get on down to City Hall."

Someone had seized Rappoport's outstretched hand and was shaking it; it was not Puttermesser. Xanthippe, practiced politician, her wide cheeks refreshed and soap-fragrant, had sped forward out of nowhere. Rappoport looked stunned; he looked interested. He slipped his fingers out of the golem's grasp and moved them upward against her chest, to catch hold of the card that twirled there: DEAF-MUTE.

"That's awfully generous of you, Ruth, adopting someone like that. You're a wonderful person. We really ought to get together again. I *will* stay for a bite, if you don't mind."

The golem did not bring her ballpoint to the table. She dealt with her soup spoon as if it were her enemy, the cook. Disgruntled, she heaped a fourth helping of mashed potatoes onto her plate. But her eye was on Rappoport, and her mouth was round with responsiveness: was it his teeth? was it his reddish mustache, turning gray? was it his wide welcoming nostrils? was it his briefcase bulging with worldly troubles?

Rappoport was talkative. His posture was straight-backed and heroic: he told of his last clandestine trip to Moscow, and of the turmoil of the oppressed.

When Puttermesser returned at midnight from the meeting on municipal bonds, the golem was asleep in her fourposter bed, her heels thrust outward in their pink socks over the footboard, and Rappoport was snoring beside her.

Eros had entered Gracie Mansion.

VIII. Xanthippe lovesick

Consider now Puttermesser's situation. What happens to an intensely private mind when great celebrity unexpectedly invades it? Absorbed in the golem's *PLAN* and its consequences—consequences beyond the marveling at, so gradual, plausible, concrete, and sensible are they, grounded in a policy of civic sympathy and urban reasonableness—Puttermesser does not readily understand that she induces curiosity and applause. She has, in fact, no expectations; only desires as strong and as strange as powers. Her desires are pristine, therefore acute; clarity is immanent. Before this inward illumination of her desires (rather, of the *PLAN*'s desires), everything else— the clash of interests that parties, races, classes, are said to give rise to—falls away into purposelessness. Another way of explaining all this is to say that Mayor Puttermesser finds virtue to be intelligible. Still another way of explaining is to say that every morning she profoundly rejoices. There is fruitfulness everywhere. Into the chaos of the void (defeat, deception, demoralization, loss) she has cast a divinely clarifying light. Out of a dunghill she has charmed a verdant citadel. The applause that reaches her is like a seasound at the farthest edge of her brain; she both hears it and does not hear it. Her angelic fame—the fame of a purifying angel—is virtue's second face. Fame makes Puttermesser happy, and at the same time it brings a forceful sense of the penultimate, the tentative, the imperiled.

It is as if she is waiting for something else: for some conclusion, or resolution, or unfolding.

The golem is lovesick. She refuses to leave the Mansion. No more for her the daily voyage into the broad green City as the Mayor's ambassador and spy. She removes the DEAF-MUTE card and substitutes another: CONTEMPLATIVE. Puttermesser does not smile at this: she is not sure whether it is meant to be a joke. There is too much gloom. There are hints of conspiracy. Anyhow the golem soon takes off the new sign. In the intervals between Rappoport's appearances Xanthippe languishes. Rappoport comes often—sometimes as often as three or four times a week. Xanthippe, moping, thumps out to greet him, trailing a loose white tail of her toga; she escorts him straight into her bedroom. She turns on the record player that Rappoport has brought her as a birthday gift. She is two years old and insatiable. God knows what age she tells her lover.

Rappoport steals out of the golem's bedroom with the dazzled inward gaze of a space traveler.

The Mayor upbraids Xanthippe: "It's enough. I don't want to see him around here. Get rid of him."

Xanthippe writes: "Jealousy!"

"I'm tired of hearing complaints from the cook. This is Gracie Mansion, it's not another kind of house."

"Jealousy! He used to be yours."

"You're stirring up a scandal."

"He brings me presents."

"If you keep this up, you'll spoil everything."

"My mother has purified the City."

"Then don't foul it."

"I am in contemplation of my future."

"Start contemplating the present! Look out the window! Fruitfulness! Civic peace! You saw it happening. You caused it."

"I can tear it all down."

"You were made to serve and you know it."

"I want a life of my own. My blood is hot."

The Mansion thickens with erotic airs. Heavy perfumes float. Has Rappoport journeyed to mysterious islands to offer the golem these lethargic scents, these attars of weighty drooping petals? The golem has discarded her sewn-together sheets and looms with gemlike eyes in darkling passage-ways, wrapped in silks, vast saris that skim the carpets as she goes; each leg is a pillar wound in a bolt of woven flowers.

The summer deepens. A dry dust settles on the leaves in the Bronx Botanical Gardens, and far away the painted carousels of Brooklyn cry their jollities.

The Mayor: "I notice Rappoport hasn't been around lately."

Xanthippe writes: "He left."

"Where?"

"He clouded over his destination. Vienna. Rome. Jerusalem. Winnipeg. What do I care? A man of low position. Factotum of refugee philanthropy, twelve bosses over him."

"What happened?"

"I wore him out."

"I need you right away," Puttermesser urges. "We're putting in new tiles on the subway line out toward Jamaica Avenue. With two-color portraits baked right into the glaze—Thoreau, Harriet Beecher Stowe, Emerson so far. You can decide who else."

"No."

"You haven't been anywhere in months."

"My mother speaks the truth. I thirst for the higher world. Office and rank. Illustrious men."

Puttermesser is blighted with melancholy. She fears. She foresees. In spite of fruitfulness and civic peace (rather, on their account), it is beginning to be revealed to her what her proper mayoral duty directs.

She does nothing.

In pity, she waits. Sometimes she forgets. How long did the Great Rabbi Judah Loew of Prague wait, how often did he forget? There are so many distinguished visitors. The Emperor of Japan takes the elevator to the top of the Empire State Building. Puttermesser gives an astronaut a medal on the steps of City Hall; he has looked into the bosom of Venus. The mayors of Dublin, San Juan, and Tel Aviv arrive. In the Blue Room, Puttermesser holds a news conference about interest rates. She explains into the television cameras that the City of New York, in its abundance, will extend interest-free loans to the Federal government in Washington.

Now and then Xanthippe disappears. She does not return to the Mansion at night. Frequently her fourposter stands empty.

Early one morning, the golem, her eyes too polished, her cheeks too red, her silk windings torn, the tiny letters on her forehead jutting like raw scars, thumps home.

"Four days gone without a word!" Puttermesser scolds.

Xanthippe writes impatiently: "Been down to Florida."

"Florida!"

"Been to visit ex-Mayor Malachy ('Matt') Mavett."

"What for?"

"Remember Marmel?"

"What's this about?"

"Been out West to visit him. Him and Turtelman."

"What *is* this?"

But Puttermesser knows.

There are curious absences, reports of exhaustion, unexplained hospital-izations. The new Commissioner of Receipts and Disbursements whispers to Puttermesser, in confidence, that he will divorce his wife. His eyeballs seem sunken, his lips drop back into a hollow face. He has lost weight overnight. He will not say what the trouble is. He resigns. The Executive Director of the Board of Education resigns. It is divulged that he suffers from catarrh and is too faint to stand. The Commissioner of the Department of Cultural Affairs has been struck stone-deaf by a horrible sound, a kind of exultant hiss; he will not say what it was. The City's managers and executives all appear to sicken together: commissioner after commissioner, department after depart-ment. Puttermesser's finest appointments—felled; depleted. There is news of an abortion in Queens. A pimp sets himself up in business on Times Square again, in spite of the cherry trees the Department of Sanitation has planted there; the Commissioner of Sanitation himself stalks under the hanging cher-ries, distracted, with a twisted spine and the start of a hunch. Two or three of the proud young men of the dancing clubs defect and return to mugging in the subways. The City's peace is unraveling. The commissioners blow their noses into bloody tissues, drive their little fingers into their ears, develop odd stammers, instigate backbiting among underlings.

The golem thirsts.

"Stay home," the Mayor pleads. "Stay out of the City."

The golem will no longer obey. She cannot be contained. "My blood is hot," Xanthippe writes; she writes for the last time. She tosses her ballpoint pen into the East River, back behind the Mansion.

IX. The golem destroys her maker

Mayor Puttermesser's reputation is ebbing. The cost of municipal borrow-ing ascends. A jungle of graffiti springs up on the white flanks of marble sculptures inside museums; Attic urns are smashed. Barbarians cruise the streets. O New York! O lost New York!

Deputy commissioners and their secretaries blanch at the sound of a heavy footstep. Morning and afternoon the golem lumbers from office to office, searching for high-level managers. In her ragged sari brilliant with woven flowers, her great head garlanded, drenched in a density of musky oils, Xanthippe ravishes prestigious trustees, committee chairmen, council members, borough presidents, the Second Deputy Comptroller's three assis-tants, the Director of the Transit Authority, the Coordinator of Criminal Justice, the Chief of the Office of Computer Plans and Controls, the Head of Intergovernmental Relations, the Chancellor of the City University, the Rector of the Art Commission, even the President of the Stock Exchange! The City is diseased with the golem's urge. The City sweats and coughs in her terrifying embrace. The City is in the pincer of the golem's love, because Xanthippe thirsts, she thirsts, she ravishes and ravages, she ambushes management level after management level. There is no Supervising Accountant or Secretary to the Minority Leader who can escape her electric gaze.

Sex! Sex! The golem wants sex! Men in high politics! Lofty officials! Elevated bureaucrats!

Mayor Putterrnesser is finished. She can never be re-elected. She is a disgrace; her Administration is wrecked. Distrust. Desolation. It is all over for Mayor Puttermesser and the life of high politics. The prisons are open again. The press howls. Mayor Puttermesser is crushed. The golem has destroyed her utterly.

X. The golem snared

Puttermesser blamed herself. She had not forestalled this devastation. She had not prepared for it; she had not acted. She had seen what had to be done, and put it off and put it off. Dilatory. She could not say to herself that she was ignorant; hadn't she read in her books, a thousand times, that a golem will at length undo its creator? The turning against the creator is an "attribute" of a golem, comparable to its speechlessness, its incapacity for procreation, its soullessness. A golem has no soul, therefore cannot die— rather, it is returned to the elements of its making.

Xanthippe without a soul! Tears came to Puttermesser, her heart in secret shook. She was ready to disbelieve. A golem cannot procreate? Ah, but its blood is as hot as human blood. Hotter! A golem lusts tremendously, as if it would wrest the flame of further being from its own being. A golem, an earthen thing of packed mud, having laid hold of life against all logic and natural expectation, yearns hugely after the generative, the fructuous. Earth is the germ of all fertility: how then would a golem not dream itself a double? It is like a panting furnace that cries out for more and more fuel, that spews its own firebrands to ignite a successor-fire. A golem cannot procreate! But it has the will to; the despairing will; the violent will. Offspring! Progeny! The rampaging energies of Xanthippe's eruptions, the furious bolts and convulsions of her visitations—Xanthippe, like Puttermesser herself, longs for daughters! Daughters that can never be!

Shall the one be condemned by the other, who is no different?

Yet Puttermesser weeps. The golem is running over the City. She never comes home at all now. A ferry on its way from the Battery to Staten Island is terrorized; some large creature, bat or succubus, assaults the captain and causes him to succumb. Is it Xanthippe? Stories about "a madwoman on the loose, venomous against authority" ("unverifiable," writes the City Hall Bureau of the *Times*) wash daily over Mayor Puttermesser's desk. The secret chamber where sleeps the President of the Chase Manhattan Bank has had its windows brutally smashed; a bit of flowered silk clings to the jagged glass.

Xanthippe! Xanthippe! Puttermesser calls in her heart.

Every night pickets parade in front of Gracie Mansion, with torches and placards:

> MAYOR PUTTERMESSER WHAT HAS HAPPENED TO THE SUBWAYS?
>
> HIGH HOPES THE HIGH ROAD TO HELL.
>
> SHE WHO SPARKED SNUFFED.
>
> PUTTERMESSER S BITTER MESSES.
>
> RUTHIE WITH SUCH A DOWN WE NEEDED YOUR UP?
>
> FROM SMASH HIT TO SMASH.
>
> KAPUT-TERMESSER!

Every day there are speakers on the steps of City Hall, haranguing; when the police chase them, they vanish for ten minutes and reappear. Mobs bubble, hobble, guffaw. Puttermesser composes a letter to ex-Mayor Malachy ("Matt") Mavett:

> Gracie Mansion
> City of New York

Dear Matt [she permits herself this liberty]:

My campaign manager's recent Florida visit may have caused you some distress. I did not authorize it. Your defeat via the ballot box, which eliminated the wrongdoers Turtelman and Marmel from City officialdom, was satisfaction enough. Please excuse any personal indignities my campaign manager (who is now on my personal staff) may have inflicted. She expresses her nature but cannot assume responsibility for it.

Dilatory! Procrastinator! Imaginary letters! Puttermesser's tears go on falling.

> Gracie Mansion
> City of New York

Dear Morris:

Please come.

> In friendship
> Ruth

She hands this to one of the window-pole thieves to mail. In a few days it brings Rappoport, out of breath, his once-pouting briefcase hollow, caved in; Rappoport himself is hollow, his stout throat caved in, as if he had ejected his Adam's apple. His nose and chin, and the furless place between his eyebrows, have a papery cast. His beautiful teeth are nicked. His mustache looks squirrelly, gray.

"Xanthippe's left home," Puttermesser announces.

"You're the Mayor. Call the Missing Persons Bureau."

"Morris. Please."

"What do you want?"

"Bring her back."

"Me?"

"You can do it."

"How?"

"Move in."

"What? Here? In Gracie Mansion?"

"In Xanthippe's bed. Morris. Please. She likes you. You're the one who started her off."

"She got too big for her britches. In more than a manner of speaking, if you don't mind my saying so. What d'you mean, started her off?"

"You excited her."

"That's not my fault."

"You created desire. Morris, bring her back. You can do it."

"What for? I've had enough. No more. Drained. Drained, believe me, Ruth."

"Lie in her bed. Just once."

"What's in it for me? I didn't come back to this rotten town for the sake of a night's sleep in Gracie Mansion. The novelty's worn off. The bloom is no longer on the rose, you follow? Besides, you've gone downhill, Ruth, did you see those pickets out there?" He shows her his sleeve—two buttons ripped off. "They treated me like a scab, walking in here—"

"Just lie down in her bed, Morris. That's all I'm asking."

"No."

"I'll make it worth your while."

"What're you getting at? You're getting at something."

"You're a fund-raiser by profession," Puttermesser says meditatively; a strangeness rises in her. A noxious taste.

"Something like that. There's a lot of different things I do."

"That's right. Plenty of experience. You're qualified for all sorts of fine spots."

"I'm qualified for what?"

"The truth is," Puttermesser says slowly, "I'm in possession of a heap of resignations. Several of my commissioners," Puttermesser says slowly, "have fallen ill."

"I hear there's typhoid in some of those buildings along Bruckner Boulevard. What've you got, an epidemic? I heard cholera in Forest Hills."

"Rumors," Puttermesser spits out. "People love to badmouth. That's what makes the City go down. The banks are leaving, nobody worries about *that.* I'm talking resignations. *Openings,* Morris. You can take your pick, in fact. How about the Department of Investigation? Run the Inspectors General. Or I can appoint you judge. How about Judge of the Criminal Court? Good spot, good pay. Prestige, God knows. Look, if you like you can take over Receipts and Disbursements."

Rappoport stared. "Commissioner of Receipts and Disbursements?"

"I can go higher if you want. Fancier. Board of Water Supply's a dandy. Nice remuneration, practically no show."

"Ruth, Ruth, what is this?"

Justice, justice shalt thou pursue!

It is Mayor Puttermesser's first political deal.

"Stay a night in Xanthippe's bed and any job you want is yours. The orchard's dropping into your lap, Morris, I'm serious. Plums."

"A spot in your Administration actually?"

"Why not? Choose."

"Receipts and Disbursements," Rappoport instantly replies.

Puttermesser says sourly, "You're at least as qualified as Turtelman."

"What about my wife?"

"Keep her in Toronto."

Standing in solitude in the night fragrance behind Gracie Mansion, Puttermesser catches river-gleams: the Circle Line yacht with its chandelier decks; a neon sign pulsing; the distant caps of little waves glinting in moonwake, in neonwake. White bread baking on the night shift casts its faintly animal aroma on the waters: rich fumes more savory than any blossom. It is so dark in the back garden that Puttermesser imagines she can almost descry Orion's belt buckle. One big moving star twins as it sails: the headlights of an airliner nosing out toward Europe. Plane after plane rises, as if out of the black river. Puttermesser counts them, each with its sharp beams like rays scattered from the brow of Moses, arching upward into the fathomless universe. She counts planes; she counts neon blinks; she counts the silhouettes of creeping scows; she counts all the mayors who have preceded her in the City of New York. Thomas Willett, Thomas Delavall . . . William Dervall, Nicholas De Meyer, Stephanus Van Cortlandt . . . Francis Rombouts . . . Isaac de Reimer, Thomas Noell, Philip French, William Peartree, Ebenezer Wilson . . . DeWitt Clinton . . . Gideon Lee . . . Smith Ely . . . Jimmy Walker . . . John P. O'Brien, Fiorello H. LaGuardia . . . Robert F. Wagner, John V. Lindsay, Abraham D. Beame, Edward I. Koch! She counts and waits. She is waiting for the golem to be lured homeward, to be ensnared, to lumber groaning with desire into her fourposter bed.

In the golem's fourposter, Commissioner Morris Rappoport, newly appointed chief of the Department of Receipts and Disbursements, lies in sheets saturated with a certain known pungency. He has been here before. He recoils from the familiar scented pillows.

Indoors and out, odors of what has been and what is about to be: the cook's worn eggplant au gratin, river smells, the garden beating its tiny wings of so many fresh hedge-leaves, airplane exhaust spiraling downward, the fine keen breath of the bread ovens, the golem's perfumed pillows—all these drifting smokes and combinations stir and turn and braid themselves into a rope of awesome incense, drawing Xanthippe to her bed. Incense? Fetor and charged decay! The acrid signal of dissolution! Intimations of the tellurian elements! Xanthippe, from wherever she has hurtled to in the savage City (savage once again), is pulled nearer and nearer the Mansion, where the portraits of dead mayors hang. Scepter and status, all the enchantments of influence and command, lead her to her undoing: in her bed lies the extremely important official whose job it is to call the tune that makes the City's money dance. She will burst on him her giant love. On the newly appointed Commissioner of Receipts and Disbursements the golem will spend her terrible ardor. Then she will fall back to rest, among the awful perfumes of her cleft bed.

Whereupon Mayor Puttermesser, her term of office blighted, her comely *PLAN* betrayed, will dismantle the golem, according to the rite.

XI. The golem undone, and the babbling of Rappoport

The City was ungovernable; the City was out of control; it was no different now for Mayor Puttermesser than it had ever been for any mayor. In confusion and hypocrisy, Puttermesser finished out what was left of her sovereign days.

One thing was different: a certain tumulus of earth introduced by the Parks Commissioner in the mournful latter half of Mayor Puttermesser's Administration.

Across the street from City Hall lies a little park, crisscrossed by paths and patches of lawn fenced off by black iron staves. There are benches set down here and there with a scattered generosity. There is even an upward-flying fountain. Perhaps because the little park is in the shadow of City Hall and, so to speak, under its surveillance, the benches have not been seriously vandalized, and the lawns not much trampled on. Best of all, and most alluring, are the flower beds, vivid rectangles of red geraniums disposed, it must be admitted, in the design of a miniature graveyard. Civil servants peering down from high windows of the elephant-gray Municipal Building can see the crimson slash that with wild brilliance cuts across the concrete bitterness below. Some distance behind the flower beds rise those great Stonehenge slabs of the Twin Towers; eastward, the standing zither that is Brooklyn Bridge.

From the Mayor's office inside City Hall the park is not visible, and for Puttermesser this is just as well. It would not have done for her to be in sight of Xanthippe's bright barrow while engaged in City business. Under the roots of the flower beds lay fresh earth, newly put down and lightly tamped. Mayor Puttermesser herself, in the middle of the night, had telephoned the Parks Commissioner (luckily just back from Paris) and ordered the ground to be opened and a crudely formed and crumbling mound of special soil to be arranged in the cavity, as in an envelope of earth. The Parks Commissioner, urgently summoned, thought it odd, when he arrived at Gracie Mansion with his sleepy diggers, that the Mayor should be pacing in the back garden behind the Mansion under a veined half-moon; and odder yet that she should be accompanied by a babbling man with a sliding tongue, who identified himself as the newly appointed Commissioner of Receipts and Disbursements, Morris Rappoport.

"Did you bring spades? And a pickup truck?" the Mayor whispered.

"All of that, yes."

"Well, the spades won't do. At least not yet. You don't shovel up a floor. You can use the spades afterward, in the park. There's some dried mud spread out on a bedroom floor in the Mansion. I want it moved. With very great delicacy. Can you make your men understand that?"

"Dried mud?"

"I grant you it's in pieces. It's already falling apart. But it's got a certain design. Be delicate."

What the Parks Commissioner saw was a very large and shapeless, or mainly shapeless, mound of soil, insanely wrapped (so the Parks Commissioner privately judged) in a kind of velvet shroud. The Parks Commissioner had been on an official exchange program in France, and had landed at Kennedy Airport less than two hours before the Mayor telephoned. The exchange program meant that he would study the enchanting parks of Paris, while his Parisian counterpart was to consider the gloomier parks of New York. The Parks Commissioner, of course, was Puttermesser's own appointee, a botanist and city planner, an expert on the hardiness of certain shade trees, a specialist in filigreed gazebos, a lover of the urban nighttime. All the same, he was perplexed by the Mayor's caprice. The mound of dirt on the bedroom floor did not suggest to him his own good fortune and near escape. In fact, though neither would ever learn this, the Parks Commissioner and his Parisian counterpart were both under a felicitous star—the Parisian because his wife's appendectomy had kept him unexpectedly and rather too lengthily in Paris so that he never arrived in New York at all (he was an anxious man), and the Parks Commissioner because he had not been at home in his lower Fifth Avenue bed when the golem came to call. Instead, he had been out inspecting the Bois de Boulogne—consequently, the Parks Commissioner was in fine mental health, and was shocked to observe that the newly appointed Commissioner of Receipts and Disbursements was not.

Rappoport babbled. He followed after Puttermesser like a dog. He had performed exactly as she had instructed, it seemed, but then her instructions became contradictory. First he was to circle. Then he was not to circle. Rather, he was to scrape with his penknife. There he was, all at once a satrap with a title; the title was as palpable as a mantle, and as sumptuous; overhead drooped the fourposter's white velvet canopy with its voluptuous folds and snowy crevices—how thickly warm his title, how powerful his office! Alone, enclosed in the authority of his rank, Rappoport awaited the visitation of the golem. Without a stitch, not a shred of sari remaining, her burnished gaze on fire with thirst for his grandeur, she burst in, redolent of beaches, noisy with a fiery hiss; Rappoport tore the white velvet from the tester and threw it over burning Xanthippe.

Rappoport babbled. He told all the rest: how they had contended; how he had endured her size and force and the horror of her immodesty and the awful sea of her sweat and the sirocco of her summer breath; and how he—or was it she?—had chanted out the hundred proud duties of his new jurisdiction: the protocol and potency of the City's money, where it is engendered, where it is headed, where it lands: it could be said that she was teaching him his job. And then the Mayor, speaking through the door, explaining the depth of tranquility after potency that is deeper than any sleep or drug or anesthesia, directing him to remove Xanthippe in all her deadweight mass from the fourposter down to the bare floor, and to wind her in the canopy.

Rappoport babbled: how he had lifted Xanthippe in her trance, the torpor that succeeds ravishment, down to the bare floor; how he had wound her in white velvet; how pale Puttermesser, her reading lenses glimmering into an old green book, directed him with sharpened voice to crowd his mind with impurity—with everything earthly, soiled, spoiled, wormy; finally how Puttermesser directed him to trail her as she weaved round Xanthippe on the floor, as if circling her own shadow.

Round and round Puttermesser went. In the instant of giving the golem life, the just, the comely, the cleanly, the Edenic, had, all unwittingly, consummated Puttermesser's aspiring reflections—even the radiant *PLAN* itself! Now all must be consciously reversed. She must think of violent-eyed loiterers who lurk in elevators with springblades at the ready, of spray cans gashing red marks of civilization-hate, of civic monuments with their heads knocked off, of City filth, of mugging, robbery, arson, assault, even murder. Murder! If, for life, she had dreamed Paradise, now she must feel the burning lance of hell. If, for life, she had walked seven times clockwise round a hillock of clay, now she must walk seven times counterclockwise round captive Xanthippe. If, for life, she had pronounced the Name, now she must on no account speak or imagine it or lend it any draught or flame of breath; she must erase the Name utterly.

And what of Rappoport, Rappoport the golem's lure and snare, Rappoport who had played himself out in the capture of Xanthippe? He too must walk counterclockwise, behind Puttermesser, just as the Great Rabbi Judah Loew had walked counterclockwise with his disciples when the time came for the golem of Prague to be undone. The golem of Prague, city-savior, had also run amok!—terrorizing the very citizens it had been created to succor. And all the rites the Great Rabbi Judah Loew had pondered in the making of the golem, he ultimately dissolved in the unmaking of it. All the permutations and combinations of the alphabet he had recited with profound and holy concentration in the golem's creation, he afterward declaimed backward, for the sake of the golem's discomposition. Instead of meditating on the building up, he meditated on the breaking down. Whatever he had early spiraled, he late unraveled: he smashed the magnetic links that formed the chain of being between the atoms.

Puttermesser, circling round the torpid Xanthippe in her shroud of white velvet, could not help glancing down into the golem's face. It was a child's face still. Ah, Leah, Leah! Xanthippe's lids flickered. Xanthippe's lips stirred. She looked with her terrible eyes—how they pulsed—up at Puttermesser.

"My mother."

A voice!

"O my mother," Xanthippe said, still looking upward at Puttermesser, "why are you walking around me like that?"

She spoke! Her voice ascended!—a child's voice, pitched like the pure cry of a bird.

Puttermesser did not halt. "Keep moving," she told Rappoport.

"O my mother," Xanthippe said in her bird-quick voice, "why are you walking around me like that?"

Beginning the fifth circle, Rappoport gasping behind her, Puttermesser said, "You created and you destroyed."

"No," the golem cried—the power of speech released!—"it was you who created me, it is you who will destroy me! Life! Love! Mercy! Love! Life!"

The fifth circle was completed; still the golem went on bleating in her little bird's cry. "Life! Life! More!"

"More," Puttermesser said bitterly, beginning the sixth circle. "More. You wanted more and more. It's more that brought us here. More!"

"You wanted Paradise!"

"Too much Paradise is greed. Eden disintegrates from too much Eden. Eden sinks from a surfeit of itself."

"O my mother! I made you Mayor!"

Completing the sixth circle, Puttermesser said, "You pulled the City down."

"O my mother! Do not cool my heat!"

Beginning the seventh circle, Puttermesser said, "This is the last. Now go home."

"O my mother! Do not send me to the elements!"

The seventh circle was completed; the golem's small voice piped on. Xanthippe lay stretched at Puttermesser's feet like Puttermesser's own shadow.

"Trouble," Puttermesser muttered. "Somehow this isn't working, Morris. Maybe because you're not a priest or a Levite."

Rappoport swallowed a tremulous breath. "If she gets to stand, if she decides to haul herself up—"

"Morris," Puttermesser said, "do you have a pocket knife?"

Rappoport took one out.

"O my mother, mother of my life!" the golem bleated. "Only think how for your sake I undid Turtelman, Marmel, Mavett!"

Huge sly Xanthippe, gargantuan wily Xanthippe, grown up out of the little seed of a dream of Leah!

Rappoport, obeying Puttermesser, blew aside the golem's bangs and with his small blade erased from Xanthippe's forehead what appeared to be no more than an old scar—the first on the right of three such scars—queerly in the shape of a sort of letter K.

Instantly the golem shut her lips and eyes.

The *aleph* was gone.

"Dead," Rappoport said.

"Returned," Puttermesser said. "Carry her up to the attic."

"The attic? *Here?* In Gracie Mansion? Ruth, think!"

"The Great Rabbi Judah Loew undid the golem of Prague in the attic of the Altneuschul. A venerable public structure, Morris, no less estimable than Gracie Mansion."

Rappoport laughed out loud. Then he let his tongue slide out, back and forth, from right to left, along the corners of his mouth.

"Bend down, Morris."

Rappoport bent down.

"Pick up her left hand. By the wrist, that's the way."

Between Rappoport's forefinger and thumb the golem's left hand broke into four clods.

"No, it won't do. This wasn't well planned, Morris, I admit it. If we try to get her up the attic stairs—well, you can see what's happening. Never mind, I'll call the Parks Commissioner. Maybe City Hall Park—"

Then began the babbling of Rappoport.

XII. Under the flower beds

Garbage trucks are back on the streets. Their ferocious grinders gnash the City's spew. Traffic fumes, half a hundred cars immobile in a single inter-section, demoralization in the ladies' lavatories of the Municipal Building, computers down, Albany at war with City Hall, a drop in fifth-grade reading scores—the City is choking. It cannot be governed. It cannot be controlled. There is a rumor up from Florida that ex-Mayor Malachy ("Matt") Mavett is scheming to recapture City Hall. As for current patronage, there is the eg-regious case of the newly appointed Commissioner of Receipts and Disburse-ments, said to be the Mayor's old lover; he resigns for health reasons even before taking office. His wife fetches him home to Toronto. Mayor Putter-messer undergoes periodontal surgery. When it is over, the roots of her teeth are exposed. Inside the secret hollow of her head, just below the eye sockets, on the lingual side, she is unendingly conscious of her own skeleton.

The *Soho News* is the only journal to note the Mayor's order, in the middle of a summer night, for an extra load of dirt to be shoveled under the red geraniums of City Hall Park. Parks Department diggers have planted a small wooden marker among the flower beds: DO NOT TOUCH OR PICK. With wanton contempt for civic decorum, passersby often flout the modest sign. Yet whoever touches or picks those stems of blood-colored blossoms soon sickens with flu virus, or sore throat, or stuffed nose accompanied by nausea—or, sometimes, a particularly vicious attack of bursitis.

And all the while Puttermesser calls in her heart: O lost New York! And she calls: O lost Xanthippe!

At Fumicaro

Frank Castle knew everything. He was an art critic; he was a book critic; he wrote on politics and morals; he wrote on everything. He was a journalist, both in print and weekly on the radio; he had "sensibility," but he was proud of being "focussed." He was a Catholic; he read Cardinal Newman and François Mauriac and Étienne Gilson and Simone Weil and Jacques Maritain and Evelyn Waugh and Graham Greene. He reread "The Heart of the Matter" a hundred times, weeping (Frank Castle could weep) for poor Scobie. He was a parochial man who kept himself inside a frame. He had few Protestant and no Jewish friends. He said he was interested in happiness, and that was why he liked being Catholic; Catholics made him happy.

Fumicaro made him happy. To get there he left New York on an Italian liner, the Benito Mussolini. Everything about it was talkative but excessively casual. The schedule itself was casual, and the ship's engines growled in the slip through a whole day before embarkation. Aboard, the passageways were packed with noisy promenaders—munchers of stuffed buns with their entrails dripping out (in all that chaos the dock peddlers had somehow pushed through), quaffers of colored fizzy waters.

At the train station in Milan he found a car, at an exorbitant rate, to take him to Fumicaro. He was already hours late. He was on his way to the Villa Garibaldi, established by a Chicago philanthropist who had set the place up for conferences of a virtuous nature. The Fascists interfered, but not much, and out of a lazy sense of duty; so far, only a convention of lepidopterists had been sent away. One of the lepidopterists had been charged with supplying information, not about butterflies, to gangs of anti-Fascists in their hideouts in the hills around Fumicaro.

There were wonders all along the road: dun brick houses Frank Castle had thought peculiar only to certain neighborhoods in the Bronx, each with its distinctive four-sided roof and, in the dooryard of each, a fig tree tightly mummified in canvas. It was still November, but not cold, and the banks along the spiralling mountain route were rich with purple flowers. As they ascended, the driver began to hum a little, especially where the curves were most hair-raising, and when a second car came hurtling into sight from the opposite direction in a space that seemed too narrow even for one, Frank Castle believed death was near; and yet they passed safely and climbed higher. The mountain grew more and more decorous, sprouting antique topiary and far flecks of white villas.

In the Villa Garibaldi the three dozen men who were to be his colleagues were already at dinner, under silver chandeliers; there was no time for him to be taken to his room. The rumbling voices put him off a bit, but he was not altogether among strangers. He recognized some magazine acquaintances and three or four priests, one of them a public charmer whom he had interviewed on the radio. After the conference—it was called "The Church and How It is Known," and would run four days—almost everyone was planning to go on to Rome. Frank Castle intended to travel to Florence first (he hoped for a glimpse of the portrait of Thomas Aquinas in the San Marco), and then to Rome, but on the fourth day, entirely unexpectedly, he got married instead.

After dinner there was a sluggish session around the huge conference board in the hall next to the dining room—Frank Castle, who had arrived hungry, now felt overfed—and then Mr. Wellborn, the American director, instructed one of the staff (a quick hollow-faced fellow who had waited on Frank Castle's table) to lead him down to the Little Annex, the cottage where he was to sleep. It was full night now; there was a stone terrace to cross, an iron staircase down, a pebbled path weaving between lofty rows of hedges. Like the driver, the waiter hummed, and Frank Castle looked to his footing. But again there was no danger—only strangeness, and a fragrance so alluring that his nostrils strained after it with appetite. The entrance to the Little Annex was an engaging low archway. The waiter set down Frank Castle's suitcase on the gravel under the arch, handed him a big cold key, and pointed upward to a circular flight of steps. Then he went humming away.

At the top of the stairs Frank Castle saw a green door, but there was no need for the key—the door was open; the lamp was on. Disorder; the bed unmade, though clean sheets were piled on a chair. An empty wardrobe; a desk without a telephone; a bedside cabinet, holding the lit gooseneck; a loud clock and a flashlight; the crash of water in crisis. It was the sound of a toilet flushing again and again. The door to the toilet gaped. He went in and found the chambermaid on her knees before it, retching; in four days she would be his wife.

He was still rather a young man, yet not so young that he was unequal to suddenness. He was thirty-five, and much of his life had flowered out of suddenness. He did not exactly know what to do, but he seized a wash-

cloth, moistened it with cold water at the sink, and pressed it against the forehead of the kneeling woman. She shook it off with an animal sound.

He sat on the rim of the bathtub and watched her. He did not feel especially sympathetic, but he did not feel disgust either. It was as if he were watching a waterfall—a thing belonging to nature. Only the odor was unnatural. Now and then she turned her head and threw him a wild look. *Condemn what thou art, that thou mayest deserve to be what thou art not,* he said to himself; it was St. Augustine. It seemed right to him to think of that just then. The woman went on vomiting. A spurt of colorless acrid liquid rushed from her mouth. Watching serenely, he thought of some grand fountain where dolphins, or else infant cherubim, spew foamy white water from their bottomless throats. He saw her shamelessly: she was a solid little nymph. She was the coarse muse of Italia. He recited to himself, *If to any man the tumult of the flesh were silenced, silenced the phantasies of earth, waters, and air, silenced, too, the poles.*

She reached back with one hand and grasped the braid that lay along her neck. Her nape, bared, was running with sweat, and also with tears that trailed from the side of her mouth and around. It was a short robust neck, like the stem of a mushroom.

"Are you over it?" he said.

She lifted her knees from the floor and sat back on her heels. Now that she had backed away from it, he could see the shape of the toilet bowl. It was, to his eyes, foreign-looking: high, much taller than the American variety, narrow. The porcelain lid, propped upright, was bright as a mirror. The rag she had been scrubbing it with was lost in her skirt.

Now she began to hiccup.

"Is it over?"

She leaned her forehead along the base of the washstand. The light was not good—it had to travel all the way from the lamp on the table in the bedchamber and through the door, dimming as it came; nevertheless her color seemed high. Surely her lips were swollen; they could not have been intended to bulge like that. He believed he understood just how such a face ought to be composed. With her head at rest on the white pillar of the sink, she appeared to him (he said these words to himself slowly and meticulously, so clarified and prolonged was the moment for him) like an angel seen against the alabaster column that upholds the firmament. Her hiccups were loud, frequent; her shoulders jerked, and still the angel did not fall.

She said, *"Le dispiace se mi siedo qui? Sono molto stanca."*

The pointless syllables—it was his first day in Italy—made him conscious of his stony stare. His own head felt stone: was she a Medusa?—those long serpents of her spew. It occurred to him that, having commenced peacefully enough, he was far less peaceful now. He was, in fact, staring with all his might, like a statue, a stare without definition or attachment, and that was foolish. There was a glass on a shelf over the sink. He stood up and stepped over her feet (the sensation of himself as great stone arch-of-triumph darkening her body) and filled the glass with water from the tap and gave it to her.

She drank as quickly as a child, absorbed. He could hear her throat race and shut on its hinge, and race again. When the glass was empty she said, *"Molto gentile da parte sua. Mi sento così da ieri. È solo un piccolo problema."* All at once she saw how it was for him: he was a foreigner and could not understand. Recognition put a smoke of anxiety over her eyes. She said loudly, *"Scusi,"* and lapsed into a brevity of English as peculiar as any he had ever heard, surprising in that it was there at all: "No belief!" She jumped up on her thick legs and let her braid hang. *"Ho vomitato!"* she called—a war cry roughened by victorious good humor. The rag separated itself from the folds of her big skirt and slid to the floor, and just then, while he was contemplating the density of her calves and the marvel of their roundness and heaviness, she seemed as he watched to grow lighter and lighter, to escape from the fine aspiring weight that had pulled her up, and she fell like the rag, without a noise.

Her lids had slapped down. He lifted her and carried her—heaved her—onto the bed and felt for her pulse. She was alive. He had never before been close to a fainted person. If he had not seen for himself how in an instant she had shut herself off, like a faucet turned, he would have been certain that the woman he had set down on the naked gray mattress, without sheets, was asleep.

The night window was no better than a blind drawn to: no sight, no breath, no help. Only the sweet grassy smells of the dark mountainside. He ran halfway down the spiral stone staircase and then thought, Suppose, while I am gone, the woman dies. She was only the chambermaid; she was a sound girl, her cheeks vigorous and plump; he knew she would not die. He locked the door and lay down beside her in the lamplight, riding his little finger up and down her temple. It was a marvel and a luxury to be stretched out there with her, unafraid. He assured himself she would wake and not die.

He was in a spiritual condition. He had been chaste for almost six months—demandingly pure, even when alone, even inside his secret mind. His mind was a secret cave, immaculately swept and spare. It was an initiation. He was preparing himself for the first stages of a kind of monasticism. He did not mean that he would go off and become a monk in a monastery: he knew how he was of the world. But he intended to be set apart in his

own privacy: to be strong and transcendent, above the body. He did not hope to grow into a saint, yet he wanted to be more than ordinary, even while being counted as "normal." He wanted to possess himself first, so that he could yield himself, of his own accord, to the forces of the spirit.

Now here was his temptation. It seemed right—foreordained—that he would come to Italy to be lured and tempted. The small rapture versus the greater rapture—the rapture in the body and the rapture in God, and he was for the immensity. Who would not choose an ocean, with its heaven-tugged tides, over a single drop? He looked down at the woman's face and saw two wet black drops, each one an opened eye.

"Do you feel sick again? Are you all right?" he said, and took away his little finger.

"No belief! No belief!"

The terrible words, in her exhausted croak, stirred him to the beginning of a fury. What he had done, what he had endured, to be able to come at last to belief! And a chambermaid, a cleaner of toilets, could cry so freely against it!

"No belief! *Ho vomitato,* no belief!"

He knew her meaning: she was abashed, shame punched out her tears, she was sunk in absurdity and riddle. But still it shook him—he turned against her—because every day of his life he had to make this same pilgrimage to belief all over again, starting out each dawn with the hard crow's call of no belief.

"No belief! No belief!" she croaked at him.

"Stop that."

She raised herself on her wrist, her arm a bent pole. "Signore, *mi scusi,* I make the room—"

"Stay where you are."

She gestured at the pile of sheets on the chair, and fell back again.

"Do they know you're sick? Does Mr. Wellborn know?"

She said laboriously, "I am two day sick." She touched her stomach and hiccupped. "I am not sick two day like now."

He could not tell from this whether she meant she was better or worse. "Do you want more water?"

"Signore, *grazie,* no water."

"Where do you stay?" He did not ask where she lived; he could not imagine that she lived anywhere.

Her look, still wet, trailed to the window. "In the town."

"That's all the way down that long road I drove up."

"*Sì.*"

He reflected. "Do you always work so late?"

"Signore, in this morning when I am sick I no make the room, I come back to make finish the room. I make finish over there all the room"—her eyes jumped in the direction of the Villa—"only the Signore's room I no make."

He let out his breath: a wind so much from the well of his ribs that it astonished him. "They don't know where you are." He was in awe of his own lung. "You can stay here," he said.

"Oh, Signore, *grazie,* no—"

"Stay," he said, and elevated his little finger. Slowly, slowly, he dragged it across her forehead. A late breeze, heavy with the lazy fragrance of some alien night-bloomer, had cooled her. He tasted no heat in the tiny salted cavern between her nose and mouth. The open window brought him the smell of water; during the taxi's climb to the Villa Garibaldi he had scarcely permitted himself a glimpse of old shining Como, but now his nostrils were free and full: he took in the breath of the lake while again letting out his own. He unbuttoned his shirt and wiped every cranny of her face with it, even inside her ears; he wiped her mushroom neck. He had worn this shirt all the way from Leghorn, where the Benito Mussolini had docked, to Milan, and from the train station in Milan to Fumicaro. He had worn it for twenty hours. By now it was dense with the exhalations of Italy, the sweat of Milan.

When he spoke of Milan she pushed away his shirt. Her mother, she told him, lived in Milan. She was a maid at the Hotel Duomo, across from the cathedral. Everyone called her Caterina, though it wasn't her name. It was the name of the last maid, the one who got married and went away. They were like that in Milan. They treated the maids like that. The Duomo was a tourist hotel; there were many Americans and English; her mother was quick with foreign noises. Her mother's English was very good, very quick; she claimed to have learned it out of a book. An American had given her his bilingual dictionary to keep, as a sort of tip.

In Milan they were not kind. They were so far north they were almost like Germans or Swiss. They cooked like the Swiss, and they had cold hearts like the Germans. Even the priests were cold. They said ordinary words so strangely: they accused Caterina of a mischief called "dialect," but the mischief was theirs, not hers. Caterina had a daughter, whom she had left behind in Calabria. The daughter lived with Caterina's old mother, but when the daughter was thirteen Caterina summoned her north to Milan, to work in the hotel. The daughter's name was Viviana Teresa Accenno, and it was she who now lay disbelieving in Frank Castle's bed in the Little Annex of the Villa Garibaldi. Viviana at thirteen was very small, and looked no more than nine or ten. The manager of the Duomo did not wish to employ

her at all, but Caterina importuned, so he put the girl into the kitchen to help the under-chefs. She washed celery and broccoli; she washed the grit out of spinach and lettuce. She reached with the scrub brush under the stove and behind it, crevices where no one else could fit. Her arm then was a little stick for poking. Unlike Caterina, she hardly ever saw any Americans or English. Despite the bilingual dictionary, Viviana did not think that her mother could read anything at all—it was only that Caterina's tongue was so quick. Caterina kept the dictionary at the bottom of her wardrobe; sometimes she picked it up and cradled it, but she never looked into it. Still, her English was very fine, and she tried to teach it to Viviana. Viviana could make herself understood, she could say what she had to, but she could never speak English like Caterina.

Because of her good English Caterina became friends with the tourists. They gave her presents—silk scarves, and boxes made of olivewood, with celluloid crucifixes resting on velveteen inside, all the useless things tourists are attracted to—and in return she took parties out in the evenings; often they gave her money. She led them to out-of-the-way restaurants in neighborhoods they would never have found on their own, and to a clever young cobbler she was acquainted with, who worked in a shoe factory by day but measured privately for shoes at night. He would cut the leather on a Monday and have new shoes ready on a Wednesday—the most up-to-date fashions for the ladies, and for the gentlemen oxfords as sober and sturdy as anyone could wish. His prices were as low as his workmanship was splendid. The tourists all supposed he stole the leather from the factory, but Caterina guaranteed his probity and assured them this could not be. His jacket pockets were heavy with bits of leather of many shapes, and also straps and buckles, and tiny corked flacons of dye.

Caterina had all these ways of pleasing tourists, but she would not allow Viviana to learn any of them. Every Easter she made Viviana go back to spend a whole week with the grandmother in Calabria, and when Viviana returned, Caterina had a new Easter husband. She had always had a separate Milan husband, even when her Calabria husband, Viviana's father, was alive. It was not bigamy, not only because Caterina's Calabria husband had died long ago but also because Caterina had never, strictly speaking, been married in the regular way to the Milan husband. It wasn't that Caterina did not respect the priests; each day she went across the street and over the plaza to the cathedral to kneel in the nave, as broad as a sunless grassless meadow. The floor was made holy by the bones of a saint shut up in a box in front of the altar. All the priests knew her, and tried to persuade her to marry the Easter husband, and she always promised that very soon she would. And they in turn promised her a shortcut: if only she showed good will and an honest faith, she could become a decent wife overnight. But she did not, and Viviana at length understood why: the Easter husband kept changing heads. Sometimes he had one head, sometimes another, sometimes again the first. You could not marry a husband who wore a different head all the time. Except for the heads, the Easter husband was uniformly very thin, from his Adam's apple all the way down to his fancy boots. One Easter he wore the cobbler's head, but Caterina threw him out. She said he was a thief. A silver crucifix she had received as a present from a Scottish minister was missing from the bottom of the wardrobe, though the bilingual dictionary was still there. But the cobbler came back with the news that he had a cousin in Fumicaro, where they were looking for maids for the American villa there; so Caterina decided to send her daughter, who was by now sixteen and putting flesh on her buttocks. For an innocent, Caterina said, the money was safer than in Milan.

And just then the grandmother died; so Caterina and Viviana and the cobbler all travelled down to Calabria for the funeral. That night, in the grandmother's tiny house, Viviana had a peculiar adventure, though as natural as rain; it only felt peculiar because it had never happened before—she had always trusted that someday it would. The cobbler and Caterina were crumpled up together in the grandmother's shabby bed; Caterina was awake, sobbing; she explained how she was a dog at loose in the gutters, she belonged nowhere, she was a woman without a place, first a widow, now an orphan and the mother of an orphan. The highfalutin priests in the cathedral could not understand how it was for a widow of long standing. If a widow of long standing, a woman used to making her own way, becomes a wife, they will not let her make her own way anymore, she will be poorer as a poor man's wife than as a widow. What can priests, those empty pots, those eunuchs, know of the true life of a poor woman? Lamenting, Caterina fell asleep, without intending to; and then the cobbler with his bony shadow slipped out from the grandmother's bed and circled to the corner where Viviana slept, though now she was as wide awake as could be, in her cot near the stove, a cot dressed up during the day in a rosy fringed spread. It had crocheted pillow covers patterned with butterflies that the grandmother had let Viviana hold at night, like dolls. Viviana's lids were tight. She felt the saint's bones had risen from their northern altar and were sliding toward her in the dark. Caterina kept on clamorously breathing through the tunnel of her throat, and Viviana squeezed her shut eyes down on the butterflies. If she pressed them for five minutes at a time, their wings would appear to flutter. She could make their wings stir just by pressing down on them. It seemed she was making the cobbler shudder now as he moved, in just that same way; her will was surely against it, and yet he was

shuddering close to the cot. He had his undershirt on, and his bony-faced smile, and he shivered, though it was only September and the cabbage-headed trees in her grandmother's yard were luxuriant in Calabrian warmth.

After this she came to Fumicaro to work as a chambermaid at the Villa Garibaldi; she had not told her mother a thing about where the cobbler had put his legs and his arms, and not only because he had shown her the heavy metal of his belt. The cobbler was not to blame; it was her mother's mourning that was at fault, because if Caterina had not worn herself out with mourning the cobbler would have done his husband business in the regular way, with Caterina; and instead he had to do it with Viviana. All men have to do husband business, even if they are not regular husbands; it is how men are. How you are also, Signore, an American, a tourist.

It was true. In less than two hours Frank Castle had become the lover of a child. He had carried her into his bed and coaxed her story from her, beginning with his little finger's trip across her forehead. Then he had let his little finger go riding elsewhere, and elsewhere, riding and riding, until her sweat returned, and he began to sweat himself; the black night window was not feeding them enough air. Air! It was like trying to breathe through a straw. He drew the key from the door and steered her, both of them bare-foot, down the curling stairs, and walked with her out onto the gravel, through the arch. There was no moon, only a sort of gliding whitish mist low to the ground, and transitory; sometimes it was there, sometimes not. At the foot of the invisible hill, below the long hairy slope of mountainside, Como stretched like a bit of black silk nailed down. A galaxy prickled over-head, though maybe not: lights of villas high up, chips of stars—in such a blackness it was impossible to know the difference. Earth and sky were without distinction. She pointed far out, to the other side of the lake: noth-ingness. Yet there, she said, stood the pinkish palace of Il Duce, filled with seventy-five Fascist servants, and a hundred soldiers who never slept.

After breakfast, at the first meeting of the morning, a young priest read a paper. It seemed he had forgotten the point of the conference—public re-lations—and was speaking devoutly, liturgically. His subject was purity. The flesh, he said, is holy bread, like the shewbread of the Israelites, meant to be consecrated for God. To put it to use for human pleasure alone is de-filement. The words inflamed Frank Castle: he had told Viviana to save his room for last and to wait for him there in the afternoon. At four o'clock, after the day's third session, while the others went down the mountain—the members of the conference had been promised a ride across Como in a motor launch—he climbed to the green door of the Little Annex and once again took the child into his bed.

He knew he was inflamed. He felt his reason had been undermined, like a crazy man's. He could not get enough of this woman, this baby. She came to him again after dinner; then he had to attend the night session, until ten; then she was in his bed again. She was perfectly well. He asked her about the nausea. She said it was gone, except very lightly, earlier that day; she was restored. He could not understand why she was yielding to him this way. She did whatever he told her to. She was only afraid of meeting Guido, Mr. Wellborn's assistant, on her way to the Little Annex: Guido was the one who kept track of which rooms were finished, and which remained, and in what order. Her job was to make the beds and change the towels and clean the floors and the tub. Guido said the Little Annex must be done first. It was easy for her to leave the Little Annex for last—it had only two rooms in it, and the other was empty. The person who was to occupy the empty room had not yet arrived. He had sent no letter or telegram. Guido had instructed Viviana to tend to the empty room all the same, in case he should suddenly make his appearance. Mr. Wellborn was still expecting him, whoever it was.

On the third day, directly after lunch, it was Frank Castle's turn to speak. He was, after all, he said, only a journalist. His paper would be primarily neither theological nor philosophical—on the contrary, it was no more than a summary of a series of radio interviews he had conducted with new converts. He would attempt, he said, to give a collective portrait of these. If there was one feature they all had in common, it was what Jacques Maritain characterized as "the impression that evil was truly and substantially someone." To put it otherwise, these were men and women who had caught sight of demons. Let us not imagine, Frank Castle said, that—at the start—it is the love of Christ that brings souls into the embrace of Christ. It is fear; sin; evil; true cognizance of the Opposer. The corridor to Christ is at bottom the Devil, just as Judas was the necessary corridor to redemption.

He read for thirty minutes, finished to a mainly barren room, and thought he had been too metaphorical; he should have tried more for the psychological—these were modern men. They all lived, even the priests, along the skin of the world. They had cleared out, he guessed, in order to walk down the mountain into the town in the brightness of midday. There was a hot-chocolate shop, with pastry and picture postcards of Fumicaro: clusters of red tiled roofs, and behind them, like distant ice-cream cones, the Alps—you could have your feet in Italy and your gaze far into Switzerland. Around the corner from the hot-chocolate place, he heard them say, there was a little box of a shop, with a tinkling bell, easily overlooked if

you didn't know about it. It was down an alley as narrow as a thread. You could buy leather wallets, and ladies' pocketbooks, also of leather, and shawls and neckties labelled *seta pura*. But the true reason his colleagues were drawn down to the town was to stand at the edge of Como. Glorious disc of lake! It had beckoned them yesterday. It beckoned today. It summoned eternally. The bliss of its flat sun-shot surface; as dazzling as some huge coin. The room had emptied out toward it; he was not offended, not even discontent. He had not come to Fumicaro to show how clever he could be (nearly all these fellows were clever), or how devout; he knew he was not devout enough. And not to discover new renunciations, and not to catch the hooks the others let fly. And not even to be tested. He was beyond these trials. He had fallen not into temptation but into happiness. Happy, happy Fumicaro! He had, he saw, been led to Fumicaro not for the Church—or not directly for the Church, as the conference brochure promised—but for the explicit salvation of one needful soul.

She was again waiting for him. He was drilled through by twin powers: the power of joy, the power of power. She was obedient, she was his own small nun. The roundness of her calves made him think of loaves of round bread, bread like domes. She asked him—it was in a way remarkable—whether his talk had been a success. His "talk." A "success." She was alert, shrewd. It was clear she had a good brain. Already she was catching on. Her mind skipped, it was not static; it was a sort of burr that attached itself to whatever passed. He told her his paper had not been found interesting. His listeners had drifted off to look at Como. Instantly she wanted to take him there—not through the town, with its lures for tourists, but down an old stone road, mostly overgrown, back behind the Villa Garibaldi, to the lake's unfrequented rim. She had learned about it from some of the kitchen staff. He was willing, but not yet. He considered who he was; where he was. A man on fire. He asked her once more if she was well. Only a little in the morning not, she said. He was not surprised; he was prepared for it. She had missed, she said, three bleedings. She believed she might be carrying the cobbler's seed, though she had washed herself and washed herself. She had cleaned out her insides until she was as dry as a saint.

She lay with her head against his neck. Her profile was very sharp. He had seen her head a hundred times before, in museums: the painted walls of Roman villas. The oversized eyes with their black oval shine, like a pair of olives, the nose broad but so splendidly symmetrical, the top lip with its two delectably lifted points. Nevertheless she was mysteriously not handsome. It was because of her caste. She was a peasant's child. Her skin was a marvel—as if a perpetual brownish shadow had dropped close against it, partly translucent. A dark lens stretched over her cheeks, through which he saw, minutely, the clarity of her youth. He thought she was too obedient; she had no pride. Meekness separated her from beauty. She urged her mouth on his neck and counted: *Settembre, Ottobre, Novembre,* all without the bleeding.

He began to explain the beginning of his plan: in a week or two she would see New York.

"New York! No belief!" She laughed—and there was her gold tooth!—and he laughed too, because of his idiocy, his recklessness; he laughed because he had really lost his reason now and was giving himself over to holy belief. She had been disclosed to him, and on her knees; it followed that he had been sent. Her laughter was all youth and clarity and relief—what she had escaped! Deliverance. His was clownishness: he was a shaman. And recognition: he was a madman, driven like a madman or an idiot.

"You're all right," he said. "You'll be all right."

She went on laughing. "No belief! No belief! *Dio, Dio!*" She laughed out the comedy of her entanglements: a girl like herself, who has no husband, and goes three bleedings without bleeding, will be she said, "finish"— she had seized the idiom out of the air. There was no place for her but the ditch. There would never be a regular husband for her—not in Fumicaro, not in Milan, not at home in Calabria, not anywhere on any piece of God's earth inhabited by the human family. No one would touch her. They would throw her into the ditch. She was in hell. Finish. God had commanded the American signore to pull her out from the furnace of hell.

He explained again, slowly (he was explaining it to himself), in a slow voice, with the plainest words he could muster, that he would marry her and take her home with him to America. To New York.

"New York!" She *did* believe him; she believed him on the instant. Her trust was electric. The beating of her belief entered his rib cage, thrashing and plunging its beak into his spine. He could not help himself: he was his own prisoner, he was inside his own ribs, pecking there. "New York!" she said. For this she had prayed to the Holy Bambino. Oh, not for New York, she had never prayed for America, who could dream it!

No belief: he would chain himself to a rock and be flung into the sea, in order to drown unbelief.

Therefore he would marry Viviana Teresa Accenno. It was his obeisance. It was what had brought him to Italy; it was what had brought him to the Little Annex of the Villa Garibaldi. There were scores of poor young women all over Italy—perhaps in Fumicaro itself—in her position. He could not marry them all. Her tragedy was a commonplace. She was a noisy aria in an eternal opera. It did not matter. This girl was the one he had been led to. Now the power travelled from him to her; he felt the pounding of her gratitude, how it fed her, how it punished him, how she widened herself for him,

how stalwart she was, how nervy! He was in her grip, she was his slave; she had the vitality of her surrender. For a few moments it made her his master.

He did not return to the salons and chandeliers of the Villa Garibaldi that day—not for the pre-dinner session or for the after-dinner session; and not for dinner either. From then on everything went like quicksilver. Viviana ran to find Guido, to report that she was short of floor wax; he gave her the key to the supplies closet, which was also the wine cellar. Easeful Fumicaro! where such juxtapositions reigned. She plucked a flask of each: wax and wine. Mr. Wellborn blinked at such pilfering; it kept the staff content. It was only Guido who was harsh. Still, it was nothing at all for her to slip into the kitchen and spirit away a fat fresh bread and a round brick of cheese. They trod on ivy that covered the path under the windows of the grand high room that held the meadow-long conference board. Frank Castle could hear the cadenced soughing of the afternoon speaker. The sun was low but steady. She took him past enormous bricked-up arches, as tall as city apartment buildings. In the kitchen, where they were so gullible, they called it the Roman aqueduct, but nobody sensible supposed that Romans had once lived here. It was *stupido,* a tale for children. They say about the Romans that they did not have God; the priests would not let them linger in holy Italy if they did not know Jesus, so they must have lived elsewhere. She did not doubt that they had once existed, the Romans, but elsewhere. In Germany, maybe in Switzerland. Only never in Italy. The Pope of those days would never have allowed infidels to stay in such a place as Fumicaro. Maybe in Naples! Far down, under their feet, they could descry a tiny needle: it was the bell tower of the ancient church in Fumicaro. Frank Castle had already inquired about this needle. It had been put there in the twelfth century. Wild irises obscured the stone road; it wound down and down, and was so spare and uneven that they had to go single file. They met no one. It was all theirs. He had a sense of wingedness: how quickly they came to the lip of Como. The lake was all gold. A sun-ball was submerged in it as still as the yolk of an egg, and the red egg on the horizon also did not move. They encamped in a wilderness—thorny bushes and a jumble of long-necked, thick-speared grasses.

The wine was the color of light, immaculately clear, and warm, and wonderfully sour. He had never before rejoiced in such a depth of sourness—after you swallowed some and contemplated it, you entered the second chamber of the sourness, and here it was suddenly applelike. Their mouths burst into orchards. They were not hungry; they never broke off even a crumb of the bread and cheese; of these they would make a midnight supper, and in the early morning he would pay something to the milk driver, who would carry them as far as he could. The rest of the trip they would go by bus, like ordinary people. Oh, they were not ordinary! And in Milan Viviana would tell Caterina everything—everything except about where the cobbler had put his legs and his arms; she would not mention the cobbler at all—and Caterina would lead them across the plaza into the cathedral, and the priests would marry them in the shortcut way they had always promised for Caterina and her Easter husband.

It was nearly night. Como had eaten the red egg; it was gone. Streaks of white and pink trailed over water and sky. There was still enough light for each to see the other's face. They passed the bottle of wine between them, back and forth, from hand to hand, stumbling upward, now and then wandering wide of the path—the stones were sometimes buried. A small abandoned shrine blocked the way. The head was eroded, the nose chipped. "This must be a Roman road," he told her. "The Romans built it."

"No belief!" It was becoming their life's motto.

The air felt miraculously dense, odorous with lake and bush. It could almost be sucked in, it was so liquidly thick. They spiralled higher, driving back the whiplike growth that snapped at their eyes. She could not stop laughing, and that made him start again. He knew he was besotted.

Directly in front of them the grasses appeared to part. Noises: rustle and flutter and an odd abrasive sound—there was no mistake, the bushes were moving. The noises ran ahead with every step they took; the disturbance in the bushes and the growling scrape were always just ahead. He thought of the malcontents who were said to have their hiding places in the mountains—thugs; he thought of small mountain beasts that might scramble about in such a space—a fox? He was perfectly ignorant of the usual habitat of foxes. Then—in what was left of the dusk—he caught sight of a silhouette considerably bigger and less animate than a fox. It was a squarish thing kicking against the vegetation and scudding on the stones. It looked to be attached to a pallid human shape, broad but without glimmer, also in silhouette.

"Hello?" said an elderly American voice. "Anybody back there speak English?"

"Hello," Frank Castle called.

The square thing was a suitcase.

"Damn cab let me off at the bottom. Said he wouldn't go up the hill in the dark. Didn't trust his brakes. Damn lazy thieving excuse—I paid him door to door. This can't be the regular way up anyhow."

"Are you headed for the Villa Garibaldi?"

"Three days late to boot. You mixed up in it? Oh, it just stirs my blood when they name a bed to sleep in after a national hero."

"I'm mixed up in it. I came on the Benito Mussolini," Frank Castle said.

"Speaking of never getting a night's sleep. So did I. Didn't see you aboard. Didn't see anyone. Stuck to the bar. Not that I can see you now, getting pitch black. Don't know where the hell I am. Dragging this damn thing. Is that a kid with you? I'll pay him to lug my bag."

Frank Castle introduced himself, there on the angle of the mountainside, on the Roman road, in the tunnelling night. He did not introduce Viviana. All his life it would be just like that. She crept back off the bit of path into the thornbushes.

"Percy Nightingale," the man said. "Thank you kindly, but never mind, if the kid won't take it, I'll carry it myself. Damn lazy types. How come you're on the loose, they haven't corralled you for the speeches?"

"You've missed mine."

"Well, I don't like to get to these things too early. I can sum up all the better if I don't sit through too many speeches—I do a summing-up column for the *All-Parish Wick*. Kindles Brooklyn and Staten Island. What've I missed besides you?"

"Three days of inspiration."

"Got my inspiration in Milan, if you want the truth. Found a little inn with a bar and had myself a bender. Listen, you've got to see the 'Last Supper'— it's just about over. Peeling. They stick the paint back down somehow, but I give it no more'n fifty years. And for God's sake don't skip the unfinished 'Pietà'—arms and legs in such a tangle you wouldn't believe. Extra legs stuck in. My God, what now?" They had come flat out against a wall.

Viviana jumped into the middle of the stone road and zigzagged leftward. An apparition of battlements: high box hedges. Without any warning they had emerged right under the iron staircase abutting the kitchen of the Villa Garibaldi.

Climbing, the man with the suitcase said, "The name's familiar. Haven't I heard you on the radio, WJZ, those interviews with convicts?"

"Converts."

"I know what I said."

Viviana had evaporated.

"Are you the one Mr. Wellborn's expecting?"

"Mister who?"

"Wellborn," Frank Castle said. "The director. You'd better go to his office first. I think we're going to be neighbors."

"Love thy neighbor as thyself. He doesn't sound like a Wop."

"He's a Presbyterian from New Jersey."

"Myself, I'm a specialist. Not that I ever got my degree. I specialize in Wops and Presbyterians. Ad hoc and à la carte. We all have to make a living."

In his cups, Frank Castle thought. Then he remembered that he was drunk himself. He dug into his pocket and said with patient annoyance, "You know you can still catch the night session if you want. Here, take my program. It lists the whole conference. They were handing these out after Mass on the first day."

Percy Nightingale said, "After Mass? Liturgy giving birth to jargon. The sublime giving birth to what you'd damn well better be late arriving at."

But it was too dark to read.

In the Little Annex, behind the green door, Frank Castle began to pack. The wine had worn off. He wondered whether his stupefying idea—his idiocy—would wear off. He tested his will: was it still firm? He had no will. He had no purpose. He did not know what he was thinking. He was not thinking of a wedding. He felt infinitely bewildered. He stood staring at his shirts. Had Viviana run down the mountain again, into Fumicaro, to fetch her things from her room? They had not planned that part. Somehow he took it for granted that she had no possessions, or that her possessions did not matter, or were invisible. He saw that he had committed the sin of heroism, which always presumes that everyone else is unreal, especially the object of rescue. She was the instrument of his carnality, the occasion of his fall; no more than that, though that was too much. He had pushed too far. A stranger, a peasant's child. He was no more capable of her salvation than of his own.

The doorknob turned. He hardly understood what he would say to her. After all she was a sort of prostitute, the daughter of a sort of prostitute. He did not know exactly what these women were—the epiphenomena, he supposed, of the gradual movement, all over the world, of the agricultural classes to the city. He was getting his reason back again. She, on her side, was entirely reasonable. An entrapment. Such women are always looking for free tickets to the New World. She had planted herself in his room—just his luck—to pretend sickness. All right, she hadn't pretended; he could see it wasn't pretense. All the more blatant. A scheme; a pit; a noose. With her bit of English she had examined the conference lists and found her eligible prey: an unmarried man. The whole roster were married men—it was only the priests and himself. So she had done her little research. A sensible girl who goes after what she wants. He was willing to give her some money, though God was his witness he didn't have so much that he could take on an extended program of philanthropy—his magazine, the *Sacral Review,* was making good his expenses. All the same he had to pinch. It was plain to him that she had never expected him to redeem the impulse of his dementia. It was his relief—the relief he felt in coming to his senses—that she

had all along meant to exploit. Relief and the return of sanity were what he had to pay for. Mild enough blackmail. He wrenched his head round.

There stood Nightingale, anxiously jubilating and terrifically white. He had, so far, been no more than an old man's voice in the night, and to the extent that a voice represents a soul, he had falsified, he had misrepresented utterly. He was no older than Frank Castle, and it was not only that he was alarmingly indistinct—his ears were blanched; his mouth was a pinkish line; his eyes, blue overrinsed to a transparency, were humps in a face as flat as zinc. He was almost blotted out. His look was a surprise: white down to his shoes, and immensely diffident. His shirt was white, his thighs were white, his shoes the same, and even shyer; he was self-effacing. He had already taken off his pants—he was without dazzle or glare. Washed out to a Celtic pallor. Frank Castle was unsure, with all this contradiction between words and appearance, where to put his confidence.

"You're right. Neighbors," Nightingale said. "You can have your program back, I've got the glory of my own now. It's a wonder *any*one shows up for these things. It puts the priests to sleep, not that you can tell the difference when they're awake. I don't mind myself forgoing the pleasure"—he shook open the little pamphlet—"of, get this, *Approaches to Bigotry. The Church and the Community, North, East, South, West. The Dioceses of Savannah, Georgia, and Denver, Colorado, Compared. Parish or Perish*. My God, I wish I could go to bed."

"No one's forcing you to attend," Frank Castle said.

"You bet they're not. If I sum up better by turning up late, I sum up best if I don't turn up at all. Listen, I like a weight on me when I sleep. No matter what the climate or the weather, put me in the tropics, I've got to have plenty of blankets on me. I told them so in the office—they're sending the chambermaid. Not that she isn't taking her own sweet time. No wonder, godforsaken place they've stuck us in, way down here. The rest get to sleep like princes in the palace. I know about me, I always get the short straw, but what's your crime, you're not up at the big house? Hey, you packing?"

Was he really packing? There were his shirts in a mound, folded and waiting to be folded, and his camera; there was his open suitcase.

"Not that I blame you, running off. Three days of it should do anyone." Nightingale tossed the pamphlet on the bed. "You've paid your dues. Especially if you got to stick in your two cents with the speechifying—what on?"

Footsteps on the circling stairs. Heavy goat hops. Viviana, obscured by blankets. She did not so much as glance in.

"Interviews with convicts," Frank Castle said.

Nightingale guffawed—the pouncing syllables of a hawk, the thread of the lips drawn covertly in. A hider. Recklessness at war with panic. Mistrusting the one, Frank Castle believed in the other. Panic. "What's your fix on these fellows? Cradle Catholics in my family since Adam, if not before, but I got my catechism from Father Leopold Robin."

"Never heard of him."

"Wouldn't expect you to. *Né* Rabinowitz."

Frank Castle felt himself heat up. The faintest rise of vertigo. It was stupid to give in to peculiar sensations just because Viviana hadn't looked in the door. He said, "Would you mind asking the chambermaid"—the word tugged at his tongue, as if it had fallen into something glutinous—"to stop by when she's finished? They haven't changed my towels—"

"A whole speech on seeing the light? That's what you did? Too pious for me."

"Scientific. I put in the statistics. Enough to please even a specialist. How many converts per parish, what kinds of converts, from what kinds of backgrounds."

But he was listening to the small sounds in the next room.

Nightingale said, "Clare Boothe Luce. There's your trophy."

"We get all sorts these days. Because of the ascent of the Devil. Everyone's scared of the Devil. The rich and the poor. The soft and the arrogant—"

"And who's the Devil? You one of these fellows think Adolf's the new Satan? At least he holds off against the Commies."

"I'm willing to think you're the Devil," Frank Castle said.

"You're a touchy one."

"Well, the Devil's in all of us."

"Touchy and pious—I told you pious. You wouldn't think it would take a year to drop two blankets on a bed! All right, I'll send you that girl." He took two steps into the corridor and turned back. "This Father Robin wore the biggest crucifix you ever saw. Maybe it only looked that big—I was just a kid. But that's how it is with those convicts—they're self-condemned, so they take their punishment more seriously than anybody. It gives me the willies when they come in hotter'n Hades. They act like a bunch of goddam Holy Rollers with lights in their sockets. Show me a convert, I'll show you a fellow out to get even with someone. They're killers."

"Killers?"

"They kill the old self for the sake of the new self. Conversion," Nightingale said, "is revenge."

"You're forgetting Christ."

"Oh Jesus God. I never forget Christ. Why else would I end up in this goddam shack in this godforsaken country? Maybe the Fascists'll make

something out of these Wops yet. Put some spine in 'em. You want that girl?
I'll get you that girl."

Left to himself, Frank Castle dropped his head into his hands. With his
eyes shut, staring into the flesh of his lids, he could see a whirligig of gold
flecks. He had met a man and instantly despised him. It seemed to him that
everyone here, not counting the handful of priests, was a sham—mounte-
banks all. And, for that matter, the priests as well. Public-relations types.
Journalists, editors. In an older time these people would have swarmed
around the marketplace selling indulgences and hawking pigs' hair.

The chambermaid came in. She was a fleshless uncomprehending spindly
woman of about forty, perspiring at the neck, with ankles like balloons.
There was a purple mark in the middle of her left cheek. "Signore?" she said.

He went into the toilet and brought out a pair of fresh bath towels. "I
won't need these. I'm leaving. You might as well do whatever you want
with them." She shook her head and backed away. He had already taken it
in that she would not be able to follow a word. And anyhow his charade
made no sense. Still, she accepted the towels with a maddening docility; she
was no different from Viviana. Any explanation, or no explanation, was all
the same to these creatures. He said, "Where's the other maid who always
comes?"

The woman stared.

"Viviana," he said.

"Ah! *L'altra cameriera.*"

"Where is she?"

With the towels stuck firmly under one armpit, she lifted her shoulders
and held out her palms; then shut the door smartly behind her. A desolation
entered him. He decided to attend the night session.

The meadow-long conference board had grown slovenly. Notebooks,
squashed paper balls, pencils without points, empty pitchers and dirty
cups, an exhausted coffee urn, languid eyeglasses lying with their ear-
pieces askew, here and there a leg thrown up on the table: formality had
vanished, decay was crawling through. The meeting was well under way;
the speaker was annunciating Pascal. It was very like a chant—he had
sharp tidy hand gestures, a grocer slicing cheese. "'Not only do we understand God only through Jesus Christ, but we understand ourselves only
through Jesus Christ. We understand life and death only through Jesus
Christ. Outside Jesus Christ we do not know what life is, nor death, nor
God, nor ourselves.' These words do not compromise; they do not try to get
along with those who are indifferent to them, or with those who would
laugh at them. They are neither polite nor gentle. They take their stand, and
their stand is eternal and absolute. Today the obligation of Catholic public

relations is not simply to defend the Church, though there is plenty of that to be done as well. In America especially we live with certain shadows, yet here in the mountains and valleys of Fumicaro, in glorious Italy, the Church is a serene mother, and it is of course easy to forget that she is troubled elsewhere. Elsewhere she is defamed as the refuge of superstition. She is accused of unseemly political advantages. She is assaulted as a vessel of archaism and as an enemy of the scientific intelligence. She is pointed to as an institution whose whole raison d'être is the advance of clerical power. Alas, the Church in her true soul, wearing her Heavenly garments, is not sufficiently understood or known.

"All this public distortion is real enough, but our obligation is even more fundamental than finding the right lens of clarification to set over the falsifying portrait. The need to defend the Church against the debasement of the ignorant or the bigoted is, how shall we call it, a mere ripple in the sacred river. Our task as opinion-makers—and we should feel no shame over this phrase, with all its American candor, for are we not Americans at an American colloquy, though we sit here charmed by the antiquity of our surroundings?—our task, then, is to show the timelessness of our condition, the applicability of our objectifying vision even to flux, even to the immediate instant. We are to come with our high banner inscribed Eternity, and demonstrate its pertinence in the short run; indeed, in the shortest run of all, the single life, the single moment. We must let flower the absolute in the concrete, in the actual rise and fall of existence. Our aim is transmutation, the sanctification of the profane."

It was impossible to listen; Nightingale was right. Frank Castle sank down into some interior chamber of mind. He was secretive; he knew this about himself. It was not that he had habits of concealment, or that, as people say, he kept his own counsel. It was instead something akin to sensation, an ache or a bump. Self-recognition. Every now and then he felt the jolt of who he was and what he had done. He was a man who had invented his own designations. He was undetermined. He was who he said he was. No one, nothing, least of all chance, had put him in his place. Like Augustine, he interpreted himself, and hotly. Oh, hotly. Whereas this glacial propagandist, reciting his noble text, bleating out "absolute" and "concrete" and "transmutation," had fallen into his slot like a messenger from fate. Once fallen, fixed. Rooted. A stalactite.

Far behind the speaker, just past the lofty brass-framed doorway—a distance of several pastures, a whole countryside—a plump little figure glimmered. Viviana! There she was; there she stood. You would need a telescope to bring her close. Even with his unaccoutred eye, Frank Castle noticed how nicely she was dressed: if he had forgotten that she might have possessions,

here was something pleasant—though it was only a blouse and skirt. She was clutching an object, he could not make out what. The blouse had a bright blue ribbon at the neck, and long sleeves. It might have been the ribbon, or the downward flow of the sleeves, or even the skirt, red as paint, which hung lower than he was used to—there was a sudden propriety in her. The wonderful calves were hidden: those hot domes he had only that afternoon drawn wide apart. Her thighs, too, were as hot and heavy as corn bread. Across such a space her head, remote and even precarious, was weighted down, like the laden head of a sunflower. She was absorbed by the marble floor tiles of the Villa Garibaldi. She would not come near. She eclipsed herself. She was a bit of shifting reflection.

He wondered if he should wait the speaker out. Instead he got up—every step a crash—and circled the table's dishevelled infinity. No one else moved. He was a scandal. Under the chandelier the speaker stuck to his paper. Frank Castle had done the same the day before, when they had all walked out on him for a ride across Como. Now here he was deserting, the only one to escape. It was almost ten o'clock at night; the whole crew of them had been up since eight. One had made a nest of his rounded arms and was carefully, sweetly, cradling his face down into it. Another was propped back with his mouth open, brazenly asleep, something between a wheeze and a snuffle puffing intermittently out.

In the hall outside he said, "You've changed your clothes."

"We go Milano!"

She was in earnest then. Her steady look, diverted downward, was patient, docile. He did not know what to make of her; but her voice was too high. He set an admonitory finger over his own mouth. "Where did you disappear to?"

"I go, I put"—he watched her labor after the words; excitement throttled her—"*fiore. Il santo!* To make *un buon viaggio.*"

He was clear enough about what a *santo* was. "A saint? Is there a saint here?"

"You see before, in the road. You see him," she insisted. She held up a metal cylinder. It was the flashlight from his bedside cabinet in the Little Annex. "Signore, come."

"Do you have things? You're taking things?"

"*La mia borsa, una piccola valigia.* I put in the Signore's room."

They could not stand there whispering. He followed where she led. She took him down the mountainside again, along the same half-buried road, to a weedy stone stump. It was the smothered little shrine he had noticed earlier. It grew right up out of the middle of the path. The head, with its rotted nose, was no more than a smudge. Over it, as tall as his hipbone, a kind of stone umbrella, a shelter like an upside-down U, or a fragment of vertical bathtub, seemed to be turning into a mound of wild ivy. Spiking out of this dense net was the iris Viviana had stuck there.

"San Francesco!" she said; the kitchen staff had told her. Such hidden old saints were all over the hills of Fumicaro.

"No," Frank Castle said.

"*Molti santi.* You no belief? Look, Signore. San Francesco."

She gave him the flashlight. In its white pool everything had a vivid glaze, like a puppet stage. He peered at the smudge. Goddess or god? Emperor's head, mounted like a milestone to mark out sovereignty? The chin was rubbed away. The torso had crumbled. It hardly looked holy. Depending on the weather, it might have been as old as a hundred years, or a thousand; two thousand. Only an archeologist could say. But he did not miss how the flashlight conjured up effulgence. A halo blazed. Viviana was on her knees in the scrub; she tugged him down. With his face in leaves he saw the eroded fragment of the base, and, half sunken, an obscure tracing, a single intact word: "DELEGI." I chose; I singled out. Who chose, what or who was singled out? Antiquity alone did not enchant him: the disintegrating image of some local Roman politico or evanescent godlet. The mighty descend to powder and leave chalk on the fingertips.

Her eyes were shut; she was now as she had been in her small faint, perfectly ordered; but her voice was crowded with intense little mutterings. She was at prayer.

"Viviana. This isn't a saint."

She stretched forward and kissed the worn-away mouth.

"You don't know *what* it is. It's an old pagan thing."

"San Francesco," she said.

"No."

She turned on him a smile almost wild. The thing in the road was holy to her. It had a power; she was in thrall to sticks and stones. "*Il santo,* he pray for us." In the halo of the flashlight her cheeks looked oiled and sleek and ripe for biting. She crushed her face down into the leaves beside his own— it was as if she read him and would consent to be bitten—and said again, "Francesco."

He had always presumed that sooner or later he would marry. He had spiritual ambition; yet he wanted to join himself to the great protoplasmic heave of human continuity. He meant to be fruitful: to couple, to procreate. He could not be continent; he could not sustain purity; he was not chaste. He had a terrible impulsiveness; his fall with Viviana was proof enough. He loved the priests, with their parched lip-corners and glossy eyes, their

enigmatic loins burning for God. But he could not become like them; he was too fitful. He had no humility. Sometimes he thought he loved Augustine more than God. *Imitatio Dei:* he had come to Christ because he was secretive, because Jesus lived, though hiddenly. Hence the glory of the thousand statues that sought to make manifest the reticent Christ. Sculptors, like priests, are least of all secretive.

Often it had seemed to Frank Castle that, marriage being so open a cell, there was no one for him to marry. Wives were famous for needing explanations. He could not imagine not being married to a bookish sort—an "intellectual"—but also he feared this more than anything. He feared a wife who could talk and ask questions and analyze and inquire after his history. Sometimes he fancied himself married to a rubber doll about his own size. She would serve him. They would have a rubber child.

A coldness breathed from the ground. Already hoarfrost was beginning to gather—a blurry veil over the broken head in the upended tub.

He said, "Get up."

"Francesco."

"Viviana, let's go." But he hung back himself. She was a child of simple intuitions, a kind of primitive. He felt how primitive she was. She was not a rubber doll, but she would keep clear of the precincts of his mind. This gladdened him. He wondered how such a deficiency could make him so glad.

She said for the third time, "Francesco." He understood finally that she was speaking his name.

They spent the night in his room in the Little Annex. At six the milk driver would be grinding down from the kitchen lot past the arch of the Little Annex. They waited under a brightening sunrise. The mist was fuming free of the mountainside; they could see all the way down to Como. Quietly loitering side by side with the peasant's child, again Frank Castle felt himself slowly churning into chaos: half an hour ago she had stretched to kiss his mouth exactly as she had stretched to kiss the mouth of the pagan thing fallen into the ground. He was mesmerized by the strangeness he had chosen for himself: a whole life of it. She was holding his hand like an innocent; her fingers were plaited into his. And then, out of the blue, as if struck by a whirlwind, they were not. She tore herself from him; his fingers were ripped raw; it seemed like a seizure of his own skin; he lost her. She had hurled herself nearly out of sight. Frank Castle watched her run—she looked flung. She ran into the road and down the road and across, behind the high hedges, away from the bricked-up vaults of the Roman aqueduct.

Percy Nightingale was descending from those vaults. Under his open overcoat a pair of bare bluish-white knees paraded.

"Greetings," he called, "from a practiced insomniac. I've been examining the local dawn. They do their dawns very nicely in these parts, I'll give 'em *that*. What detritus we travellers gather as we move among the realms—here you are with two bags, and last night I'm sure I saw you with only one. You don't happen to have any extra booze in one of those?" He stamped vaguely round in an uneven try at a circle. "Who was that rabbit who fled into the bushes?"

"I think you scared it off," Frank Castle said.

"The very sight of me? It's true I'm not dressed for the day. I intend to pull on my pants in time for breakfast. You seem to be waiting for a train."

"For the milk driver."

"Aha. A slow getaway. You'd go quicker with the booze driver. I'd come along for kicks with the booze driver."

"The fact of the matter," Frank Castle said in his flattest voice, "is that you've caught me eloping with the chambermaid."

"What a nice idea. Satan, get thee behind me and give me a push. Long and happy years to you both. The scrawny hag with the pachyderm feet and the birthmark? She made up my bed very snugly—I'd say she's one of the Roman evidences they've got around here." He pointed his long chin upward toward the aqueduct. "Since you didn't invite me to the exhumation, I won't expect to be invited to the wedding. Believe it or not, here's your truck."

Frank Castle picked up Viviana's bag and his own and walked out into the middle of the road, fluttering his green American bills; the driver halted.

"See you in the funny papers," Nightingale yelled.

He sat in the seat next to the driver's and turned his face to the window. The road snaked left and then left again: any moment now a red-skirted girl would scuttle out from behind a dip in the foliage. He tried to tell this to the driver, but the man only chirped narrowly through his country teeth. The empty steel milk cans on the platform in the back of the truck jiggled and rattled; sometimes their flanks collided—a robust clang like cymbals. It struck him then that the abyss in his belly was his in particular: it wasn't fright at being discovered and judged that had made her bolt but practical inhibition—she was canny enough, she wasn't about to run off with a crazed person. Lust! He had come to his senses yesterday, though only temporarily; she had come to hers today, and in the nick of time. After which it occurred to him that he had better look in his wallet. Duped. She had robbed him and escaped. He dived into his pocket.

Instantly the driver's open palm was under his nose.

"I paid you. *Basta,* I gave you *basta.*"

The truck wobbled perilously around a curve, but the hand stayed.

"Good God! Keep hold of the wheel, can't you? We'll go off the road!"

He shook out a flood of green bills onto the seat. Now he could not know how much she had robbed him of. He did not doubt she was a thief. She had stolen cheese from the kitchen and wine from a locked closet. He thought of his camera. It would not surprise him if she had bundled it off in a towel or a pillowcase in the night. Thievery had been her motive from the beginning. Everything else was ruse, snare, distraction, flimflam; she was a sort of gypsy, with a hundred tricks. He would never see her again. He was relieved. The freakishness of the last three days stung him; he grieved. Never again this surrender to the inchoate; never again the abyss. A joke! He had almost eloped with the chambermaid. Damn Nightingale!

They rattled—sounding now like a squad of carillons—into Fumicaro. Here was the promenade; here was the hot-chocolate shop; here was the church with its bell tower; here was morning-dazzled Como—high and pure the light that rose from it. "Autobus," he commanded the driver. He had spilled enough green gold to command. The country teeth showed the bliss of the newly rich. He was let out at an odd little turn of gossipy street, which looked as if it had never in all its existence heard tell of a bus; and here—"No belief!"—was Viviana, panting hard. She could not catch her breath, because of the spy. A spy had never figured in their fears, God knows! A confusion and a danger. The spy would be sure to inform Guido, and Guido would be sure to inform Mr. Wellborn, or, worse yet, the cobbler's cousin, who, as it happened, was Guido's cousin, too, only from the other side of the family. And then they would not let her go. No, they would not! They would keep her until her trouble became visible and ruinous, and then they would throw her into the ditch. The spy was an untrustworthy man. He was the man they had met on the hill, who took her for a boy. He was the man in the empty room of the Little Annex. The other *cameriera* had told her that on top of all the extra blankets she had brought him he had put all the towels there were, and then, oh! he pulled down the curtains and piled them on top of the towels. And he stood before the other *cameriera* shamelessly, without his *pantaloni!* And so what could she do? She flew down the secret stone path, she flew right past San Francesco without stopping, to get to the autobus piazza before the milk driver.

Droplets of sweat erupted in a phalanx on her upper lip. She gave him the sour blink of an old woman; he glimpsed the Calabrian grandmother, weathered by the world's suspiciousness. "You think I no come?"

He would not tell that he thought she had stolen.

"No belief!" Out tumbled her hot laugh, redolent of his bed in the Little Annex. "When *questo bambino* finish"—she pressed the cushion of her belly—"you make new *bambino*, O.K.?"

* * *

In Milan that evening (his fourth in Italy), in a cramped cold chapel in the cathedral, within sight of the relic, they were married by a priest who was one of Caterina's special friends.

Caterina herself surprised him: she was dressed like a businesswoman. She wore a black felt hat with a substantial brim; she was substantial everywhere. Her head was set alertly on a neck that kept turning, as if wired to a generator; there was nothing she did not take in with her big powerful shining eyes. He felt that she took *him* in, all in a gulp. Her arm shot out to smack Viviana, because Viviana, though she had intended to continue not to tell about the cobbler, on her wedding day could not dissemble. The arm drew back. Caterina would not smack Viviana in front of a tourist, an American, on her wedding day. She was respectful. Still, it was a slander—the cobbler did not go putting seeds into the wombs of innocent girls. Twisting her neck, Caterina considered the American.

"Three days? You are friend of my Viviana three days, Signore?" She tapped her temple, and then made circles in the air with her forefinger. "For what you want to marry my Viviana if you no put the seed?"

He knew what a scoundrel he seemed. The question was terrifying; but it was not meant for him. They went at it, the mother and the daughter, weeping and shrieking, in incomprehensible cascades: it was an opera, extravagant with drama, in a language he could not fathom. All this took place in Caterina's room in the Hotel Duomo, around the corner from a linen closet as capaciously fitted with shelves as a library; he sat in a chair face to face with the wardrobe in which the bilingual dictionary was secreted. The door was at his right hand—easy enough to grab the knob and walk away. For nearly an hour he sat. The two barking mouths went on barking. The hands clenched, grasped, pushed. He felt detached, distant; then, to his amazement, at a moment of crescendo, when the clamor was at its angriest, the two women fell into each other's embrace. Implausible as it was, preposterous as it was, Caterina was sending Viviana to America. *Un colpo di fulmine! Un fulmine a ciel sereno!*

Just before the little ceremony, the priest asked Frank Castle how he would feel about a baby that was—as he claimed—not his. Frank Castle could not think what to say. The priest was old and exhausted. He spoke of sin as of an elderly dog who is too sick to be companionable—yet you are used to him, you can't do without him, you can't bring yourself to get rid of him. The wedding ring was Caterina's.

Frank Castle exchanged his return ticket for two others on the Stella Italiana, sailing for New York in ten days. It was all accident and good luck: someone had cancelled. There were two available places. That left time for

the marriage to be accorded a civil status: the priest explained to Caterina that though in the eyes of God Viviana was now safe, they had to fetch a paper from the government and get it stamped. This was the law.

There was time for Milan. It was very queer: Viviana had been brought to this northern treasure-city as a girl of thirteen and still did not know where the "Last Supper" was. Caterina knew; she even knew who had made it. "Leonardo da Vinci," she recited proudly. But she had never seen it. She took Viviana away to shop for a trousseau; they bought everything new but shoes, because Viviana was stubborn. She refused to go to the cobbler. *"Ostinata!"* Caterina said, but a certain awe had begun to creep into her fury. Viviana had found an American husband who talked on the radio in New York! Il Duce talked on the radio, too, and they could hear him as far away as America. Viviana a bride! Married, and to a tourist! These were miracles. Someone, Caterina said, had kissed a saint.

The "Last Supper" was deteriorating. It had to be looked at from behind a velvet rope. Viviana said it was a pity the camera hadn't yet been invented when Our Lord walked the earth—a camera would get a *much* better picture of Our Lord than the one in the flaking scene on the wall. Frank Castle taught her how to use his camera, and she snapped him everywhere; they snapped each other. They had settled into Caterina's room, but they had to come and go with caution, so that the manager would not know. It cost them nothing to stay in Caterina's room. Caterina did not say where she went to sleep; she said she had many friends who would share. When Viviana asked her who they were, Caterina laughed. "The priests!" she said. All over the Duomo, Frank Castle was treated with homage, as a person of commercial value. He was an American with an Italian wife. In the morning they had coffee in the dining room. The waiter gave his little bow. Viviana was embarrassed. At the Villa Garibaldi she had deferred to the waiters; no one was so low as the *cameriera*. It made her uncomfortable to be served. Frank Castle told her she was no longer a *cameriera;* soon she would be an American. Unforgiving, she confided that Caterina had gone to stay with the cobbler.

He took her—it was still Nightingale's itinerary—to see the unfinished "Pietà" in a castle with bartizans and old worn bricks; schoolchildren ran in and out of the broad grassy trench that had once been the moat, but Viviana was unmoved. It was true that she admired the lustre of Our Lady's perfect foot, as polished as the marble flagging of the Villa Garibaldi; the rest was mainly rough rock. She thought it ridiculous to keep a thing like that on display. Our Lord didn't have a face. The Virgin didn't have a face. They looked like two ghouls. And this they called religion! What sense was it that the *muratore* who made it was famous—his sprawling Jesus was no more beautiful or *sacro* than a whitewashed wall falling down. And without a face! She let Frank Castle take her picture in her new bird-speckled dress in front of all that rubble, and meanwhile she described the statue of Our Lady that had stood on a shelf in her own plain room at Fumicaro. The Madonna's features were perfect in every detail—there were even wonderfully tiny eyelashes glued on, made of actual human hair. And all in the nicest brightest colors, the eyes a sweet blue, the cheeks rosy. The Holy Bambino was just as exact. He had a tiny belly button with a blue rhinestone in it, to match Our Lady's blue robe, and under his gauzy diaper he even had a lacquered penis that showed through, the color of a human finger, though much tinier. He had tiny celluloid fingernails! A statue like that, Viriana said, is *molto sacro*—she had kneeled before it a thousand times. She had cried penitential floods because of the bleeding that did not come. She had pleaded with Our Lady for intercession with the Holy Bambino, and the Holy Bambino had heard her prayer. She had begged the Holy Bambino, if He could not make the bleeding come, to send a husband, and He had sent a husband.

They walked through rooms of paintings: voluptuous Titians; but Frank Castle was startled only by the solidity of Viviana. Ardor glowed in her. He had arrived in Italy with two little guidebooks, one for Florence and one for Rome, but he had nothing for Milan. Viviana herself was unmapped. Everything was a surprise. He could not tell what lay around the corner. He marvelled at what he had done. On Monday, at Fumicaro, Augustine and philosophy; on Thursday, the chattering of a brown-eyed bird-speckled simple-minded girl. His wife. His little peasant wife, a waif with a baby inside her! All his life he would feel shame over her. To whom could he show her without humiliation?

Her ignorance moved and elevated him. He thought of St. Francis rejoicing in the blows and ridicule of a surly innkeeper: *Willingly and for the love of Christ let me endure pains and insults and shame and want, inasmuch as in all other gifts of God we may not glory, since they are not ours but God's.* Frank Castle understood he would always be mocked because of this girl; he went on snapping his camera at her. How robust she was, how gleaming, how happy! She was more hospitable to God than anyone who hoped to find God in books. She gave God a home everywhere—in old Roman tubs, in painted wooden dolls: it did not matter. Sticks and stones. He saw that no one had taught her to clean under her fingernails. He puzzled over it: she was the daughter of a trader in conveniences, she was herself a kind of commodity; she believed herself fated, a vessel for anyone's use. He had married shame. Married! It was what he had done. But he felt no remorse; none. He was exhilarated—to have had the courage for such a humbling!

In front of them, hanging from a crossbar, was a corpse made of oak. It was the size of a real man, and had the head of a real man. It wore a wreath made of real brambles, and there were real holes in its body, with real nails beaten into them.

Viviana dropped to the floor and clasped her hands.

"Viviana, people don't pray here."

Her mouth went on murmuring.

"You don't *do* that in a place like this."

"Una chiesa," she said.

"People don't pray in museums." Then it came to him that she did not know what a museum was. He explained that the pictures and statues were works of art. And he was married to her! "There aren't any priests," he said.

She shot him a look partly comical and partly shocked. Even priests have to eat, she protested. The priests were away, having their dinner. Here it was almost exactly like the *chiesa* at Fumicaro, only more crowded. At the other *chiesa,* where they kept the picture of the "Last Supper," there were also no priests to be seen, and did that prove it wasn't a *chiesa?* Caterina had always told her how ignorant tourists were. Now she would have to put in an extra prayer for him, so that he could feel more sympathy for the human hunger of priests.

She dipped her head. Frank Castle circled all around the medieval man of wood. Red paint, dry for seven centuries, spilled from the nail holes. Even the back of the figure had its precision: the draw of muscles stretching in fatigue. The carver had not stinted anywhere. Yet the face was without a grain of pious inspiration. It was as if the carver had cared only for the carving itself, and not for its symbol. The man on the crossbar was having his live body imitated, and that was all. He was a copy of the carver's neighbor perhaps, or else a cousin. When the carving was finished, the neighbor or cousin stepped down, and together he and the carver hammered in the nails.

The nails. Were they for pity? They made him feel cruel. He reflected on their cruelty—a religion with a human corpse at the center, what could that mean? The carver and his model, beating and beating on the nails.

In the streets there were all at once flags, and everywhere big cloth posters of Il Duce flapping on the sides of buildings. Il Duce had a frog's mouth and enormous round Roman eyes. Was it a celebration? He could learn nothing from Viviana. Some of the streets were miraculously enclosed under a glass dome. People walked and shopped in a greenish undersea twilight. Masses of little tables freckled the indoor sidewalks. Mobs went strolling, all afternoon and all night, with an exuberance that stunned him. All of Milan was calling out under glass. They passed windows packed with umbrellas, gloves, shoes, pastries, silk ties, marzipan. There was the cathedral itself, on a giant platter, made all of white marzipan. He bought a marzipan goose for Viviana, and from a peddler a little Pinocchio on a string. Next to a bookstore, weaving in and out of the sidewalk coffee-drinkers—*"Turista? Turista?"*—boys were handing out leaflets in French and English. Frank Castle took one and read: "Only one of my ancestors interests me: there was a Mussolini in Venice who killed his wife who had betrayed him. Before fleeing he put two Venetian *scudi* on her chest to pay for her funeral. This is how the people of Romagna are, from whom I descend."

They rode the elevator to the top of the cathedral and walked over the roofs, among hundreds of statues. Behind each figure stood a dozen others. There were saints and martyrs and angels and gryphons and gargoyles and Romans; there were Roman soldiers whose decorated sword handles and buskins sprouted the heads of more Roman soldiers. Viviana peered out through the crenellations at the margins of the different roofs, and again there were hundreds of sculptures; thousands. The statues pullulated. An army of carvers had swarmed through these high stones, century after century, striking shape after amazing shape. Some were reticent, some ecstatic. Some were motionless, some flew. It was a dream of proliferation, of infinity: of figures set austerely inside octagonal cupolas, and each generative flank of every cupola itself lavishly friezed and fructified; of limbs erupting from limbs; of archways efflorescing; of statues spawning statuary. What had looked, from the plaza below, like the frothiest lacework or egg-white spume here burst into solidity, weight, shadow and dazzlement: a derangement of plenitude tumbling from a bloated cornucopia.

A huge laughter spurted out of Frank Castle's lung. On the hot copper roof he squatted down and laughed.

"What? What?" Viviana said.

"You could be here years and years," he said. "You would never finish! You would have to stay up in the air your whole life!"

"What?" she said. "What I no finish?"

He had pulled out his handkerchief and was pummelling his wet eyes. "If—if—" But he could not get it out.

"What? What? Francesco—"

"If—suppose—" The laughter felt like a strangulation; he coughed out a long constricted breath. "Look," he said, "I can see you falling on your goddam knees before every goddam *one* of these! Viviana," he said, "it's a *chiesa!* The priests aren't eating dinner! The priests are down below! Under our feet! You could be up here," he said—now he understood exactly what had happened at Fumicaro; he had fixed his penance for life—"a thousand years!"

ESSAYS

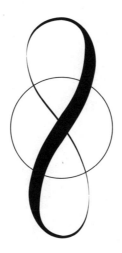

Mrs. Virginia Woolf:
A Madwoman and
Her Nurse

No recent biography has been read more thirstily by readers and writers of fiction than Quentin Bell's account of the life of his aunt Virginia. Reviewing it, Elizabeth Hardwick speaks of "the present exhaustion of Virginia Woolf," and compares the idea of Bloomsbury—it "wearies"—to a pond run out of trout. But for most American writers, bewildered by the instability of what passes for culture and literature, envious of the English sense of place and of being placed, conscious of separations that yet lack the respectability of "schools" or even the interest of alien perspectives, stuck mainly with the crudity of being either For or Against Interpretation, the legend of Bloomsbury still retains its inspiriting powers. Like any Golden Age, it promises a mimetic future: some day again, says Bloomsbury of 1905, there will be friends, there will be conversation, there will be moods, and they will all again *really matter,* and fall naturally, in the way of things that matter, into history.

Part of the special history of the Bloomsbury of mood is pictorial—and this has nothing to do with the art critic Roger Fry, or the painter Duncan Grant. It is not what the painters painted or what the writers wrote about painting that hangs on: it is the photographs, most of them no more official than snapshots, of the side of a house, two people playing checkers on an old kitchen chair set out in the yard, three friends and a baby poking in the sand. The snapshots are all amateur. Goblets of brightness wink on eaves, fences, trees, and wash out faces in their dazzle; eyes are lost in blackened sockets. The hem of a dress is likely to be all clarity, but the heads escape— under hat brims, behind dogs, into mottled leaf-shade. And out of the blur of those hopeless poses, cigarettes, hands on knees, hands over books, anxious little pups held up to the camera, walking sticks, long grotesque nose-shadows, lapels, outdoor chairs and tables, there rises up—no, leaks down—so much tension, so much ambition, so much fake casualness, so much heartbreaking attention to the momentariness of the moment. The people in the snapshots knew, in a way we do not, who they were. Bloomsbury was self-conscious in a way we are not. It sniffed at its own perceptions, even its own perceived posterity. Somewhere early in the course of her diaries, Virginia Woolf notes how difficult it would be for a biographer to understand her—how little biographers can know, she said—only from the evidence of her journals. Disbelieving in the probity of her own biography, she did not doubt that she would have her own biographer.

She did not doubt; she knew; they knew. Hatched from the last years of the reign of Victoria, Bloomsbury was still a world where things—if not people, then ideas—could be said to reign. Though old authority might be sneered at (or something worse even than a sneer—Virginia Woolf declared her certainty that she could not have become a writer had her father lived), though proprieties might be outrageously altered ("Semen?" asked Lytton Strachey, noticing a stain on Vanessa Bell's skirt one afternoon), though sex was accessible and often enough homoerotic, though freedom might be proclaimed on Gordon Square, though livings were earned, there was nonetheless a spine of authority to support Bloomsbury: family, descent, class and community—the sense of having-in-common. Bloomsbury, after all, was an inheritance. Both E. M. Forster's and Virginia Woolf's people were associated with the liberal and intellectual Clapham Sect of the century before. Cambridge made a kind of cousinship—the staircase at Trinity that drew together Clive Bell, Saxon Sydney-Turner, and Virginia Woolf's brother Thoby Stephen was the real beginning of the gatherings at Gordon Square. Bloomsbury was pacifist and busy with gossip about what it always called "buggery," but it was not radical and it did not harbor rebels. Rebels want to make over; the Bloomsburyites reinforced themselves with their like. The staircase at Trinity went on and on for the rest of their lives, and even Virginia Woolf, thinking to make over the form of the novel, had to have each newly completed work ratified by Morgan Forster and sometimes Maynard Keynes before she could breathe at ease again. The authority of one's closest familiars is the unmistakable note of Bloomsbury. It was that sure voice she listened for. "Virginia Woolf was a Miss Stephen," Quentin Bell begins, in the same voice; it is an opening any outsider could have written, but not in that sharp cadence. He is not so much biographer as a later member of the circle—Virginia Woolf's sister's son, the child of Vanessa and Clive Bell. He knows, he does not doubt. It is the note of self-recognition; of confidence; of inheritance. Everything is in his grip.

And yet—as she predicted—Virginia Woolf's biographer fails her. He fails her, in fact, more mournfully than any outsider could. It is his grip that fails her. This is not only because, sticking mainly to those matters he has sure authority over, he has chosen to omit a literary discussion of the body of work itself. "I have found the work of the biographer sufficiently difficult without adventuring in other directions," he tells us, so that to speak of Quentin Bell's "sure authority" is not to insinuate that all his data are, perhaps, out of childhood memory or family reminiscence, or that he has not mined library after library, and collection after collection of unpublished papers. He is, after all, of the next generation, and the next generation is always in some fashion an outsider to the one before. But what *is* in his grip is something more precise, curiously, than merely data, which the most impersonal research can reliably throw up: it is that particular intimacy of perspective—of experience, really—which characterizes not family information, but family bias. Every house has its own special odor to the entering guest, however faint—it sticks to the inhabitants, it is in their chairs and in their clothes. The analogy of bias to scent is chiefly in one's unconsciousness of one's own. Bell's Woolf is about Virginia, but it has the smell of Vanessa's house. The Virginia Woolf that comes off these pages is a kind of emanation of a point of view, long settled, by now, into family feeling. Stephens, Pattles, Fishers—all the family lines—each has its distinct and legendary scent. The Stephens are bold, the Pattles are fair, the Fishers are self-righteous. And Virginia is mad.

She was the family's third case of insanity, all on the Stephen side. Leslie Stephen, Virginia Woolf's celebrated father—a man of letters whose career was marked not least by the circumstance that Henry James cherished him—was married twice, the second time to Julia Duckworth, a widow with children. Together they produced Vanessa and Virginia, Thoby and Adrian. A child of Leslie Stephen's first marriage, the younger of Virginia's two half-sisters, was born defective—it is not clear whether backward or truly insane—and was confined to an asylum, where she died old. Virginia's first cousin—the child of her father's brother—went mad while still a young man, having struck his head in an accident. But one wonders, in the retrograde and rather primitive way one contemplates families, whether there might not have been a Stephen "taint." In a family already accustomed to rumor of aberration, Virginia Woolf, in any case, was incontrovertibly mad. Her madness was distinguished, moreover, by a threatening periodicity: at any moment it could strike, disabling everyone around her. Vanessa had to leave her children and come running, nurses had to be hired, rest homes interviewed, transport accomplished. The disaster was ten times wider than its victim.

And just here is the defect in writing out of family authority. The odor is personal, hence partial. Proust says somewhere that the artist brings to the work his whole self, to his familiars only those aspects that accommodate them. The biographer close to his subject has the same difficulty; the aspect under which Quentin Bell chiefly views his aunt Virginia is not of accommodation but of a still narrower partiality: discommodity, the effect on family perspective of Virginia Woolf's terrible and recurrent insanity. It was no mere melancholia, or poetic mooning—as, reading Leonard Woolf's deliberately truncated edition of her diary, we used to guess. A claustrophilic though inspired (also self-inspiring) document, it made us resent the arbitrary "personal" omissions: was it the madness he was leaving out? Certainly we wanted the madness too, supposing it to be the useful artistic sort: grotesque moods, quirks—epiphanies really. But it was not that; it was the usual thing people get put away for, an insanity characterized by incoherent howling and by violence. She clawed her attendants and had to be restrained; she would not touch food; she was suicidal. Ah, that cutting difference: not that she longed for death, as poets and writers sometimes do for melancholy's sake, but that she wanted, with the immediacy of a method, to be dead.

Bell's Woolf, then, is not about the Virginia Woolf of the diaries, essays, and novels—not, in the Proustian sense, about the writer's whole self. And surely this is not simply because literary criticism is evaded. Bell's Woolf is not about a writer, in fact; it is about the smell of a house. It is about a madwoman and her nurse.

The nurse was Leonard Woolf. Upon him Quentin Bell can impose no family aspects, rumors, characteristics, old experience, inherited style. He does not trail any known house-scent, like Stephens, Pattles, Fishers. Though he shared the Cambridge stairs—Thoby Stephen, Saxon Sydney-Turner, Clive Bell, Lytton Strachey, and Leonard Woolf together briefly formed the Midnight Society, a reading club that met on Saturday evenings in Clive Bell's rooms—he was not an inheritor of Cambridge. Cambridge was not natural to him, Bloomsbury was not natural to him, even England was not natural to him—not as an inheritance; he was a Jew. Quentin Bell has no "authority" over Leonard Woolf, as he has over his aunt; Leonard is nowhere in the biographer's grip.

The effect is unexpected. It is as if Virginia Woolf escapes—possessing her too selectively, the biographer lets her slip—but Leonard Woolf somehow stays to become himself. Which is to say, Bell's Virginia Woolf can be augmented by a thousand other sources—chiefly by her own work—but we learn as much about Leonard Woolf here as we are likely to know from any other source. And what we learn is a strange historical judgment, strange but unfragmented, of a convincing wholeness: that Leonard Woolf was a family sacrifice. Without him—Quentin Bell's clarity on this point is ineffaceable—

Virginia Woolf might have spent her life in a mental asylum. The elder Stephens were dead, Thoby had died at twenty-six, Adrian married a woman apparently indifferent to or incompatible with the Bloomsburyites; it was Vanessa on whom the grimness fell. Leonard Woolf—all this is blatant—got Vanessa off the hook. He was, in fact, deceived: he had no inkling he was being captured for a nurse.

> Neither Vanessa nor Adrian gave him a detailed and explicit account of Virginia's illnesses or told him how deadly serious they might be. . . . Her insanity was clothed, like some other painful things in that family, in a jest. . . . Thus, in effect if not in intention, Leonard was allowed to think of Virginia's illnesses as something not desperately serious, and he was allowed to marry her without knowing how fearful a care such a union might be. In fairness to all parties it must be said that, even if Virginia's brother and sister had been as explicit and circumstantial as they ought to have been, Leonard would certainly not have been deflected from his purpose of marrying Virginia. . . . As it was, he learnt the hard way and one can only wonder, seeing how hard it was, and that he had for so long to endure the constant threat of her suicide, to exert constant vigilance, to exercise endless persuasive tact at mealtimes and to suffer the perpetual alternations of hope and disappointment, that he too did not go mad.
>
> In fact he nearly did, although he does not mention it.

"He does not mention it." There was in Leonard Woolf an extraordinary silence, a containment allied to something like concealment, and at the same time open to a methodical candor. This is no paradox; candor is often the mode of the obtuse person. It is of course perilous to think of Leonard Woolf as obtuse: he was both activist and intellectual, worldly and introspective; his intelligence, traveling widely and serenely over politics and literature, was reined in by a seriousness that makes him the most responsible and conscientious figure among all the Bloomsburyites. His seriousness was profound. It was what turned a hand press "small enough to stand on a kitchen table" into the Hogarth Press, an important and innovative publishing house. It was what turned Leonard Woolf himself from a highly able agent of colonialism—at the age of twenty-four he was an official of the British ruling apparatus in Ceylon—into a convinced anti-imperialist and a fervent socialist. And it was what turned the Jew into an Englishman.

Not that Leonard Woolf is altogether without ambivalence on this question; indeed, the word "ambivalence" is his own. Soon after his marriage to Virginia Stephen, he was taken round on a tour of Stephen relations— among them Virginia's half-brother, Sir George Duckworth, in his large house in Dalingridge Place, and "Aunt Anny," who was Lady Ritchie,

Thackeray's daughter, in St. George's Square. He suffered in these encounters from an "ambivalence in my attitude to the society which I found in Dalingridge Place and St. George's Square. I disliked its respectability and assumptions while envying and fearing its assurance and manners." And: "I was an outsider to this class, because, although I and my father before me belonged to the professional middle class, we had only recently struggled up into it from the stratum of Jewish shopkeepers. We had no roots in it." This looks like candor—"we had no roots"—but it is also remarkably insensible. Aware of his not belonging, he gives no evidence anywhere that the people he moved among were also aware of it. It is true that his own group of selfconsciously agnostic Cambridge intellectuals apparently never mentioned it to his face. Thoby Stephen in a letter to Leonard in Ceylon is quick enough to speak of himself, mockingly, as a nonbelieving Christian— "it's no good being dainty with Christians and chapel's obviously rot"—but no one seems ever to have teased Leonard about his being an agnostic Jew. In the atmosphere of that society, perhaps, teasing would have too dangerously resembled baiting; levity about being a Christian was clearly not interchangeable with levity about being a Jew. Fair enough: it never is. But Virginia, replying to a letter in which Leonard implores her to love him, is oddly analytical: ". . . of course, I feel angry sometimes at the strength of your desire. Possibly, your being a Jew comes in also at this point. You seem so foreign." Was he, like all those dark lubricious peoples whose origins are remote from the moderating North, too obscurely other? She corrects herself at once, with a kind of apology: "And then I am fearfully unstable. I pass from hot to cold in an instant, without any reason; except that I believe sheer physical effort and exhaustion influence me." The correction—the retraction—is weak, and fades off; what remains is the blow: "You seem so foreign."

We do not know Leonard's response to this. Possibly he made none. It would have been in keeping had he made none. Foreignness disconcerted him—like Virginia he was at moments disturbed by it and backed away— and if his own origins were almost never mentioned to his face, his face was nevertheless *there,* and so, in those striking old photographs, were the faces of his grandparents. Leonard Woolf is bemused in his autobiography by his paternal grandfather, "a large, stern, black-haired, and black-whiskered, rabbinical Jew in a frock coat." Again he speaks of this "look of stern rabbinical orthodoxy," and rather prefers the "round, pink face of an incredibly old Dutch doll," which was the face of his Dutch-born maternal grandmother— about whom he speculates that it was "possible that she had a good deal of non-Jewish blood in her ancestry. Some of her children and grandchildren were fair-haired and facially very unlike the 'typical' Jew." Her husband, however, was a different case: "No one could have mistaken him for any-thing but a Jew. Although he wore coats and trousers, hats and umbrellas, just like those of all the other gentlemen in Addison Gardens, he looked to me as if he might have stepped straight out of one of those old pictures of caftaned, bearded Jews in a ghetto. . . ." Such Jews, he notes, were equipped with "a fragment of spiritual steel, a particle of passive and uncon-querable resistance," but otherwise the character, and certainly the history, of the Jews do not draw him. "My father's father was a Jew," he writes, ex-empting himself by two generations. "I have always felt in my bones and brain and heart English and, more narrowly, a Londoner, but with a nostal-gic love of the city and civilization of ancient Athens." He recognizes that his "genes and chromosomes" are something else; he is a "descendant" of "the world's official fugitives and scapegoats."

But a "descendant" is not the same as a member. A descendant shares an origin, but not necessarily a destiny. Writing in his eighties, Leonard Woolf recollects that as a schoolboy he was elected to an exclusive debating so-ciety under the thumb of G. K. Chesterton and his brother, and "in view of the subsequent violent anti-Semitism of the Chestertons" he finds this "amusing"; he reports that he was "surprised and flattered." Sixty-three years afterward he is still flattered. His description of the public school that flattered him shows it to be a detestable place, hostile to both intellect and feeling: "I got on quite well with the boys in my form or with whom I played cricket, football, and fives, but it would have been unsafe, prac-tically impossible, to let them know what I really thought or felt about anything which seemed to me important." *Would have been unsafe*. It was a risk he did not take—unlike Morgan Forster, who, in the same situ-ation in a similar school, allowed himself to be recognized as an intellectual and consequently to suffer as a schoolboy pariah. Leonard Woolf did not intend to take on the role of pariah, then or later. Perhaps it was cowardice; or perhaps it was the opposite, that "fragment of spiritual steel" he had in-herited from the ghetto; or perhaps it was his sense of himself as exempt from the ghetto.

Certainly he always thought of himself as wholly an Englishman. In the spring of 1935 he and Virginia drove to Rome. "I was astonished then (I am astonished still)," Quentin Bell comments, "that Leonard chose to travel by way of Germany." They were on German soil three days; near Bonn they en-countered a Nazi demonstration but were unharmed, and entered Italy safely. What prompted Leonard Woolf to go into Germany in the very hour Jews were being abused there? Did he expect Nazi street hoodlums to distin-guish between an English Jewish face and a German Jewish face? He carried with him—it was not needed and in the event of street hoodlumism would anyhow have been useless—a protective letter from an official of the German embassy in London. More than that, he carried—in his "bones and brain and heart"—the designation of Englishman. It was a test, not of the inherited fragment of spiritual steel, but of the strength of his exemption from that heritage. If Quentin Bell is twice astonished, it may be because he calculated the risk more closely than Leonard; or else he is not quite so persuaded of the Englishness of Leonard Woolf as is Leonard Woolf.

And, superficially at least, it is difficult to be persuaded of it. One is drawn to Leonard's face much as he was drawn to his grandfather's face, and the conclusion is the same. What Leonard's eyes saw was what the eyes of the educated English classes saw. What Leonard felt on viewing his grandfather's face must have been precisely what Clive Bell and Thoby Stephen would have felt. There is an arresting snapshot—still another of those that make up the pictorial history of Bloomsbury—of Leonard Woolf and Adrian Stephen. They are both young men in their prime; the date is 1914. They are standing side by side before the high narrow Gothic-style windows of Asham House, the Sussex villa Leonard and Virginia Woolf owned for some years. They are dressed identically (vests, coats, ties) and positioned identically—feet apart, hands in pockets, shut lips gripping pipe or cigarette holder. Their shoes are lost in the weedy grass, and the sunlight masks their faces in identical skull-shadows. Both faces are serene, holding back amusement, indulgent of the photographer. And still it is not a picture of two cultivated Englishmen, or not only that. Adrian is incredibly tall and Vikinglike, with a forehead as broad and flat as a chimney tile; he looks like some blueblood American banker not long out of Princeton; his hair grows straight up like thick pale straw. Leonard's forehead is an attenuated wafer under a tender black forelock, his nose is nervous and frail, he seems younger and more vulnerable than his years (he was then thirty-four) and as recognizably intellectual as—well, how does one put the contrast? Following Leonard, one ought to dare to put it with the clarity of a certain cultural bluntness: he looks like a student at the yeshiva. Leonard has the unmistakable face of a Jew. Like his grandfather—and, again like him, despite his costume—Leonard Woolf might have stepped out of one of those pictures of caftaned Jews in the ghetto.

The observation may be obvious and boring but it is not insignificant, if only because it is derived from Leonard himself; it is his own lesson. What can be learned from it is not merely that he was himself conscious of all that curious contrast, but that his fellows could not have been indifferent to it. In a 1968 review of the penultimate volume of Leonard Woolf's memoirs, Dan Jacobson wonders, "Did his being a Jew never affect . . . his career or social life in the several years he spent as a colonial offficer in Ceylon, his only companions during that time being other colonial civil servants—not in general the most enlightened, tolerant, or tactful of British social groups? Did it not arise in the political work he carried out later in England, especially during the rise of Nazism?" On all these matters Leonard is mute; he does not mention it. Not so Virginia. "He's a penniless Jew," she wrote in a letter to a friend announcing her marriage, and we know that if she had married a poor man of her own set she would not have called him a penniless Englishman. She called Leonard a Jew not to identify or explain him, but because, quite simply, that is how she saw him; it was herself she was explaining. And if she wrote light-heartedly, making a joke of marriage without inheritance, it was also a joke in general about unaccoutered Jews—from her point of view, Leonard had neither inheritance nor heritage. He was—like the Hogarth Press later on—self-created.

Of course, in thinking about Leonard Woolf, one is plainly not interested in the question of the acculturated Jew (". . . nearly all Jews are both proud and ashamed of being Jews," Leonard writes—a model of the type); it is not on the mark. What *is* to the point is the attitude of the class Leonard aspired to join. "Virginia for her part," Quentin Bell notes—and it is unnecessary to remind oneself that he is her nephew—

> had to meet the Woolf family. It was a daunting experience. Leonard himself was sufficiently Jewish to seem to her disquietingly foreign; but in him the trait was qualified. He had become so very much a citizen of her world. . . . But Leonard's widowed mother, a matriarchal figure living with her large family in Colinette Road, Putney, seemed very alien to Virginia. No place could have been less like home than her future mother-in-law's house.
>
> And how did the Woolfs regard her? Did they perceive that she thought their furniture hideous? Did she seem to them a haughty goy thinking herself too good for the family of their brilliant son? I am afraid that they probably did.
>
> [Here follows an account of Virginia's response—aloof and truculent—upon learning the character of the dietary laws, which Mrs. Woolf observed.]
>
> Virginia was ready to allow that Mrs. Woolf had some very good qualities, but her heart must have sunk as she considered what large opportunities she would have for discovering them.
>
> "Work and love and Jews in Putney take it out of me," she wrote, and it was certainly true.

This aspect of Virginia Stephen's marriage to Leonard Woolf is usually passed over in silence. I have rehearsed it here at such length not to emphasize it for its own sake—there is nothing novel about upper-class English distaste for Jews—but to make a point about Leonard. He is commonly depicted as, in public, a saintly socialist, and, in private, a saintly husband. He was probably both; but he also knew, like any percipient young man in love with a certain segment of society, how to seize vantage ground. As a schoolboy he was no doubt sincerely exhilarated by the playing field, but he hid his intellectual exhilarations to make it look as if the playing field were all there was to esteem; it was a way, after all, of buying esteem for himself. And though he was afterward no doubt sincerely in love with Virginia Stephen (surely a woman less intelligent would not have satisfied him), it would be a mistake to suppose that Virginia herself—even given her brilliance, her splendid head on its splendid neck, the radiance of her first appearance in Thoby's rooms in Cambridge wearing a white dress and round hat and carrying a parasol, astonishing him, Leonard says, as when "in a picture gallery you suddenly come face to face with a great Rembrandt or Velasquez"—it would be ingenuous, not to say credulous, to think that Virginia alone was all there was to adore. Whether Leonard Woolf fell in love with a young woman of beauty and intellect, or more narrowly with a Stephen of beauty and intellect, will always be a formidable, and a necessary, question.

It is a question that, it seems to me, touches acutely on Leonard Woolf in his profoundly dedicated role as nurse. He was dedicated partly because he was earnestly efficient at everything, and also because he loved his wife, and also because he was a realist who could reconcile himself to any unlooked-for disaster. He came to the situation of Virginia's health determinedly and unquestioningly, much as, years later, when the German bombings had begun, he joined up with the Local Defence Volunteers: it was what had to be done. But in the case of Virginia more than merely courage was at issue; his "background" had equipped him well to be Virginia Stephen's nurse. When things were going badly he could take on the burden of all those small code-jottings in his diary—"V.n.w.," "b.n.," "V.sl.h."—and all the crises "Virginia not well," "bad night," "Virginia slight headache" horrendously implied, for the simple reason that it was worth it to him. It was worth it because she was a genius; it was worth it because she was a Stephen.

The power and allure of the Stephen world lay not in its distance from the Jews of Putney—Bloomsbury was anyhow hardly likely to notice the Jews of Putney, and if Virginia did notice, and was even brought to tea there, it was through the abnormal caprice of a freakish fate—but in its illustriousness. Virginia was an illustrious young woman: had she had no gift of her own, the luster of her father's situation, and of the great circle of the aristocracy of intellect into which she was born, would have marked her life. It was additionally marked by her double fortune of genius and insanity, and though her primary fortune—the circle into which she was born—

attracted, in the most natural way, other members of that circle, the biting and always original quality of her mind put the less vivid of them off. Her madness was not public knowledge, but her intellect could not be hidden. Her tongue had a fearful and cutting brilliance. "I was surprised to find how friendly she made herself appear," said Walter Lamb, another of Thoby Stephen's Cambridge friends, amazed on one occasion to have been undevoured. He courted her for a time, pallidly, asking frightened questions: "Do you want to have children and love in the normal way?"—as if he expected nothing usual from Virginia Stephen. "I wish," she wrote to Lytton Strachey, after reporting Lamb's visits, "that earth would open her womb and let some new creature out." The courtship was brief and ended in boredom. Lamb's offer was one of at least four proposals of marriage from differing sources; Strachey himself had tendered her one. Since he preferred stableboys to women, a fact they both understood very well, it was a strange mistake. Sydney Waterlow, still another Cambridge name, was a suitor; she regarded him as "amiable." Hilton Young, a childhood friend—cast, says Quentin Bell, from a "smooth and well-proportioned mould"—might have been an appropriate match, mixing politics with poetry and gaining a peerage; he was merely "admirable." Meanwhile, Virginia was thoughtfully flirting with her sister's husband. At twenty-nine, despite all these attentions, she was depressed at being still unmarried; she was despondent, as she would be for the rest of her life, over her childlessness. Not one of those triflings had turned to infatuation, on either side.

It was fortunate. There was lacking, in all these very intelligent men, and indeed in their type in general, the kind of sexual seriousness that is usually disparaged as uxoriousness. It was a trait that Leonard invincibly possessed and that Clive Bell despised as "provincial and puritanical, an enemy to all that was charming and amusing in life." Clive was occupied by a long-standing affair and lived apart from Vanessa, who, at various times, lived with Roger Fry and with Duncan Grant—who was (so closely was this group tied) Lytton Strachey's cousin, and who may have been (so Quentin Bell allows us to conjecture) the father of Quentin's sister, Angelica. Vanessa typed and distributed copies of Lytton Strachey's indecent verse; once at a party she did a topless dance; it was legendary that she had at another party fornicated with Maynard Keynes *"coram publico"*—the whole room looking on. It may have been in honor of these last two occasions that Virginia Woolf, according to Quentin Bell, pronounced human nature to have been "changed in or about December 1910."

It was not a change Leonard Woolf approved of. Four years after this crucial date in human history he published a novel critical of "unnatural cultured persons" given to "wild exaggerated talk" and frivolous behavior;

it was clearly an assault on Vanessa and Clive Bell and their circle. The novel, called *The Wise Virgins,* was about *not* marrying Virginia. Instead the hero is forced to marry a Putney girl, and lives unhappily ever after—only because, having been infected with Bloomsbury's licentious notions, he has carelessly gotten her with child. The fictional Leonard loses the heroine who represents Virginia, and is doomed to the drabness of Putney; in the one act he both deplores Bloomsbury and laments his deprivation of it. The real Leonard tried to pick his way between these soul-cracking contradictions. He meant to have the high excitement of Bloomsbury— and certainly "frivolity" contributed to Bloomsbury's dash and éclat—without the frivolity itself. He meant to be master of the full brilliant breadth of all that worldliness, and at the same time of the more sober and limiting range of his native seriousness.

That he coveted the one while requiring the other was—certainly in her biographer's eyes—the salvation of Virginia. No one else in that milieu could have survived—surely not as husband—her illnesses. Roger Fry, for instance, put his own mad wife away and went to live with Vanessa. As for Lamb, Waterlow, Young—viewed in the light of what Virginia Woolf's insanity extracted from her caretaker, their possibilities wither. Of all her potential husbands, only Leonard Woolf emerged as fit. And the opposite too can be said: of Bloomsbury's potential wives, only Virginia emerged as fit for Leonard. He was fit for her because her madness, especially in combination with her innovative genius, demanded the most grave, minutely persevering and attentive service. She was fit for him not simply because she represented Bloomsbury in its most resplendent flowering of originality and luminousness; so, after all, did Vanessa, an accomplished painter active with other painters in the revolutionary vitality of the Post-Impressionists. But just as no marriage could survive Vanessa for long, so Leonard married to Vanessa would not have survived Bloomsbury for long. What Leonard needed in Virginia was not so much her genius as her madness. It made possible for him the exercise of the one thing Bloomsbury had no use for: uxoriousness. It allowed him the totality of his seriousness unchecked. It *used* his seriousness, it gave it legitimate occupation, it made it both necessary and awesome. And it made *her* serious. Without the omnipresent threat of disintegration, freed from the oppression of continuous vigil against breakdown, what might Virginia's life have been? The flirtation with Clive hints at it: she might have lived, at least outwardly, like Vanessa. It was his wife's insanity, in short, that made tenable the permanent—the secure— presence in Bloomsbury of Leonard himself. Her madness fed his genius for responsibility; it became for him a corridor of access to her genius. The spirit

of Bloomsbury was not Leonard's, his temperament was against it—Bloomsbury could have done without him. So could a sane Virginia.

The whole question of Virginia's sexuality now came into Leonard's
hands. And here too he was curiously ambivalent. The honeymoon was not
a success; they consulted Vanessa, Vanessa the sexual creature—when had
she had her first orgasm? Vanessa could not remember. "No doubt," she reflected, "I sympathised with such things if I didn't have them from the time I
was 2." "Why do you think people make such a fuss about marriage & cop-
ulation?" Virginia was writing just then; ". . . certainly I find the climax
immensely exaggerated." Vanessa and Leonard put their heads together over
it. Vanessa said she believed Virginia "never had understood or sympathised
with sexual passion in men"; this news, she thought, "consoled" Leonard.
For further consolation the two of them rehearsed (and this was before England had become properly aware of Freud) Virginia's childhood trauma
inflicted by her elder half-brother George Duckworth, who had, under cover
of big-brotherly affection, repeatedly entered the nursery at night for intimate fondlings, the nature of which Virginia then hardly comprehended;
she knew only that he frightened her and that she despised him. Apparently
this explanation satisfied Leonard—the "consolation" worked—if rather too
quickly; the ability to adjust speedily to disappointment is a good and useful
trait in a colonial officer, less so in a husband. It does not contradict the
uxorious temperament, however, and certainly not the nursing enterprise: a
wife who is seen to be frigid as well as mad is simply taken for that much
sicker. But too ready a reconcilement to bad news is also a kind of abandon-
ment, and Leonard seems very early to have relinquished, or allowed Virginia to relinquish, the sexual gratifications of marriage. All the stranger
since he repeatedly speaks of himself as "lustful." And he is not known to
have had so much as a dalliance during his marriage.

On the other hand, Quentin Bell suggests—a little coyly, as if only blame-
lessly hinting—that Virginia Woolf's erotic direction was perhaps toward
women rather than men. The "perhaps" is crucial: the index to the first
volume lists "passion for Madge Vaughan," "passion for Violet Dickinson,"
but the corresponding textual passages are all projections from the most
ordinary sort of data. Madge Vaughan was a cousin by marriage whom Virginia knew from the age of seven; at sixteen she adored her still, and once
stood in the house paralyzed by rapture, thinking, "Madge is here; at this
moment she is actually under this roof"—an emotion, she once said, that
she never equaled afterward. Many emotions at sixteen are never equaled
afterward. Of Virginia's intense letter-writing to Violet Dickinson—a friend
of her dead half-sister—Quentin Bell says: ". . . it is clear to the modern

reader, though it was not at all clear to Virginia, that she was in love and that her love was returned." What is even clearer is that it is possible to be too "modern," if that is what enables one to read a sensual character into every exuberant or sympathetic friendship between women. Vita Sackville-West, of course, whom Virginia Woolf knew when both writers were already celebrated, was an established sapphist, and was plainly in pursuit of Virginia. Virginia, she wrote, "dislikes the quality of masculinity," but that was the view of one with a vested interest in believing it. As for Virginia, she "felt," according to her biographer, "as a lover feels—she desponded when she fancied herself neglected, despaired when Vita was away, waited anxiously for letters, needed Vita's company and lived in that strange mixture of elation and despair which lovers—and one would have supposed only lovers—can experience." But all this is Quentin Bell. Virginia herself, reporting a three-day visit from Sackville-West, appears erotically detached: "These Sapphists *love* women; friendship is never untinged with amorosity. . . . I like her and being with her and the splendour—she shines in the grocer's shop . . . with a candle lit radiance." She acknowledged what she readily called Vita's "glamour," but the phrase "these Sapphists" is too mocking to be lover's language. And she was quick to criticize Vita (who was married to Harold Nicolson) as a mother: ". . . she is a little cold and off-hand with her boys." Virginia Woolf's biographer nevertheless supposes—he admits all this is conjecture—"some caressing, some bedding together." Still, in the heart of this love, if it was love, was the ultimate withdrawal: "In brain and insight," Virginia remarked in her diary, "she is not as highly organised as I am." Vita was splendid but "not reflective." She wrote "with a pen of brass." And: "I have no enormous opinion of her poetry." Considering all of which, Quentin Bell notes persuasively that "she could not really love without feeling that she was in the presence of a superior intellect." Sackville-West, for her part, insisted that not only did Virginia not like the quality of masculinity, but also the "possessiveness and love of domination in men."

Yet Leonard Woolf dominated Virginia Woolf overwhelmingly—nor did she resist—not so much because his braininess impressed her (his straightforwardly thumping writing style must have claimed her loyalty more than her admiration), but because he possessed her in the manner of—it must be said again—a strong-minded nurse with obsessive jurisdiction over a willful patient. The issue of Virginia Woolf's tentative or potential lesbianism becomes reduced, at this point, to the merest footnote of possibility. Sackville-West called her "inviolable"; and the fact is she was conventionally married, and had conventional expectations of marriage. She wanted children. For a wedding present Violet Dickinson sent her a cradle. "My baby shall sleep in [it]," she said at thirty. But it stood empty, and she felt, all her life, the ache of the irretrievable. "I don't like the physicalness of having children of my own," she wrote at forty-five, recording how "the little creatures"—Vanessa's children—"moved my infinitely sentimental throat." But then, with a lurch of candor: "I can dramatise myself a parent, it is true. And perhaps I have killed the feeling instinctively; or perhaps nature does." Two years after declaring the feeling killed, during a dinner party full of worldly conversation with the Webbs and assorted eminences, she found herself thinking: "L. and myself . . . the pathos, the symbolical quality of the childless couple."

The feeling was not killed; it had a remarkable durability. There is no record of her response to the original decision not to have children. That decision was Leonard's, and it was "medical." He consulted three or four people variously qualified, including Vanessa's doctor and the nurse who ran the home to which Virginia was sent when most dangerously disturbed (and to whom, according to Bell, Leonard ascribed "an unconscious but violent homosexual passion for Virginia"—which would, one imagines, make one wonder about the disinterestedness of her advice). Leonard also requested the opinion of Dr. George Savage, Virginia's regular physician, whom he disliked, and was heartily urged to have babies; soon after we find him no longer in consultation with Dr. Savage. Bell tells us that "in the end Leonard decided and persuaded Virginia to agree that, although they both wanted children, it would be too dangerous for her to have them." The "too dangerous" is left unexplained; we do not even know Leonard's ostensible reason. Did he think she could not withstand pregnancy and delivery? She was neither especially frail nor without energy, and was a zealous walker, eight miles at a time, over both London and countryside; she hefted piles of books and packed them for the Hogarth Press; she had no organic impediments. Did he believe she could not have borne the duties of rearing? But in that class there was no household without its nanny (Vanessa had two), and just as she never had to do a housekeeping chore (she never laid a fire, or made a bed, or washed a sock), she need not have been obliged to take physical care of a child. Did he, then, fear an inherited trait—diseased offspring? Or did he intend to protect the phantom child from distress by preventing its birth into a baleful household? Or did he mean, out of some curious notion of intellectual purity, not to divide the strength of Virginia's available sanity, to preserve her undistracted for her art?

Whatever the reason, and to spare her—or himself—what pains we can only guess at, she was in this second instance released from "normality." Normality is catch-as-catch-can. Leonard, in his deliberateness, in his responsibility, was more serious than that, and surrendered her to a program of omissions. She would be spared the tribulations both of the conjugal bed and of childbed. She need not learn ease in the one; she need not, no, must not, venture into the other. In forbidding Virginia maternity, Leonard abandoned her to an unparalleled and unslakable envy. Her diary again and again records the pangs she felt after visits with Vanessa's little sons—pangs, defenses, justifications: she suffered. Nor was it a social suffering—she did not feel deprived of children because she was expected to. The name "Virginia Woolf" very soon acquired the same resonance for her contemporaries ("this celebrity business is quite chronic," she wrote) as it has for us—after which she was expected to be only Virginia Woolf. She learned, after a while, to be only that (which did not, however, prevent her from being an adored and delightful aunt), and to mock at Vanessa's mothering, and to call it obsessive and excessive. She suffered the envy of the childless for the fruitful, precisely this, and nothing societally imposed; and she even learned to transmute maternal envy into a more manageable variety—literary begrudging. This was directed at Vanessa's second son, Julian Bell, killed in the Spanish Civil War, toward whose literary ambitions Virginia Woolf was always ungenerous, together with Leonard; a collection of Julian's essays, prepared after his death, Leonard dubbed "Vanessa's necrophily." Vanessa-envy moved on into the second generation. It was at bottom a rivalry of creatureliness, in which Virginia was always the loser. Vanessa was on the side of "normality," the placid mother of three, enjoying all the traditional bourgeois consolations; she was often referred to as a madonna; and at the same time she was a thorough-going bohemian. Virginia was anything but placid, yet lived a sober sensible domestic life in a marriage stable beyond imagining, with no trace of bohemianism. Vanessa the bohemian madonna had the best of both hearth-life and free life. Virginia was barred from both.

Without the authoritative domestic role maternity would have supplied, with no one in the household dependent on her (for years she quarreled with her maid on equal or inferior terms), and finding herself always—as potential patient—in submission, Virginia Woolf was by degrees nudged into a position of severe dependency. It took odd forms: Leonard not only prescribed milk at eleven in the morning, but also topics for conversation in the evening. Lytton Strachey's sister-in-law recalls how among friends Leonard would work up the "backbone" of a subject "and then be happy to let [Virginia] ornament it if she wanted to." And he gave her pocket money every week. Her niece Angelica reports that "Leonard kept Virginia on very short purse-strings," which she exercised through the pleasures of buying "coloured string and sealing-wax, notebooks and pencils." When she came to the end of writing a book, she trembled until Leonard read it and gave his approval. William Plomer remembers how Leonard would grow alarmed if, watching Virginia closely, he saw her laugh a little too convulsively. And once she absentmindedly began to flick bits of meat off her dinner plate; Leonard hushed the company and led her away.*

—All of which has given Leonard his reputation for saintliness. A saint who successively secures acquiescence to frigidity, childlessness, dependency? Perhaps; probably; of course. These are, after all, conventual vows—celibacy, barrenness, obedience. But Leonard Woolf was a socialist, not an ascetic; he had a practical political intelligence; he was the author of books called *Empire and Commerce in Africa* and *Socialism and Co-operation;* he ran the Hogarth Press like a good businessman; at the same time he edited a monthly periodical, *The International Review;* he was literary editor of *The Nation.* He had exactly the kind of commonsensical temperament that scorns, and is repelled by, religious excess. And of Virginia he made a shrine; of himself, a monk. On the day of her death Virginia walked out of the house down to the river Ouse and drowned herself; not for nothing was that house called Monk's House. The letter she left for Leonard was like almost every other suicide note, horribly banal, not a writer's letter at all, and rich with guilt—"I feel certain I am going mad again. I feel we can't go through another of those terrible times. . . . I can't go on spoiling your life any longer." To Vanessa she wrote, "All I want to say is that Leonard has been so astonishingly good, every day, always; I can't imagine that anyone could have done more for me than he has. . . . I feel he has so much to do that he will go on, better without me. . . ."

Saints make guilt—especially when they impose monkish values; there is nothing new in that. And it was the monk as well as her madness she was fleeing when she walked into the Ouse, though it was the saint she praised. "I don't think two people could have been happier than we have been," the note to Leonard ended. A tragic happiness—such a thing is possible: cheerful invalids are a commonplace, and occasionally one hears of happy inmates. A saintly monk, a monkish nurse? All can be taken together, and all are true together. But the drive toward monkishness was in Leonard. What was natural for himself he prescribed for Virginia, and to one end only: to prevent her ongoing nervous crises from reaching their extreme state; to keep her sane. And to keep her sane was, ultimately, to keep her writing. It is reasonable to imagine that without Leonard Woolf there would have been very little of that corpus the name Virginia Woolf calls to mind—there would have been no *Mrs. Dalloway,* no *To the Lighthouse,* no *The Waves,* no *Common Reader.* And it may be that even the word

---

*Joan Russell Noble, ed., *Recollections of Virginia Woolf by Her Contemporaries* (William Morrow & Company, Inc., 1972).

Bloomsbury—the redolence, the signal—would not have survived, since she was its center. "She would not have been the symbol" of Bloomsbury, T. S. Eliot said, "if she had not been the maintainer of it." For Bloomsbury as an intellectual "period" to have escaped oblivion, there had to be at least one major literary voice to carry it beyond datedness. That voice was hers.

The effort to keep her sane was mammoth. Why did Leonard think it was worth it? The question, put here for the second time, remains callous but inevitable. Surely it would have been relieving at last (and perhaps to both of them) to let her slide away into those rantings, delusions, hallucinations; she might or might not have returned on her own. It is even possible that the nursing was incidental, and that she recovered each time because she still had the capacity to recover. But often enough Leonard—who knew the early symptoms intimately—was able to prevent her from going under; each pulling-back from that brink of dementia gained her another few months of literary work. Again and again he pulled her back. It required cajolery, cunning, mastery, agility, suspiciousness, patience, spoon-feeding, and an overwhelming sensitiveness to every flicker of her mood. Obviously it drained him; obviously he must have been tempted now and then to let it all go and give up. Almost anyone else would have. Why did he not? Again the answer must be manifold. Because she was his wife; because she was the beloved one to whom he had written during their courtship, "You don't know what a wave of happiness comes over me when I see you smile";* because his conscience obliged him to; because she suffered; because—this before much else—it was in his nature to succor suffering. And also: because of her gift; because of her genius; for the sake of literature; because she was unique. And because she had been a Miss Stephen; because she was Thoby Stephen's sister; because she was a daughter of Leslie Stephen; because she was, like Leonard's vision of Cambridge itself, "compounded of . . . the atmosphere of long years of history and great traditions and famous names [and] a profoundly civilized life"; because she was Bloomsbury; because she was England.

For her sake, for art's sake, for his own sake. Perhaps above all for his own sake. In her he had married a kind of escutcheon; she represented the finest grain of the finest stratum in England. What he shored up against disintegration was the life he had gained—a birthright he paid for by spooning porridge between Virginia Woolf's resisting lips.

---

*From an unpublished letter in the Berg Collection. Quoted in *The New York Times,* June 14, 1973.

* * *

Proust is right to tell us to go to a writer's books, not to his loyalties. Wherever Leonard Woolf is, there Virginia Woolf is not. The more Leonard recedes or is not present, the more Virginia appears in force. Consequently Quentin Bell's biography—the subversive strength of which is Leonard—demands an antidote. The antidote is, of course, in the form of a reminder—that Virginia Woolf was a woman of letters as well as a patient; that she did not always succumb but instead could be an original fantasist and fashioner of an unaccustomed way of seeing; that the dependency coincided with a vigorous intellectual autonomy; that together with the natural subordination of the incapacitated she possessed the secret confidence of the innovator.

Seen through Leonard's eyes, she is, in effect, always on the verge of lunacy. "I am quite sure," he tells us in his autobiography, "that Virginia's genius was closely connected with what manifested itself as mental instability and insanity. The creative imagination in her novels, her ability to 'leave the ground' in conversation, and the voluble delusions of the breakdown all came from the same place in her mind—she 'stumbled after her own voice' and followed 'the voices that fly ahead.'" At the same time her refusal to eat was associated with guilt—she talked of her "faults"—and Leonard insists that "she remained all through her illness, even when most insane, terribly sane in three-quarters of her mind. The point is that her insanity was in her premises, in her beliefs. She believed, for instance, that she was not ill. . . ."

Seen through the books, she is never "ill," never lunatic. Whether it was mental instability or a clear-sighted program of experiment in the shape of the novel that unhinged her prose from the conventional margins that had gone before is a question not worth speculating over. Leonard said that when mad she heard the birds sing in Greek. The novels are not like that: it is not the data that are altered, but the sequence of things. When Virginia Woolf assaulted the "old" fiction in her famous *Mr. Bennett and Mrs. Brown,* she thought she was recommending getting rid of the habit of data; she thought this was to be her fictive platform. But when she grappled with her own inventions, she introduced as much data as possible and strained to express it all under the pressure of a tremendous simultaneity. What she was getting rid of was consecutiveness; precisely the habit of premises. If clinging to premises was the sanity of her insanity, then the intent of her fiction was not an extension of her madness, as Leonard claimed, but its calculated opposite. The poetry of her prose may have been like the elusive poetry of her dementia, but its steadfast design was not. "The design," she wrote of *Mrs. Dalloway,* "is so queer and so masterful"; elated, she saw ahead. She was an artist; she schemed, and not through random contractions or inflations of madness, but through the usual methods of art: inspired intellection, the breaking down of expectation into luminous segments of shock.

A simpler way of saying all this is that what she achieved as a stylist cannot really be explained through linking it with madness. The diaries give glimpses of rationalized prefigurations; a letter from Vanessa suggests moths, which metamorphosed into *The Moths,* which became *The Waves.* She knew her destination months before she arrived; she was in control of her work, she did what she meant to do. If the novels are too imaginatively astonishing to be persuasive on this point, the essays will convince. They are read too little, and not one of them is conceptually stale, or worn in any other way. In them the birds do not sing in Greek either, but the Greek— the sign of a masterly nineteenth-century literary education—shows like a spine. In the essays the control of brilliant minutiae is total—historical and literary figures, the particulars of biography, society, nationality, geography. She is a courier for the past. In Volume III of the *Collected Essays,* for instance, the range is from Chaucer through Montaigne through some Eliz- abethans major and minor, through Swift and Sterne and Lord Chesterfield, Fanny Burney and Cowper. She was interested also in the lives of women, especially writers. She studies Sara Coleridge, the poet's daughter; Harriette Wilson, the mistress of the Earl of Craven; Dr. Johnson's Mrs. Thrale; and Dorothy Osborne, a talented letter-writer of the seventeenth century. The language and scope of the essays astound. If they are "impressionistic," they are not self-indulgent; they put history before sensibility. When they are ironic, it is the kind of irony that enlarges the discriminatory faculty and does not serve the cynical temper. They mean to interpret other lives by the annihilation of the crack of time: they are after what the novels are after, a compression of then and now into the simultaneity of a singular recogni- tion and a single comprehension. They mean to make every generation, and every instant, contemporaneous with every other generation and in- stant. And yet—it does not contradict—they are, taken all together, the Eng- lish Essay incarnate.

The autonomous authority of the fiction, the more public authority of the essays, are the antidotes to Bell's Woolf, to Leonard's Virginia. But there is a third antidote implicit in the whole of the work, and in the drive behind the work, and that is Virginia Woolf's feminism. It ought to be said at once that it was what can now be called "classical" feminism. The latter-day choice of Virginia Woolf, on the style of Sylvia Plath, as a current women's-movement avatar is inapposite and mistaken. Classical feminism is inimical to certain developing strands of "liberation." Where feminism repudiates the conceit of the "gentler sex," liberation has come to reaffirm it. Where feminism asserts a claim on the larger world, liberation shifts to separatism. Where feminism scoffs at the plaint of "sisters under the skin," and maintains individuality of condition and temperament, liberation reinstates sisterhood and sameness. Where feminism shuns self-preoccupation, liberation experiments with self-examination, both psychic and medical. Classical feminism as represented by Virginia Woolf meant one thing only: access to the great world of thinking, being, and doing. The notion of "male" and "female" states of intellect and feeling, hence of prose, ultimately of culture, would have been the occasion of a satiric turn for Virginia Woolf; so would the idea of a politics of sex. Clive Bell reports that she licked envelopes once or twice for the Adult Suffrage League, but that she "made merciless fun of the flag-waving fanaticism" of the activists. She was not political—or, perhaps, just political enough, as when Chekhov notes that "writers should engage themselves in politics only enough to protect themselves from politics." Though one of her themes was women in history (several of her themes, rather; she took her women one by one, not as a race, species, or nation), presumably she would have mocked at the invention of a "history of women"—what she cared for, as *A Room of One's Own* both lucidly and passionately lays out, was access to a unitary culture. Indeed, *Orlando* is the metaphorical expression of this idea. History as a record of division or exclusion was precisely what she set herself against: the Cambridge of her youth kept women out, and all her life she preserved her resentment by pronouncing herself undereducated. She studied at home, Greek with Janet Case, literature and mathematics with her father, and as a result was left to count on her fingers forever—but for people who grow up counting on their fingers, even a Cambridge education cannot do much. Nevertheless she despised what nowadays is termed "affirmative action," granting places in institutions as a kind of group reparation; she thought it offensive to her own earned prestige, and once took revenge on the notion. In 1935 Forster, a member of the Committee of the London Library, informed her that a debate was under way concerning the admission of women members. No women were admitted. Six years later Virginia Woolf was invited to serve; she said she would not be a "sop"—she ought to have been invited years earlier, on the same terms as Forster, as a writer; not in 1941, when she was already fifty-nine, as a woman.

Nor will she do as martyr. Although Cambridge was closed to her, literary journalism was not; although she complains of being chased off an Oxbridge lawn forbidden to the feet of women, no one ever chased her off a page. Almost immediately she began to write for the *Times Literary Supplement* and for *Cornhill;* she was then twenty-two. She was, of course, Leslie Stephen's daughter, and it is doubtful whether any other young writer, male or female, could have started off so auspiciously: still, we speak here not of "connections" but of experience. At about the same time she was sum-moned to teach at Morley, a workers' college for men and women. One of her reports survives, and Quentin Bell includes it as an appendix. "My four women," she writes, "can hear eight lectures on the French Revolution if they wish to continue their historical learning"—and these were working-class women, in 1905. By 1928, women had the vote, and full access to uni-versities, the liberal professions, and the civil service. As for Virginia Woolf, in both instances, as writer and teacher, she was solicited—and this cannot be, after all, only because she was Leslie Stephen's daughter. She could use on the spot only her own gifts, not the rumor of her father's. Once she de-termined to ignore what Bell calls the "matrimonial market" of upper-class partying, into which for a time her half-brother George dragooned her, she was freed to her profession. It was not true then, it is not true now, that a sublime and serious pen can be circumscribed.

Virginia Woolf was a practitioner of her profession from an early age; she was not deprived of an education, rather of a particular college; she grew rich and distinguished; she developed her art on her own line, accord-ing to her own sensibilities, and was acclaimed for it; though insane, she was never incarcerated. She was an elitist, and must be understood as such. What she suffered from, aside from the abysses of depression which char-acterized her disease, was not anything like the condition of martyrdom—unless language has become so flaccid that being on occasion patronized begins to equal death for the sake of an ideal. What she suffered from really was only the minor inflammations of the literary temperament. And she was not often patronized: her fame encouraged her to patronize others. She could be unkind, she could be spiteful, she could envy—her friendship with Katherine Mansfield was always unsure, being founded on rivalry. Mansfield and her husband, the journalist John Middleton Murry, "work in my flesh," Virginia Woolf wrote, "after the manner of the jigger insect. It's annoying, indeed degrading, to have these bitternesses." She was bitter also about James Joyce; she thought him, says Bell, guilty of "atrocities." Her diary speaks of "the damned egotistical self; which ruins Joyce," and she saw *Ulysses* as "insistent, raw, striking and ultimately nauseating." But she knew Joyce to be moving in the same direction as herself; it was a race that, despite her certainty of his faults, he might win. By the time of her death she must have understood that he *had* won. Still, to be outrun in fame is no martyrdom. And her own fame was and is in no danger, though, unlike Joyce, she is not taken as a fact of nature. Virginia Woolf's reputation in the thirty and more years since her death deepens; she becomes easier to read, more complex to consider.

To Charlotte Brontë, born sixty-six years before Virginia Woolf, Robert Southey, then Poet Laureate, had written, "Literature cannot be the business of a woman's life, and it ought not to be." No one addressed Virginia Woolf of Bloomsbury in this fashion; she was sought out by disciples, editors, litterateurs; in the end Oxford and Cambridge asked her to lecture before their women's colleges. If the issue of martyrdom is inappropriate (implying as it does that a woman who commits suicide is by definition a martyr), what of heroism? Virginia Woolf's death was or was not heroic, depending on one's view of suicide by drowning. The case for Leonard's heroism is more clear-cut: a saint is noble on behalf of others, a hero on behalf of himself. But if Virginia Woolf is to be seen as a heroine, it must be in those modes outside the manner of her death and even the manner of her life as a patient in the house.

If she is to be seen as a heroine, it must be in the conjuring of yet another of those Bloomsbury photographs—this time one that does not exist. The picture is of a woman sitting in an old chair holding a writing board; the point of her pen touches a half-filled page. To gaze at her bibliography is, in a way, to conjure this picture that does not exist—hour after hour, year after year, a life's accumulation of stupendous visionary toil. A writer's heroism is in the act of writing; not in the finished work, but in the work as it goes.

Vanessa's son gives us no heroine: only this stubborn and sometimes querulous self-starving madwoman, with so stoic, so heroic, a male nurse. And when she runs away from him to swallow the Ouse, the heroism of both of them comes to an end.

Justice (Again) to Edith Wharton

Nearly forty years ago, Edmund Wilson wrote a little essay about an under-rated American novelist and called it "Justice to Edith Wharton." She was in need of justice, he claimed, because "the more commonplace work of her later years had had the effect of dulling the reputation of her earlier and more serious work." During this last period—a stretch of about seventeen years, from (roughly) 1920 to her death in 1937—Edith Wharton's novels were best sellers, her short stories commanded thousands of dollars; but both in mode and motivation she remained, like so many others in the twenties and thirties, a nineteenth-century writer. She believed in portraying character, her characters displayed the higher values, her prose was a plat-form for her own views. In 1937, when Wilson undertook to invigorate her reputation, the machinery of nineteenth-century fiction was beginning to be judged not so much as the expression of a long tradition, or (as nowadays we seem to view it) as the exhausted practice of a moribund convention, but more bluntly as a failure of talent. Wilson accounted for that apparent failure in Edith Wharton by speculating on the psychological differences between male and female writers:

> It is sometimes true of women writers—less often, I believe, of men—that a manifestation of something like genius may be stimulated by some exceptional emotional strain, but will disappear when the stimulus has passed. With a man, his professional, his artisan's life is likely to persist and evolve as a partially in-dependent organism through the vicissitudes of his emotional experience. Henry James in a virtual vacuum continued to possess and develop his *métier*. But Mrs. Wharton had no *métier* in this sense.

What sort of "justice" is this? A woman typically writes best when her emotions are engaged; the barren female heart cannot seize the writer's trade? Only a decade ago, such a declaration would have been derided by old-fashioned feminists as a passing insolence. But even the satiric reader, contending in one fashion or another with this passage, would have been able, ten years ago, to pluck the offending notion out as a lapse in the texture of a measured and generally moderating mind.

No longer. Wilson's idea returns only to hold, and it holds nowhere so much as among the literary proponents of the current women's movement: Wilson's lapse is exalted to precept. The idea of Edith Wharton as a "woman writer" in need of constantly renewable internal stimuli, whose gifts are best sustained by "exceptional emotional strain"—all this suits the newest doctrine of sexual exclusiveness in literature. Indeed, one of the outstanding tenets of this doctrine embraces Wilson unrelentingly. "Rarely in the work now being written by women," according to an article called "Toward a Definition of the Female Sensibility,"

> does one feel the presence of writers genuinely penetrating their own experience, risking emotional humiliation and the facing-down of secret fears, unbearable wisdoms. . . . There are works, however, . . . in which one feels the heroic effort stirring,*

and there follow numerous examples of women writing well because of the stimulus of some exceptional emotional strain.

Restitution, then (one supposes), is to come to Edith Wharton not from the old-fashioned feminists, but from the newer sort, who embrace the proposition that strong emotion in women, emotion uniquely female, is what will best nourish a female literature. What we are to look for next, it follows, is an ambitious new-feminist critical work studying Wharton's "vicissitudes of . . . emotional experience" and correlating the most fevered points with the most accomplished of the fictions.

Such a work, it turns out, more extensive and more supple than Wilson's pioneer brief would suggest, has just made its appearance: Ellen Moers's *Literary Women*. Like other new feminists, Moers believes that there is such an entity as the "history of women," that there are poetic images uniquely female, and even "landscapes charged with female privacy." She writes of "how much the freedom and tactile sensations of near-naked sea bathing has meant to modern women," and insists that a scene recounting the sensation of walking through a field of sea-like grass provides that "moment when Kate Chopin reveals herself most truly a woman writer." Edith Wharton's life—a buried life—ought, properly scrutinized, to feed such a set of sympathies, and to lure the attention of restitution. *Literary Women*, after all, is conceived of in part as a rescue volume, as a book of rehabilitation

---

*Vivian Gornick, *The Village Voice*, May 31, 1973.

and justice: a number of writers, Moers explains, "came to life for me as women writers as they had not done before. Mrs. Gaskell and Anne Brontë had once bored me; Emily Dickinson was an irritating puzzle, as much as a genius; I could barely read Mary Shelley and Mrs. Browning. Reading them anew as women writers taught me how to get excited about these five, and others as well."

Others as well. But Edith Wharton is omitted from *Literary Women*. Her name appears only once, as an entry in an appendix. Only *The House of Mirth* is mentioned there, along with a reference, apparently by way of explanation of the larger omission, to the chapter on Edith Wharton in Alfred Kazin's *On Native Grounds*. Pursuing the citation, one discovers that Kazin, like Wilson, like the new feminists, speaks of "the need that drove her to literature." Whatever the need, it does not engage Moers; or Kazin. He advances the notion that "to Edith Wharton, whose very career as a novelist was the tenuous product of so many personal maladjustments, the novel became an involuted expression of self." Unlike the new feminists, Kazin will not celebrate this expression; it represents for him a "failure to fulfill herself in art." Wharton, he concludes, "remains not a great artist but an unusual American, one who brought the weight of her personal experience to bear upon a modern American literature to which she was spiritually alien."

Justice to Edith Wharton: where, then, is it to come from? Not taken seriously by the dominant criticism, purposefully ignored by the radical separatist criticism of the new feminists*—she represents an antagonism. The antagonism is not new. Wharton describes it herself in her memoir, *A Backward Glance*:

> My literary success puzzled and embarrassed my old friends far more than it impressed them, and in my own family it created a kind of constraint which increased with the years. None of my relations ever spoke to me of my books, either to praise or blame—they simply ignored them; and among the immense tribe of my cousins, though it included many with whom I was on terms of affectionate intimacy, the subject was avoided as if it were a kind of family disgrace, which might be condoned but could not be forgotten. Only one eccentric widowed cousin, living a life of lonely invalidism, turned to my novels for occasional distraction, and had the courage to tell me so.

She continues: "At first I felt this indifference acutely; but now I no longer cared, for my recognition as a writer had transformed my life."

---

*Though, to be fair, I have heard of at least one new-feminist literature class that has studied *The House of Mirth*—evidently because it is so easy to interpret its heroine as the ideal victim.

So it is here—in this uplifting idea, "my life," this teleological and novelistic idea above all—that one will finally expect to look for Wharton's restitution "as a writer." The justice that criticism perversely fails to bring, biography will achieve.

Perhaps. The biography of a novelist contains a wonderful advantage: it accomplishes, when well executed, a kind of mimicry. A good biography is itself a kind of novel. Like the classic novel, a biography believes in the notion of "a life"—a life as a triumphal or tragic story with a shape, a story that begins at birth, moves on to a middle part, and ends with the death of the protagonist.

Despite the reliable pervasiveness of birth and death, hardly any "real" life is like that. Most simply unfold, or less than that, dreamwalk themselves out. The middle is missing. What governs is not pattern but drift. Most American lives, moreover, fail to recognize that they are sticks in a stream, and are conceived of as novels-of-progress, as purposeful *Bildungsromane* saturated with an unending hopefulness, with the notion of infinite improvement on the way toward a salubrious goal; the frontier continues to inhabit the American mentality unfailingly.

And most American biographies are written out of this same source and belief. A biography that is most like a novel is least like a life. Edith Wharton's life, though much of it was pursued outside of America, is an American life in this sense: that, despite certain disciplines, it was predicated on drift, and fell out, rather than fell into place. If other American lives, less free than hers, drift less luckily between the Scylla and Charybdis of obligation and crisis, hers drifted in a setting all horizon, in a perpetual noncircumstance clear of external necessity. She had to invent her own environment and its conditions, and while this may seem the reverse of rudderlessness, what it signifies really is movement having to feign a destination. A life with a "shape" is occasioned by what is present in that life; drift grows out of what is absent. For Edith Wharton there was—outside the writing—no destination, and no obligation to get there. She had houses, she had wealth; she chose, rather than "had," friends. She had no family (she was estranged from her brothers, and we hear nothing further about the affectionate cousins), she had no husband (though she was married to one for more than half her life), she had no children. For a long time she resented and disliked children, and was obsessed by a love for small dogs. She was Henry James's ideal American heroine: she was indeed his very heiress of all the ages, she was "free," she was cultivated both in the conventional and the spiritual sense, she was gifted, acute, mobile; she appeared to be mistress of her destiny.

The destiny of such freedom is drift, and though her life was American in this, it was European in its resignation: she had no illusion that—outside the writing—she was doing more than "filling in." Her one moment of elevated and secure purpose occurred when, inspired by the model of Walt Whitman in the hospitals of the Civil War, she founded war relief agencies in France during the First World War. She supervised brilliantly: she supervised her friendships, her gardeners, her guests, the particulars of her dinner parties, her households; she even, to a degree, supervised the insurmountable Henry James—she took him for long rides in her car, she demanded hours in London and tea at Lamb House, she finagled with his publisher to provide him with a handsome advance (she herself was the secret philanthropist behind the scenes), she politicked to try and get him the Nobel Prize for Literature. She supervised and commanded, but since no one demanded anything of *her* (with a single exception, which, like the Gorgon's head, was not to be gazed at), she was captain, on an uncharted deep, of a ship without any imaginable port. She did everything on her own, to no real end; no one ever asked her to accommodate to any pressure of need, she had no obligations that she did not contrive or duty that she did not devise. Her necessities were self-imposed. Her tub went round and round in a sea of self-pleasing.

All this was outside the writing. One learns it from R. W. B. Lewis's prize-winning biography,* which is, like a posthumously uncovered Wharton novel, sustained by the idea of "a life." It has the fecund progression, the mastery of incident, the affectionate but balanced devotion to its protagonist, the power of suspenseful development, even the unraveling of a mysterious love story, that the "old" novel used to deliver—the novel before it became a self-referring "contemporary" art-object. In its own way it is a thesis novel: it is full of its intention to bring justice to Edith Wharton. A massive biography, almost by its weight, insists on the importance of its subject. Who would dare pass that writer by to whom a scholar-writer has dedicated, as Lewis has, nearly a decade of investigation and discovery? "They are among the handsomest achievements in our literature," he remarks of her major fictions. And adds: "I have wondered, with other admirers of Edith Wharton, whether her reputation might today stand even higher if she had been a man."

If the last statement has overtones of the new feminism—glory but for the impediment of sex—the book does not. Lewis sets out to render the life of an artist, not of a "woman artist." Unexpectedly, though it is the artist he is after, what he succeeds chiefly in giving us is the life of a woman. The "chiefly" is no small thing: it is useful to have a documented narrative of an

---

Edith Wharton: A Biography (Harper & Row, 1975). The prizes are the Pulitzer, the National Book Critics Circle Award, and Columbia University's Bancroft Prize.

exceptional upper-class woman of a certain American period. Still, without romanticizing what is meant by the phrase "an artist's life," there is a difference between the biography of a writer and the mode of living of a narrow American class.

Can the life justify the writer then? Or, to put it otherwise, can biography take the place of literary judgment? Lewis's book is a straightforward "tale," not a critical biography. Nor is it "psychobiography": though it yields new and revealing information about Edith Wharton's sexual experience, it does not propose to illumine the hidden chambers of the writer's sentience—as, for example, Ruby V. Redinger's recent inquiry into George Eliot's relationship to her brother Isaac, with its hunches and conjectures, purports to do, or Quentin Bell's half-study, half-memoir of Virginia Woolf. Lewis has in common with these others the revelation of a secret. In the case of Quentin Bell, it is the exact extent of Virginia Woolf's insanity; in the volume on George Eliot, the secret is the dense burden of humiliation imposed by an adored brother more cruel and rigid than society itself. And in Lewis, the secret is an undreamed-of, now minutely disclosed, adulterous affair with a journalist. In all three accounts, the writer is on the whole not there. It is understandable that the writer is mainly absent for the psychobiographer; something else is being sought. It is even more understandable that the writer should be absent for a nephew-biographer, whose preoccupation is with confirming family stories.

But if, for Lewis, the writer is not there, it is not because he fails to look for her but because she is very nearly invisible. What, through luck and diligence, he causes to become visible is almost not the point, however unpredictable and startling his discoveries are. And they are two: the surprising place of Morton Fullerton in Edith Wharton's middle years, and the appearance of a candid manuscript, written in her seventies, describing, with the lyrical explicitness of an enraptured anatomist, a fictional incestuous coupling. The manuscript and the love affair are so contrary to the established Wharton legend of cold propriety that they go far to make us look again—but only at the woman, not at the writer.

The real secret in Lewis's biography is devoid of sex, lived or imagined, though its centerpiece is a bed; and it concerns not the woman but the writer. The secret is divulged on page 353, when Wharton is fifty-one, and occupies ten lines in a volume of nearly six hundred pages. The ten lines recount a perplexing incident—"a minor fit of hysterics." The occasion is mysterious: Edith Wharton and Bernard Berenson, touring the great cities and museums of Europe together, arrive at the Hotel Esplanade in Berlin. They check into their respective rooms, and Edith Wharton, ignoring the view of the city though she has never been there before, begins to rage because the bed in her hotel room was not properly situated; not until it had been moved to face the window did she settle down and begin to find Berlin "incomparable." Berenson thought this an absurd performance; but because Edith never harped upon the physical requirements of her literary life, he did not quite realize that she worked in bed every morning and therefore needed a bed which faced the light. It had been her practice for more than twenty years; and for a woman . . . who clung so tenaciously to her daily stint, the need was a serious one.

The fit and its moment pass; the ensuing paragraphs tell of German politics snubbed and German music imbibed—we are returned, in short, to the life of an upper-class American expatriate tourist, privileged to travel in the company of a renowned connoisseur. But the plangent moment—an outcry over the position of a bed—dominates the book: dominates what has gone before and what is to come, and recasts both. Either the biographer can stand up to this moment—the woman revealed *as writer*—or the book falls into the drifting ash of "a life."

It falls, but it is not the biographer's fault; or not his fault alone. Edith Wharton—as writer—is to blame. She put a veil over the bed that was her workplace, and screened away the real life that was lived in it. What moves like a long afterimage in the wake of reading Lewis is a procession of stately majesties: Edith Wharton always standing, always regal, always stiffly dressed and groomed, standing with her wonderfully vertical spine in the hall of one of her great houses, or in the drawing room of her Paris apartment, with her fine hand out to some equally resplendent guest, or in her gardens, not so much admiring her flowers as instructing or reprimanding the servants of her flowers; or else "motoring" through the dust of some picturesque lane in the French countryside, her chauffeur in peaked hat and leather goggles, like blinders, on a high seat in front of her, indistinguishable from the horse that still headed most vehicles on the road.

If this is the Wharton myth, she made it; she wove it daily. It winds itself out like a vivid movie, yet darkly; it leaves out the window-lit bed. What went on outside the bed does not account for what went on in it. She frequented literary salons, and on a smaller scale held them (after dinner, Henry James reading aloud in the library); she talked bookishly, and with fervor; she was an intellectual. But she was not the only brilliant woman of her time and status; all of that, in the biography of a writer, weighs little.

Visualize the bed: she used a writing board. Her breakfast was brought to her by Gross, the housekeeper, who almost alone was privy to this inmost secret of the bedchamber. (A secretary picked up the pages from the floor for typing.) Out of bed, she would have had to be, according to her code, properly dressed, and this meant stays. In bed, her body was free, and freed her pen.

There is a famous photograph of Edith Wharton seated at a desk; we know now, thanks to the "minor fit of hysterics" at the Hotel Esplanade, how the camera lies—even though it shows us everything we might want to know about a way of life. The time is in the 1890s, the writer is in her early thirties. The desk is vast, shining, with a gold-tooled leather top; at the rear of its far surface is a decorated rack holding half a dozen books, but these are pointless—not only because anyone using this desk would need an impossibly long reach, but because all the volumes are faced away from the writer, with their backs and titles to the open room. Two tall electrified candlestick-lamps (the wire drags awkwardly) stand sentinel over two smaller candlesticks; there is a single letter, already stamped; otherwise the desk is clear, except for a pair of nervous ringed hands fiddling with a bit of paper.

The hands belong to a young woman got up, to our eyes, as theatrically as some fanciful notion of royalty: she is plainly a lady of fashion, with a constricted waist and a constricting tall collar; her dress is of the whitest fabric, all eyeleted, embroidered, sashed; her hair is elaborately rolled and ringleted; an earring makes a white dot below the high dark eave of her hair; her back is straight, even as she leans forward with concentrated mouth and lost eyes, in the manner of a writer in trance. Mellifluous folds hide her feet; a lady has no legs. She is sitting on a graceful chair with whorled feet— rattan framed by the most beautiful carved and burnished wood. (A rattan chair with not a single hole? No one could ever have *worked* in such a chair; the photographer defrauds us—nothing more important than a letter will ever be written at this desk.) The Oriental carpet, with its curious and dense figures, is most explicitly in focus, and over the edge of it a tail of skirt spills, reflected white on a floor as sleek as polished glass. In the background, blurred to the camera's lens but instructive to ours: a broad-shouldered velvet chair, a marble bust on an ebony pedestal, a table with a huge porcelain sculpture, a lofty shut oak or walnut door.—In short, an "interior," reminding us that the woman at the unused desk has undertaken, as her first writing venture, a collaborative work called *The Decoration of Houses*.

There are other portraits in this vein, formal, posed, poised, "intellectual" (meaning the subject muses over a seeming letter or book), all jeweled clips and chokers and pearls in heavy rows, pendants, feathered hats, lapdogs, furs, statuesque burdens of flounced bosom and grand liquescent sleeve, queenly beyond our bourgeois imaginings. And the portraits of houses: multiple chimneys, balconies, cupolas, soaring Romanesque windows, immense stone staircases, summer awnings of palatial breadth, shaped ivy, topiary like oversized chess pieces, walks, vistas, clouds of flower beds.

What are we (putting aside Marxist thoughts) to make of this avalanche of privilege? It is not enough to say: money. The class she derived from never talked of money; the money was invisible, like the writing in bed, and just as secret, and just as indispensable. The "love of beauty," being part of class habit, does not explain it; perhaps the class habit does. It was the class habit that kept her on the move: the class habit that is restlessness and drift. She wore out houses and places, or else her spirit wore out in them: New York, Newport, Lenox—finally America. In France there was the Paris apartment in the Rue de Varenne, then a small estate in St. Bricesous-Forêt, in the country north of Paris, then an old chateau in Hyères, on the warm Mediterranean coast. Three times in her life she supervised the total renovation of a colossal mansion and its grounds, in effect building and furnishing and landscaping from scratch; and once, in Lenox, she bought a piece of empty land and really did start from scratch, raising out of the earth an American palace called The Mount. All of this exacted from her the energy, attentiveness, and insatiable governing impulses of a corporation chief executive; or the head of a small state.

In an architectural lull, she would travel. All her life she traveled compulsively, early in her marriage with her husband, touring Europe from February to June, afterward with various male companions, with the sense, and with the propriety, of leading a retinue. Accumulating "scenes"— hotels, landscapes, seascapes, museums, villages, ruins—she saw all the fabled cities of Europe, the islands of the Aegean, Tunis, Algiers, Carthage, the Sahara.

And all the while she was surrounded by a crowd. Not simply while traveling: the crowd was part of the daily condition of her houses and possessions. She had a household staff consisting of maids ("housemaids" and "chambermaids"—there appears to be a difference), a chief gardener and several under-gardeners, cook, housekeeper, major-domo, chauffeur, personal maid, "traveling" maid, secretary, "general agent," footmen. (One of the latter, accompanying her to I Tatti, the Berenson villa in Italy, inconveniently fell in love with a Berenson maid, and had to be surrendered.) These "establishments," Lewis remarks, "gave her what her bountiful nature desired: an ordered life, a carefully tended beauty of surroundings, and above all, total privacy." The "above all" engenders skepticism. Privacy? Surveying that mob of servants, even imagining them crossing silent carpets on tiptoe, one takes the impression, inevitably, of a hive. Her solitude was the congested solitude of a monarch; she was never, like other solitary-minded American writers (one thinks of Poe, or of course Emily Dickinson, or even

Scott Fitzgerald), completely alone in the house. But these hectic move-
ments of the hive were what she required; perhaps she would not have
known how to do without them. Chekhov could sit at a table in the middle
of the din of a large impoverished family, ignoring voices and footsteps in
order to concentrate on the scratch of his pen. Edith Wharton sat up in bed
with her writing board, in the middle of the active business of a house
claiming her attention, similarly shutting out the only family she had. A hired
family, an invented one. When she learned that her older brother Freddy,
living not far away in Paris, had suffered a stroke, she was "unresponsive";
but when Gross, her housekeeper of long standing, and Elise, her personal
maid, both grew fatally ill within a short space, she wrote in her diary, "All
my life goes with those two dying women."

Nicky Mariano, in her memoir of her life as secretary-companion to Berenson, recalls how Edith Wharton treated her with indifference—until one
day, aboard a yacht near Naples, she happened to ask after Elise. She was
at once dispatched to the cabin below to visit with the maid. "From then on
I became aware of a complete change in Edith's manner to me. There was
a warmth, a tone of intimacy that I had never heard before." And again, describing how Wharton "looked after her servants with affectionate zeal and
took a lively interest in all their joys and sorrows," she produces another
anecdote:

> I remember how once during one of our excursions with her, she was deeply
> hurt and angry when on leaving a villa near Siena after a prolonged visit she
> discovered that neither her maid nor her chauffeur had been asked into the
> house.

What is the effect on a writer of being always encircled by servants?
What we are to draw from this is not so much the sadness of purchased
affections, or even the parasitism (once, left without much help for a brief
period, she was bewildered about her daily survival), but something more
perplexing: the moment-by-moment influence of continuous lower-class
companionship. Room ought to be given to considering this; it took room
in Wharton's life: she was with her servants all the time, she was with
her friends and peers only some of the time. E. M. Forster sought out the
common people in the belief that too much education atrophies the senses;
in life and in art he went after the lower orders because he thought them
the embodiment of the spontaneous gods of nature. In theory, at least—
perhaps it was only literary theory—Forster wanted to become "instinctual,"
and instinct was with the working class. But Edith Wharton kept her distance even as she drew close; she remained mistress always. It made her a
kind of double exile. As an expatriate settled in France, she had cut herself

off from any direct infusion of the American sensibility and the American language. Through her attachment to her servants, she became intimately bound to illiterate lives remote from her mentality, preoccupations, habitual perceptions—a second expatriation as deliberate as the more obvious one. Nor did her servants give her access to "ordinary" life (she was no Lady Chatterley, there was no gamekeeper for her)—no one is "ordinary" while standing before the monarch of the house. Still, she fussed over her army of hirelings; it was a way of inventing claims. For her servants she provided pensions; she instituted a trust fund as a private charity for three Belgian children; she sent regular checks to her sister-in-law, divorced from her brother a quarter of a century and therefore clearly not to be taken for family. For family, in short, she substituted claims indisputably of her own making. She could feel responsible for servants and acquired dependents as others feel responsible for parents, brothers, children: but there was a tether made of money, and the power-end of the tether was altogether in her hand. With servants, there is no murkiness—as there sometimes is in friendship—about who is beholden to whom.

With her friends it was more difficult to invent claims; friendship has a way of resisting purchase, and she had to resort to ruses. When she wanted to release Morton Fullerton from the entangling blackmail of his former French mistress, she arranged with Henry James to make it seem as if the money were coming impersonally from a publisher. Fullerton having been, however briefly, her lover, it was hardly possible to hand over one hundred pounds and call it a "pension"; the object was not so much to keep Fullerton's friendship free as to establish the illusion of such freedom. It was enough for the controlling end of the money tether to know the tether was there; and anyhow the tether had a witness and an accomplice. "Please consider," James wrote, entering into the plot, "that I will play my mechanical part in your magnificent combination with absolute piety, fidelity, and punctuality."

But when it was James himself who came to be on the receiving end of the golden tether, he thundered against the tug of opulence, and the friendship was for a while impaired. The occasion was a proposal for his seventieth birthday: Edith Wharton, enlisting about forty moneyed Americans, thought to raise "not less than $5000," the idea being "that he should choose a fine piece of old furniture, or something of the kind"—but to James it all smelled blatantly of charity, meddling, pity, and cash. Once he got wind of the plan he called it a "reckless and indiscreet undertaking," and announced in a cable that he was beginning "instant prohibitive action. Please express to individuals approached my horror. Money absolutely returned."

It was returned, but within a few months James was hooked anyhow on that same line—hooked like Morton Fullerton, without being aware of it. This time the accomplice was Charles Scribner, who forwarded to James a phoney "advance" of eight thousand dollars intended to see him through the writing of *The Ivory Tower*—but the money was taken out of Wharton's own advance, from another publisher, of fifteen thousand dollars. The reluctant agent of the scheme, far from celebrating "your magnificent combination," saw it rather as "our fell purpose." "I feel rather mean and caddish and must continue so to the end of my days," Charles Scribner grumbled. "Please never give me away." In part this sullenness may have been guilt over not having himself volunteered, as James's publisher, to keep a master artist free from money anxiety, but beyond that there was a distaste for manipulation and ruse.

This moral confusion about proprieties—whom it is proper to tip, and whom not—expressed itself in other strange substitutions. It was not only that she wanted to pay her lover and her friend for services rendered, sexual or literary—clearly she had little overt recognition of the *quid pro quo* uses of philanthropy. It was not only that she loved her maid Gross more than her mother, and Arthur White her "man" more than her brother—it is understood that voluntary entanglements are not really entanglements at all. But there were more conspicuous replacements. Lacking babies, she habitually fondled small dogs: there is an absurd photograph of Edith Wharton as a young woman of twenty-eight, by then five years into her marriage, with an angry-looking Pekingese on each mutton-leg shoulder; the animals, pressed against her cheeks, nearly obscure her face; the face is cautious and contemplative, as of one not wanting to jar precious things. A similar photograph shows her husband gazing straight out at us with rather empty pale eyes over a nicely trimmed mustache and a perfect bow tie—on his lap, with no special repugnance, he is holding three small dogs, two of them of that same truculent breed, and though the caption reads "Teddy Wharton with his dogs," somehow we know better whose dogs they are. His body is detached; his expression, very correct and patient, barely hides—though Lewis argues otherwise—how he is being put upon by such a pose.

Until late in life, she never knew a child. Effie, the little girl in *The Reef*, is a child observed from afar—she runs, she enters, she departs, she is sent, she is summoned, at one moment she is presented as very young, at another she is old enough to be having lessons in Latin. She is a figment of a child. But the little dogs, up to the end of Edith Wharton's life, were always understood, always thought to have souls, always in her arms and in her bed; they were, Lewis says, "among the main joys of her being." Drawing up a list of her "ruling passions" at forty-four, she put "Dogs" second after

"Justice and Order." At sixty-two she wrote in her journal of "the *us*ness" in the eyes of animals, "with the underlying *not-us*ness which belies it," and meditated on their "eternal inarticulateness and slavery. Why? their eyes seem to ask us."

The fellow feeling she had for the *not-us*ness of her Pekingese she did not have for her husband, who was, from her point of view, also *"not-us."* He too was inarticulate and mired in the slavery of a lesser intellect. He was a good enough man, interested (like his wife) in being perfectly clothed, vigorous and humorous and kind and compliant (so compliant that he once actually tried to make his way through James's *The Golden Bowl*)—undistinguished in any jot, the absolute product of his class. He had no work to do, and sought none. One of Edith Wharton's friends—a phrase instantly revealing, since her friends were practically never his; the large-hearted Henry James was nearly the only one to cross this divide—observed that Teddy Wharton's "idleness was busy and innocent." His ostensible employment was the management of his wife's trust funds, but he filled his days with sports and hunting, and his glass with fine wine. Wine was the one thing he had a connoisseur's familiarity with; and, of all the elegant good things of the world, wine was the one thing his wife disliked. When he was fifty-three he began to go mad, chiefly, it would seem, because he had married the wrong wife, with no inkling that she would turn out to be the wrong wife. Edith Newbold Jones at twenty-three was exactly what Edward Wharton, a dozen years older, had a right to expect for himself: she had heritage (her ancestor, Ebenezer Stevens, was an enterprising artillery officer in the Revolutionary War), she had inheritance (the Joneses owned the Chemical Bank of New York and much of the West Side). In brief, family and money. The dominant quality—what he had married her for, with that same idle innocence that took note only of the pleasantly obvious—was what Edith Wharton was afterward to call "tribe." The Whartons and the Joneses were of the same tribe—old Protestant money—and he could hardly predict that his wife would soon replace him in the nuptial bed with a writing board. At first he was perplexed but proud: Louis Auchincloss quotes a description of Teddy Wharton from Consuelo Vanderbilt's memoirs as "more of an equerry than an equal, walking behind [his wife] and carrying whatever paraphernalia she happened to discard," and once (Lewis tells us), walking as usual behind her, Teddy exclaimed to one of her friends, "Look at that waist! No one would ever guess that she had written a line of poetry in her life." She, meanwhile, was driven to writing in her journal, "Oh, Gods of derision! And you've given me over twenty years of it!" This outcry occurred immediately after she had shown her husband, during a wearying train journey, "a particularly interesting passage" in a scientific volume called *Heredity and*

Variation. His response was not animated. "I heard the key turn in my prison-lock," she recorded, in the clear metaphorical style of her fiction.

A case can be made that it was she who turned the key on him. His encroaching madness altered him—he began to act oddly, out of character; or, rather, more in character than he had ever before dared. The equerry of the paraphernalia undertook to behave as if he were master of the paraphernalia—in short, he embezzled a part of the funds it had been his duty to preserve and augment. And, having been replaced in bed by a writing board, he suddenly confessed to his wife (or perhaps feverishly bragged) that he had recently gone to live with a prostitute in a Boston apartment, filling its remaining rooms with chorus girls; the embezzled funds paid for the apartment. The story was in the main confirmed. His madness had the crucial sanity of needs that are met.

His wife, who—granted that philanthropy is not embezzlement—was herself capable of money ruse, and who had herself once rapturously fallen from merely spiritual friendship, locked him up for it. Against his protestations, and those of his sister and brother, he was sent to a sanitorium. Teddy had stolen, Teddy had fallen; he was an adulterer. She had never stolen (though there is a robust if mistaken critical tradition that insists she stole her whole literary outlook from Henry James); but she had fallen, she was an adulteress. Teddy's sexual disgrace was public; hers went undivulged until her biographer came upon it more than three decades after her death. But these sardonic parallels and opposites illumine little beyond the usual ironies of the pot and the kettle. What had all at once happened in Edith Wharton's life was that something *had* happened. Necessity intervened, her husband was irrefutably a manic-depressive. He had hours of excitement and accusation; more often he was in a state of self-castigation. He begged her for help, he begged to be taken back and to be given a second chance. ". . . when you came back last year," she told him, "I was ready to overlook everything you had done, and to receive you as if nothing had happened." This referred to the Boston apartment; she herself had been in a London hotel with Fullerton at nearly the same time. In the matter of her money she was more unyielding. Replying to his plea to be allowed to resume the management of her trusts and property, she took the tone of a mistress with a servant who has been let go, and who is now discovered still unaccountably loitering in the house. "In order that no further questions of this kind should come up, the only thing left for me to do is to suggest that you should resign your Trusteeship. . . . Your health unfortunately makes it impossible for you to take any active part in the management of my affairs." Gradually, over months, she evolved a policy: she did everything for him that seemed sensible, as long as it was cold-hearted. He was removed, still uncured, from the sanitorium, and subjected to a regime of doctors, trips, traveling companions, scoldings. In the end, when he was most sick and most desperate, she discarded him, handing him over to the doctors the way one hands over impeding paraphernalia to an equerry. She discarded him well before she divorced him; divorce, at that period and in her caste, took deliberation. She discarded him because he impeded, he distracted, he was a nuisance, he drained her, he wore her out. As a woman she was contemptuous of him, as a writer she fought off his interruptions. The doctors were more polite than Henry James, who characterized Teddy Wharton as able to "hold or follow no counter-proposal, no plan of opposition, of his own, for as much as a minute or two; he is immediately *off*—irrelevant and childish . . . one's pity for her is at the best scarce bearable."

She too pitied herself, and justly, though she forgot to pity *him*. He had lost all trust in himself, whatever he said he timidly or ingratiatingly or furiously took back. He was flailing vainly after the last flashes of an autonomy his wife had long ago stripped from him. And during all that angry space, when she was bitterly engaged in fending off the partisan ragings of his family, and coldly supervising his medical and traveling routines, she, in the stern autonomy of her morning bed, was writing *Ethan Frome,* finishing *The Reef,* bringing off short stories. She could do all this because she did not look into her husband's eyes and read there, as she had read in the eyes of her little dogs, the helpless pathos of "Why?" It was true that she did not and could not love him, but her virtue was always according to principle, not passion. Presumably she also did not love the French soldiers who were sick with tuberculosis contracted in the trenches of the First World War; nevertheless for them she organized a cure program, which she termed "the most vital thing that can be done in France now." Whatever the most vital thing for Teddy might have been—perhaps there was nothing—she relinquished it at last. The question of the tubercular soldiers was, like all the claims on her spirit that she herself initiated, volitional and opportune. She had sought out these tragedies, they were not implicated in the conditions of her own life, that peculiar bed she had made for herself—"such a great big uncompromising 4-poster," James called it. For the relief of tubercular soldiers and other good works, she earned a French medal, and was made a Chevalier of the Legion of Honor. An arena of dazzling public exertion. But in the lesser frame of private mess she did nothing to spare her husband the humiliation of his madness. It is one thing to go mad, it is another to be humiliated for it. The one time in her life drift stopped dead in its trackless spume, and a genuine claim made as if to seize her—necessity, redder in tooth and claw than any sacrifice one grandly chooses for oneself—she turned away. For her, such a claim was the Gorgon's head, to gaze on which was death.

Writer's death. This is something most writers not only fear but sweat to evade, though most do not practice excision with as clean a knife-edge as cut away "irrelevant and childish" Teddy from Edith Wharton's life. "Friend, client, child, sickness, fear, want, charity, all knock at once at thy closet door and say—'Come out unto us.' But keep thy state," Emerson advised, "come not into their confusion." And Mann's Tonio Kröger declaims that "one must die to life to be utterly a creator." This ruthless romantic idea—it cannot be lived up to by weaklings who succumb to conscience, let alone to love—is probably at bottom less romantic than pragmatic. But it is an idea very nearly the opposite of Wilson's and Kazin's more affecting view of Edith Wharton: that joylessness was her muse, that her troubles energized her for fiction—the stimulus of "some exceptional emotional strain," according to Wilson, "so many personal maladjustments," according to Kazin, which made the novelist possible. If anything made the novelist possible, it was the sloughing off of the sources of emotional strain and personal maladjustment. As for the parallel new-feminist opinion that a woman writes best when she risks "unbearable wisdoms," it does not apply: what wisdom Edith Wharton found unbearable she chose not to bear.

The rest was chatter. Having turned away from the Gorgon's head, she spent the remainder of her life—indeed, nearly the whole of it—in the mainly insipid, sometimes inspired, adventure of elevated conversation. She had her friends. There were few women—whether because she did not encounter her equals among women, or because she avoided them, her biographer yields no hint. The majority were men (one should perhaps say "gentlemen")—Lapsley, Lubbock, Berenson, Fullerton, Simmons, James, Bourget, D'Humières, Berry, Sturgis, Hugh-Smith, Maynard, Gregory, Grant, Scott . . . the list is longer still. Lewis fleshes out all these names brilliantly, particularly Berry and Fullerton; the great comic miraculous James needs no fleshing out. James was in a way afraid of her. She swooped down on him to pluck him away for conversation or sightseeing, and he matched the "commotion and exhaustion" of her arrivals against the vengeance of Bonaparte, Attila, and Tamerlane. "Her powers of devastation are ineffable," he reported, and got into the habit of calling her the Angel of Devastation. She interrupted his work with the abruptness of a natural force (she might occur at any time) and at her convenience (she had particular hours for her work, he had all hours for his). He read her novels and dispatched wondrous celebrating smokescreens of letters ("I applaud, I mean I value, I egg you on") to hide the insufficiency of his admiration. As for her "life," it was a spectacle that had from the beginning upset him: her "desolating, ravaging, burning and destroying energy." And again: "such a nightmare of perpetually renewable choice and decision, such a luxury of bloated alternatives." "*What* an incoherent life!" he summed it up. Lewis disagrees, and reproaches James for partial views and a probable fear of strong women; but it may be, on all the lavish evidence Lewis provides, that the last word will after all lie with drift, exactly as James perceived it in her rushing aimlessness aimed at him.

Before Lewis's landmark discovery of the Wharton-Fullerton liaison, Walter Van Rensselaer Berry—Wharton's distant cousin, an international lawyer and an aristocrat—was commonly regarded as the tender center and great attachment of her life. Lewis does not refute this connection, though he convincingly drains it of sexual particularity, and gives us the portrait of a conventionally self-contained dry-hearted lifelong bachelor, a man caught, if not in recognizable drift, then in another sort of inconclusiveness. But Walter Berry was Edith Wharton's first literary intellectual—a lightning bolt of revelation that, having struck early, never lost its electrical sting. Clearly, she fed on intellectuals—but in a withdrawn and secretive way: she rarely read her work aloud, though she rejoiced to hear James read his. She brooded over history and philosophy, understood everything, but was incapable in fiction or elsewhere of expressing anything but the most commonplace psychology. This was, of course, her strength: she knew how human beings behave, she could describe and predict and surprise. Beyond that, she had a fertile capacity for thinking up stories. Plots and permutations of plots teemed. She was scornful of writers who agonized after subject matter. Subjects, she said, swarmed about her "like mosquitoes," until she felt stifled by their multiplicity and variety.

The truth is she had only one subject, the nineteenth century's unique European literary subject: society. Standard American criticism, struggling to "place" Edith Wharton in a literary environment unused to her subject, has contrived for her the role of a lesser Henry James. This has served to indict her as an imitative figure. But on no significant level is the comparison with James pertinent, except to say that by and large they wrote about the same kinds of people, derived from the same class. Otherwise the difference can be seized in a breath: James was a genius, Wharton not. James invented an almost metaphysical art, Wharton's insights lay close against their molds: what she saw she judged. James became an American in the most ideal sense, Wharton remained an estranged New Yorker. James was an uncanny moralist, Wharton a canny realist. James scarcely ever failed—or, at least, his few failures when they occurred were nevertheless glorious in aspiration and seamless in execution. When Wharton failed, she fell into an embarrassing triteness of language and seeing.

It is a pity that her name is attached so unrelentingly—thanks to the American high school—to *Ethan Frome*, a desolate, even morbid, narrow, soft-at-the-center and at the last unsurprising novella not at all typical of her range. It is an outdoor book that ends mercilessly indoors; she was an indoor novelist. She achieved two permanent novels, one—*The House of Mirth*—a spoiled masterpiece, a kind of latterday reverse *Scarlet Letter*, very direct yet eerie, the other *The Age of Innocence*, a combination of ode and elegy to the New York of her childhood, affirmation and repudiation both. A good many of her short stories and some of the novellas ("The Old Maid," for instance) are marvels of shapeliness and pointedness. This applies also to stories written during her late period, when she is widely considered to have debased her gift. The common accusation—Wilson makes it—is that her prose finally came to resemble women's-magazine fiction. One can venture that she did not so much begin to sound like the women's magazines, as that they began to sound like her, a condition that obtains until this moment. No one has explored Wharton's ongoing subliminal influence on current popular fiction (see almost any issue of *Redbook*); such an investigation would probably be striking in its disclosure of the strength of her legacy. Like any hokey imitation long after the model is lost to consciousness, it is not a bad compliment, though it may be awkward to admit it. (One of the least likely tributes to the Roman Empire, after all, is the pervasiveness of nineteenth-century American civic architecture.) But *The House of Mirth* and *The Age of Innocence* are, like everything unsurpassable because deeply idiosyncratic, incapable of spawning versions of themselves; in these two novels she is in command of an inwardness commensurate with structure. In them she does not simply grab hold of society, or judge it merely; she turns society into an exulting bird of prey, with blood on its beak, steadily beating its wings just over our heads; she turns society into an untamable *idea*. The reader, apprehensive, yet lured by the bird's lyric form, covers his face.

She could do all that; she had that power. Lewis, writing to justify and defend, always her sympathetic partisan, nevertheless hedges. Having acknowledged that she had "begun to locate herself—with a certain assurance, though without vanity—in the developing course of American literature," he appends a doubt:

> But in another part of her, there remained something of the conviction drilled into her in old New York that it was improper for a lady to write fiction. One could do so only if one joked about it—if one treated it, to borrow Lubbock's word, as "an amusement." She sometimes sounded as if her writing were her entertainingly guilty secret, and in her memoirs she referred to it (borrowing

the title of a popular children's book of her own New York youth) as her "secret garden."

But in the winter of 1911 [she was then at work on *The Reef*], as on perhaps half a dozen other occasions, it was the believing artist that was in the ascendancy during the hard-driving morning hours.

Somehow it is easy to doubt that she had this doubt—or, if she once had it, that she held it for long. To believe in her doubt is to make the bad case of the orthodox critics who, unlike Lewis, have shrunk from taking her seriously as an artist because as an American aristocrat she was born shockingly appurtenanced, and therefore deserves to be patronized for her sorrows. To believe in her doubt is to make the bad case of the new feminists, for whom female sex is, always and everywhere, an impediment difficult to transcend—even when, for an obsessed writer of talent, there is nothing to transcend. To believe in her doubt is to reverse the terms of her life and her work. Only "half a dozen other occasions" when Wharton was a "believing artist"? Only so few? This would mean that the life outside her bed—the dressed life of conversation and travel, the matchstick life of drift—was the primary life, and the life with her writing board—the life of the believing artist—the deviation, the anomaly, the distraction.

But we know, and have always known (Freud taught us only how to reinforce this knowledge), that the secret self is the true self, that obsession is confession. For Edith Wharton that is the only acceptable evaluation, the only possible justice. She did not doubt her allegiance. The writing came first. That she kept it separate from the rest was a misrepresentation and a mistake, but it may also have been a species of holy instinct—it was the one uncontaminated zone of her being: the place unprofaned. Otherwise she can be defined only by the horrific gyrations of "a life"—by the spiraling solipsism and tragic drift that led her to small dogs instead of babies, servants instead of family, high-minded male distance instead of connubial friendship, public virtue instead of private conscience, infatuation instead of the love that sticks. Only the writing board could justify these ugly substitutions. And some would say—myself not among them—that not even the writing board justified them.

Literature and the Politics of Sex: A Dissent

Women who write with an overriding consciousness that they write *as women* are engaged not in aspiration toward writing, but chiefly in a politics of sex. A new political term makes its appearance: *woman writer,* not used descriptively—as one would say "a lanky brown-haired writer"—but as part of the language of politics.

Now a politics of sex can be very much to the point. No one would deny that the movement for female suffrage was a politics of sex, and obviously any agitation for equality in employment, in the professions, and in government is a politics of sex.

But the language of politics is not writer's language. Politics begins with premises; imagination goes in search of them. The political term *woman writer* signals in advance a whole set of premises: that, for instance, there are "male" and "female" states of intellect and feeling, hence of prose; that individuality of condition and temperament do not apply, or at least not much, and that all writing women possess—not by virtue of being writers but by virtue of being women—an instantly perceived common ground; that writers who are women can best nourish other writers who are women.

"There is a human component to literature," according to Ellen Moers, "which a woman writer can more easily discuss with another woman writer, even across an ocean, than she can with the literary man next door."*

I deny this. There is a human component to literature that does not separate writers by sex, but that—on the contrary—engenders sympathies from sex to sex, from condition to condition, from experience to experience, from like to like, and from unlike to unlike. Literature universalizes. Without disparaging particularity or identity, it universalizes; it does not divide.

---

*Literary Women.

But what, with respect to particularity or identity, is a "woman writer"? Outside its political uses, "woman writer" has no meaning—not intellectually, not morally, not historically. A writer is a writer.

Does a "woman writer" have a separate psychology—by virtue of being a woman? Does a "woman writer" have a separate body of ideas—by virtue of being a woman? It was these misleading currencies that classical feminism was created to deny.

Does a "woman writer" have a body of separate experience—by virtue of being a woman? It was this myth-fed condition of segregation that classical feminism was created to bring an end to.

Insofar as some women, and some writers who are women, have separate bodies of experience or separate psychologies, to that degree has the feminism of these women not yet asserted itself. In art, feminism is that idea which opposes segregation; which means to abolish mythological divisions; which declares that the imagination cannot be "set" free, because it is already free.

To say "the imagination is free" is, in fact, a tautology. The imagination is by definition, by nature, freedom and autonomy. When I write, I am free. I am, as a writer, whatever I wish to become. I can think myself into a male, or a female, or a stone, or a raindrop, or a block of wood, or a Tibetan, or the spine of a cactus.

In life, I am not free. In life, female or male, no one is free. In life, female or male, I have tasks; I have obligations and responsibilities; I have a toothache, being contingent on nature; I am devoured by drudgery and fragmentation. My freedom is contingent on need. I am, in short, claimed. Female or male, I am subject to the disciplines of health or disease, of getting and spending, of being someone's child and being someone's parent. Society—which is not yet utopia—tells me to go stand there and do that, or else keep my distance and not do this. In life, I accept those dictums of Society which seem to me to be the same as Civilization, and quarrel with the rest.

But when I write, what do Society and its protocol mean to me? When I write, I am in command of a grand *As If*. I write *As If* I were truly free. And this *As If* is not a myth. As soon as I proclaim it, as soon as my conduct as a writer expresses it, it comes into being.

A writer—I mean now a fiction writer or a poet, an *imagining* writer—is not a sociologist, or a social historian, or a literary critic, or a journalist, or a politician. The newspeak term "woman writer" has the following sociological or political message: "Of course we believe in humanity-as-a-whole. Of course we believe that a writer is a writer, period. But let us for a little while gather together, as women, to become politically strong, strong in morale, a visible, viable social factor; as such, we will separate ourselves only temporarily, during this strengthening period, and then, when we can rejoin the world with power and dignity in our hands, we *will* rejoin it, and declare ourselves for the unity of the human species. This temporary status will be our strategy in our struggle with Society."

That is the voice of the "woman writer." But it is a mistaken voice. Only consider: in intellectual life, a new generation comes of age every four or five years. For those who were not present at the inception of this strategy, it will not seem a strategy at all; it will be the only reality. Writers will very soon find themselves born into one of two categories, "woman writer" or "writer," and all the "writers" will be expected to be male—an uninspiring social and literary atmosphere the world has known before. "Literature cannot be the business of a woman's life, and it ought not to be," the Poet Laureate Robert Southey scolded Charlotte Brontë. But that was the early half of the nineteenth century. Only twenty years ago, an anthologist of Russian literature, speaking of a Russian writer's international influence, re-marked that "in the case of certain British lady-writers it may be said to have been nothing short of disastrous." He does not tell us about those British gentleman-writers who were also bad literary imitators. One could raise a mountain of such quotations, all specializing in the disparagement that in-evitably emerges out of segregation. The success of feminism inhibited such views, but regression will be made easy once the pure, unqualified, unpo-lemical, unpoliticized word "writer" begins all over again to refer to only half the writers there are.

And not only this. The strategy is based on a temporary assumption of an untruth. When the strategy's utility passes, we are assured, the natural condition of unity will be resumed. But it is dangerous to accommodate to a falsehood even for a single minute. The so-called temporary has an ineluc-table inclination to turn into long-range habit. All politicians know that every "temporary" political initiative promised as a short-term poultice stays on the books forever. *Strategies become institutions.* If writers promise them-selves that they will organize as "women writers" only "temporarily," that they will yoke themselves to a misleading self-definition only for the sake of a short-term convenience, it is almost certain that the temporary will become the long-term status quo, and "convenience" will be transmogrified into a new truth.

But worse than that. Belief in a "new truth" nearly always brings authori-tarianism in its wake. As the temporary-segregation strategy more and more loses its character both as to "temporary" and as to "strategy," it begins also to lay claim to a full, in fact to the only, definition of feminism. More and more, apartness is perceived as the dominant aim, even the chief quality, of feminism. More and more, women are urged to think of themselves in tribal terms, as if anatomy were the same as culture. More and more, artists who are women are made to feel obliged to deliver a "women's art," as if ten thousand other possibilities, preoccupations, obsessions, were inauthentic for women, or invalid, or, worse yet, lyingly evasive. We grow familiar, currently, with the presumption of a "women's photography";* will there eventually arise a women's entomology, or a women's astrophysics? Or will only the sciences, in their objective universalism, retain the freedom of the individual mind, unfettered by *a priori* qualification?

Art formed or even touched by any inflexibility—any topical or social expectation, any extrinsic burden, any axiom or presumption or political nuance, any prior qualification at all—will always make for a debased culture. Sometimes history gives this inflexibility the name of "dogma"; sometimes "party line"; sometimes, alas, "truth."

Classical feminism—i.e., feminism at its origin, when it saw itself as justice and aspiration made universal, as mankind widened to humankind—rejected anatomy not only as destiny, but as any sort of governing force; it rejected the notion of "female sensibility" as a slander designed to shut women off from access to the delights, confusions, achievements, darknesses, and complexities of the great world. Classical feminism was conceived of as the end of false barriers and boundaries; as the end of segregationist fictions and restraints; as the end of the Great Multiple Lie.

What was the Great Multiple Lie? It applied to all women, and its premise was that there is a "female nature" which is made manifest in all art by women. For imaginative writers, its assertions were especially limiting and corrosive. For example:

1. It assumed a psychology and an emotional temper peculiar to women.

2. It assumed a prose or verse style endemic in, and characteristic of, women.

3. It assumed a set of preoccupations appropriate, by nature, to female poets and novelists—e.g., female friendship, female madness, motherhood, love and romance, domestic conflict, duty, religiosity, etc.

4. It assumed a natural social community grounded in biology and reproductive characteristics ("sisters under the skin"), rather than in intellect or temperament or derivation or societal experience.

---

*Molly Haskell, *Ms.,* September 1977: "There is a tendency (and this is true of women's films as well) toward a novelistic rather than dramatic organization of material, meaning that character is conveyed evocatively through an accumulation of small gestures, half notes, and ordinary details rather than through the climactic scenes of confrontation and revelation." Since all of this is also an excellent description of the short stories and plays of, say, Chekhov, the attempt to prove female "tendency" through illustration turns out to be just as unimpressive when performed by a female critic as by a male critic.

5. It took for granted the difference (from "male" writing) of "women's" poetry and "women's" novels by assuming a "woman's" separate sensibility.

6. It posited for intellect and imagination a purely sexual base. It assumed the writer's gender inherently circumscribed and defined and directed the writer's subject matter, perspective, and aspiration.

All this emits a certain melancholy familiarity: the old, old prejudices, after all. Their familiarity in voices hostile to women is melancholy, and usual, enough; but now, more and more, the voices that carry these convictions are women's voices. With some small modifications (for love and romance, substitute sex; for domestic conflict, substitute home-and-career clashes; for female madness, female rage; and omit duty and religiosity altogether), these ideas make up the literary credo of the new feminism. More and more, there are writers and artists and other masters of imagination who declare themselves freed by voluntary circumscription. "Up till now I was mistaken," they will testify; "I was trying to write like a man. Then I began to write about myself as a daughter, as a lover, as a wife, as a mother, as a woman in relation to other women; as a *self*. I learned to follow the contours of my emotional life. I began to write out of my femaleness."

Thurber once wrote a story about a bear who leaned so far backward that he ended up by falling on his face. Now we are enduring a feminism so far advanced into "new truths" that it has arrived at last at a set of notions indistinguishable from the most age-encrusted, unenlightened, and imprisoning antifeminist views.

Occasionally one hears of prisoners who decline parole, preferring fences and cells. Having returned, they still continue, sensibly and sanely, to call their comfortable old cages "prison." Artists who insist on defining themselves as "women" artists may, after a fashion, flourish under that designation, but they should not stumble into the misnomer of calling voluntary circumscription "feminism." Classical feminism, while not denying the body, while not precluding self-image and self-knowledge, never dreamed of engaging these as single-minded objectives. Feminism means, has always meant, access to possibilities beyond self-consciousness. Art, freed of restrictions, grows in any space, even the most confined. But polemical self-knowledge is restricted knowledge. Self-discovery is only partial discovery. Each human being is a particle of a generation, a mote among the revealing permutations of Society. When you know yourself, when you have toiled through "the contours of emotional life," where are you, what is it that you know, how far can it take you? Self-consciousness—narcissism, solipsism—is small nourishment for a writer. Literature is hungrier than that: a writer with an ambitious imagination needs an appetite beyond the self.

For writers who are women, the "new truth" of self-regard, of biologically based self-confinement, is the Great Multiple Lie freshly got up in drag.

For writers there *are* no "new truths." There is only one very old truth, as old as Sappho, as old as Homer, as old as the Song of Deborah, as old as the Songs of David—that the imagination is free, that the gift of making literature is accessible to every kind and condition of human being, that when we write we are not women or men but blessèd beings in possession of a Promethean art, an art encumbered by peril and hope and fire and, above all, freedom. What we ought to do, as writers, is not wait for freedom, meanwhile idling in self-analysis; the freedom one waits for, or builds strategies toward, will never come. What we ought to do, as writers, is seize freedom now, immediately, by recognizing that we already have it.

The Lesson of the Master

There was a period in my life—to purloin a famous Jamesian title, "The Middle Years"—when I used to say, with as much ferocity as I could muster, "I hate Henry James and I wish he was dead."

I was not to have my disgruntled way. The dislike did not last and turned once again to adoration, ecstasy, and awe; and no one is more alive than Henry James, or more likely to sustain literary immortality. He is among the angels, as he meant to be.

But in earlier days I felt I had been betrayed by Henry James. I was like the youthful writer in "The Lesson of the Master" who believed in the Master's call to live immaculately, unspoiled by what we mean when we say "life"—relationship, family mess, distraction, exhaustion, anxiety, above all disappointment. Here is the Master, St. George, speaking to his young disciple, Paul Overt:

> "One has no business to have any children," St. George placidly declared. "I mean, of course, if one wants to do anything good."
> "But aren't they an inspiration—an incentive?"
> "An incentive to damnation, artistically speaking."

And later Paul inquires:

> "Is it deceptive that I find you living with every appearance of domestic felicity—blest with a devoted, accomplished wife, with children whose acquaintance I haven't yet had the pleasure of making, but who *must* be delightful young people, from what I know of their parents?"
> St. George smiled as for the candour of his question. "It's all excellent, my dear fellow—heaven forbid I should deny it. . . . I've got a loaf on the shelf; I've got everything in fact but the great thing."
> "And the great thing?" Paul kept echoing.
> "The sense of having done the best—the sense which is the real life of the artist and the absence of which is his death, of having drawn from his intellectual instrument the finest music that nature had hidden in it, of having played it as it should be played. He either does that or he doesn't—and if he doesn't he isn't worth speaking of."

Paul pursues:

> "Then what did you mean . . . by saying that children are a curse?"
>
> "My dear youth, on what basis are we talking?" and St. George dropped upon the sofa at a short distance from him. . . . "On the supposition that a certain perfection's possible and even desirable—isn't it so? Well, all I say is that one's children interfere with perfection. One's wife interferes. Marriage interferes."
>
> "You think, then, the artist shouldn't marry?"
>
> "He does so at his peril—he does so at his cost."

Yet the Master who declares all this is himself profoundly, inextricably, married; and when his wife dies, he hastens to marry again, choosing Life over Art. Very properly James sees marriage as symbol and summary of the passion for ordinary human entanglement, as experience of the most commonplace, most fated kind.

But we are also given to understand, in the desolation of this comic tale, that the young artist, the Master's trusting disciple, is left both perplexed and bereft: the Master's second wife is the young artist's first love, and the Master has stolen away his disciple's chance for ordinary human entanglement.

So the Lesson of the Master is a double one: choose ordinary human entanglement, and live; or choose Art, and give up the vitality of life's passions and panics and endurances. What I am going to tell now is a stupidity, a misunderstanding, a great Jamesian life-mistake: an embarrassment and a life-shame. (Imagine that we are in one of those lavishly adorned Jamesian chambers where intimate confessions not accidentally but suspensefully take place.) As I have said, I felt myself betrayed by a Jamesian trickery. Trusting in James, believing, like Paul Overt, in the overtness of the Jamesian lesson, I chose Art, and ended by blaming Henry James. It seemed to me James had left out the one important thing I ought to have known, even though he was saying it again and again. The trouble was that I was listening to the Lesson of the Master at the wrong time, paying powerful and excessive attention at the wrong time; and this cost me my youth.

I suppose a case can be made that it is certainly inappropriate for anyone to moan about the loss of youth and how it is all Henry James's fault. All of us will lose our youth, and some of us, alas, have lost it already; but not all of us will pin the loss on Henry James.

I, however, do. I blame Henry James.

Never mind the sublime position of Henry James in American letters. Never mind the Jamesian prose style—never mind that it too is sublime, nuanced, imbricated with a thousand distinctions and observations (the reason H. G. Wells mocked it), and as idiosyncratically and ecstatically redolent of the spirals of past and future as a garlic clove. Set aside also the Jamesian impatience with idols, the moral seriousness active in both the work and the life. (I am thinking, for example, of Edith Wharton's compliance in the face of their mutual friend Paul Bourget's anti-Semitism, and James's noble and definitive dissent.) Neglect all this, including every other beam that flies out from the stupendous Jamesian lantern to keep generations reading in rapture (which is all right), or else scribbling away at dissertation after dissertation (which is not so good). I myself, after all, committed a Master's thesis, long ago, called "Parable in Henry James," in which I tried to catch up all of James in the net of a single idea. Before that, I lived many months in the black hole of a microfilm cell, transcribing every letter James ever wrote to Mr. Pinker, his London agent, for a professorial book; but the professor drank, and died, and after thirty years the letters still lie in the dark.

All that while I sat cramped in that black bleak microfilm cell, and all that while I was writing that thesis, James was sinking me and despoiling my youth, and I did not know it.

I want, parenthetically, to recommend to the Henry James Society—there is such an assemblage—that membership be limited: no one under age forty-two and three-quarters need apply. Proof of age via birth certificate should be mandatory; otherwise the consequences may be harsh and horrible. I offer myself as an Extreme and Hideous Example of Premature Exposure to Henry James. I was about seventeen, I recall, when my brother brought home from the public library a science-fiction anthology, which, through an odd perspective that perplexes me still, included "The Beast in the Jungle." It was in this anthology, and at that age, that I first read James— fell, I should say, into the jaws of James. I had never heard of him before. I read "The Beast in the Jungle" and creepily thought: Here, here is my autobiography.

From that time forward, gradually but compellingly—and now I yield my scary confession—I became Henry James. Leaving graduate school at the age of twenty-two, disdaining the Ph.D. as an acquisition surely beneath the concerns of literary seriousness, I was already Henry James. When I say I "became" Henry James, you must understand this: though I was a near-sighted twenty-two-year-old young woman infected with the commonplace intention of writing a novel, I was *also* the elderly bald-headed Henry James. Even without close examination, you could see the light glancing off my pate; you could see my heavy chin, my watch chain, my walking stick, my tender paunch.

I had become Henry James, and for years and years I remained Henry James. There was no doubt about it: it was my own clear and faithful truth. Of course, there were some small differences: for one thing, I was not a genius. For another, even in my own insignificant scribbler class, I was not prolific. But I carried the Jamesian idea, I was of his cult, I was a worshiper of literature, literature was my single altar; I was, like the elderly bald-headed James, a priest at that altar; and that altar was all of my life. Like John Marcher in "The Beast in the Jungle," I let everything pass me by for the sake of waiting for the Beast to spring—but unlike John Marcher, I knew what the Beast was, I knew exactly, I even knew the Beast's name: the Beast was literature itself, the sinewy grand undulations of some unraveling fiction, meticulously dreamed out in a language of masterly resplendence, which was to pounce on me and turn me into an enchanted and glorious Being, as enchanted and glorious as the elderly bald-headed Henry James himself.

But though the years spent themselves extravagantly, that ambush never occurred: the ambush of Sacred and Sublime Literature. The great shining Beast of Sacred and Sublime Literature did not pounce. Instead, other beasts, lesser ones, unseemly and misshapen, sprang out—all the beasts of ordinary life: sorrow, disease, death, guilt, responsibility, envy, grievance, grief, disillusionment—the beasts that are chained to human experience, and have nothing to do with Art except to interrupt and impede it, exactly according to the Lesson of the Master.

It was not until I read a certain vast and subtle book that I understood what had happened to me. The book was not by Henry James, but about him. Nowadays we give this sort of work a special name: we call it a non-fiction novel. I am referring, of course, to Leon Edel's ingenious and beautiful biography of Henry James, which is as much the possession of Edel's imagination as it is of the exhilaratingly reported facts of James's life. In Edel's rendering, I learned what I had never before taken in—but the knowledge came, in the Jamesian way, too late. What I learned was that Henry James himself had not always been the elderly bald-headed Henry James!—that he too had once been twenty-two years old.

This terrible and secret knowledge instantly set me against James. From that point forward I was determined to eradicate him. And for a long while I succeeded.

What had happened was this: in early young-womanhood I believed, with all the rigor and force and stunned ardor of religious belief, in the old Henry James, in his scepter and his authority. I believed that what *he* knew at sixty I was to encompass at twenty-two; at twenty-two I lived like the elderly bald-headed Henry James. I thought it was necessary—it was imperative, there was no other path!—to be, all at once, with no progression or evolution, the author of the equivalent of *The Ambassadors* or

The Wings of the Dove, just as if "A Bundle of Letters," or "Four Meetings," or the golden little "The Europeans" had never preceded the great late Master.

For me, the Lesson of the Master was a horror, a Jamesian tale of a life of mishap and mistake and misconceiving. Though the Master himself was saying, in *The Ambassadors*, in Gloriani's garden, to Little Bilham, through the urgent cry of Strether, "Live, live!"—and though the Master himself was saying, in "The Beast in the Jungle," through May Bartram, how ghastly, how ghostly, it is to eschew, to evade, to turn from, to miss absolutely and irrevocably what is all the time there for you to seize—I mistook him, I misheard him, I missed, absolutely and irrevocably, his essential note. What I heard instead was: *Become a Master*.

Now the truth is it could not have been done, even by a writer of genius; and what a pitiful flicker of the flame of high ambition for a writer who is no more than the ordinary article! No one—not even James himself—springs all at once in early youth into full Mastery, and no writer, whether robustly gifted, or only little and pale, should hope for this implausible fate.

All this, I suppose, is not at all a "secret" knowledge, as I have characterized it, but is, rather, as James named it in the very person of his naïve young artist, most emphatically *overt*—so obvious that it is a mere access of foolishness even to talk about it. Still, I offer the implausible and preposterous model of myself to demonstrate the proposition that the Lesson of the Master is not a lesson about genius, or even about immense ambition; it is a lesson about misreading—about what happens when we misread the great voices of Art, and suppose that, because they speak of Art, they *mean* Art. The great voices of Art never mean *only* Art; they also mean Life, they always mean Life, and Henry James, when he evolved into the Master we revere, finally meant nothing else.

The true Lesson of the Master, then, is, simply, never to venerate what is complete, burnished, whole, in its grand organic flowering or finish—never to look toward the admirable and dazzling end; never to be ravished by the goal; never to worship ripe Art or the ripened artist; but instead to seek to be young while young, primitive while primitive, ungainly when ungainly— to look for crudeness and rudeness, to husband one's own stupidity or ungenius.

There *is* this mix-up most of us have between ourselves and what we admire or triumphantly cherish. We see this mix-up, this mishap, this mishmash, most often in writers: the writer of a new generation ravished by the genius writer of a classical generation, who begins to dream herself, or himself, as powerful, vigorous and original—as if being filled up by the genius

writer's images, scenes, and stratagems were the same as having the capacity to pull off the identical magic. To be any sort of competent writer one
must keep one's psychological distance from the supreme artists.

If I were twenty-two now, I would not undertake a cannibalistically ambitious Jamesian novel to begin with; I would look into the eyes of Henry
James at twenty-two, and see the diffident hope, the uncertainty, the marveling tentativeness, the dream that is still only a dream; the young man
still learning to fashion the Scene. Or I would go back still further, to the
boy of seventeen, misplaced in a Swiss Polytechnic School, who recalled in
old age that "I so feared and abhorred mathematics that the simplest arith-
metical operation had always found and kept me helpless and blank." It is
not to the Master in his fullness I would give my awed, stricken, desperate
fealty, but to the faltering, imperfect, dreaming youth.

If these words should happen to reach the ears of any young writer
dumbstruck by the elderly bald-headed Henry James, one who has hungrily
heard and ambitiously assimilated the voluptuous cathedral-tones of the
developed organ-master, I would say to her or him: put out your lean
and clumsy forefinger and strike your paltry, oafish, feeble, simple, skeletal,
single note. Try for what Henry James at sixty would scorn—just as he
scorned the work of his own earliness, and revised it and revised it in the
manner of his later pen in that grand chastisement of youth known as the
New York Edition. Trying, in youth, for what the Master in his mastery
would condemn—that is the only road to modest mastery. Rapture and
homage are not the way. Influence is perdition.

Washington Square, 1946

. . . this portion of New York appears to many persons the most delectable. It has a kind of established repose which is not of frequent occurrence in other quarters of the long, shrill city; it has a riper, richer, more honorable look than any of the upper ramifications of the great longitudinal thoroughfare—the look of having had something of a social history.

—HENRY JAMES, *Washington Square*

I first came down to Washington Square on a colorless February morning in 1946. I was seventeen and a half years old and was carrying my lunch in a brown paper bag, just as I had carried it to high school only a month before. It was—I thought it was—the opening day of spring term at Washington Square College, my initiation into my freshman year at New York University. All I knew of N.Y.U. then was that my science-minded brother had gone there; he had written from the Army that I ought to go there too. With master-of-ceremonies zest he described the Browsing Room on the second floor of the Main Building as a paradisal chamber whose bookish loungers leafed languidly through magazines and exchanged high-principled witticisms between classes. It had the sound of a carpeted Olympian club in Oliver Wendell Holmes's Boston, Hub of the Universe, strewn with leather chairs and delectable old copies of *The Yellow Book.*

On that day I had never heard of Oliver Wendell Holmes or *The Yellow Book,* and Washington Square was a faraway bower where wounded birds fell out of trees. My brother had once brought home from Washington Square Park a baby sparrow with a broken leg, to be nurtured back to flight.

It died instead, emitting in its last hours melancholy faint cheeps, and leaving behind a dense recognition of the minute explicitness of mortality. All the same, in the February grayness Washington Square had the allure of the celestial unknown. A sparrow might die, but my own life was luminously new: I felt my youth like a nimbus.

Which dissolves into the dun gauze of a low and sullen city sky. And here I am flying out of the Lexington Avenue subway at Astor Place, just a few yards from Wanamaker's, here I am turning the corner past a second-hand bookstore and a union hall; already late, I begin walking very fast toward the park. The air is smoky with New York winter grit, and on clogged Broadway a mob of trucks shifts squawking gears. But there, just ahead, crisscrossed by paths under high branches, is Washington Square; and on a single sidewalk, three clear omens; or call them riddles, intricate and redolent. These I will disclose in a moment, but before that you must push open the heavy brass-and-glass doors of the Main Building, and come with me, at a hard and panting pace, into the lobby of Washington Square College on the earliest morning of the freshman year.

On the left, a bank of elevators. Straight ahead, a long burnished corridor, spooky as a lit tunnel. And empty, all empty. I can hear my solitary footsteps reverberate, as in a radio mystery drama: they lead me up a short staircase into a big dark ghost-town cafeteria. My brother's letter, along with an account of the physics and chemistry laboratories (I will never see them), has already explained that this place is called Commons—and here my heart will learn to shake with the merciless newness of life. But not today; today there is nothing. Tables and chairs squat in dead silhouette. I race back through a silent maze of halls and stairways to the brass-and-glass doors—there stands a lonely guard. From the pocket of my coat I retrieve a scrap with a classroom number on it and ask the way. The guard announces in a sly croak that the first day of school is not yet; come back tomorrow, he says.

A dumb bad joke: I'm humiliated. I've journeyed the whole way down from the end of the line—Pelham Bay, in the northeast Bronx—to find myself in desolation, all because of a muddle: Tuesday isn't Wednesday. The nimbus of expectation fades off. The lunch bag in my fist takes on a greasy sadness. I'm not ready to dive back into the subway—I'll have a look around.

Across the street from the Main Building, the three omens. First, a pretzel man with a cart. He's wearing a sweater, a cap that keeps him faceless—he's nothing but the shadows of his creases—and wool gloves with the fingertips cut off. He never moves; he might as well be made of papier-mâché, set up and left out in the open since spring. There are now almost no pretzels for sale, and this gives me a chance to inspect the construction of his bare pretzel poles. The pretzels are hooked over a column of gray cardboard cylinders, themselves looped around a stick, the way horseshoes drop around a post. The cardboard cylinders are the insides of toilet paper rolls.

The pretzel man is rooted between a Chock Full o' Nuts (that's the second omen) and a newsstand (that's the third).

The Chock Full: the doors are like fans, whirling remnants of conversation. *She will marry him. She will not marry him.* Fragrance of coffee and hot chocolate. *We can prove that the senses are partial and unreliable vehicles of information, but who is to say that reason is not equally the product of human limitation?* Powdered doughnut sugar on their lips.

Attached to a candy store, the newsstand. Copies of *Partisan Review*: the table of the gods. Jean Stafford, Mary McCarthy, Elizabeth Hardwick, Irving Howe, Delmore Schwartz, Alfred Kazin, Clement Greenberg, Stephen Spender, William Phillips, John Berryman, Saul Bellow, Philip Rahv, Richard Chase, Randall Jarrell, Simone de Beauvoir, Karl Shapiro, George Orwell! I don't know a single one of these names, but I feel their small conflagration flaming in the gray street: the succulent hotness of their promise. I mean to penetrate every one of them. Since all the money I have is my subway fare—two nickels—I don't buy a copy (the price of *Partisan* in 1946 is fifty cents); I pass on.

I pass on to the row of houses on the north side of the Square. Henry James was born in one of these, but I don't know that either. Still, they are plainly old, though no longer aristocratic: haughty last-century shabbies with shut eyelids, built of rosy-ripe respectable brick, down on their luck. Across the park bulks Judson Church, with its squat squarish bell tower; by the end of the week I will be languishing at the margins of a basketball game in its basement, forlorn in my blue left-over-from-high-school gym suit and mooning over Emily Dickinson:

> There's a certain Slant of light,
> Winter Afternoons—
> That oppresses, like the Heft
> Of Cathedral Tunes—

There is more I don't know. I don't know that W. H. Auden lives just down *there*, and might at any moment be seen striding toward home under his tall rumpled hunch; I don't know that Marianne Moore is only up the block, her doffed tricorn resting on her bedroom dresser. It's Greenwich Village—I know *that*—no more than twenty years after Edna St. Vincent Millay has sent the music of her name (her best, perhaps her only, poem) into these bohemian streets: bohemia, the honey pot of poets.

On that first day in the tea-leafed cup of the town I am ignorant, ignorant! But the three riddle-omens are soon to erupt, and all of them together will illumine Washington Square.

Begin with the benches in the Park. Here, side by side with students and their loose-leafs, lean or lie the shadows of the pretzel man, his creased ghosts or doubles: all those pitiables, half-women and half-men, neither awake nor asleep, the discountable, the repudiated, the unseen. No more notice is taken of any of them than of a scudding fragment of newspaper in the path. Even then, even so long ago, the benches of Washington Square are pimpled with this hell-tossed crew, these Mad Margarets and Cokey Joes, these volcanic coughers, shakers, groaners, tremblers, droolers, blasphemers, these public urinators with vomitous breath and rusted teeth-stumps, dead-eyed and self-abandoned, dragging their makeshift junkyard shoes, their buttonless layers of raggedy ratfur. The pretzel man with his toilet paper rolls conjures and spews them all—he is a loftier brother to these citizens of the lower pox, he is guardian of the garden of the jettisoned. They rattle along all the seams of Washington Square. They are the pickled City, the true and universal City-below-Cities, the wolfish vinegar-Babylon that dogs the spittled skirts of bohemia. The toilet paper rolls are the temple-columns of this sacred grove.

Next, the whirling doors of Chock Full o' Nuts. Here is the marketplace of Washington Square, its bazaar, its roiling gossip parlor, its matchmaker's office and arena—the outermost wing, so to speak, evolved from the Commons. On a day like today, when the Commons is closed, the Chock Full is thronged with extra power, a cello making up for a missing viola. Until now, the fire of my vitals has been for the imperious tragedians of the *Aeneid*; I have lived in the narrow throat of poetry. Another year or so of this oblivion, until at last I am hammer-struck with the shock of Europe's skull, the bled planet of death camp and war. Eleanor Roosevelt has not yet written her famous column announcing the discovery of Anne Frank's diary. The term "cold war" is new. The Commons, like the college itself, is overcrowded, veterans in their pragmatic thirties mingling with the reluctant dreamy young. And the Commons is convulsed with politics: a march to the docks is organized, no one knows by whom, to protest the arrival of Walter Gieseking, the German musician who flourished among Nazis. The Communists—two or three readily recognizable cantankerous zealots—stomp through with their daily leaflets and sneers. There is even a Monarchist, a small poker-faced rectangle of a man with secretive tireless eyes who, when approached for his views, always demands, in perfect Bronx tones, the restoration of his king. The engaged girls—how many of them there seem to be!—flash their rings and tangle their ankles in their long

New Look skirts. There is no feminism and no feminists; I am, I think, the only one. The Commons is a tide: it washes up the cold war, it washes up the engaged girls' rings, it washes up the several philosophers and the numerous poets. The philosophers are all Existentialists; the poets are all influenced by "The Waste Land." When the Commons overflows, the engaged girls cross the street to show their rings at the Chock Full.

Call it density, call it intensity, call it continuity: call it, finally, society. The Commons belongs to the satirists. Here, one afternoon, is Alfred Chester, holding up a hair, a single strand, before a crowd. (He will one day write stories and novels. He will die young.) "What is that hair?" I innocently ask, having come late on the scene. "A pubic hair," he replies, and I feel as Virginia Woolf did when she declared human nature to have "changed in or about December 1910"—soon after her sister Vanessa explained away a spot on her dress as "semen."

In or about February 1946 human nature does not change; it keeps on. On my bedroom wall I tack—cut out from *Life* magazine—the wildest Picasso I can find: a face that is also a belly. Mr. George E. Mutch, a lyrical young English teacher twenty-seven years old, writes on the blackboard: "When lilacs last in the dooryard bloom'd," and "Bare, ruined choirs, where late the sweet birds sang," and "A green thought in a green shade"; he tells us to burn, like Pater, with a hard, gemlike flame. Another English teacher— his name is Emerson—compares Walt Whitman to a plumber; next year he will shoot himself in a wood. The initial letters of Washington Square College are a device to recall three of the Seven Deadly Sins: Wantonness, Sloth, Covetousness. In Commons they argue the efficacy of the orgone box. Eda Lou Walton, sprightly as a bird, knows all the Village bards, and is a Village bard herself. Sidney Hook is an intellectual rumble in the logical middle distance. Homer Watt, chairman of the English Department, is the very soul who, in a far-off time of bewitchment, hired Thomas Wolfe.

And so, in February 1946, I make my first purchase of a "real" book— which is to say, not for the classroom. It is displayed in the window of the secondhand bookstore between the Astor Place subway station and the union hall, and for weeks I have been coveting it: *Of Time and the River*. I am transfigured; I am pierced through with rapture; skipping gym, I sit among morning mists on a windy bench a foot from the stench of Mad Margaret, sinking into that cascading syrup: "Man's youth is a wonderful thing: It is so full of anguish and of magic and he never comes to know it as it is, until it is gone from him forever. . . . And what is the essence of that strange and bitter miracle of life which we feel so poignantly, so unutterably, with such a bitter pain and joy, when we are young?" Thomas Wolfe, lost, and by the wind grieved, ghost, come back again! In Washington

Square I am appareled in the "numb exultant secrecies of fog, fog-numb air filled with solemn joy of nameless and impending prophecy, an ancient yellow light, the old smoke-ochre of the morning. . . ."

The smoke-ochre of the morning. Ah, you who have flung Thomas Wolfe, along with your strange and magical youth, onto the ash heap of juvenilia and excess, myself among you, isn't this a lovely phrase still? It rises out of the old pavements of Washington Square as delicately colored as an eggshell.

The veterans in their pragmatic thirties are nailed to Need; they have families and futures to attend to. When Mr. George E. Mutch exhorts them to burn with a hard, gemlike flame, and writes across the blackboard the line that reveals his own name,

> The world is too much with us; late and soon,
> Getting and spending, we lay waste our powers,

one of the veterans heckles, "What about getting a Buick, what about spending a buck?" Chester, at sixteen, is a whole year younger than I; he has transparent eyes and a rosebud mouth, and is in love with a poet named Diana. He has already found his way to the Village bars, and keeps in his wallet Truman Capote's secret telephone number. We tie our scarves tight against the cold and walk up and down Fourth Avenue, winding in and out of the rows of secondhand bookshops crammed one against the other. The proprietors sit reading their wares and never look up. The books in all their thousands smell sleepily of cellar. Our envy of them is speckled with longing; our longing is sick with envy. We are the sorrowful literary young.

Every day, month after month, I hang around the newsstand near the candy store, drilling through the enigmatic pages of *Partisan Review*. I still haven't bought a copy; I still can't understand a word. I don't know what "cold war" means. Who is Trotsky? I haven't read *Ulysses;* my adolescent phantoms are rowing in the ablative absolute with *pius* Aeneas. I'm in my mind's cradle, veiled by the exultant secrecies of fog.

Washington Square will wake me. In a lecture room in the Main Building, Dylan Thomas will cry his webwork syllables. Afterward he'll warm himself at the White Horse Tavern. Across the corridor I will see Sidney Hook plain. I will read the Bhagavad Gita and Catullus and Lessing, and, in Hebrew, a novel eerily called *Whither?* It will be years and years before I am smart enough, worldly enough, to read Alfred Kazin and Mary McCarthy.

In the spring, all of worldly Washington Square will wake up to the luster of little green leaves.

The Question of
Our Speech:
The Return to Aural Culture

When I was a thirteen-year-old New Yorker, a trio of women from the provinces took up, relentlessly and extravagantly, the question of my speech. Their names were Miss Evangeline Trolander, Mrs. Olive Birch Davis, and Mrs. Ruby S. Papp (pronounced *pop*). It was Mrs. Papp's specialty to explain how to "breathe from the diaphragm." She would place her fingers tip-to-tip on the unyielding hard shell of her midriff, hugely inhaling: how astonishing then to see how the mighty action of her lungs caused her fingertips to spring apart! This demonstration was for the repair of the New York voice. What the New York voice, situated notoriously "in the throat," required above everything was to descend, pumping air, to this nether site, so that "Young Lochinvar came out of the WEST" might come bellowing out of the pubescent breast.

The New York palate, meanwhile, was consonantally in neglect. *T*'s, *d*'s, and *l*'s were being beaten out against the teeth, European-fashion—this was called "dentalization"—while the homeless *r* and *n* went wandering in the perilous trough behind the front incisors. There were corrective exercises for these transgressions, the chief one being a liturgical recitation of "Tillie the Toiler took Tommy Tucker to tea," with the tongue anxiously flying up above the teeth to strike precisely on the lower ridge of the upper palate.

The diaphragm; the upper palate; and finally the arena in the cave of the mouth where the vowels were prepared. A New Yorker could not say a proper *a*, as in "paper"—this indispensable vibration was manufactured somewhere back near the nasal passage, whereas civility demanded the *a* to emerge frontally, directly from the lips' vestibule. The New York *i* was worst of all: how Mrs. Davis, Mrs. Papp, and Miss Trolander mimicked and ridiculed the New York *i*! "Oi loik oice cream," they mocked.

All these emendations, as it happened, were being applied to the entire population of a high school for girls in a modest Gothic pile on East Sixty-eighth Street in the 1940s, and no one who emerged from that pile after four years of daily speech training ever sounded the same again. On the eve of graduation, Mrs. Olive Birch Davis turned to Mrs. Ruby S. Papp and said: "Do you remember the *ugliness* of her *diction* when she came to us?" She meant me; I was about to deliver the Class Speech. I had not yet encountered Shaw's *Pygmalion,* and its popular recrudescence in the form of *My Fair Lady* was still to occur; all the same, that night, rehearsing for commencement, I caught in Mrs. Davis and Mrs. Papp something of Professor Higgins's victory, and in myself something of Eliza's humiliation.

Our teachers had, like young Lochinvar, come out of the West, but I had come out of the northeast Bronx. Called on to enunciate publicly for the first time, I responded with the diffidence of secret pleasure; I liked to read out loud, and thought myself not bad at it. Instead, I was marked down as a malfeasance in need of overhaul. The revisions and transformations that followed were not unlike an evangelical conversion. One had to be willing to be born again; one had to be willing to repudiate wholesale one's former defective self. It could not be accomplished without faith and shame: faith in what one might newly become, shame in the degrading process itself—the dedicated repetition of mantras. "Tillie the Toiler took Tommy Tucker to tea," "Oh! young LOCHinvar has come out of the WEST, Through all the wide BORDER HIS steed was the BEST." All the while pneumatically shooting out one's diaphragm, and keeping one's eye (never one's *oi*) peeled for the niggardly approval of Miss Evangeline Trolander.

In this way I was, at an early age, effectively made over. Like a multitude of other graduates of my high school, I now own a sort of robot's speech—it has no obvious native county. At least not to most ears, though a well-tutored listener will hear that the vowels hang on, and the cadence of every sentence has a certain laggardly northeast Bronx drag. Brooklyn, by contrast, is divided between very fast and very slow. Irish New York has its own sound, Italian New York another; and a refined ear can distinguish between Bronx and Brooklyn Irish and Bronx and Brooklyn Jewish: four separate accents, with the differences to be found not simply in vowels and consonants, but in speed and inflection. Nor is it so much a matter of ancestry as of neighborhood. If, instead of clinging to the green-fronded edge of Pelham Bay Park, my family had settled three miles west, in a denser "section" called Pelham Parkway, I would have spoken Bronx Jewish. Encountering City Island, Bronx Jewish said Ciddy Oilen. In Pelham Bay, where Bronx Irish was almost exclusively spoken in those days, it was Ciddy Allen. When Terence Cooke became cardinal of New York, my heart leaped up: Throggs Neck! I had assimilated those sounds long ago on a pebbly beach. No one had ever put the cardinal into the wringer of speech repair. I knew him through and through. He was my childhood's brother, and restored my orphaned ear.

Effectively made over: these noises that come out of me are not an overlay. They do not vanish during the free play of dreams or screams. I do not, cannot, "revert." This may be because Trolander, Davis, and Papp caught me early; or because I was so passionate a devotee of their dogma.

Years later I tried to figure it all out. What did these women have up their sleeves? An aesthetic ideal, perhaps: Standard American English. But behind the ideal—and Trolander, Davis, and Papp were the strictest and most indefatigable idealists—there must have been an ideology; and behind the ideology, whatever form it might take, a repugnance. The speech of New York streets and households soiled them: you could see it in their proud pained meticulous frowns. They were intent on our elevation. Though they were dead set on annihilating Yiddish-derived "dentalization," they could not be said to be anti-Semites, since they were just as set on erasing the tumbling consonants of Virginia Greene's Alexander Avenue Irish Bronx; and besides, in our different styles, we *all* dentalized. Was it, then, the Melting Pot that inspired Trolander, Davis, and Papp? But not one of us was an "immigrant"; we were all fully Americanized, and our parents before us, except for the handful of foreign-born "German refugees." These were marched off to a special Speech Clinic for segregated training; their *r*'s drew Mrs. Davis's eyes toward heaven, and I privately recognized that the refugees were almost all of them hopeless cases. A girl named Hedwig said she *didn't care,* which made me conclude that she was frivolous, trivialized, not serious; wasn't it ignominious enough (like a kind of cheese) to be called "Hedwig"?

Only the refugees were bona fide foreigners. The rest of us were garden-variety subway-riding New Yorkers. Trolander, Davis, and Papp saw us nevertheless as tainted with foreignness, and it was the remnants of that foreignness they meant to wipe away: the last stages of the great turn-of-the-century alien flood. Or perhaps they intended that, like Shaw's Eliza, we should have the wherewithal to rise to a higher station. Yet, looking back on their dress and manner, I do not think Trolander, Davis, and Papp at all sought out or even understood "class"; they were reliably American, and class was nothing they were capable of believing in.

What, then, did these ferrywomen imagine we would find on the farther shore, once we left behind, through artifice and practice, our native speech? Was it a kind of "manners," was it what they might have called "breeding"? They thought of themselves as democratic noblewomen (nor did they suppose this to be a contradiction in terms), and they expected of us, if not the same, then at least a recognition of the category. They trusted in the power of models. They gave us the astonishing maneuvers of their teeth, their tongues, their lungs, and drilled us in imitation of those maneuvers. In the process, they managed—this was their highest feat—to break down embarrassment, to deny the shaming theatricality of the ludicrous. We lost every delicacy and dignity in acting like freaks or fools while trying out the new accent. Contrived consonants began freely to address feigned vowels: a world of parroting and parody. And what came of it all?

What came of it was that they caused us—and here was a category *they* had no recognition of—they caused us to exchange one regionalism for another. New York gave way to Midwest. We were cured of Atlantic Seaboard, a disease that encompassed north, middle, and south; and yet only the middle, and of that middle only New York, was considered to be on the critical list. It was New York that carried the hottest and sickest inflammation. In no other hollow of the country was such an effort mounted, on such a scale, to eliminate regionalism. The South might have specialized in Elocution, but the South was not ashamed of its idiosyncratic vowels; neither was New England; and no one sent missionaries.

Of course this was exactly what our democratic noblewomen were: missionaries. They restored, if not our souls, then surely and emphatically our *r*'s—those *r*'s that are missing in the end syllables of New Yorkers, who call themselves Noo Yawkizz and nowadays worry about muggizz. From Boston to New York to Atlanta, the Easterner is an Eastinna, his mother is a mutha, his father a fahtha, and the most difficult stretch of anything is the hahd paht; and so fawth. But only in New York is the absent *r*—i.e., the absent *aw*—an offense to good mannizz. To be sure, our missionaries did not dream that they imposed a parochialism of their own. And perhaps they were right not to dream it, since by the forties of this century the radio was having its leveling effect, and Midwest speech, colonizing by means of "announcers," had ascended to the rank of standard speech.

Still, only forty years earlier, Henry James, visiting from England after a considerable period away, was freshly noticing and acidly deploring the pervasively conquering *r*:

> . . . the letter, I grant, gets terribly little rest among those great masses of our population that strike us, in the boundless West especially, as, under some strange impulse received toward consonantal recovery of balance, making it present even in words from which it is absent, bringing it in everywhere as with the small vulgar effect of a sort of morose grinding of the back teeth. There are, you see, sounds of a mysterious intrinsic meanness, and there are

sounds of a mysterious intrinsic frankness and sweetness; and I think the re-current note I have indicated—fatherr and motherr and otherr, waterr and matterr and scatterr, harrd and barrd, parrt, starrt and (dreadful to say) arrt (the repetition it is that drives home the ugliness), are signal specimens of what becomes of a custom of utterance out of which the principle of taste has dropped.

In 1905, to drop the *r* was to drop, for the cultivated ear, a principle of taste; but for our democratic noblewomen four decades on, exactly the reverse was true. James's New York/Boston expectations, reinforced by southern England, assumed that Eastern American speech, tied as it was to the cultural reign of London, had a right to rule and to rule out. The history and sociolinguistics governing this reversal is less pressing to examine than the question of "standard speech" itself. James thought that "the voice *plus* the way it is employed" determined "positively the history of the national character, almost the history of the people." His views on all this, his alarms and anxieties, he compressed into a fluid little talk ("The Question of Our Speech") he gave at the Bryn Mawr College commencement of June 8, 1905—exactly one year and two days before my mother, nine years old, having passed through Castle Garden, stood on the corner of Battery Park, waiting to board the horsecar for Madison Street on the Lower East Side.

James was in great fear of the child waiting for the horsecar. "Keep in sight," he warned, "the so interesting historical truth that no language, so far back as our acquaintance with history goes, has known any such ordeal, any such stress or strain, as was to await the English in this huge new community it was to help, at first, to father and mother. It came *over,* as the phrase is, came over originally without fear and without guile—but to find itself transplanted to spaces it had never dreamed, in its comparative humility, of covering, to conditions it had never dreamed, in its comparative innocence, of meeting." He spoke of English as an "unfriended heroine," "our transported medium, our unrescued Andromeda, our medium of utterance, . . . disjoined from all the associations, the other presences, that had attended her, that had watched for her and with her, that had helped to form her manners and her voice, her taste and her genius."

And if English, orphaned as it was and cut off from its "ancestral circle," did not have enough to contend with in its own immigrant situation, arriving "without fear and without guile" only to be ambushed by "a social and political order that was both without previous precedent and example and incalculably expansive," including also the expansiveness of a diligent public school network and "the mighty maniac" of journalism—if all this was not threatening enough, there was the special danger my nine-year-old mother posed. She represented an unstable new ingredient. She represented violation, a kind of linguistic Armageddon. She stood for disorder and promiscuity. "I am perfectly aware," James said at Bryn Mawr,

> that the common school and the newspaper are influences that shall often have been named to you, exactly, as favorable, as positively and actively contributive, to the prosperity of our idiom; the answer to which is that the matter depends, distinctively, on what is meant by prosperity. It is prosperity, of a sort, that a hundred million people, a few years hence, will be unanimously, loudly—above all loudly, I think!—speaking it, and that, moreover, many of these millions will have been artfully wooed and weaned from the Dutch, from the Spanish, from the German, from the Italian, from the Norse, from the Finnish, from the Yiddish even, strange to say, and (stranger still to say), even from the English, for the sweet sake, or the sublime consciousness, as we may perhaps put it, of speaking, of talking, for the first time in their lives, *really* at their ease. There are many things our now so profusely important and, as is claimed, quickly assimilated foreign brothers and sisters may do at their ease in this country, and at two minutes' notice, and without asking any one else's leave or taking any circumstance whatever into account—any save an infinite uplifting sense of freedom and facility; but the thing they may best do is play, to their heart's content, with the English language, or, in other words, dump their mountain of promiscuous material into the foundation of the American.

"All the while we sleep," he continued, "the vast contingent of aliens whom we make welcome, and whose main contention, as I say, is that, from the moment of their arrival, they have just as much property in our speech as we have, and just as good a right to do what they choose with it . . . all the while we sleep the innumerable aliens are sitting up (*they* don't sleep!) to work their will on their new inheritance." And he compared the immigrants' use of English to oilcloth—"highly convenient . . . durable, tough, cheap."

James's thesis in his address to his audience of young aristocrats was not precisely focused. On the one hand, in describing the depredations of the innumerable sleepless aliens, in protesting "the common schools and the 'daily paper,'" he appeared to admit defeat—"the forces of looseness are in possession of the field." Yet in asking the graduates to see to the perfection of their own speech, he had, he confessed, no models to offer them. Imitate, he advised—but whom? Parents and teachers were themselves not watchful. "I am at a loss to name you particular and unmistakable, edifying and illuminating groups or classes," he said, and recommended, in the most general way, the hope of "encountering, blessedly, here and there, articulate individuals, torch-bearers, as we may rightly describe them, guardians of the sacred flame."

As it turned out, James not only had no solution; he had not even put the right question. These young women of good family whom he was exhorting to excellence were well situated in society to do exactly what James had described the immigrants as doing: speaking "*really* at their ease," playing, "to their heart's content, with the English language" in "an infinite uplifting sense of freedom and facility." Whereas the "aliens," hard-pressed by the scramblings of poverty and cultural confusions, had no notion at all of linguistic "freedom and facility," took no witting license with the English tongue, and felt no remotest ownership in the language they hoped merely to earn their wretched bread by. If they did not sleep, it was because of long hours in the sweatshops and similar places of employment; they were no more in a position to "play" with English than they were to acquire bona fide *Mayflower* ancestry. Ease, content, facility—these were not the lot of the unsleeping aliens.

To the young people of Bryn Mawr James could offer nothing more sanguine, nothing less gossamer, than the merest metaphor—"guardians of the sacred flame." Whom then should they imitate but himself, the most "articulate individual" of them all? We have no record of the graduates' response to James's extravagant "later style" as profusely exhibited in this address: whatever it was, they could not have accepted it for standard American. James's English had become, by this time, an invention of his own fashioning, so shaded, so leafy, so imbricated, so brachiate, so filigreed, as to cast a thousand momentary ornamental obscurities, like the effect of the drill-holes in the spiraled stone hair of an imperial Roman portrait bust. He was the most eminent torchbearer in sight, the purest of all possible guardians of the flame—but a model he could not have been for anyone's everyday speech, no more than the Romans talked like the Odes of Horace. Not that he failed to recognize the exigencies of an active language, "a living organism, fed by the very breath of those who employ it, whoever these may happen to be," a language able "to respond, from its core, to the constant appeal of time, perpetually demanding new tricks, new experiments, new amusements." He saw American English as the flexible servant "of those who carry it with them, on their long road, as their specific experience grows larger and more complex, and who need it to help them to meet this expansion." And at the same time he excluded from these widened possibilities its slangy young native speakers and the very immigrants whose educated children would enrich and reanimate the American language (eight decades later we may judge how vividly), as well as master and augment its literature.

Its literature. It is striking beyond anything that James left out, in the course of this lecture, any reference to reading. Certainly it was not overtly his subject. He was concerned with enunciation and with idiom, with syllables, with vowels and consonants, with tone and inflection, with *sound*—but he linked the American voice to such "underlying things" as "proprieties and values, perfect possessions of the educated spirit, clear humanities," as well as "the imparting of a coherent culture." Implicit was his conviction that speech affects literature, as, in the case of native speakers, it inevitably does: naturalism in the dialogue of a novel, say, is itself always a kind of dialect of a particular place and time. But in a newly roiling society of immigrant speakers, James could not see ahead (and why should he have seen ahead? Castle Garden was unprecedented in all of human history) to the idea that a national literature can create a national speech. The immigrants who learned to read learned to speak. Those who only learned to speak did not, in effect, learn to speak.

In supposing the overriding opposite—that quality of speech creates culture, rather than culture quality of speech—James in "The Question of Our Speech" slighted the one formulation most pertinent to his complaints: the uses of literature. Pressing for "civility of utterance," warning against "influences round about us that make for . . . the confused, the ugly, the flat, the thin, the mean, the helpless, that reduce articulation to an easy and ignoble minimum, and so keep it as little distinct as possible from the grunting, the squealing, the barking or roaring of animals," James thought it overwhelmingly an issue of the imitation of oral models, an issue of "the influence of *observation*," above all an issue of manners—"for that," he insisted, "is indissolubly involved." How like Mrs. Olive Birch Davis he is when, at Bryn Mawr, he hopes to inflame his listeners to aspiration! "At first dimly, but then more and more distinctly, you will find yourselves noting, comparing, preferring, at last positively emulating and imitating." Bryn Mawr, of course, was the knowing occasion, not the guilty target, of this admonition—he was speaking of the young voices he had been hearing in the street and in the parlors of friends, and he ended with a sacred charge for the graduates themselves: "you may, sounding the clearer note of intercourse as only women can, become yourselves models and missionaries [sic], perhaps even a little martyrs, of the good cause."

But why did he address himself to this thesis exclusively in America? Could he not, even more emphatically, have made the same declarations, uttered the same dooms, in his adopted England? No doubt it would not have been seemly; no doubt he would have condemned any appearance of ingratitude toward his welcoming hosts. All true, but this was hardly the reason the lecture at Bryn Mawr would not have done for Girton College. In Britain, regionalisms are the soul of ordinary English speech, and in James's time more than in our own. Even now one can move from hamlet to hamlet and hear the vowels chime charmingly with a different tone in each village. Hull, England, is a city farther from London in speech—though in distance only 140 miles to the north—than Hull, Massachusetts, is from San Francisco, 3,000 miles to the west. Of England, it is clear, James had only the expectations of class, and a single class set the standard for cultivated speech. Back home in America, diversity was without enchantment, and James demanded a uniform sound. He would not have dreamed of requiring a uniform British sound: English diversity was *English* diversity, earned, native, beaten out over generations of the "ancestral circle"—while American diversity meant a proliferating concatenation of the innumerable sleepless aliens and the half-educated slangy young. With regard to England, James knew whence the standard derived. It was a quality—an emanation, even—of those who, for generations, had been privileged in their education. As Virginia Woolf acknowledged in connection with another complaint, the standard was Oxbridge. To raise the question of "our" speech in England would have been a superfluity: both the question and the answer were self-evident. In England the question, if anyone bothered to put it at all, was: Who sets the standard? And the answer, if anyone bothered to give it at all, was: Those who have been through the great public schools, those who have been through either of the great pair of ancient universities—in short, those who run things.

This was perhaps what led James, in his American reflections, to trip over the issues, and to miss getting at the better question, the right and pertinent question: *the* question, in fact, concerning American speech. In Britain, and in the smaller America of his boyhood that strained to be a mirror of the cousinly English culture, it remained to the point to ask who sets the standard. And the rejoinder was simple enough: the people at the top. To risk the identical question in the America of 1905, with my mother about to emerge from Castle Garden to stand waiting for the horsecar on the corner of Battery Park, was unavoidably to hurtle to the very answer James most dreaded and then desperately conceded: the people at the bottom.

The right and pertinent question for America was something else. If, in politics, America's Enlightenment cry before the world was to be "a nation of laws, not of men," then it was natural for culture to apply in its own jurisdiction the same measure: unassailable institutions are preferable to models or heroes. To look for aristocratic models for common speech in the America of 1905 was to end exactly where James *did* end: "I am at a loss to name you particular and unmistakably edifying and illuminating groups or classes." It could not be done. As long as James believed—together with Trolander, Davis, and Papp, his immediate though paradoxical heirs: paradoxical because their ideal was democratic and his was the-people-at-the-top—as long as he believed in the premise of "edifying and illuminating" models, his analysis could go nowhere. Or, rather, it could go only into the rhapsody of vaporous hope that is the conclusion of "The Question of Our Speech"—"become yourselves models and missionaries, even a little martyrs, of the good cause." Holy and resplendent words I recognize on the instant, having learned them—especially the injunction to martyrdom—at the feet of Trolander, Davis, and Papp.

No, it was the wrong question for America, this emphasis on *who;* the wrong note for a campus (however homogeneous, however elite) just outside Philadelphia, that Enlightenment citadel, whose cracked though mighty Bell was engraved with a rendering of the majestic Hebrew word *dror:* a word my nine-year-old mother, on her way to Madison Street, would have been able to read in the original, though presumably James could not—a deprivation of literacy my mother might have marked him down for. "All life," James asserted on that brilliant June day (my mother's life was that day still under the yoke of the Czar; the Kishinev pogrom, with its massacre and its maimings, had occurred only two years earlier), "all life comes back to the question of our speech, the medium through which we communicate with each other; for all life comes back to the question of our relations with each other." And: "A care for tone is part of a care for many things besides; for the fact, for the value, of good breeding, above all, as to which tone unites with various other personal, social signs to bear testimony. The idea of good breeding . . . is one of the most precious conquests of civilization, the very core of our social heritage."

Speech, then, was *who;* it was breeding; it was "relations"; it was manners; and manners, in this view, make culture. As a novelist, and particularly as a celebrated practitioner of "the novel of manners" (though to reduce James merely to this is to diminish him radically as a recorder of evil and to silence his full moral genius), it was requisite, it was the soul of vitality itself, for James to analyze in the mode of *who*. But for a social theorist—and in his lecture social theory was what James was pressing toward—it was a failing and an error. The absence of models was not simply an embarrassment; it should have been a hint. It should have hinted at the necessary relinquishment of *who* in favor of *what:* not who appoints the national speech, but what creates the standard.

If, still sticking to his formulation, James had dared to give his private answer, he might have announced: "Young women, I, Henry James, am that august Who who fixes the firmament of our national speech. Follow me, and you follow excellence." But how had this vast substantial Who that was Henry James come to be fashioned? It was no Who *he* followed. It was instead a great cumulative corporeal What, the voluminous and manifold heritage of Literature he had been saturated in since childhood. In short, he *read:* he was a reader, he had always read, reading was not so much his passion or his possession as it was his bread, and not so much his bread as it was the primordial fountain of his life. Ludicrous it is to say of Henry James that he read, he was a reader! As much say of Vesuvius that it erupted, or of Olympus that it kept the gods. But reading—just that, *what is read*—is the whole, the intricate, secret of his exemplum.

The vulgarity of the low press James could see for himself. On the other hand, he had never set foot in an American public school (his education was, to say the least, Americanly untypical), and he had no inkling of any representative curriculum. Nevertheless it was this public but meticulous curriculum that was to set the standard; and it was a curriculum not far different from what James might have found for himself, exploring on his own among his father's shelves.

A year or so after my mother stepped off the horsecar into Madison Street, she was given Sir Walter Scott's "The Lady of the Lake" to read as a school assignment. She never forgot it. She spoke of it all her life. Mastering it was the triumph of her childhood, and though, like every little girl of her generation, she read *Pollyanna,* and in the last months of her eighty-third year every word of Willa Cather, it was "The Lady of the Lake" that enduringly typified achievement, education, culture.

Some seventy-odd years after my mother studied it at P. S. 131 on the Lower East Side, I open "The Lady of the Lake" and take in lines I have never looked on before:

> Not thus, in ancient days of Caledon,
> > Was thy voice mute amid the festal crowd,
> When lay of hopeless love, or glory won,
> > Aroused the fearful, or subdued the proud.
> At each according pause was heard aloud
> > Thine ardent symphony sublime and high!
> Fair dames and crested chiefs attention bowed;
> > For still the burden of thy minstrelsy
> Was Knighthood's dauntless deed, and Beauty's matchless eye.
>
> O wake once more! how rude soe'er the hand
> > That ventures o'er thy magic maze to stray;
> O wake once more! though scarce my skill command
> > Some feeble echoing of thine earlier lay;
> Though harsh and faint, and soon to die away,
> > And all unworthy of thy nobler strain,
> Yet if one heart throb higher at its sway,

The wizard note has not been touched in vain.
Then silent be no more! Enchantress, wake again!

My mother was an immigrant child, the poorest of the poor. She had
come in steerage; she knew not a word of English when she stepped off
the horsecar into Madison Street; she was one of the innumerable unsleeping aliens. Her teachers were the entirely ordinary daughters of the Irish
immigration (as my own teachers still were, a generation on), and had no
special genius, and assuredly no special training (a certain Miss Walsh was
in fact ferociously hostile), for the initiation of a Russian Jewish child into
the astoundingly distant and incomprehensible premises of such poetry.
And yet it was accomplished, and within the briefest period after the voyage
in steerage.

What was accomplished was not merely that my mother "learned" this
sort of poetry—i.e., could read and understand it. She learned what it represented in the widest sense—not only the legendary heritage implicit in
each and every word and phrase (to a child from Hlusk, where the
wooden sidewalks sank into mud and the peasants carried water buckets
dangling from shoulder yokes, what was "minstrelsy," what was "Knight-
hood's dauntless deed," what on earth was a "wizard note"?), but what it
represented in the American social and tribal code. The quickest means of
stitching all this down is to say that what "The Lady of the Lake" stood for,
in the robes and tapestries of its particular English, was the received tradition exemplified by Bryn Mawr in 1905, including James's presence there as
commencement speaker.

The American standard derived from an American institution: the public
school, free, democratic, open, urgent, pressing on the young a program of
reading not so much for its "literary value," though this counted too, as for
the stamp of Heritage. All this James overlooked. He had no firsthand sense
of it. He was himself the grandson of an ambitiously money-making Irish
immigrant; but his father, arranging his affluent life as a metaphysician, had
separated himself from public institutions—from any practical idea, in fact,
of institutions *per se*—and dunked his numerous children in and out of
school on two continents, like a nomad in search of the wettest oasis of all.
It was hardly a wonder that James, raised in a self-enclosed clan, asserted
the ascendancy of manners over institutions, or that he ascribed to personal
speech "positively the history of the national character, almost the history of
the people," or that he spoke of the "ancestral circle" as if kinship were the
only means to transmit that national character and history.

It was as if James, who could imagine nearly everything, had in this
instance neglected imagination itself: kinship as construct and covenant,

kinship imagined—and what are institutions if not invented kinship circles: society as contract? In the self-generating Enlightenment society of the American founding philosophers, it was uniquely the power of institutions to imagine, to create, kinship and community. The Constitution, itself a kind of covenant or imaginatively established "ancestral circle," created peoplehood out of an idea, and the public schools, begotten and proliferated by that idea, implemented the Constitution; and more than the Constitution. They implemented and transmitted the old cultural mesh. Where there was so much diversity, the institution substituted for the clan, and discovered—through a kind of civic magnetism—that it could transmit, almost as effectively as the kinship clan itself, "the very core of our social heritage."

To name all this the principle of the Melting Pot is not quite right, and overwhelmingly insufficient. The Melting Pot called for imitation. Imagination, which is at the heart of institutionalized covenants, promotes what is intrinsic. I find on my shelves two old textbooks used widely in the "common schools" James deplored. The first is *A Practical English Grammar,* dated 1880, the work of one Albert N. Raub, A.M., Ph.D. ("Author of 'Raub's Readers,' 'Raub's Arithmetics,' 'Plain Educational Talks, Etc.'"). It is a relentless volume, thorough, determined, with no loopholes; every permutation of the language is scrutinized, analyzed, accounted for. It is also a commonplace book replete with morally instructive quotations, some splendidly familiar. Each explanatory chapter is followed by "Remarks," "Cautions," and "Exercises," and every Exercise includes a high-minded hoard of literary Remarks and Cautions. For instance, under Personal Pronouns:

> Though the mills of God grind slowly,
>   yet they grind exceedingly small;
> Though with patience He stands waiting,
>   with exactness grinds He all.

> This above all, to thine own self be true,
> And it must follow, as the night the day,
> Thou canst not then be false to any man.

> These are thy glorious works, Parent of good,
>   Almighty! Thine this universal frame.

> Alas! they had been friends in youth,
> But whispering tongues can poison truth;
> And constancy lives in realms above,
>   And life is thorny, and youth is vain;
> And to be wroth with one we love
>   Doth work like madness on the brain.

So much for Longfellow, Shakespeare, Milton, and Coleridge. But also Addison, Cowper, Pope, Ossian, Scott, Ruskin, Thomson, Wordsworth, Trollope, Gray, Byron, Whittier, Lowell, Holmes, Moore, Collins, Hood, Goldsmith, Bryant, Dickens, Bacon, Franklin, Locke, the Bible—these appear throughout, in the form of addenda to Participles, Parsing, Irregular Verbs, and the rule of the Nominative Independent; in addition, a handful of lost presences: Bushnell, H. Wise, Wayland, Dwight, Blair, Mrs. Welby (nearly the only woman in the lot), and Anon. The *content* of this volume is not its subject matter, neither its syntactic lesson nor its poetic maxims. It is the voice of a language; rather, of language itself, language as texture, gesture, innateness. To read from beginning to end a schoolbook of this sort is to recognize at once that James had it backwards and upside down: it is not that manners lead culture; it is culture that leads manners. What shapes culture—this is not a tautology or a redundancy—is culture. "Who makes the country?" was the latent question James was prodding and poking, all gingerly; and it was the wrong—because unanswerable—one. "What kind of country shall we have?" was Albert N. Raub's question, and it *was* answerable. The answer lay in the reading given to the children in the schoolhouses: the institutionalization, so to say, of our common speech at its noblest.

My second text is even more striking: *The Etymological Reader*, edited by Epes Sargent and Amasa May, dated 1872. "We here offer to the schools of the United States," begins the Preface, "the first systematic attempt to associate the study of etymology with exercises in reading." What follows is a blitz of "vocabulary," Latin roots, Saxon roots, prefixes, and suffixes, but these quickly subside, and nine-tenths of this inventive book is an anthology engaging in its richness, range, and ambition. "Lochinvar" is here; so are the Declaration of Independence and selections from Shakespeare; so is Shelley's "To a Skylark"; so is the whole "Star-Spangled Banner." But also: "Description of a Bee Hunt," "Creation a Continuous Work," "The Sahara," "Anglo-Saxon and Norman French," "Conversation," "Progress of Civilization," "Effects of Machinery," "On the Choice of Books," "Our Indebtedness to the Greeks," "Animal Heat," "Corruptions of Language," "Jerusalem from the Mount of Olives," "On the Act of Habeas Corpus," "Individual Character," "Going Up in a Balloon," and dozens of other essays. Among the writers: Dickens, Macaulay, Wordsworth, Irving, Mark Twain, Emerson, Channing, John Stuart Mill, Carlyle, De Quincey, Tennyson, Mirabeau, and so on and so on.

It would be foolish to consider *The Etymological Reader* merely charming, a period piece, "Americana"—it is too immediately useful, too uncompromising, and, for the most part, too enduring to be dismissed with condescension.

> It was one of those heads which Guido has often painted—mild, pale, penetrating, free from all commonplace ideas of fat, contented ignorance, looking downward upon the earth; it looked forward, but looked as if it looked at something beyond this world. How one of his order came by it, Heaven above, who let it fall upon a monk's shoulders, best knows; but it would have suited a Brahmin, and had I met it upon the plains of Hindostan, I had reverenced it.

To come upon Sterne, just like this, all of a sudden, for the first time, pressed between Southey's sigh ("How beautiful is night!") and Byron's "And the might of the Gentile, unsmote by the sword, / Hath melted like snow in the glance of the Lord"—to come upon Sterne, just like that, is to come upon an unexpected human fact. Such textbooks filled vessels more fundamental than the Melting Pot—blood vessels, one might venture. Virtuous, elevated, striving and stirring, the best that has been thought and said: thus the voice of the common schools. A fraction of their offerings had a heroic, or monumental, quality, on the style perhaps of George Washington's head. They stood for the power of civics. But the rest were the purest belles-lettres: and it was belles-lettres that were expected to be the fountainhead of American civilization, including civility. Belles-lettres provided style, vocabulary, speech itself; and also the themes of Victorian seriousness: conscience and work. Elevated literature was the model for an educated tongue. Sentences, like conscience and work, were demanding.

What did these demanding sentences do in and for society? First, they demanded to be studied. Second, they demanded sharpness and cadence in writing. They promoted, in short, literacy—and not merely literacy, but a vigorous and manifold recognition of literature as a *force*. They promoted an educated class. Not a hereditarily educated class, but one that had been introduced to the initiating and shaping texts early in life, almost like the hereditarily educated class itself.

All that, we know, is gone. Where once the *Odyssey* was read in the schools, in a jeweled and mandarin translation, Holden Caulfield takes his stand. He is winning and truthful, but he is not demanding. His sentences reach no higher than his gaze. The idea of belles-lettres, when we knock our unaccustomed knees against it, looks archaic and bizarre: rusted away, like an old car chassis. The content of belles-lettres is the property of a segregated caste or the dissipated recollections of the very old.

Belles-lettres in the schools fashioned both speech and the art of punctuation—the sound and the look of nuance. Who spoke well pointed well; who pointed well spoke well. One was the skill of the other. No one now punctuates for nuance—or, rather, whoever punctuates for nuance is "corrected." Copy editors do not know the whole stippled range of the colon or the semicolon, do not know that "O" is not "oh," do not know that not all juxtaposed adjectives are coordinate adjectives; and so forth. The degeneration of punctuation and word-by-word literacy is pandemic among English speakers: this includes most poets and novelists. To glimpse a typical original manuscript undoctored by a copy editor is to suffer a shock at the sight of ignorant imprecision; and to examine a densely literate manuscript after it has passed through the leveling hands of a copy editor is again to suffer a shock at the sight of ignorant imprecision.

In 1930 none of this was so. The relentlessly gradual return of aural culture, beginning with the telephone (a farewell to letter-writing), the radio, the motion picture, and the phonograph, speeded up by the television set, the tape recorder, and lately the video recorder, has by now, after half a century's worth of technology, restored us to the pre-literate status of face-to-face speech. And mass literacy itself is the fixity of no more than a century, starting with the advancing reforms following the industrial revolution—reforms introducing, in England, the notion of severely limited leisure to the classes that formerly had labored with no leisure at all. Into that small new recreational space fell what we now call the "nineteenth-century novel," in both its supreme and its lesser versions. The act of reading—the *work,* in fact, of the act of reading—appeared to complicate and intensify the most ordinary intelligence. The silent physiological translation of letters into sounds, the leaping eye encoding, the transmigration of blotches on a page into the story of, say, Dorothea Brooke, must surely count among the most intricate of biological and transcendent designs. In 1930 the so-called shopgirl, with her pulp romance, is habitually engaged in this electrifying webwork of eye and mind. In 1980 she reverts, via electronics, to the simple speaking face. And then it is all over, by and large, for mass literacy. High literacy has been the province of an elite class since Sumer; there is nothing novel in having a caste of princely readers. But the culture of mass literacy, in its narrow period from 1830 to 1930, was something else: Gutenberg's revolution did not take effect in a popular sense—did not properly begin—until the rise of the middle class at the time, approximately, of the English Reform Act of 1832. Addison's *Spectator,* with its Latin epigraphs, was read by gentlemen, but Dickens was read by nearly everyone. The almost universal habit of reading for recreation or excitement conferred the greatest complexity on the greatest number, and the thinnest sliver of history expressed it: no more than a single century. It flashed by between aural culture and aural culture, no longer-lived than a lightning bug. The world of the VCR is closer to the pre-literate society of traveling mummers than it is to that of the young Scott Fitzgerald's readership in 1920.

When James read out "The Question of Our Speech" in 1905, the era of print supremacy was still in force, unquestioned; the typewriter and the electric light had arrived to strengthen it, and the telephone was greeted only as a convenience, not a substitute. The telephone was particularly welcome—not much was lost that ought not to have been lost in the omission of letters agreeing to meet the 8:42 on Tuesday night on the east platform. Since then, the telephone has abetted more serious losses: exchanges between artists and thinkers; documents of family and business relations; quarrels and cabals among politicians; everything that in the past tended to be preserved for biographers and cultural historians. The advent of the computer used as word processor similarly points toward the wiping out of any *progressive* record of thought; the grain of a life can lie in the illumination of the crossed-out word.

But James, in the remoteness of post-Victorian technology, spoke unshadowed by these threatened disintegrations among the community of the literate; he spoke in the very interior of what seemed then to be a permanently post-aural culture. He read from a manuscript; later that year, Houghton, Mifflin published it together with another lecture, this one far more famous, "The Lesson of Balzac." We cannot hear his voice on a phonograph record, as we can hear his fellow self-exile T. S. Eliot's; and this, it might be said, is another kind of loss. If we cherish photographs of Henry James's extraordinarily striking head with its lantern eyes, we can regret the loss of a filmed interview of the kind that nowadays captures and delivers into the future Norman Mailer and John Updike. The return to an aural culture is, obviously, not *all* a question of loss; only of the most significant loss of all: the widespread nurture by portable print; print as water, and sometimes wine. It was, in its small heyday (we must now begin to say *was*), the most glorious work of the eye-linked brain.

And in the heyday of that glorious work, James made a false analysis. In asking for living models, his analysis belonged to the old aural culture, and he did not imagine its risks. In the old aural culture, speech *was* manner, manner *was* manners, manners *did* teach the tone of the civilized world. In the new aural culture, speech remains manner, manner becomes manners, manners go on teaching the tone of the world. The difference is that the new aural culture, based, as James urged, on emulation, is governed from below. Emulation as a principle cannot control its sources. To seize on only two blatancies: the guerrilla toy of the urban underclass, the huge and hugely loud portable radio—the "ghetto blaster"—is adopted by affluent middle-class white adolescents; so is the locution "Hey, man," which now crosses both class and gender. James worried about the replacement in America of "Yes" by "Yeah" (and further by the comedic "Yep"), but its source was the drawl endemic to the gilt-and-plush parlors of the upper middle class. "Yeah" did not come out of the street; it went into the street. But it is also fairly certain that the "Yeah"-sayers, whatever their place in society, could not have been strong readers, even given the fissure that lies between reading and the style of one's talk. The more attached one is to the community of readers, the narrower the fissure. In a society where belles-lettres are central to education of the young, what controls speech is the degree of absorption in print. Reading governs speech, governs tone, governs manner and manners and civilization. "It is easier to overlook any question of speech than to trouble about it," James complained, "but then it is also easier to snort or neigh, to growl or 'meaow,' than to articulate and intonate."

And yet he overlooked the primacy of the high act of reading. No one who, in the age of conscience and work, submitted to "The Lady of the Lake," or parsed under the aegis of Albert N. Raub, or sent down a bucket into *The Etymological Reader,* was likely to snort or neigh or emit the cry of the tabby. Agreed, it was a more publicly formal and socially encrusted age than ours, and James was more publicly formal and socially encrusted than many of his contemporaries: he was an old-fashioned gentleman. He had come of age during the Civil War. His clothes were laid out by a manservant. His standard was uncompromising. All the same, he missed how and where his own standard ruled. He failed to discover it in the schoolhouses, to which it had migrated after the attenuation of the old aural culture. To be sure, the school texts, however aspiring, could not promise to the children of the poor, or to the children of the immigrants, or to the children of working men, any hope of a manservant; but they *did* promise a habit of speech, more mobilizing and organizing, even, than a valet. The key to American speech was under James's nose. It was at that very moment being turned in a thousand locks. It was opening gate after gate. Those who could read according to an elevated standard could write sufficiently accomplished sentences, and those who could write such sentences could "articulate and intonate."

"Read, read! Read yourself through all the stages of the masters of the language," James might have exhorted the graduates. Instead, he told them to seek "contact and communication, a beneficent contagion," in order to "bring about the happy state—the state of sensibility to tone." It offended him, he confessed, that there were "forces assembled to make you believe that no form of speech is provably better than another." Forty years on, Trolander, Davis, and Papp set their own formidable forces against the forces of relativism in enunciation. Like James, they were zealous to impose their own parochialisms. James did not pronounce the *r* in "mother"; it was, therefore, vulgar to let it be heard. Our Midwestern teachers *did* pronounce the *r*; it was, therefore, vulgar *not* to let it be heard. How, then, one concludes, *is* any form of speech "provably better than another"? In a relativist era, the forces representing relativism in enunciation have for the moment won the argument, it seems; yet James has had his way all the same. With the exception of the South and parts of the East Coast, there is very nearly a uniform *vox Americana*. And we have everywhere a uniform "tone." It is in the streets and in the supermarkets, on the radio and on television; and it is low, low, low. In music, in speech, in manner, the upper has learned to imitate the lower. Cheapened imprecise speech is the triumph of James's tribute to emulation; it is the only possible legacy that could have come of the principle of emulation.

Then why did James plead for vocal imitation instead of reading? He lived in a sea of reading, at the highest tide of literacy, in the time of the crashing of its billows. He did not dream that the sea would shrink, that it was impermanent, that we would return, through the most refined technologies, to the aural culture. He had had his own dealings with a continuing branch of the aural culture—the theater. He had written for it as if for a body of accomplished readers, and it turned on him with contempt. "Forget not," he warned in the wake of his humiliation as a playwright, "that you write for the stupid—that is, your maximum of refinement must meet the minimum of intelligence of the audience— the intelligence, in other words, of the biggest ass it may conceivably contain. It is a most unholy trade!" He was judging, in this outcry, all those forms that arrange for the verbal to bypass the eye and enter solely through the ear. The ear is, for subtlety of interpretation, a coarser organ than the eye; it follows that nearly all verbal culture designed for the ear is broader, brighter, larger, louder, simpler, less intimate, more insistent—more *theatrical*—than any page of any book.

For the population in general, the unholy trades—they are now tremendously in the plural, having proliferated—have rendered reading nearly obsolete, except as a source of data and as a means of record-keeping— "warehousing information." For this the computer is an admittedly startling advance over Pharaoh's indefatigably meticulous scribes, notwithstanding the lofty liturgical poetry that adorned the ancient records, offering a tendril of beauty among the granary lists. Pragmatic reading cannot die, of course, but as the experience that feeds *Homo ridens,* reading is already close to moribund. In the new aural culture of America, intellectuals habitually define "film" as "art" in the most solemn sense, as a counterpart of the literary novel, and ridicule survivors of the age of "movies" as naïfs incapable of making the transition from an old form of popular entertainment to a new form of serious expression meriting a sober equation with written art—as if the issue had anything to do with what is inherently complex in the medium, rather than with what is inherently complex in the recipient of the medium. Undoubtedly any movie is more "complicated" than any book; and also more limited by the apparatus of the "real." As James noted, the maker of aural culture brings to his medium a "maximum of refinement"—i.e., he does the best he can with what he has to work with; sometimes he is even Shakespeare. But the job of sitting in a theater or in a movie house or at home in front of a television set is not so reciprocally complex as the wheels-within-wheels job of reading almost anything at all (including the comics). Reading is an act of imaginative conversion. That specks on a paper can turn into tale or philosophy is as deep a marvel as alchemy or wizardry. A secret brush construes phantom portraits. In the proscenium or the VCR everything is imagined *for* one: there is nothing to do but see and hear, and what's there is what is literally there. When film is "poetic," it is almost never because of language, but rather because of the resemblance to paintings or engravings—one thinks of the knight on a horse in a field of flowers in Bergman's *The Virgin Spring*. Where film is most art, it is least a novelty.

The new aural culture is prone to appliance-novelty—a while ago who could have predicted the video recorder or the hand-held miniature television set, and who now knows what variations and inventions lie ahead? At the same time there is a rigidity to the products of the aural culture—like those static Egyptian sculptures, stylistically unaltered for three millennia, that are brilliantly executed but limited in imaginative intent.

In the new aural culture there is no prevalent belles-lettres curriculum to stimulate novel imaginative intent, that "wizard note" of the awakened Enchantress; what there is is replication—not a reverberation or an echo, but a copy. The Back to Basics movement in education, which on the surface looks as if it is calling for revivification of a belles-lettres syllabus, is not so much reactionary as lost in literalism, or *trompe l'oeil:* another example of the replication impulse of the new aural culture, the culture of theater. Only in a *trompe l'oeil* society would it occur to anyone to "bring back the old values" through bringing back the McGuffey Reader—a scenic designer's idea, and still another instance of the muddle encouraged by the notion of "emulation." The celebration of the McGuffey Reader can happen only in an atmosphere where "film," a copyist's medium, is taken as seriously as a book.

A book is not a "medium" at all; it is far spookier than that, one of the few things-in-themselves that we can be sure of, a Platonic form that can inhabit a virtual infinity of experimental incarnations: any idea, any story, any body of poetry, any incantation, in any language. Above all, a book is the riverbank for the river of language. Language without the riverbank is only television talk—a free fall, a loose splash, a spill. And that is what an aural society, following a time of complex literacy, finally admits to: spill and more spill. James had nothing to complain of: he flourished in a period when whoever read well could speak well; the rest was provincialism—or call it, in kindness, regional exclusiveness. Still, the river of language—to cling to the old metaphor—ran most forcefully when confined to the banks that governed its course. But we who come after the hundred-year hegemony of the ordinary reader, we who see around us, in all these heaps of appliances (each one a plausible "electronic miracle"), the dying heaves of the caste-free passion for letters, should know how profoundly—and possibly how irreversibly—the mummers have claimed us.

Crocodiled Moats in the Kingdom of Letters

> For constantly I felt I was moving among two groups—comparable in intelligence, identical in race, not grossly different in social origin, earning about the same incomes, who had almost ceased to communicate at all, who in intellectual, moral and psychological climate had so little in common that . . . one might have crossed an ocean.
>
> —C. P. Snow, *The Two Cultures and the Scientific Revolution*

Disraeli in his novel *Sybil* spoke of "two nations," the rich and the poor. After the progress of more than a century, the phrase (and the reality) remains regrettably apt. But in the less than three decades since C. P. Snow proposed his "two cultures" thesis—the gap of incomprehension between the scientific and literary elites—the conditions of what we still like to call culture have altered so drastically that Snow's arguments are mostly dissolved into pointlessness. His compatriot and foremost needler, the Cambridge critic F. R. Leavis, had in any case set out to flog Snow's hypothesis from the start. Snow, he said, "rides on an advancing swell of cliché," "doesn't know what literature is," and hasn't "had the advantage of an intellectual discipline of any kind." And besides—here Leavis emitted his final boom—"there is only one culture."

In the long run both were destined to be mistaken—Leavis perhaps more than Snow. In 1959, when Snow published *The Two Cultures*, we had already had well over a hundred years to get used to the idea of science as a multi-divergent venture—dozens and dozens of disciplines, each one nearly a separate nation with its own governance, psychology, entelechy. It might have been possible to posit, say, a unitary medical culture in the days when barbers were surgeons; but in recent generations we don't expect our dentist to repair a broken kneecap, or our orthopedist to practice cardiology. And nowadays we are learning that an ophthalmologist with an understanding of the cornea is likely to be a bit shaky on the subject of the retina. Engineers are light-years from astrophysicists. Topology is distinct from topography, paleobotany from paleogeology. In reiterating that scientific culture is specialist culture—who doesn't know this?—one risks riding an advancing swell of cliché. Yet science, multiplying, fragmented, in hot pursuit of split ends, is in a way a species of polytheism, or, rather, animism: every grain of matter, every path of conceptualization, has its own ruling spirit, its differentiated lawgiver and traffic director. Investigative diversity and particularizing empiricism have been characteristic of science since—well, since alchemy turned into physical chemistry (and lately into superconductivity); since the teakettle inspired the locomotive; since Icarus took off his wax wings to become Pan Am; since Archimedes stepped out of his tub into Einstein's sea.

Snow was in command of all this, of course—he was pleased to identify himself as an exceptional scientist who wrote novels— and still he chose to make a monolith out of splinters. Why did he do it? In order to have one unanimity confront another. While it may have been a polemical contrivance to present a diversiform scientific culture as unitary, it was patently not wrong, thirty years ago, to speak of literary culture as a single force or presence. That was what was meant by the peaceable word "humanities." And it was what Leavis meant, too, when he growled back at Snow that one culture was all there was worth having. "Don't mistake me," Leavis pressed, "I am not preaching that we should defy, or try to reverse, the accelerating movement of external civilization (the phrase sufficiently explains itself, I hope) that is determined by advancing technology. . . . What I am saying is that such a concern is not enough—disastrously not enough." Not enough, he argued, for "a human future . . . in full intelligent possession of its full humanity." For Leavis, technology was the mere outer rind of culture, and the job of literature (the hot core at the heart of culture) was not to oppose science but to humanize it. Only in Snow's wretchedly deprived mind did literature stand apart from science; Snow hardly understood what literature was *for*. And no wonder: Snow's ideas about literary intellectuals came, Leavis sneered, from "the reviewing in the Sunday papers."

It has never been easy to fashion a uniform image of science—which is why we tend to say "the sciences." But until not very long ago one could take it for granted (despite the headlong decline of serious high art) that there was, on the humanities side, a concordant language of sensibility, an embracing impulse toward integration, above all the conviction of human connectedness—even if that conviction occasionally partook of a certain crepuscular nostalgia we might better have done without. Snow pictured literature and science as two angry armies. Leavis announced that there was only one army, with literature as its commander in chief. Yet it was plain that both Leavis and Snow, for all their antagonisms, saw the kingdom of letters as an intact and enduring power.

This feeling for literary culture as a glowing wholeness—it *was* a feeling, a stirring, a flush of idealism—is now altogether dissipated. The fragrant term that encapsuled it—belles-lettres—is nearly archaic and surely effete: it smacks of leather tooling for the moneyed, of posturing. But it was once useful enough. "Belles-lettres" stood for a binding thread of observation and civilizing emotion. It signified not so much that letters are beautiful as that the house of letters is encompassingly humane and undivisive, no matter how severally its windows are shaped, or who looks out or in. Poets, scholars, journalists, librarians, novelists, playwrights, art critics, philosophers, writers for children, historians, political theorists, and all the rest, may have inhabited different rooms, differently furnished, but it was indisputably one house with a single roof and plenty of connecting doors and passageways. And sometimes—so elastic and compressive was the humanist principle— poet, scholar, essayist, philosopher, etc., all lived side by side in the same head. Seamlessness (even if only an illusion) never implied locked and separate cells.

And now? Look around. Now "letters" suggests a thousand enemy camps, "genres" like fortresses, professions isolated by crocodiled moats. The living tissue of intuition and inference that nurtured the commonalty of the humanities is ruptured by an abrupt invasion of specialists. In emulation of the sciences? But we don't often hear of astronomers despising molecular biologists; in science, it may be natural for knowledge to run, like quicksilver, into crannies.

In the ex-community of letters, factions are in fashion, and the business of factions is to despise. Matthew Arnold's mild and venerable dictum, an open-ended, open-armed definition of literature that clearly intends a nobility of inclusiveness—"the best that is known and thought in the world"—earns latter-day assaults and jeers. What can all that mean now but "canon," and what can a received canon mean but reactionary, racist, sexist, elitist closure? Politics presses against disinterestedness; what claims to be intrinsic is counted as no more than foregone conclusion. All categories are suspect, no category is allowed to display its wares without the charge of vested interest or ideological immanence. What Arnold called the play of mind is asked to show its credentials and prove its legitimacy. "Our organs of criticism," Arnold complained in 1864 (a period as uninnocent as our own), "are organs of men and parties having practical ends to serve, and with them those practical ends are the first thing and the play of mind the second."

And so it is with us. The culture of the humanities has split and split and split again, always for reasons of partisan ascendancy and scorn. Once it was not unusual for writers—Dreiser, Stephen Crane, Cather, Hemingway!—to turn to journalism for a taste of the workings of the world. Today novelists and journalists are alien breeds reared apart, as if imagination properly belonged only to the one and never to the other; as if society and instinct were designed for estrangement. The two crafts are contradictory even in method: journalists are urged to tell secrets in the top line; novelists insinuate suspensefully, and wait for the last line to spill the real beans. Dickens, saturated in journalism, excelled at shorthand; was a court reporter; edited topical magazines.

In the literary academy, Jacques Derrida has the authority that Duns Scotus had for medieval scholastics—and it is authority, not literature, that mainly engages faculties. In the guise of maverick or rebel, professors kowtow to dogma. English departments have set off after theory, and use culture as an instrument to illustrate doctrinal principles, whether Marxist or "French Freud." The play of mind gives way to signing up and lining up. College teachers were never so cut off from the heat of poets dead or alive as they are now; only think of the icy distances separating syllables by, say, Marianne Moore, A. R. Ammons, May Swenson, or Amy Clampitt from the papers read at last winter's Modern Language Association meeting—viz., "Written Discourse as Dialogic Interaction," "Abduction, Transference, and the Reading Stage," "The Politics of Feminism and the Discourse of Feminist Literary Criticism."

And more: poets trivialize novelists, novelists trivialize poets. Both trivialize critics. Critics trivialize reviewers. Reviewers retort that they *are* critics. Short-story writers assert transfigurations unavailable to novelists. Novelists declare the incomparable glories of the long pull. Novelizing aestheticians, admitting to literature no claims of moral intent, ban novelizing moralists. The moralists condemn the aestheticians as precious, barren, solipsist. Few essayists essay fiction. Few novelists hazard essays. Dense-language writers vilify minimalists. Writers of plain prose ridicule complex sentences. Professors look down on commercial publishers. Fiction writers dread university presses. The so-called provinces envy and despise the provinciality of New York. New York sees sour grapes in California and everywhere else. The so-called mainstream judges which writers are acceptably universal and which are to be exiled as "parochial." The so-called parochial, stung or cowardly or both, fear all particularity and attempt impersonation of the acceptable. "Star" writers—recall the 1986 International PEN Congress in New York—treat lesser-knowns as invisible, negligible. The lesser-knowns, crushed, disparage the stars.

And even the public library, once the unchallenged repository of the best that is known and thought, begins to split itself off, abandons its mandate, and rents out Polaroid cameras and videotapes, like some semi-philanthropic Crazy Eddie. My own local library, appearing to jettison the basic arguments of the age, flaunts shelf after shelf prominently marked Decorating, Consumer Power, How To, Cookery, Hooray for Hollywood, Accent on You, What Makes Us Laugh, and many more such chitchat categories. But there are no placards for Literature, History, Biography; and Snow and Leavis, whom I needed to moon over in order to get started on this essay, were neither one to be had. (I found them finally in the next town, in a much smaller if more traditionally bookish library.)

Though it goes against the grain of respected current belief to say so, literature is really *about* something. It is about us. That may be why we are drawn to think of the kingdom of letters as a unity, at least in potential. Science, teeming and multiform, is about how the earth and the heavens and the microbes and the insects and our mammalian bodies are constructed, but literature is about the meaning of the finished construction. Or, to set afloat a more transcendent vocabulary: science is about God's work; literature is about our work. If our work lies untended (and what is our work but aspiration?), if literary culture falls into a heap of adversarial splinters—into competing contemptuous clamorers for turf and mental dominance—then what will be left to tell us that we are one human presence?

To forward that strenuous telling, Matthew Arnold (himself now among the jettisoned) advised every reader and critic to "try and possess one great literature, at least, besides his own; and the more unlike his own, the better." Not to split off from but to add on to the kingdom of letters: so as to uncover its human face.

An idea that—in a time of ten thousand self-segregating literary technologies—may be unwanted, if not obsolete.

Portrait of the Artist as a Bad Character

Finally there is something new to say about Mona Lisa's smile. A current theory holds that La Gioconda is a self-portrait—Leonardo without his beard—and that the smile is, in fact, a trickster's derisive glimmer, a transvestite joke: five centuries of pulling the wool over everyone's eyes.

Well, all right, suppose it's really so: a da Vinci witticism unmasked at last. What would that mean for all those duped dead generations who marveled at Mona Lisa for her harmonious specificity as a woman, or, more romantically, as Woman? If they believed in the innocence they saw, was it a lie they were seeing? Or, because he fooled the ages, ought we to send the hangman after Leonardo's ghost? And what of us—we who are advantaged, or, conceivably, deprived—in the wake of this putative discovery? In recognizing the artist's ruse, are we seeing Mona Lisa plain for the first time in the history of her unflagging secret laughter? Or do we tamper with intention when we superimpose what we may now know on that unaccoutered loveliness? Mona Lisa mustached! The graffiti vandal's dream.

Moonings like these may be of little use to da Vinci scholars, but they are charged with a certain literary irritation. They prod us to recall that the work of art is in its nature figment and fraud—but figment and fraud we have pointedly agreed to surrender to. If the fraud ends up a screw-twist more fraudulent than bargained for, that is what happens when you strike a bargain with someone dressed up in cap and bells. The Mona Lisa is made out of five-hundred-year-old paint, no matter who the model was, and it's the viewer who assents to the game of her being there at all. A portrait, like a novel, is a fiction, and what we call fiction is rightly named. In the compact between novelist and reader, the novelist promises to lie, and the reader promises to allow it.

These are notations so conspicuous and so stale that they are inscribed, no doubt, among the sacred antlers on neolithic cave walls; but they raise somewhat less obvious questions about the writer's potential for decent citizenship—the writer, that is, of fiction. Literary essayists, critical and social thinkers, historians, journalists, and so forth, don't in general, or at least not ideally, set out to defraud. The essayist's contract is exactly contrary to the novelist's—a promise to deliver ideas and "issues," implicit in which is a promise to show character. Fiction writers may easily begin as persons of character—more easily, say, than political columnists who are tempted to put a finger lightly on the scale—but the likelihood is that in the long run fiction bruises character. Novelists invent, deceive, exaggerate, and impersonate for several hours every day, and frequently on the weekend. Through the creation of bad souls they enter the demonic as a matter of course. They usurp emotions and appropriate lives.

As to the latter: "We all like to pretend we don't use real people," E. M. Forster once confessed, "but one does actually. I used some of my family. Miss Bartlett was my Aunt Emily—they all read the book but none of them saw it. . . . Mrs. Honeychurch was my grandmother. The three Miss Dickinsons condensed into two Miss Schlegels. Philip Herriton I modeled on Professor Dent. He knew this, and took an interest in his own progress." That may sound benign, but more often Professor Dent turns out to be sour and litigious, eager to muzzle, maim, or brain the writer into whose inspirations he has been unfortunate enough to fall. Saul Bellow's ingenious Shawmut, the put-down expert of "Him with His Foot in His Mouth," a self-described vatic type who stands for the artist, deduces that "I don't have to say a word for people to be insulted by me . . . my existence itself insults them. I come to this conclusion unwillingly, for God knows that I consider myself a man of normal social instincts and am not conscious of any will to offend." Yet Shawmut acknowledges he is in the grip of a manic force—a frenzy—signifying "something that is inaccessible to revision."

Good citizens are good—the consequence of normal social instincts—because they are usually accessible to revision; they are interested in self-improvement. Fiction writers have a different program for ego: not to polish it up for public relations, but to make it serve rapture—the rapture of language and drama, and also the rapture of deceit. The drive to rapture is resistant to revision in a big way, and will nail grandmothers and condense ladies no matter what. Professor Dent is right to look sweetly to his progress; he never had a chance to escape it. A well-worked fable is nothing but outright manipulation of this sort, not simply because it is all theater—what seems to be happening never actually happened—but because readers of fiction are forcibly dispossessed of a will of their own, and are made to think and feel whatever the writer commands. The characters in a novel are ten thousand times freer than their readers. Characters are often known to mutiny against the writer by taking charge of their books;

readers, never. Readers are docile in succumbing to the responses prescribed for them; or else the book uncompromisingly closes its gates and
shuts them out. In either case the writer is master.

Letters and diaries are not necessarily less fraudulent than works of fiction. It might be worthwhile for a scholar of deception—some ambitious
graduate student in American literature, say—to compare a writer's journal
entry on a particular day with a letter sent that same day. "Dear W: Your
new poems have just come. Supernal stuff! You surpass yourself," the letter
will start off. And the journal entry: "This a.m. received bilgewater from W;
wrote him some twaddle." But even journals may not be trustworthy; a
journal is a self-portrait, after all, and can white out the wens. I once met a
young novelist who admitted that he was ashamed to tell his private diary
his real secrets. On the other hand, the absence of abashment in a writer's
diary is not the same as truth: who will measure Thomas Mann by the
record of his flatulence, or the bite of Edmund Wilson by his compulsive
nature pastels ("Mountains stained by blue shade—and, later, the pale
brown rungs of the eucalyptus screens all pink in the setting sun")?

Storytellers and novelists, when on the job, rely on a treacherous braid
of observation and invention; or call it memory and insinuation. Invention
despoils observation, insinuation invalidates memory. A stewpot of bad
habits, all of it—so that imaginative writers wind up, by and large, a shifty
crew, sunk in distortion, misrepresentation, illusion, imposture, fakery.
Those who—temporarily—elude getting caught out as bad characters are
the handful of mainly guileless writers who eat themselves alive, like Kafka
or Bruno Schulz. Such creatures neither observe nor invent. They never impersonate. Instead, they use themselves up in their fables, sinew by sinew.
They are not in the world at all, or, if for a time they seem to be, it is only
a simulacrum of a social being, and another lie.

Who will blame Leonardo for fooling us? The work was a sham to begin
with. Those granules of chemicals on canvas were never Mona Lisa. She
comes to life only with our connivance. And if the artist shows no character at all, and piles a second trick on the first, isn't he exactly the rascal we
know him for?

A Selected Bibliography of the Writings of Cynthia Ozick

Compiled, with additions, from "A Bibliography of Writings by Cynthia Ozick," by Susan Currier and Daniel J. Cahill, in *Contemporary American Women Writers: Narrative Strategies*, edited by Catherine Rainwater and William J. Scheick (copyright © 1985 by The University Press of Kentucky), and by permission of The University Press of Kentucky.

BOOKS

Trust. New York: New American Library, 1966; Dutton/Obelisk, 1983.
The Pagan Rabbi and Other Stories. New York: Knopf, 1971; Schocken Books, 1976; Dutton/Obelisk 1983.
Bloodshed and Three Novellas. New York: Knopf, 1976; Dutton/Obelisk, 1983.
Levitation: Five Fictions. New York: Knopf, 1982; Dutton/Obelisk, 1983.
Art & Ardor: Essays. New York: Knopf, 1983; Dutton/Obelisk, 1984.
The Cannibal Galaxy. New York: Knopf, 1983; Dutton/Obelisk 1984.
The Messiah of Stockholm. New York: Knopf, 1987.
Metaphor & Memory: Essays. New York: Knopf, 1989.
The Shawl. New York: Knopf, l989.
Epodes: First Poems. Columbus, OH: Logan Elm Press, 1992.
What Henry James Knew, and Other Essays on Writers. London: Jonathan Cape, 1993.
Portrait of the Artist as a Bad Character and Other Essays on Writing. London/New York: Vintage, 1994.

DRAMA

Blue Light. A Play based on *The Shawl*. Producers: Kathy Levin, David Brown; Director: Don Scardino; Artistic Director: Playwrights Horizons. Staged reading, Playwrights Horizons, October 1993. Premiere production, Bay Street Theatre, Sag Harbor, Long Island, August 1994. Director: Sidney Lumet. A New York production, retitled *The Shawl,* is in preparation.

SHORT STORIES

"The Sense of Europe." *Prairie Schooner* 30 (June 1956): 126–38.

"Stone." *Botteghe Oscure* 20 (Autumn 1957), 388-414.

"The Butterfly and the Traffic Light." *Literary Review* 5 (Autumn 1961): 46–54. Reprinted in *The Pagan Rabbi and Other Stories;* in *Faith and Fiction: The Modern Short Story,* ed. Robert Detweiler and Glenn Meeter (1979).

"The Pagan Rabbi." *Hudson Review* 19 (Autumn 1966): 425–54. Reprinted in *Explorations: An Annual on Jewish Themes,* ed. Murray Mindlin and Chaim Bermont (1968); in *My Name Aloud: Jewish Stories by Jewish Writers,* ed. Harold U. Ribalow (1969); in *Best SF: 1971,* ed. Harry Harrison and Brian W. Aldiss (1972); in *The Pagan Rabbi and Other Stories;* in *Jewish American Stories,* ed. Irving Howe (1977); in *The Penguin Book of Jewish Stories,* ed. Emanuel Litvinoff (1979); in *More Wandering Stars: An Anthology of Jewish Fantasy and Science Fiction,* ed. Jack Dann (1981).

"Envy; or, Yiddish in America." *Commentary* 48 (November 1969): 35–53. Reprinted in *The Best American Short Stories, 1970,* ed. M. Foley and D. Burnett (1970); in *The Pagan Rabbi and Other Stories.*

"The Dock-Witch." *Event* 1 (Spring 1971): 40-73. Reprinted in *The Pagan Rabbi and Other Stories;* in *Best American Short Stories, 1972,* ed. M. Foley (1972).

"The Doctor's Wife." Midstream 17 (February 1971): 53–71. Reprinted in *The Pagan Rabbi and Other Stories.*

"Virility." *Anon.,* February 1971. Reprinted in *The Pagan Rabbi and Other Stories.*

"An Education." *Esquire* 77 (April 1972): 98–l02. Reprinted in *Bitches and Sad Ladies: An Anthology of Fiction by and about Women,* ed. Pat Rotter (1975); in *Bloodshed and Three Novellas;* in *Familiar Faces: Best Contemporary American Short Stories* (1979).

"Freud's Room." *American Journal,* 8 May 1973: 12–14. Reprinted as the first of two fragments and retitled "From a Refugee's Notebook," in *Levitation: Five Fictions.*

"Usurpation." *Esquire* 81 (May 1974): 124–28. Reprinted in *Prize Stories 1975: The O. Henry Awards* (1975); in *Bloodshed and Three Novellas;* in *All Our Secrets Are the Same: New Fiction from Esquire,* ed. Gordon Lish (1976).

"A Mercenary." *American Review* 23 (October 1975): 1–37. Reprinted in *Best American Short Stories, 1976,* ed. M. Foley (1976); in *Bloodshed and Three Novellas.*

"Bloodshed." *Esquire* 85 (January 1976): 100–101. Reprinted in *Bloodshed and Three Novellas;* in *All Our Secrets Are the Same: New Fiction from Esquire,* ed. Gordon Lish (1976).

"Puttermesser: Her Work History, Her Ancestry, Her Afterlife." *New Yorker* 53 (9 May 1977): 38–44. Reprinted in *Levitation: Five Fictions.*

"Shots." Quest/77 1 (July-August 1977): 68–72. Reprinted in *Levitation: Five Fictions.*

"The Sewing Harems." *Triquarterly* 40 (Fall 1977): 237–44. Reprinted as the second of two fragments and retitled "From a Refugee's Notebook," in *Levitation: Five Fictions.*

"Levitation." *Partisan Review* 46 (1979): 391–405. Reprinted in *The Pushcart Prize 5* ed. Bill Henderson (1980); in *Levitation: Five Fictions.*

"The Laughter of Akiva." *New Yorker* 56 (10 November 1980): 50–173. Revised version published in *The Cannibal Galaxy.*

"The Shawl." *New Yorker* 56 (26 May 1980): 33–34. Reprinted in *Best American Short Stories 1981* (1981); with "Rosa," in *The Shawl,* 1989.

"Puttermesser and Xanthippe." *Salmagundi* 55 (Winter 1982): 163–225. Reprinted in *Levitation: Five Fictions.*

"Rosa." *New Yorker* 59 (21 March 1983): 38–71. Reprinted in *The Shawl,* 1989.

"At Fumicaro." *New Yorker* 60 (6 August 1984): 32–58.
"Puttermesser Paired." *The New Yorker* (8 October 1990): 40–75.

POEMS

"The Fish in the Net." *Epoch* 9 (Spring 1958): 36–37.
"Apocalypse." *Commentary* 28 (September 1959): 242.
"O Talk to Me of Angels." *San Francisco Review* 1 (September 1959): 81–82.
"The Street Criers." *Noble Savage* 2 (1960): 132–34.
"The Artist, Ha Ha." *Literary Review* 5 (Spring 1962): 407–8.
"The Engineers." *Literary Review* 5 (Spring 1962): 403–4.
"To My Uncle, A Craftsman." *Literary Review* 5 (Spring 1962): 405–6.
"The Arrest." *Literary Review* 5 (Summer 1962): 545.
"The Coming." *Literary Review* 5 (Summer 1962): 544.
"O." *Antioch Review* 22 (Summer 1962): 206.
"Short Historical Essay On Obtuseness." *Literary Review* 5 (Summer 1962): 543–44.
"Visitation." *Prairie Schooner* 36 (Fall 1962): 271.
"Footnote to Lord Acton." *Virginia Quarterly Review* 38 (Winter 1962): 100. Reprinted in *Of Poetry and Power: Poems Occasioned by the Presidency and by the Death of John F. Kennedy,* ed. Edwin Glikes and Paul Schwaber (1964).
"Revisiting." *Virginia Quarterly Review* 38 (Winter 1962): 99.
"The Seventeen Questions of Rabbi Zusya." *Midstream* 8 (Winter 1962): 70.
"Stile." *Virginia Quarterly Review* 38 (Winter 1962): 99–100.
"Commuters' Train through Harlem." *Mutiny* 12 (1963): 15–16.
"Filling in the Lake." *Mutiny* 12 (1963): 15–16.
"Caryatid." *New Mexico Quarterly* 33 (Winter 1963-64): 426.
"Bridled." *Chelsea Review* 15 (June 1964): 64.
"Red-Shift." *Chelsea Review* 15 (June 1964): 65
"A Riddle." *Judaism* 14 (Fall 1965): 436. Reprinted in *Voices within the Ark: The Modern Jewish Poets,* ed. Howard Schwartz and Anthony Rudolf (1980).
"Origins, Divergences." *Judaism* 14 (Fall 1965): 433.
"The Wonder Teacher." *Judaism* 14 (Fall 1965): 432–33. Reprinted in *Voices within the Ark: The Modern Jewish Poets,* ed. Howard Schwartz and Anthony Rudolf (1980).
"When That with Tragic Rapture Moses Stood." *Judaism* 14 (Fall 1965): 434–435.
"Yom Kippur, 5726." *Judaism* 14 (Fall 1965): 433.
"In the Synagogue." *Jewish Spectator* 35 (December 1970): 9.
"Chautauqua Poems." *Field* 8 (Spring 1973): 52.
"Fire-Foe." *Literary Review* 25 (Summer 1982): 611.
"In the Yard." *Literary Review* 25 (Summer 1982): 612.
"Urn-Burial." *Literary Review* 25 (Summer 1982): 613-16.
"Greeks." In *Epodes: First Poems,* 1992.

ESSAYS

"Geoffrey, James, or Stephen."*Midstream* 3 (Winter 1957): 70–76.
"We Ignoble Savages." *Evergreen Review* 3 (November–December 1959): 48–52.
"The Jamesian Parable: *The Sacred Fount.*" *Bucknell Review* 11 (May 1963): 55–70.
"The College Freshman: Portrait of a Hero as a Collection of Old Saws." *Confrontation* 1 (Spring 1968) 40–50. Reprinted as "The College Freshman: A Teacher's

Complaint" in *Reading, Writing, and Rewriting,* ed. W. Moynihan, D. Lee, and H. Weil (1969); as "The College Freshman" in *The Conscious Reader,* ed. C. Shrodes, H. Finestone, and M. Shugrue (1974).

"An Opinion on the Ovarian Mentality." *Mademoiselle* 66 (March 1968): 20, 25.

"Women and Creativity: The Demise of the Dancing Dog." *Motive* 29 (March–April 1969): 7–16. Reprinted in *Woman in Sexist Society,* ed. Vivian Gornick and Barbara Moran (1971).

"American: Toward Yavneh." *Judaism* 19 (Summer 1970): 264–82. Reprinted in *Congress Bi-Weekly,* 26 February 1971; condensed and reprinted as "New Yiddish: Language for American Jews" in *Jewish Digest* 18 (February 1973); in *Art & Ardor.*

"Alumnus as Dodo Bird." *Change: A Magazine of Higher Learning* 3 (Summer 1971): 35–39.

"24 Years in the Life of Lyuba Bershadskaya." *New York Times Magazine,* 14 March 1971: 27–29. (Written under the pseudonym Trudie Vocse.)

"Intermarriage and the Issue of Apostasy." *Sh'ma,* 19 March 1971, 74–75.

"We Are the Crazy Lady and Other Feisty Feminist Fables." *Ms.* 1 (Spring 1972): 40–44. Reprinted in *The First Ms. Reader,* ed. Francine Klagsbrun (1973); in *The Conscious Reader: Readings Past and Present,* ed. C. Shrodes, H. Finestone, and M. Shugrue (1974); in *Woman as Writer,* ed. Jeannette Webber and Joan Grumman (1978).

"Four Questions of the Rabbis." *Reconstructionist,* 18 February 1972, 20–23. See also "Rabbis Answer Cynthia Ozick," *Reconstructionist,* 19 May 1971, 35–37.

"Literary Blacks and Jews." *Midstream* 18 (June–July 1972): 10–24. Reprinted in *Bernard Malamud: Twentieth-Century Views,* ed. Joyce Field and Leslie Field (1975); in *Art & Ardor.*

"A Bintel Brief for Jacob Glatstein." *Jewish Heritage* 14 (September 1972): 58–60.

"Germany Even without Munich." *Sh'ma,* 13 October 1973, 150–52.

"The Hole/Birth Catalogue" *Ms.* 1 (October 1972): 55–60. Reprinted in *The First Ms. Reader,* ed. Francine Klagsbrun (1973); in *Motherhood: A Reader for Men and Women,* ed. Susan Cahill (1982); in *Art & Ardor.*

"Some Antediluvian Rejections Intending to Shove Up the Generation Gap Certain Current Notions Not Held by the Writer." *American Journal,* 1 December 1972, 22–28.

"If You Can Read This, You Are Too Far Out." *Esquire* 79 (January 1973): 74, 78.

"Reconsideration: Truman Capote." *New Republic,* 27 January 1973, 31–34.

"Israel: Of Myth and Data." *Congress Bi-Weekly,* 15 June 1973, 4–8.

"All the World Wants the Jews Dead." *Esquire* 82 (November 1974): 103–7.

"Culture and the Present Moment: A Roundtable Discussion." *Commentary* 58 (December 1974): 35.

"Palestine Issue: A 'Spectacular Falsehood.'" *New York Times,* 22 November 1974, Sec. C, 38.

"A Response to Josephine Knopp's 'The Jewish Stories of Cynthia Ozick.'" *Studies in American Jewish Literature* 1 (1975): 49–50.

"A Liberal's Auschwitz." *Confrontation* 10 (Spring 1975): 125–29. Condensed and reprinted in *Jewish Digest* 21 (November 1975); reprinted in *The Pushcart Prize 1* (1976).

"The Riddle of the Ordinary." *Moment* 1 (July–August 1975): 55–59. Reprinted in *Art & Ardor.*

"Hadrian and Hebrew." *Moment* 1 (September 1975): 77–79.

"Notes towards a Meditation on Forgiveness." In *The Sunflower,* by Simon Wisenthal, with a Symposium. New York: Schocken Books, 1976, 183–90.

"Hanging the Ghetto Dog." *New York Times Book Review,* 21 March 1976, 48–57.

"Writers and Critics." *Commentary* 62 (September 1976): 8, 10.

"Justice (Again) to Edith Wharton." *Commentary* 62 (October 1976): 48–57. Reprinted in *Art & Ardor.*

(Response to "What Three Books Did You Most Enjoy This Year?") in "Authors' Authors." *New York Times Book Review,* 5 December 1976, 103.

"How to Profit More from the Teachings of Clara Schacht than from All the Wisdom of Aristotle, Montaigne, Emerson, Seneca, Cicero, et al." *Esquire* 87 (May 1977): 92ff.

"Passage to the New World." *Ms.* 6 (August 1977): 70ff.

(Introduction to *Escape from Czarist Russia,* by Siphra Rigelson Ozick.) *Ms.* 6 (August 1977): 72.

"Does Genius Have a Gender?" *Ms.* 6 (December 1977): 56.

"Justice to Feminism: 2. Literature and the Politics of Sex: A Dissent." *Ms.,* December 1977. Reprinted in *Art & Ardor.*

(Response to "Who Is the Living Writer You Most Admire?") *New York Times Book Review,* 4 December 1977, 66.

"Query: Where Are the Serious Readers?" *Salmagundi* 42 (Summer–Fall 1978): 72–73.

"The Biological Premises of Our Sad Earth-Speck." *Confrontation* 15 (Fall–Winter 1978): 166–70. Reprinted in *Art & Ardor.*

"What Has Mysticism to Do with Judaism?" *Sh'ma,* 17 February 1978, 69–71.

"Letter to a Palestinian Military Spokesman." *New York Times,* 16 March 1978, Sec. A, 23.

"My Grandmother's Pennies." *McCall's* 106 (December 1978): 30–34.

"The Holidays." (Reply to "Christmas Comes to a Jewish Home," by Anne Riophe.) *New York Times,* 28 December 1978, Sec. C, 1, 6.

"Notes toward Finding the Right Question (A Vindication of the Rights of Jewish Women)." *Forum* 35 (Spring–Summer 1979): 37–60. Reprinted in *Lilith* 6 (1979).

"Judaism and Harold Bloom." *Commentary* 67 (January 1979): 43–51.

(Response to "What Made You Decide to Become a Writer and Why?") *New York Times Book Review,* 2 December 1979, 59.

"Pay Fair." *Savvy* 1 (January 1980): 80.

"Carter and the Jews: An American Political Dilemma." *New Leader,* 30 June 1980, 3–23.

"George Steiner's Either/Or: A Response." *Salmagundi* 50–51 (Fall 1980–Winter 1981): 90–95.

"Helping T.S. Eliot Write Better: Notes towards a Definitive Bibliography." *American Poetry Review* 10 (May–June 1981): 10–13. Reprinted in *The Pushcart Prize* 7 (1982).

"I Call You 'Beloved.'" *The Hunter Magazine* 2 (September 1982): 3–5.

"What Literature Means." *Partisan Review* 49 (1982): 294–97.

"Spells, Wishes, Goldfish, Old School Hurts: The Making of a Writer." *New York Times Book Review,* 31 January 1982, 9.

"Works in Progress." *New York Times Book Review,* 6 June 1982, 11.

"The Lesson of the Master." *New York Review of Books,* 12 August 1982, 20–21. Reprinted in *Art & Ardor.*

"Bialik's Hint." *Commentary* 75 (February 1983): 22–28.

(Response to Meron Benvenisti's claim that removal to Israel of contents of PLO's Palestine Research Center in East Beirut was erasure of Palestinian culture and history.) *New York Times,* 3 March 1983, Sec. A, 26.

"Writers Domestic and Demonic." *New York Times Book Review,* 25 March 1983, 1.

(Response to Don Peretz and others rebutting identification of Palestine Research Center in Beirut as PLO intelligence matrix.) *New York Times,* 9 April 1983, Sec. A, 22.

(Response to query about what books novelists enjoy rereading.) *New York Times Book Review*, 12 June 1983, 15.

"Torah as Feminism, Feminism as Torah." *Congress Monthly*, September–October 1984: 7–10.

"The Question of Our Speech: The Return to Aural Culture." *Partisan Review*, Fiftieth Anniversary Issue, 1984–85. Reprinted in *Metaphor & Memory*.

"The First Day of School: Washington Square 1946." *Harper's*, September 1985. Reprinted as "Washington Square, 1946," in *Metaphor & Memory*.

"Poetry and the Parochial." *Congress Monthly*, November–December 1986: 7–10.

"Good Novelists, Bad Citizens." *New York Times Book Review*, 15 February 1987. Reprinted as "Portrait of the Artist as a Bad Character" in *Metaphor & Memory*; in *Portrait of the Artist as a Bad Character*.

"Science and Letters: God's Work—and Ours." *New York Times Book Review*, 27 September 1987: 3, 51. Reprinted as "Crocodiled Moats in the Kingdom of Letters" in *Metaphor & Memory*.

"Sholom Aleichem's Revolution." *New Yorker*, 28 March 1988. Reprinted in *Metaphor & Memory*.

"T.S. Eliot at 101." *New Yorker*, 20 November 1989.

"Alfred Chester's Wig." *New Yorker*, 30 March 1992.

"What Henry James Knew." *New Criterion*, January 1993. Appeared also as Introduction to the Knopf Everyman edition of Henry James's *The Awkward Age*. Reprinted in *What Henry James Knew, and Other Essays on Writers*.

"Rushdie in the Louvre." *New Yorker*, 13 December 1993.

"The American Academy in the Twenties." *New Criterion*, September 1994.

"The Way We Live Now." [On Anthony Trollope.] *New York Times Book Review*, January 1995.

"The Writer as Playwright." *Washington Post Book Review*, January 1995.

"Mark Twain's Vienna." Introduction to *The Man That Corrupted Hadleyburg and Other Stories and Essays*. Oxford University Press, forthcoming. Also in *Commentary*, May 1995: 56.

"The Year of Writing Dangerously: Isaac Babel and Identity." *New Republic*, 8 May 1995: 31.

REVIEWS

[Review of *Works and Days and Other Poems*, by Irving Feldman.] *New Mexico Quarterly* 32 (Autumn–Winter 1962–63): 235–37.

"Literature or Segregated Writing" [*Soon, One Morning: New Writing by American Negroes, 1940-1962*, ed. Herbert Hill]. *Midstream* 9 (September 1963): 97–101.

"Cheever's Yankee Heritage" [*The Wapshot Scandal*, by John Cheever.] *Antioch Review* 24 (Summer 1964): 263–67.

"Novels for Adults" [*The Crossing Point* and *A Slanting Light*, by Gerda Charles.] *Midstream* 10 (March 1964): 101–4.

"America Aglow" [*The Wapshot Scandal*, by John Cheever.] *Commentary* 38 (July 1964): 66–67.

"A Contraband Life" [*Other People's Houses*, by Lore Segal]. *Commentary* 39 (March 1965): 89.

"Of Skill and Vision" [*Where Mist Clothes Dream* and *Song Runs Naked*, by Sara; *Stop Here My Friend*, by Merrill Joan Gerber]. *Midstream* 11 (June 1965): 106-8.

"The Evasive Jewish Story" [*Modern Jewish Stories*, ed. Gerda Charles]. *Midstream* 12 (February 1966): 78–80.

"Against the Grain" [*Testimony: The United States, 1885–1890,* by Charles Reznikoff]. *Congress Bi-Weekly,* 9 May 1966, 18.

[*The Children,* by Charity Blackstone; *We Came as Children,* by Karen Gershon.] *Book Week,* 30 October 1966, 16.

"Full Stomachs and Empty Rites" [*The Jewish Cookbook,* by Mildred G. Bellin]. *Congress Bi-Weekly,* 23 January 1967, 17–19. Reprinted in *Jewish Digest* 12 (August 1967).

"Assimilation and Downward Mobility" [*The Carpenter Years,* by Arthur A. Cohen]. *Congress Bi-Weekly,* 6 March 1967, 16–17.

"From Anger to Truth" [*Digging Out,* by Ann Richardson]. *Midstream* 13 (August–September 1967): 76–79.

"The Unresplendent Dynasties of 'Our Crowd'" [*Our Crowd,* by Stephen Birmingham]. *Congress Bi-Weekly,* 18 December 1967, 3–6.

"Reflections Pleasant and Unpleasant on Jewish Marriage and Divorce" [*The Jewish Wedding Book,* by Lilly S. Routtenberg; *Jews and Divorce,* by Jacob Fried]. *Congress Bi-Weekly,* 13 January 1969, 16–17. See also letter in reply to R.R. Seldin on *The Jewish Wedding Book, Congress Bi-Weekly,* 24 March 1969, 23.

"The Uses of Legend: Elie Wiesel as Tsaddik" [*Legends of Our Time,* by Elie Wiesel]. *Congress Bi-Weekly,* 9 June 1969, 16–20.

"Hortense Calisher's Anti-Novel" [*The New Yorkers,* by Hortense Calisher]. *Midstream* 15 (November 1969): 77–80.

"Ethnic Joke" [*Bech: A Book,* by John Updike]. *Commentary* 50 (November 1970): 106–14.

"Jews and Gentiles" [*The Goy,* by Mark Harris]. *Commentary* 51 (June 1971): 104–8.

"Forster as Homosexual" [*Maurice,* by E.M. Forster]. *Commentary* 52 (December 1971): 81-85. See also letter in reply to Albert Sherrard (about Forster), *Commentary* 53 (March 1972): 30–32; letter in reply to Anne Farber (about Forster), *Commentary* 53 (May 1972): 32–42; letter in reply to Leo Skir (about Forster), *Commentary* (May 1972): 42.

[Review of *In the Reign of Peace,* by Hugh Nissenson.] *New York Times Book Review,* 19 March 1972, 4.

[Review of *Open Heart,* by Frederick Buechner.] *New York Times Book Review,* 11 June 1972, 4.

[Review of *In the Days of Simon Stern,* by Arthur A. Cohen.] *New York Times Book Review,* 3 June 1973, 6.

"Mrs. Virginia Woolf" [*Virginia Woolf: A Biography,* by Quentin Bell]. *Commentary* 56 (August 1973): 33–44. Reprinted in *Art & Ardor.*

"Slouching toward Smyrna" [*Sabbatai Sevi: The Mystical Messiah,* by Gershom Scholem.] *New York Times Book Review,* 24 February 1974, 27–28.

"Book Month Forum." *Sh'ma,* 12 December 1975, 22–23.

[Review of *The Street of Crocodiles,* by Bruno Schulz.] *New York Times Book Review,* 13 February 1977, 4–5.

"The Loose Drifting Material of Life" [*The Diary of Virginia Woolf,* vol. 1, ed. Anne Olivier Bell]. *New York Times Book Review,* 2 October 1977, 7.

"The Mystic Explorer" [*From Berlin to Jerusalem: Memories of My Youth,* by Gershom Scholem]. *New York Times Book Review,* 21 September 1980, 1.

"Fistfuls of Masterpieces" [*The Collected Stories of Isaac Bashevis Singer*]. *New York Times Book Review,* 21 March 1982, 1.

[Review of *Pipers at the Gates of Dawn,* by Jonathan Cott.] *New York Times Book Review,* 1 May 1983, 7.

[Review of *Life and Times of Michael K.,* by J. M. Coetzee.] *New York Times Book Review,* 11 December 1983, 1.

TRANSLATIONS

"The Coat," "Elegy for the Soviet Yiddish Writers," by Chaim Grade. Translated by Cynthia Ozick. In *A Treasury* of *Yiddish Poetry*. Edited by Irving Howe and Eliezer Greenberg. New York: Holt, Rinehart and Winston, 1969: 338–45.

"The Last to Sing," "And All of These Are Gone," "A Prayer," by David Einhorn. Translated by Cynthia Ozick. In *A Treasury of Yiddish Poetry*. Edited by Irving Howe and Eliezer Greenberg. New York: Holt, Rinehart and Winston, 1969: 82–85.

"On the Road to Siberia," "God, a Boy," "A Voice," "Cain and Abel," by H. Leivick. Translated by Cynthia Ozick. In *A Treasury of Yiddish Poetry*. Edited by Irving Howe and Eliezer Greenberg. New York: Holt, Rinehart and Winston, 1969: 118, 123–26.

"A Song about Elijah the Prophet," by Itzik Manger. Translated by Cynthia Ozick. *Congress Monthly,* 28 April 1969: 13.

"Father-Legend," by H. Leivick. Translated by Cynthia Ozick. *Midstream* 17 (April 1971): 4.

"Tradition and Revolt in Yiddish Poetry," by Tabachnik. Translated by Cynthia Ozick. In *Voices from the Yiddish: Essays, Memoirs, Diaries*. Edited by Irving Howe and Eliezer Greenberg. Ann Arbor: University of Michigan Press, 1972: 269–89.